FRACKOPOLY

ALSO BY WENONAH HAUTER

Foodopoly: The Battle Over the Future of Food and Farming in America

FRACKOPOLY

The Battle for the Future of
Energy and the Environment

Wenonah Hauter

THE NEW PRESS

NEW YORK
LONDON

Requests for permission to reproduce selections from this book should be mailed to:
Permissions Department, The New Press, 120 Wall Street, 31st floor, New York, NY 10005.

Published in the United States by The New Press, New York, 2016
Distributed by Perseus Distribution

LIBRARY OF CONGRESS CATALOGING-IN-PUBLICATION DATA

Names: Hauter, Wenonah, author.
Title: Frackopoly : the battle for the future of energy and the environment /
    Wenonah Hauter.
Description: New York : The New Press, 2016. | Includes bibliographical
    references and index.
Identifiers: LCCN 2015050032 (print) | LCCN 2016000020 (e-book) |
    ISBN 9781620970072 (hardback) | ISBN 9781620970171 (e-book)
Subjects: LCSH: Energy development—Environmental aspects—United States. |
    Hydraulic fracturing—Environmental aspects—United States. | Energy
    industries—Environmental aspects—United States. | Environmental
    policy—United States. | United States—Environmental conditions. | BISAC:
    SCIENCE / Environmental Science. | TECHNOLOGY & ENGINEERING /
    Environmental / General.
Classification: LCC TD195.E49 H39 2016 (print) | LCC TD195.E49 (ebook) | DDC
    363.738—dc23
LC record available at http://lccn.loc.gov/2015050032

The New Press publishes books that promote and enrich public discussion and understanding of
the issues vital to our democracy and to a more equitable world. These books are made possible
by the enthusiasm of our readers; the support of a committed group of donors, large and small;
the collaboration of our many partners in the independent media and the not-for-profit sector;
booksellers, who often hand-sell New Press books; librarians; and above all by our authors.

www.thenewpress.com

Composition by dix!
This book was set in Minion

Printed in the United States of America

10   9   8   7   6   5   4   3   2   1

This book is dedicated to the people on the front lines of drilling and fracking and those dedicated activists who are fighting to ban fracking and to move into a clean energy future.

CONTENTS

20. The Ban Movement Grows, Stretching Coast to Coast   239

21. A Global Movement to Ban Fracking   260

22. The Way Forward   270

    Notes   277

    Index   347

ACKNOWLEDGMENTS

In researching and writing *Frackopoly*, I am indebted to so many people, especially my colleagues at Food & Water Watch. I am doubly grateful to Patrick Woodall, research director extraordinaire, who helped in many facets of the project and greatly improved my very long manuscript through superb editing and masterful coordination of fact-checking sources. My talented research assistant, Francesca Buzzi, was always gracious and long-suffering as she searched for obscure documents, read boring transcripts, and traipsed across town to the Library of Congress. I deeply appreciate the many kinds of assistance that my amazing colleagues Emily Wurth and Mark Schlosberg provided in shaping the book—from reading drafts to providing much-needed advice. Hugh MacMillian, our industry expert, cheerfully found material and fact-checked and read the manuscript for accuracy. Lily Boyce, who is both artistic and versatile in manipulating data, created the many charts and graphs in the book. I offer thanks to Geert DeCock and Darcey O'Callaghan for helping to assemble the international stories. I am very appreciative of all the many ways that Royelen Boykie helped me during the writing process, always going above and beyond. Much thanks to Darcey Rakestraw, who even when she was rushed gave important feedback on chapters, and to Kim Girton for her guidance on graphics design. Over the two years that I worked on *Frackopoly*, Lane Brooks was always willing to take up the slack in running a national organization when I was bogged down in research and writing. Patty Lovera often stepped in and covered speaking engagements and events.

In the last rush to check sources and fact-check, several Food & Water Watch research staff and interns worked weekends and overtime to get the job done: Brendan Agnew, Elizabeth Duffy, Alison Grass, Genna Reed, Tim Schwab, Tyler Shannon, Oakley Shelton-Thomas, and Ron Zucker. Many other Food & Water Watch staff played an important role in helping provide information on campaigns, reading draft chapters, or doing other tasks: Jorge Aguilar, Sarah Alexander, Allison Auciello, Alex Beauchamp, Sam Bernhardt, Eleanor Bravo, Amanda Byrnes, Miranda Carter,

Katherine Cirullo, Emily Coralyne, Rachel Dawn Davis, Julia DeGraw, Elizabeth Duffy, Scott Edwards, Kate Fried, Jessica Fujan, Seth Gladstone, Mary Grant, Mitch Jones, Lynna Kaucheck, Doug Lakey, Tia Lebherz, Renee Maas, Vicki Machado, Michele Merkel, Eve Mitchell, Alex Nagy, Brenna Norton, Matt Ohloff, Lauren Petrie, William Robinson, David Sanchez, Sam Schabacker, Liz Schuster, Adam Scow, Matt Smith, Liz Solorio, Nisha Swinton, Jim Walsh, Eric Weltman, and Rita Yelda.

I am very appreciative of the help offered by the hardworking Frack Action crew: Julia Walsh, John Armstrong, and Renee Vogelsang. Besides their stalwart opposition to fracking, they were always ready to answer questions, fact-check, and critique. I am grateful to Josh Fox and Mark Ruffalo, whose contributions to the anti-fracking movement and this book are legion. I'm greatly indebted to those I interviewed—the brave people on the front lines of fracking and the many activists fighting for the future. They include Maude Barlow, David Braun, Jonathan Deal, John Fenton, Karen Feridun, Andy Gheorghiu, Wes Gillingham, Earl Hatley, Barb Jarmoska, Ray Kemble, Steve Lipsky, Roxanne Marino, Tammy Manning, Marc McCord, Eve McNamara, Kathryn McWhirter, Charles Metcalfe, Don Morrison, Maria Olteanu, Borislav Sandov, Maureen Seaberg, William J. Snape, Sandra Steingraber, Samuel Martín-Sosa Rodriguez, Claire Sandberg, Craig Stevens, Doreen Stopforth, Ling Tsou, Barbara VanHanken, Sharon Wilson and Tony Young.

Eugene Coyle gave generously of his time in reconstructing the events we lived through during the electricity deregulation debacle of the 1990s and helping to analyze the consequences. I owe a great deal to Lisa Mastny, who read and edited every chapter as I wrote it.

I owe a debt of gratitude to many other individuals who gave their time for interviews or for providing information. They include James Abourezk, Lynn Hargis, Steve Horn, Robert Howarth, John Howatt, Tony Ingraffea, Georgeta Ionescu, Jennifer Krill, Pavlo Khazan, Michael Lemov, Ralph Nader, Tyson Slocum, and Tom "Smitty" Smith.

Thank you to my loving friends and family. A special thank-you to Sue and Tom Hays for all the moral support. I am very grateful to Christy Nichols for her many gifts, sunny texts, and pep talks. As always, I am enormously thankful for my loyal children, Adrina and Che Miller, whose unconditional love and support I can always depend on. And I am especially grateful for the love, patience, and endless encouragement offered by my husband, Leigh Hauter.

FRACKOPOLY

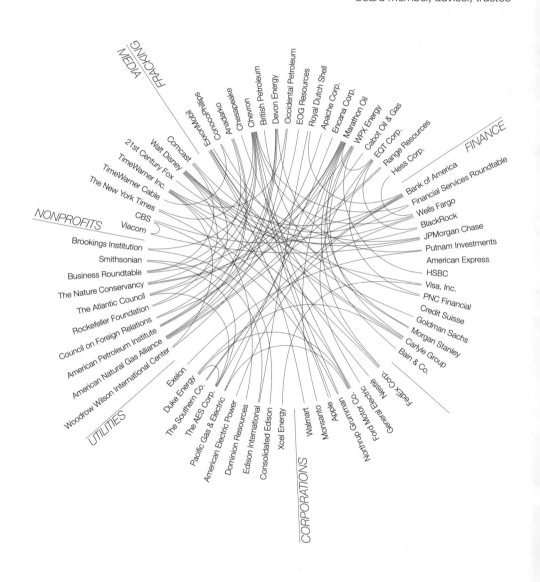

Big Oil Interlock

*Each line represents a common
board member, advisor, trustee*

INTRODUCTION

Over my decades of work in the public interest, I have developed a thick skin. If we are doing our job in the environmental movement, it is par for the course to be sneered at and called names. So when I heard that I had been pegged as "too strident" by the president of one of the largest energy and environment funders in the country, I was hardly surprised, as it has long been an institution that funds groups promoting policies to incentivize natural gas. In fact, I was pleased. I thought: *Yes, it's time to become much more forceful in protecting our threatened planet. It's time for everyone to be strident about keeping fossil fuels in the ground and eliminating the dirty energy technologies of the twentieth century.*

Unfortunately, even as hundreds of grassroots groups are battling to stop fracking, some of the largest environmental groups in the nation and many of their funders tout fracked natural gas as a "bridge fuel" or at least tacitly accept its use. Rather than focusing on an all-out effort to move away from fossil fuels, some of these groups provide cover to the fracking industry, claiming that fracking can be done safely or ignoring fracking's implications for the global climate.

Meanwhile, the communities that are living with the effects of the technology, or the ones fighting the coming wave of fracking and the associated infrastructure, feel betrayed when the place where they live becomes a sacrificial zone—with the implicit approval of some environmental organizations. A closer look at the path that these groups have laid out reveals that it will take us down the road to an environmental and climate disaster. Instead, we should aggressively deploy technologies for clean and renewable resources, reorient the energy system around conservation and efficiency, and leave fossil fuels in the ground, where they belong.

That's why I wrote this book.

In many ways, fracking looms as the environmental issue of our times. It touches every aspect of our lives—the water we drink, the air we breathe, and the health of our communities—and it ominously threatens our global climate. It pits the largest corporate interests—big energy and Wall

Street—against people and the environment in a long-term struggle for survival. Understanding the impacts of fracking and the policy decisions that have led to this dangerous point in time are key to moving beyond extreme energy.

Frackopoly describes the dangers inherent in fracking and why pursuing this harmful practice threatens public health, natural resources, and the climate. Beginning in the earliest days of the industry, it tells the story of how the largest oil and gas interests have maintained monopoly control over petroleum products and political decisions about energy. It unveils the complex set of events that have enabled the corporate progeny of John D. Rockefeller's Standard Oil to morph into some of the largest frackers of oil and natural gas today. It describes a political system rigged in favor of laissez-faire economics, allowing a juggernaut of polluters and other greedy economic forces to dominate the media, educational institutions, and our government. It describes how these selfish interests have marshaled their vast political power and resources to push fracking on every continent across the globe. It is a sordid tale about the grasp that the fossil fuel industry has had on federal dollars for energy research and development.

Frackopoly also gives voice to the many people who have been harmed by the impacts of fracking and to the brave community activists who are fighting to protect their homes and communities. It tells how a powerful movement to ban fracking has emerged, poised to challenge the pursuit of fracking and extreme energy and determined to move the nation to a sustainable energy path.

Scientific evidence continues to mount about the potential of fracking to both intensify and hasten the climate crisis. Although burning natural gas to produce electricity releases about half as much carbon dioxide (CO_2) as burning coal, this CO_2 reduction is offset by the leakage of methane during the process of drilling, fracking, processing, and transporting the gas to the power plant. Methane—the main component of natural gas—leaks into the atmosphere up to twice the rate estimated by the U.S. Environmental Protection Agency (EPA).[1] Degrading much faster in the atmosphere than CO_2, methane is, pound for pound, more efficient at trapping heat. The Intergovernmental Panel on Climate Change estimates that a pound of methane traps eighty-seven times as much heat as a pound of CO_2 in the twenty years after being emitted, and thirty-six times as much heat as a pound of CO_2 over a hundred-year time frame.[2]

Recent climate science shows that switching to natural gas is unlikely to reduce greenhouse gas emissions for decades, a crucial time frame for stopping runaway climate disruption. When the entire life cycle of producing natural gas is examined, the damage from methane leakage puts it on par with coal, or worse.[3] The most conservative estimate from atmospheric measurements—not from the inventorying based on oil and gas company data—is that natural gas leakage in 2010, averaged over the country, amounted to more than 3 percent of U.S. production that year.[4] Even if methane leakage can be brought down significantly over time—a debatable scenario—the threat to the global climate in the short term is very real. The rapid transition to natural gas is sending us to a tipping point when climate change cannot be reversed.

We have reached this critical juncture because, for more than a century, the entrenched position of the oil and gas industry in politics and the economy, and its privileged status under the law, have given it an iron grip on public policies. In recent years the stranglehold that the industry has had on politicians in both parties has propelled the fracking boom, defying common sense and the scientific evidence. Research financed by federal agencies provided the foundation for the technologies used in fracking, monies that could have been used to further the development of clean technologies. Former vice president Dick Cheney helped facilitate the exemption of fracking from national environmental laws, while states provide little oversight.

Over the past decade, oil and gas production has surged as a result of the unprecedented use of new fracking techniques and technologies, combined with long-range horizontal drilling. Fracking employs a science-fiction-like process where drillers inject millions of gallons of water, dangerous chemicals, and sand under extreme pressure to extract oil and natural gas from rock formations deep underground. After a deep vertical well is drilled, fracking takes place in multiple stages along a tunnel several inches wide that runs horizontally for a mile or more through the targeted rock formation thousands of feet underground. The incredible depth at which fracking takes place means that it is impossible to predict or know all of the unintended consequences.

Using as much as fifty times more water than conventional natural gas drilling, fracking threatens scarce water resources, especially in water-stressed areas of the country.[5] Water use varies by region, but nationally half the wells use more than 1.7 million gallons.[6] In the Pennsylvania Marcellus shale, drillers use between 3.8 million and 5.5 million gallons; some wells in

Texas have been fracked with more than 13 million gallons.[7] The industry claims that water use is low relative to overall consumption, but statistics that are based on averages over large regions are deceptive. The use of water for fracking is intensive, happening all in a local hotspot for drilling and fracking, and all at once for each new well. Oil and gas companies often compete with agriculture for the use of limited freshwater resources. In 2012, during the severe drought, frackers were the top bidders at a Colorado auction of water rights, driving up water prices for the state's farmers.

Vital aquifers are put at risk for generations to come from the toxic fracking fluid and the unleashing of toxic substances deep underground. Fractures from the process can create new and undetected pathways for contaminants to flow over time. The industry uses a multitude of different chemicals in fracking fluids, some of which are documented human health hazards or carcinogens, such as benzene and toluene, as well as endocrine disruptors. Acids also are commonly used in the injected fluids to eat away pathways for the fossil fuel to flow.[8]

Depending on the rock formation, between 5 and 50 percent of the water used in fracking returns to the surface in the initial days and weeks afterward.[9] Besides the toxic fracking fluid, the process brings to the surface corrosive salts, radioactive material, and toxic metals that had been deep underground. Thousands of leaks, blowouts, and spills from the industry involve these extremely hazardous wastes. The liquid wastes that are not spilled are typically sent to industrial treatment facilities, processed for reuse, or injected deep underground into disposal wells.

Numerous peer-reviewed studies document the explosion of earthquake "swarms" from deep-well disposal in parts of the nation that historically have experienced little if any seismic activity, especial the Midwest. Before 2009, Oklahoma annually had on average one to two earthquakes of 3.0 magnitude and twenty smaller earthquakes that mostly went unnoticed by the public. In 2014, with the increased use of deep-well injection, 585 larger earthquakes—3.0 magnitude or greater—shook the state, while more than five thousand smaller earthquakes registered on seismic equipment. In the first few months of 2015, an average of two earthquakes of magnitude 3.0 or greater occurred each day, causing impacts beyond where wells are drilled.[10]

Even in regions not targeted for fracking, a surge of deadly oil-train explosions represents a real and growing danger to communities. According to the federal Energy Information Administration (EIA), there was a fiftyfold increase in oil transport by rail between January 2010 and January 2015, with more than a million barrels of crude transported in 2014.[11] Catastrophic accidents such as the one in Lac-Mégantic, Quebec, which destroyed several blocks of the town and killed forty-seven people, demonstrate the potential threat from what are essentially bomb trains.[12] The epidemic of serious fracked-oil train accidents has sparked a debate over the tightening of federal rules governing rail transportation of the highly volatile crude. Although oil pipelines are being constructed, the industry has begun to prefer transporting oil by train because of the flexibility it offers.[13]

Meanwhile, scientific evidence continues to mount on the devastating impacts of fracking. More than 550 peer-reviewed studies have been published on the effects of fracking, with 80 percent of the research having been published since January 2013. Of the sixty-two studies on the health effects of fracking, 94 percent showed risks or adverse effects.[14] The health of thousands of people continues to be compromised by fracking. A 2013 analysis by the *Wall Street Journal* found that more than 15 million Americans are living within one mile of a well drilled since the year 2000.[15] Many more live near the other polluting infrastructure that supports fossil fuel production: processing plants, compressor stations, and refineries.

Those living near fracking sites breathe air poisoned from fracking operations. Exhaust from the diesel generators and large trucks crowding well sites, and smoke from flaring at well sites, processing plants, and compressor stations create a stream of toxic air emissions. These plumes contain variable amounts of hazardous air pollutants that include nitrogen dioxide, carbon monoxide, particulate matter, and volatile organic compounds such as benzene, toluene, and xylenes. Clouds of silica dust form at well sites as sand is managed and prepared for mixing into fracking fluid. Researchers at the National Institute of Occupational Safety and Health measured silica levels at eleven well sites as the sand was being managed, and found that exposures exceeded thresholds set to protect worker health, in some cases by a factor of ten.[16]

Silica sand mining has broadened the reach of fracking's impacts, with large amounts of silica—a fine white sand—mined from or processed in Illinois, Iowa, Minnesota, and Wisconsin. A recent review of the public health impacts of drilling and fracking summarizes that "respirable silica can cause silicosis and lung cancer and has been associated with tuberculosis, chronic obstructive pulmonary disease, kidney disease and autoimmune disease." [17]

Communities hosting fracking operations are plagued by thousands of heavy trucks crowding rural roads and by out-of-state workers flooding small towns, overwhelming local housing, police, and public health capacities. The influx of transient workers with disposable income and little to do in their off hours has been a recipe for trouble in small-town America from Pennsylvania to North Dakota, where alcohol-related crimes, sexual assaults, traffic accidents, emergency room visits, and sexually transmitted infection have all been on the rise.

Despite the hazards, oil and gas corporations frack between 25,000 and 30,000 wells each year.[18] As the primary technology used for extracting oil and natural gas from onshore wells, it also is being used to an unknown extent offshore. As this book goes to print, fracking operations are ongoing in twenty-nine states, and at least ten more states are likely to be targeted in the future. Currently 81 percent of fracking is used for extracting oil, while the other fracking activities are focused on natural gas.[19]

The decade-long surge in production of fracked natural gas and oil has temporarily brought a price collapse, resulting in less drilling in the short run. But in December 2015, the forty-year oil export ban in the United States was lifted by Congress in a victory for the Frackopoly. Less than two weeks later, oil was loaded on a tanker in Texas and delivered to Europe, opening the floodgates of exports. It will not be long before the glut ends, prices rebound, and the fracking frenzy resumes. This boom-bust cycle has plagued the oil and gas industry since the federal government's role in pricing was eliminated, long before fracking technologies were employed. Today, as in the past, smaller drillers will go bankrupt and the larger, more heavily capitalized companies will acquire them, becoming even larger and even more powerful in pushing their political agenda.

Jobs have been the big political selling point for communities risking adverse environmental impacts from fracking. Yet not only have the job numbers been greatly exaggerated, but transient oil workers fill most of the higher-paying jobs. During the boom, as the population increases, communities expand housing and other infrastructure, but once the drilling and fracking is finished, workers move on to the next location. After the short-lived boom, optimistic local political leaders hope that 20 to 30 percent of the workers there will stay to maintain wells. When prices crash, boomtowns become ghost towns, left to pay for and maintain the empty houses, apartment buildings, hotels, and other unnecessary infrastructure.

But despite the temporarily low prices, the long-term plan of the fossil fuel industry—and of the policy makers who serve their interests—is to drill and frack for every last drop. The EIA estimates that bringing the projected amounts of technically recoverable gas and oil into production will require 630,000 new onshore wells.[20] The industry is banking on increased extraction in the future, coupled with oil and natural gas exports that will push up prices. Oil and gas corporations piled up more than $160 billion in debt by 2014, in large part to support fracking and related infrastructure.[21] Their profits and ability to survive depend on the long-term systemic dependence on fossil fuels.

Despite the overwhelming evidence of the harms of fracking, the Environmental Protection Agency has thus far ignored the science. Obama's energy secretary Ernest Moniz has close ties with the industry and has claimed that he has "not seen any evidence of fracking *per se* contaminating groundwater" and that the environmental footprint is "manageable."[22] Obama's interior secretary Sally Jewell has bragged about fracking wells in her prior career in the industry and has, despite radical changes in how fracking is done, called it a "an important tool in the toolbox for oil and gas for over fifty years" and even implied that directional drilling and fracking can result in "a softer footprint on the land."[23] And the person charged with protecting communities' water, EPA administrator Gina McCarthy, has claimed that "there's nothing inherently dangerous in fracking that sound engineering practices can't accomplish,"[24] all while the EPA has ignored or buried findings that fracking has contaminated water in Texas, Wyoming, and Pennsylvania.

This support for fracking at the highest levels has caused unnecessary confusion and has provided political space for several Democratic governors who claim to care about the environment—including Jerry Brown in California and Tom Wolf in Pennsylvania—to pursue fracking. And so far, except for Senator Bernie Sanders, all of the presidential contenders for 2016, both Democratic and Republican, are fully in favor of fracking. The names of the political appointees who head the federal regulatory agencies will change, but the policies are likely to remain the same. Only a powerful grassroots insurgency focused on building the political power to hold the candidates of political parties accountable can bring about the policy changes necessary to stop the menace of fracking and dirty energy.

Fortunately, a powerful movement has emerged to ban fracking that is quickly gaining momentum. And this movement is increasingly global, with organizing efforts happening on every continent. France and Bulgaria have banned fracking, while activists are organizing to stop fracking across

Europe, from the UK and Germany to Poland and Romania. In Africa, resistance against fracking has arisen in several countries, including South Africa and Tunisia. In Latin America, a powerful coalition has emerged in Argentina, where more than thirty local fracking bans have been passed. Australian fracking activists are fighting to stop extreme energy and to protect the country's dwindling water resources.

In the United States, the movement began in those places threatened by fracking, as grassroots activists organized to protect their communities by passing local bans and other actions. To date, almost 470 local measures against fracking, wastewater disposal, and frac sand mining have passed in communities across the country. Building on this momentum, opponents of fracking scored a tremendous victory when New York governor Andrew Cuomo announced in 2014 that he intended to ban fracking in the state. This came after years of organizing and movement-building and followed a review of the science conducted by acting health commissioner Howard Zucker, which showed that the risks of fracking made the practice too dangerous to pursue. Concluding that he would not want his children to live near a fracking site, Zucker stated, "I cannot support [fracking] in the great state of New York." [25]

Across the United States, the New York victory has energized activists to work for a ban on fracking—from California to Pennsylvania. Food & Water Watch, which in 2011 was the first national organization to call for a ban—has worked to have legislation introduced in Congress to ban fracking on public lands. This is a necessary step at the federal level to educate (and pressure) members of Congress on the need to take strong action. But, much more must be done, including reversing all of the policy decisions that are incentivizing the switch to natural gas.

If we are to tackle the enormous threat posed by fracking and the fossil-fuel industry, it is crucial to understand how the policy decisions of the last forty years have led us away from sustainable energy and toward a reliance on natural gas. The devil truly is in the details. While many well-meaning environmentalists believe that we are making real progress on renewable energy, the data on the percentage of electricity generated by nonrenewable energy sources tells a different story. Although the emphasis on individual action—putting solar on rooftops—is a step in the right direction, serious policy changes must be made to displace the large amount of energy produced by natural gas, coal, and dangerous nuclear power.

Solar power generated only 0.2 percent of the nation's electricity on average between 2010 and 2014, and wind energy supplied 3.6 percent.[26] If geothermal energy is added to the equation, the renewable share grows to 4.2 percent. Hydropower generates 7 percent of the nation's electricity, but this amount may decrease over time because of the impacts on river ecosystems. Over the past five years, fossil fuels continued to power two-thirds of America's electric sockets. Coal power generated almost 42 percent of electricity, and natural gas generated nearly 26 percent.

Percent of Total Energy Use 2014

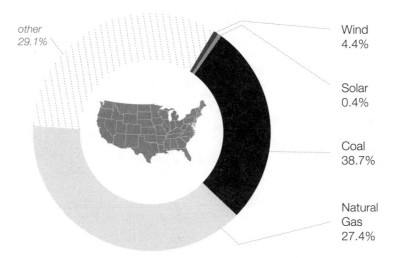

other 29.1%

Wind 4.4%

Solar 0.4%

Coal 38.7%

Natural Gas 27.4%

Some green groups claimed if electricity was deregulated, renewables would thrive and nuclear plants would be retired, but a close examination of the numbers shows that this has never happened. Nuclear power has hovered at around 20 percent of electricity production since the 1990s and is expected to increase little if at all. Old plants will be taken out of production over the next twenty years, although if nuclear power is allowed to benefit from cap-and-trade policies, new plants may be built, subsidized by taxpayer money.

Coal electricity has declined from 53 percent of generation between 1995 and 1999 to almost 42 percent over the most recent five years. It will continue to decline as a result of the adoption of the Obama administration's Clean Power Plan—a set of policies designed to replace coal-generated electricity with natural gas. Lower natural gas prices and federal mandates to reduce mercury and carbon dioxide are shifting electricity production toward natural gas and away from coal-fired generation.[27]

Natural gas has been the big winner, with generation increasing every five years since natural gas was deregulated in the 1980s. Natural gas generation has doubled from about 13 percent in the late 1990s to nearly 26 percent in recent years. Natural gas production increased an average of 5 percent a year beginning in 2000.[28]

According to a 2014 report by the EIA, between 2012 and 2040, 42 percent of the total increase in electricity generation will be from natural gas. Coal-fired generation's share of total generation will decline to 34 percent in 2040, while natural gas will rise to 31 percent.[29] But the predictions for renewables are shockingly low, with EIA predicting that solar will still make up 1 percent of electricity generation and wind 7 percent in 2040.[30]

Predictions about energy use are often proven wrong, and the complexity of energy use and production means that changes in policy frequently have many unplanned consequences. But one thing is certain: over the past forty years, the schemes favoring the use of natural gas, and to provide cheap energy to the largest industrial users of natural gas and electricity have proven successful, with dire consequences for the environment, consumers, and our democracy.

The Koch brothers have been major funders of the scheme that has landed us where we are today. Ideologically opposed to any regulation, they also have sought policy changes that would benefit their bottom line—seeking changes in natural gas and electricity policies that would facilitate cutting special deals for cheaper energy, while shifting costs to residential and small-business consumers. David Koch founded the Cato Institute in 1974, one of the think tanks pushing deregulatory policies and working with other right-wing actors such as the Heritage Foundation.[31]

Mindful of the tactics used by public interest groups, Charles and David Koch eventually decided to pursue a similar strategy by founding Citizens for a Sound Economy (CSE) in 1984, leading a grassroots-style campaign to oppose regulation and taxes.* David Koch explained of their thinking:

---

* In 2004, CSE merged with Empower America to become another right-wing action group, FreedomWorks.

"What we needed was a sales force that participated in political campaigns or town hall meetings, in rallies, to communicate to the public at large much of the information that these think tanks were creating. Almost like a door-to-door sales force."[32]

The fossil fuel industry had been attempting to deregulate the natural gas industry since the presidency of Franklin D. Roosevelt. After three decades of bitter legislative, regulatory, and legal battles, progressive forces lost the long fight over the pricing of natural gas and oversight of pipelines, beginning with the passage of the Natural Gas Act of 1978. By 1990, after a series of deregulatory policy changes, a highly speculative wholesale market in natural gas developed, with Wall Street gambling determining the price that consumers paid for natural gas and incentivizing future natural gas development. The New York Mercantile Exchange (NYMEX), a commodity futures exchange, applied to the U.S. Commodities Future Trading Commission to trade natural gas futures on February 29, 1984, and trading commenced on April 4, 1990.[33]

Between 1985 and 1990, the Federal Energy Regulatory Commission (FERC) had also made deregulatory changes to the rules for moving natural gas from wellheads to end users. Pipeline companies were required to separate gas sales, transportation, and storage services, giving large industrial customers an advantage and creating an incentive to build more pipelines. The deregulatory policies spurred a frenzy of pipeline construction that has continued unabated through the fracking boom, creating widespread habitat damage and posing safety risks. Between 1984 and 2014, gas companies added at least 936,000 miles of pipeline—about 85 miles every day—and there are now 2.5 million miles of transmission, distribution, and gathering lines.[34]

Further, thousands of miles of unregulated high-pressure pipelines with much larger capacity for transferring natural gas to processing facilities— referred to as gathering lines—have proliferated since fracking, although no cumulative record of the mileage exists.

The radical changes in the rules governing the natural gas industry inspired a ferocious lobbying campaign to make similar changes to the electric industry, changes that would eventually drive the use of natural gas for electricity. Breaking up the $200 billion (more than $300 billion adjusted for inflation) electric industry offered an opportunity to create a battle of titans, as they fought among themselves over the rules that would benefit their particular economic interest. Using a politically loaded vocabulary to win converts, they claimed that it would unleash competition, broaden consumer choice, and lower the cost of electricity.

Spearheaded by institutions affiliated with the Koch brothers, including CSE and the Cato Institute, a politically powerful coalition emerged in the 1990s to restructure the electric industry. Large coal utilities like American Electric Power Inc., and natural-gas-power marketers—companies like discredited and bankrupt Enron—were at the forefront of the lobbying machine to transform the electric industry. Proponents of deregulation sought to separate power generation from transmission and distribution, creating an unregulated wholesale market where middlemen could speculate on buying and selling electricity. Wall Street—investment houses, rating agencies, and financial analysts—fueled the drive to make electricity another tradable commodity. The changes that they wrought created a market where power producers, retailers, and other financial intermediaries could speculate on short-and long-term contracts for electricity. After deregulation, the marketplace was supposed to be self-governing, begetting cheap and reliable electricity.

The turning point began in 1992, when C. Boyden Gray, the White House counsel to President George H.W. Bush, engineered the inclusion of provisions in the Energy Policy Act of 1992 that fast-forwarded electricity deregulation.[35] Gray, a millionaire heir to a tobacco fortune, has been closely affiliated with the Koch-funded front groups throughout his long career as a corporate lobbyist, presidential adviser, and U.S. diplomat.[36] Concealed within the compromise legislation was language removing important limitations on the ownership of electricity generation, which had protected consumers. It also authorized FERC to issue orders that changed the structure of the electric industry over the second half of the decade, creating a casino-like atmosphere in the wholesale electricity market and driving construction of new gas-fired power plants. The FERC orders allowed states, if there was the desire, to rewrite the rules by which residential and small business purchased electricity.

The natural gas industry, led by Enron, launched a massive lobbying campaign to "unleash market forces," pushing for even more deregulation at the state level. Claiming that a new era of competition would replace bloated and inefficient utilities with lean and mean power marketers like Enron, California became the first state to succumb to the rhetoric, allegedly giving consumers a choice about their electricity provider. The large investor-owned utilities wrote the legislation, however, protecting their favored economic position. Between 1999 and 2001 a small cartel of energy companies was able to use the new layer that had been created between the producing and distributing of electricity to make billions of dollars by price-gouging consumers. Californians were overcharged by almost $25 billion during the first five years of deregulation, as power marketers manipulated electricity supply and natural gas prices, causing a series of rolling blackouts throughout the state. In the end, California and several other states that had deregulated this essential service instituted some form of regulation again.[37]

CSE, Enron, and the other advocates of state-based deregulation had pushed for federal legislation that would force states to forsake cost-based regulation, which limits energy company profiteering. According to the Center for Responsive Politics, the powerful coalition promoting electricity deregulation spent $50 million between 1998 and 2000 on lobbying to change the rules under which electric utilities operate.[38] Although the calamity in California set back industry efforts to pass federal legislation compelling states to restructure the electric industry, new efforts are afoot to push this agenda.

In the meantime, the creation of the wholesale electricity market has led to a dramatic increase in natural gas–fired electricity, making the fracking industry one of the biggest beneficiaries of FERC's deregulatory changes. Although companies must go through a weak permitting process that varies depending on each state's rules, no calculation of how the plan fits into a national plan for reducing pollution is made. And since the Obama administration's Clean Power Plan leaves decisions to the states, no overall examination is done on the impacts to our global climate.

Advocates who warned against the unintended consequences of electricity deregulation—both for the environment and for consumers—were ignored or scorned. Foreshadowing the future support for fracked natural gas, influential foundations and public interest advocates signed on to the efforts to deregulate electricity. Without a large grassroots campaign, the green groups negotiated from a very weak position. They naively bought the argument that, by compromising, deals could be cut to expose dirty power plants to competitive forces, and that sustainable energy would be the winner.

These same groups failed to oppose the elimination of a 1935 law, the Public Utility Holding Company Act (PUHCA). Restricting speculative ventures with ratepayer dollars and restraining electric utilities from operating outside of the geographic area that they served, this obscure law offered major protection to consumers and limited the already significant political power of the electric industry. It was repealed in the Energy Policy Act of 2005, at the same time that fracking was exempted from national environmental laws. This has created a handful of enormous electric utility companies that dominate political decision making about energy-related issues.

The chilling predictions about PUHCA's elimination are tragically coming true as the electric corporations consolidate at a rapid rate. Eugene Coyle, formerly an economist at the California utility watchdog group TURN, predicted in 1997, "What we are looking at is the shift from a situation where there are more than a thousand utilities nationwide, over which rate-payers have some control, to a future where there will be perhaps 10 big power companies operating free of regulation and acting like the oil cartels of old."[39]

The largest of these behemoths, Exelon, operating in forty-eight states, has both regulated and unregulated subsidiaries, including a large fleet of nuclear power plants. An energy trader and large electricity generator, it has subsidiaries that sell electricity and natural gas to more than 7.8 million customers.[40] Duke Energy, a giant power generator and energy trader with regulated and unregulated businesses, is headquartered in North Carolina. Serving 7.3 million customers, the company has announced that it is considering getting into the fracking business through one of its regulated subsidiaries.[41]

NextEra, a large energy company with regulated and unregulated subsidiaries, claims to be a "sustainable" energy company because it is the largest owner of wind farms. Although it produces 19 percent of the electricity it sells from wind, 50 percent of the company's generation comes from natural gas plants, and 25 percent comes from nuclear power.[42] Recently, in Florida, its regulated subsidiary, Florida Power & Light, was given permission by the Florida Public Service Commission (PSC) to go into the controversial fracking business in Oklahoma and to charge its customers for the risky business venture.[43] The PSC commissioners actually rushed their vote, not waiting for the agency's staff analysis, and now the utility is lobbying for the ability to charge customers for fracking investments without authorization from the PSC.

The companies above—each with $1 billion or more in profits—are representative of the other giant energy corporations that operate in all aspects of energy production, sales, and trading. The disturbing trends in the energy business, in which these companies play in multiple arenas, always with an eye on quarterly profits, means that they have a hugely disproportionate impact on public policy. Fracking is among the dangerous outcomes of the deregulation that has taken place over the last forty years.

Reversing bad energy policy and banning fracking will take a massive grassroots mobilization that holds accountable Democrats and Republicans alike and that takes power back from the Koch brothers and their ilk. It means challenging the entrenched political establishment that grovels to the dirty energy industry and facilitates its ability to operate without sufficient oversight, transparency, or accountability. It means working shoulder to shoulder with the brave activists across the country who are challenging extreme energy rather than worrying about the opinions of mainstream funders or other institutions that have close ties to dirty energy. With mounting evidence about the harms of fracking, and the immediacy of the impending climate crisis, it is time for the major green groups to fight for a transition to real sources of renewable energy and energy efficiency, not to depend on market-based schemes with no track record of working.

We can and we must build the political power to change the course of history—our survival depends on it.

1

IN THE BEGINNING . . .

The healthful balm, from Nature's veriest spring.
The bloom of health and life to man will bring.
As from her depths the magic liquid flows.
To calm our sufferings, and assuage our woes.
— advertisement for Kier's Petroleum,
early nineteenth century [1]

Through the ages, long before methane was removed from deep in the earth through a process known as hydraulic fracturing or "fracking," its seemingly strange properties confounded those who happened upon it seeping from the ground. In ancient Greece, or so the story goes, a goatherd moving his flock stumbled upon a burning flame on Mount Parnassus in Delphi, and he knew that he had witnessed the divine. Local wise men built a temple to Apollo at the site where the fumes of methane and other gases seeped from the ground.

From roughly 700 B.C. to A.D. 380, a long succession of priestesses, all named Pythia, went deep into the bowels of the temple and breathed deeply of the vapors that made the sacred flame burn. In 458 B.C., the clever Greek playwright Aeschylus wrote that the priestess, known as the Oracle of Delphi, would breathe fumes from a crack in the ground; upon deeply inhaling the magic vapors, she would go into a trance and become the voice of Apollo. Another Greek writer described how Pythia drank water with magic properties as it flowed from a spring into the temple chamber. The mythmakers of ancient Greece documented pilgrims coming from far and wide to learn their fates or to be given wise advice.

This incident was dismissed as legend until a team of scientists investigated the geology beneath the temple ruins and found evidence that methane had fueled the long-ago flame. They tested the nearby spring water and the mineral deposits on the ruins and discovered evidence of methane and ethane, as well as traces of the hallucinogenic gas ethylene. Traversing faults had shifted and collided, creating intense heat that, over eons, cooked the remnants of living matter from ancient seas into these hydrocarbon vapors. The gases escaped through faults, fractures, and other natural pathways to seep into the air and into the nearby spring.[2]

The bewitching properties of methane vapors escaping from the ground and ignited by lightning played a role in many of the world's oldest religions—from the burning bush in Exodus to the eternal flames worshiped by the Hindus and Zoroastrians.

Today soothsayers are still divining the magic of methane. Across the globe, self-serving modern oracles—from the financial centers that power the global economy to the powerful governments that make public policy—prophesy that natural gas will do everything from fixing the economy to solving the crisis of global climate change.

Odorless and colorless, natural gas expands to fill the area where it is contained. Unlike oil and water, it can be compressed, so its volume depends on the surrounding pressure and temperature. Naturally occurring gas is mostly methane, but it can include other components in various amounts, such as butane, hexane, propane, helium, carbon dioxide, and hydrogen sulfide, as well as benzene, toluene, ethylbenzene and xylenes, which are extremely toxic hydrocarbons collectively known as BTEX.[3] Over millions of years, layers of buried plants, sea animals, rocks, mud, and sand were subjected to extreme heat and pressure. The original energy taken in by these plants from the sun was transformed and stored deep underground in the form of oil, coal, and natural gas. That is, the sun's energy was stored in the strength of the molecular bonds between the hydrogens and carbons that make up those hydrocarbon fuels. Once discovered, the desire to exploit this ancient energy has grown exponentially with each passing century.

It was the Chinese who first recognized the energy-giving properties of natural gas around 400 B.C., when they used it to boil saltwater in order to extract salt. Within a few centuries, the Chinese began methodically looking for gas, piping the fuel through bamboo tubes and in some cases refining it with the first known carburetor.[4] They also pioneered drilling technologies in their search for water, drilling as deep as three thousand feet by dropping a heavy chiseling tool from a tall bamboo structure to pulverize the rock.[5]

The mysterious properties of gas also were known in North America. In 1626 French explorers noted that Native Americans lit gas seepages in the Lake Erie region, ironically where fracking is being pursued today. Long before settlers intruded into this region, the Mound Builders, then the Erie, and eventually the Iroquois inhabited it and made use of the gas rising from the ground. During his time as a surveyor, George Washington recorded a "burning spring" on the banks of the Kanawha River near where Charleston, West Virginia, is located today.[6]

No resourceful European colonists are recorded taking advantage of the seeping gas until William Aaron Hart came along. A talented gunsmith, he also invented and patented the percussion cap—a lock-and-ignition system for guns. Hart observed gas bubbles in a creek in western New York. In 1825 he hand-dug a well that was almost thirty feet deep and used hollowed-out logs to transport the gas a short distance to provide lighting in the small village of Fredonia, New York.

Hart soon built a rudimentary storage vat to hold the gas, called a gasometer, and transported it through lead and tin pipes to thirty-six gaslights in Fredonia. When the town was incorporated in 1829, the city fathers included five oil-light burners in the town seal, and there is still a street near the well's location named after him. Hart eventually moved to Buffalo, becoming a successful businessman with the Buffalo Gas Lighting Company.[7]

Although Hart moved on, the modern story of gas in the area around Fredonia was just beginning, and the battle over fracking was far in the future. In 1857, a distant relative of Hart's through marriage, twenty-six-year-old Preston Barmore, convinced prosperous local residents to invest in a gas company. A graduate of Fredonia Academy, a forerunner of the State University of New York at Fredonia, he obviously had done his research. Barmore and his associates were not content to rely on gas seepages for their new business. Based on a geological report, they purchased property and began using a crude method of drilling. A four-inch-diameter hole was bored more than 120 feet into the hard rock, and when no gas appeared, Barmore used gunpowder to create an explosion to release the gas (and water), creating the first gas well.[8]

By 1858 Barmore had drilled two wells that produced enough gas and water to pipe into the town. He incorporated the first gas company in the country, eventually named the Fredonia Natural Gas Company. By 1859, gas-flame lights had been installed in most stores and businesses in Fredonia.[9]

Around the same time, sixty miles from Fredonia, Colonel Edwin Drake drilled the first oil and gas well in Titusville, Pennsylvania.[10] A colorful character, Drake had never served in the military but adopted the title of colonel to impress the local townspeople with his respectability. Even so, they began to call him crazy as he struggled to capture the oil that they had seen seeping from the ground.[11] Drake had been hired by a group of speculators who secured land leases after hearing reports of oil in western Pennsylvania and were privy to a Yale chemistry professor's report of its use for lighting and lubrication. After many false starts, Drake decided that the methods used in salt mining were the solution.[12]

Salt recovery was a thriving business in many regions of the country, and oil and gas were often waste products. Drake traveled to a salt mine in nearby Tarentium, Pennsylvania, to observe the techniques and look for equipment and workers. He hired an experienced salt driller, William "Uncle Billy" Smith, to help manage the drilling project.[13] Drake and Smith refined the cable-tool drilling technique employed by the nineteenth-century salt industry, in a process very similar to the one used by the Chinese centuries before. Fueled by a steam engine, a two-foot chisel hanging by a rope from a wooden structure was lifted and dropped, creating a deeper hole each time. He encountered the same problem that Barmore had experienced: water filled the hole as he went deeper. So Drake pounded a pipe into the bedrock and drilled within it—an innovative solution that protected the upper part of the well from cave-ins and kept the water outside of the pipe's perimeter.[14]

Although the local townspeople laughed at "Drake's Folly," on August 27, 1859, he made history as the oil and gas began to flow at sixty-nine feet. The well was destroyed in a fire when Uncle Billy's lamp ignited the gas. Drake never patented his casing idea, and in his old age, while others were acquiring fortunes in the region, he was sick and poor. In 1873, at the urging of the residents of Titusville, the Pennsylvania General Assembly authorized a $1,500 annual payment to him.[15]

Although the oil boom began almost immediately after Drake hit oil, it was not until 1872 that the gas from the area where he drilled was utilized. Transmitted in the first-ever long-distance metal pipe, it flowed five miles in a two-inch iron pipe to Newton, Pennsylvania.[16]

Interest in piping gas intensified, and other natural gas companies were organized. The United Natural Gas Company, a direct forerunner of the National Fuel Gas Company, built a pipeline between McKean County, Pennsylvania, and Buffalo, New York. At eighty-seven miles, it was the longest on record during this period, and, frighteningly, parts of it are still in use. In 1899 the company improved long-distance transmission by using a compressor to pump the gas at a constant pressure.[17] Today National Fuel Gas Company operates through many subsidiaries and is deeply involved in fracking.[18]

At almost the same time, in Indiana, Elwood Haynes invented a meter to measure gas flow and pressure as well as one of the first gas-regulating thermostats. A talented scientist, he studied chemistry, biology, and German at Johns Hopkins University. Although Haynes is remembered for creating Stellite, a hard metal used in toolmaking, in the 1890s, as a manager and owner of the Portland Natural Gas and Oil Company, he oversaw construction of one of the earliest natural gas pipelines. Extending from near Portland, Indiana, to Chicago, Illinois, it went a distance of 120 miles.[19]

Yet the wide use of long-distance pipelines was still many decades in the future. Gas is difficult to corral and pipe, and during this period it was usually viewed as a waste product to be vented, burned, or left in the ground. Most of the gas used in urban areas during the nineteenth century and the early part of the twentieth century was so-called manufactured gas, derived from coal, oil, and sometimes wood, and should not be confused with natural gas. During this period, manufactured gas for local use was produced in thousands of facilities in the United States and Europe.

The new magic of chemistry was used in these community-based facilities to create a combination of gases that could be burned for lighting, heating, or cooking. Created during a complex and highly polluting process, it left behind a legacy of toxic coal-tar components that include arsenic, benzene, leads, phenols, toluene, xylenes, and even cyanide. Once natural gas became available, the use of manufactured gas diminished in the 1920s, but its toxic legacy is still being remediated in some locations today.[20]

Although manufactured gas was the primary fuel for lighting cities, natural gas had been discovered in seventeen states by the turn of the twentieth century.[21] Attempts to capture it depended largely on location, availability, and the cost of other fuels such as kerosene. Gas was used widely in the central Appalachians, the Gulf Coast, Southern California,

Kansas, Oklahoma, and Texas. Between 1920 and 1940, as the population grew where gas was available, its use tripled.[22]

Beginning in the early decades of the twentieth century, Congress answered the demands of the oil and gas industry to financially support technological advancements for the industry. The Bureau of Mines was established in 1910, and by 1913 included a petroleum division aimed at the "problems bearing on the increase of safety and efficiency and the lessening of waste in the development of oil and gas fields, and the storage, transportation, and use of petroleum and petroleum products, including natural gas."[23] Congress passed the Foster Act in 1915, creating ten new research facilities across the nation to study the development of raw materials. One of these research stations, the Bartlesville Petroleum Experiment Station (BERC), located in Oklahoma, opened its doors in 1918. Over the next six decades the facility was an important source of federally funded inventions, patents, and demonstration projects for the oil and gas industry. Initially it delivered valuable technical information about drilling, transport, and pipeline engineering. Projects included research on water intrusion in wells, increased output from water flooding, geologic resource mapping, detection and prevention of leaks in natural gas pipelines, geophysical methods of prospecting, and the mechanics of extracting crude oil and natural gas.[24]

By the 1920s, improvements in pipe technology made long-distance pipelines economically feasible. Seams in steel pipes could be welded electrically for durability, and problems with corrosion had been solved by a joint research program between the U.S. Bureau of Standardization and the natural gas and utilities industries.[25] In 1925 Magnolia Gas of Dallas, Texas, laid the first all-welded steel gas pipeline, reaching 217 miles from northern Louisiana to Beaumont, Texas.[26]

The first truly long-distance pipe was constructed in 1931, spanning one thousand miles; it reached from the Texas Panhandle to Chicago. Built at the cost of $75 million, it was funded by a number of smaller gas companies, such as Peoples Gas in Chicago. Fabricated from twenty-four-inch steel pipe, it crossed the Mississippi and required 2,600 right-of-way agreements.[27]

Industry capture of important federal institutions intensified during this early period and the syndrome of a revolving door between industry and government was spawned.[28] Many experienced researchers left their jobs in government research for the higher salaries offered by industry.

Later many returned to the public sector as regulators, bringing their company loyalty and personal relationships with industry leaders to their jobs.

Federal research temporarily waned in the 1920s as one of the frequent
boom-and-bust cycles hit the industry. New wells were drilled and then
abandoned once the "easy" oil was gone. By the end of the decade, as the
stock market plunged, Texas oil was dumped on the market, resulting in
the lowest oil prices in history.[29] Research resumed in the 1930s and 1940s
when the Bartlesville Station teamed up with the American Gas Association (AGA) to create mathematical formulas to characterize flows through
gas pipelines, and to determine new ways of gauging and controlling the
flow from natural gas wells. The government subsidized the lion's share of
the research, with the industry contributing only 20 percent of the funds.[30]

Federal funding was also used to address safety-related problems, an
area that industry was not interested in financing research on. The invis-
ibility and lack of odor of gas could cause asphyxiation, fires, and explosions. When the AGA asked the federal government to do more research
in the 1920s, researchers investigated eighty-nine different compounds,
choosing fifty-seven to be tested between 1926 and 1930. They determined
that ethyl mercaptan was the most effective, least corrosive, and most practical odorant to add to natural gas.[31]

In spite of the research, the industry did not go to the expense of adding
the odorant until a long sequence of mass-casualty accidents had taken
place. Odorants began to be used in the 1940s, but it was not until 1970 that
the use of a warning agent was mandated.[32]

World War II Stimulates Petroleum Development

In the lead up to the war, government officials worked with industry to
increase fossil fuel production. A field office was established in Franklin,
Pennsylvania, in 1942. A natural gas specialist was among the staff hired at
the research center to examine the geology of reservoirs—an expansion of
work being done in other regions of the country. The researchers analyzed
rocks to determine their physical and chemical composition and explored
the most promising sites for water flooding. In these experiments, pressurized water was injected into the well to drive the oil or gas resource to the
surface, the precursor to today's fracking techniques.[33]

Congress also took several steps to encourage more exploration and
production of oil and gas, especially on public lands, including updating

the Mineral Leasing Act of 1920. The royalty payments of at least 12.5 percent were maintained, but the complex system of prospecting permits was replaced by a system allowing oil and gas companies to lease undeveloped public lands. In 1946 Congress further simplified the leasing process, making it more attractive to petroleum interests.[34]

Although the Bureau of Mines had been tasked earlier in the century to survey and document petroleum resources, the U.S. Geological Survey (USGS) began to play an increased role in petroleum mapping as the war approached. Created in 1879, it had been charged to survey the 1 billion acres of federal land (including unmapped land acquired from the Louisiana Purchase and the Mexican War) that remained unsurveyed. After the United States entered the war, the USGS strategic minerals program—a program authorized in 1939—was expanded from minerals to include petroleum.[35]

World War II also drove major developments in welding, pipe rolling, and metallurgy that made extremely long-distance pipelines feasible. Attacks on oil tankers and the increasing need for fuel during the war led the federal government to launch a huge pipeline project that included funding, designing, and constructing two legendary pipelines. The Big Inch pipeline was twenty-four inches in diameter and took oil 1,254 miles from East Texas to Illinois. Its companion, the twenty-inch Little Big Inch, stretched from Texas through Illinois to New Jersey.[36]

After the war, a bitter battle was waged over the fate of the pipelines with several rounds of bidding and a debate over using them for gas or oil. Suspicion of unethical behavior and conflicts of interests marked the privatization of the pipelines. Both pipelines were sold to Texas Eastern Transmission Corporation at a price just over $143 million—about $2 million less than the government invested in them during the war.[37] Following several mergers, the original company is now part of Spectra Energy.[38]

Oil and gas developments offshore can also be traced to projects initiated during World War II. Operation Pluto (for "pipe line under the ocean") in Britain, a huge research and engineering project, created the technical know-how that eventually would allow the nascent offshore North Sea and Gulf of Mexico industries to flourish after the war. The project involved building numerous pipelines across the English Channel that could be connected to the more than one-thousand-mile network of pipelines in England during the war, taking fuel from the ports of Liverpool and Bristol to France, in support of the Allied invasion of Normandy. More than a million gallons of fuel was transmitted every day through the undersea pipes during the war.[39]

After World War II

With the deep commitment to oil and gas buttressed by improved technology and favorable policies, the use of these fuels grew dramatically during the decades after the war. But by the 1970s a convergence of current events that included the Middle East oil embargo and alleged natural gas scarcity, created tremendous political pressure to rethink energy policy. In 1975, a new program was funded to work on improving directional drilling and hydraulic fracturing. Government researchers also experimented with "massive hydraulic fracturing," applying extreme pressure with pressurized water.[40]

In the midst of all of this activity, Jimmy Carter was elected president, and in 1977, after much controversy, his large new energy policy program passed in Congress. It created the cabinet-level Department of Energy, reorganized programs scattered throughout the government, and coordinated new energy research.[41] The technologies necessary for fracking were jump-started by the taxpayer-funded research during this period and into the 1980s. One project involved drilling test wells to locate and identify the chemical nature of shale and placing the information in a large database correlated with existing maps.[42] Sophisticated seismic tools and mapping software were created to show three-dimensional maps of shale formations.[43] The technologies necessary for drilling horizontal wells were developed.[44]

To grease the wheels, in 1980 Congress provided a production tax credit for unconventional gas that remained in place for more than two decades, which quadrupled drilling during this period.[45] In contrast to fossil fuels, renewable energy has received only a small share of government research-and-development dollars. The Congressional Research Service reported that in the sixty-five years between 1948 and 2012, federal agencies spent the bulk of their dollars on fossil fuels and nuclear technologies, but only 12 percent of their research budget was spent on renewables and 10 percent on energy efficiency.[46]

This is a story about political expedience, influence peddling, and greed.

Political decisions on energy policy and expenditures on decades of research directly led to the commercialization of fracking technologies. In recent years, federal dollars have been spent making new information and technology available to the oil and gas industry on shale geology, seismic imaging, and directional shale drilling techniques. The industry dismisses the role that the U.S. government has played in the research and promotion of fossil fuels, however. Among their reasons is the fear of how government involvement will promote a transition to sustainable energy.

2

SETTING THE STAGE

Anyone wishing to see what is to come should examine what has been.
—Niccolò Machiavelli

Early twentieth-century utility mogul Samuel Insull served as a prototype for twenty-first-century wheeler-dealers, from Enron's Ken Lay to Chesapeake Energy's Aubrey McClendon. While he is remembered for working with Thomas Edison to create the electric industry, his questionable business dealings paved the way for New Deal regulation of electric and gas utilities.[1] Insull arranged construction of Natural Gas Pipeline Company of America's thousand-mile-long pipe from West Texas to the Midwest, the long-distance pipeline owned by the same company that George Mitchell contracted with in 1954 for almost forty years, making him a millionaire.[2] (See Chapter 7.)

Insull admired monopoly power, as reflected in his 1910 speech titled "Sell Your Product at a Price Which Will Enable You to Get a Monopoly." Insull hated city government interference in his local utilities, but he gambled on advocating weak state-based regulation that could be influenced by a man of his stature and cunning. He believed that public ownership would be the result of failing to regulate. When challenged about this strategy, he boasted that in 1917 utility commissions had approved 90 percent of rate increases for regulated utilities. His vision of corporate-dominated utility regulation still operates today.[3]

A brilliant manager and unscrupulous financier, Insull built a network of nearly five thousand gas, coal, and electric utilities located in thirty states.[4] Using the holding company as an instrument of high finance, he stacked one leveraged company on top of another, milking profits from the entire structure. His gas and electric companies gouged consumers because their parent company forced them to borrow money at high interest rates and to pay exorbitant prices for trumped-up services. Even as the operating utility was cheated, it was required to pay high dividends to the holding company.[5] Ultimately, as the scheme lurched to a tragic ending, Insull had businesses worth a half billion dollars on paper with only $27 million of actual equity. With the stock market crash his empire imploded, ruining six hundred thousand investors.[6]

Holding companies were masters at monopoly. Those associated with J.D. Rockefeller's Standard Oil of New Jersey and Columbia Gas and Electric, two of the largest in the country, divided the market in two and drove competitors out of business.* They kept wildcatters from accessing pipeline connections in their monopoly fiefdoms and wrested financial control of the independent pipeline firms.[7]

After Franklin D. Roosevelt's election, his administration launched a Federal Trade Commission (FTC) investigation into utility holding companies, culminating in an enormous ninety-six-volume report cataloguing the abuses.[8] Evidence of outrageous profiteering emerged. A holding company could receive from 50 percent to more than 300 percent profit from utility subsidiaries it controlled.[9] Eleven holding companies produced more than half of all natural gas and controlled three-quarters of the fifty thousand miles of interstate gas pipelines. Four of these giants controlled 58 percent of the pipeline miles. They distributed the majority of electricity and often also controlled coal and oil.[10]

The stunning crash of Insull's empire and the FTC's investigation provided a justification for Roosevelt's allies to introduce legislation outlawing holding companies and regulating utilities. A two-hundred-day battle was waged in Congress with more than six hundred lobbyists—more than one for every congressman—threatening to oust members who dared support a "death sentence" for holding companies. They spent an estimated $1.5 million to defeat the legislation, the equivalent of $26 million today.[11]

Senator Hugo Black—later a Supreme Court justice—headed an investigation that collected evidence about the corruption and the fact that ratepayers would pick up the tab.[12] Black's investigation inflamed public opinion, making a compromise possible. In 1935 the Public Utility Holding Company Act passed, allowing the holding company structure (parent

---

* Standard Oil of New Jersey became Exxon in 1972. Columbia Gas and Electric became part of Duke Energy after a series of mergers and acquisitions.

company with subsidiaries) to be used but forbidding parent companies from cheating ratepayers by charging high fees to their affiliates. Those operating utilities in multiple states had to have contiguous service territories, and they were regulated by the Securities and Exchange Commission (SEC).[13] PUHCA required holding companies to simplify their structures, submit financial information to the SEC, and focus on their core businesses, which effectively prohibited oil companies and non-utilities from owning gas or electric utilities. To facilitate oversight, it restricted the size and geography of gas and electric utilities, requiring them to incorporate in the state where they operated.[14]

Decades of lobbying for its repeal attests to the law's effectiveness. It was eventually repealed by the Energy Policy Act of 2005, leading to the growth of mega-utilities.[15]

Pipeline Power

When PUHCA passed without pipeline regulation, their owners continued to charge gas distribution companies exorbitant rates that were paid by consumers. A group of urban cities organized to push for federal regulation of the gas transmitted in interstate pipelines, while independent gas producers also lobbied to regulate the monopolies that were cheating them. After much wrangling, the Natural Gas Act of 1938 was signed into law, giving the Federal Power Commission (FPC, later renamed the Federal Energy Regulatory Commission, or FERC) authority to ensure "just and reasonable rates" on pipelines.[16] The agency was also given authority to permit the building of new gas pipelines—an authority that FERC is abusing today as it allows the construction of a massive new network of unnecessary and dangerous interstate pipelines.[17]

World War II drove a surge in natural gas production, with Appalachia hosting 70 percent of new wells drilled between 1942 and 1945.[18] After World War II, America's status as an economic powerhouse triggered an expansion of pipeline infrastructure and profiteering.

Complaints about how the FPC established fair and reasonable gas prices precipitated a study of the gas industry that was released in 1948, sharply dividing the FPC. Conflicting reports emerged, one focused on cost-based pricing that allowed regulators to set the price of gas based on production costs and then to add a fair rate of return. (Between 1945 and 1960, it was 5.7 to 6.5 percent.)[19] Meanwhile, the Federal Trade Commission was pursuing an antitrust investigation of the petroleum industry, sparking action in Congress. In 1948, President Truman had been reelected and Democrats gained control of Congress. Powerful oil and gas allies had been put into leadership positions in Congress, and Oklahoma Democrat Robert Kerr, the millionaire owner of Kerr-McGee Oil Industries and great-uncle of Chesapeake Energy's founder and former CEO, Aubrey McClendon,* was elected to the Senate.[20] (See Chapter 9.) Industry shills introduced legislation to prevent the regulation of gas prices at the wellhead by the FPC, but it failed to pass in 1948.[21]

The next year Kerr introduced new legislation to exempt gas from regulation. It was drafted by a lawyer for Phillips Petroleum,† one of the largest producers of gas with operations in the Midwest, Southwest, Rocky Mountains, and Gulf Coast states and the owner of 4,380 miles of pipelines.[22] Leland Olds, a brave FPC commissioner, testified that the legislation was about a craving for higher profits that would allow a $500 million surcharge on consumers. Senator Kerr retorted, "That will be admitted." The media backlash prompted Truman to veto the bill in 1950.[23]

Kerr and the gas producers had their revenge when Olds was up for reappointment for his fourth term at the FPC. Foreshadowing the worst of the McCarthy-era red-baiting, Olds, a New Deal progressive, was mercilessly smeared and attacked.[24] A Texas lawmaker charged that Olds "has not believed in our constitution, our government, our Congress, our representative form of government, our churches, our flag, our schools, our system of free enterprise."[25]

Although Olds was strongly defended by many allies, his appointment was rejected by a vote of 53 to 15. The attack on Olds was significant because it served as a warning about the growing and fierce opposition to allowing the FPC to regulate the industry on behalf of consumers—opposition that

---

* In 2006, Houston-based Anadarko Petroleum Corporation acquired Kerr-McGee in a cash transaction totaling $16.4 billion plus the assumption of $1.6 billion in debt. The company is involved in uranium mining and milling and has been involved in several controversies, including the alleged murder of whistle-blower Karen Silkwood in 1974.

† In 2002, Phillips Petroleum merged with Conoco to become ConocoPhillips. ConocoPhillips split into two separate companies in 2012, with the legacy company maintaining the name and continuing to develop and produce crude oil and natural gas. The company that was spun off, named Phillips 66, kept the refinery, chemical, and pipeline assets of the former ConocoPhillips.

ultimately led to more tepid and less consumer-friendly oversight.[26] During the ongoing controversies, Phillips Petroleum tested the waters for dramatically raising the wellhead price for natural gas. The state of Wisconsin and several local jurisdictions petitioned the FPC to prevent this unjustified increase, but the politicized FPC decided against them. Wisconsin then sued the FPC in 1951 and won, meaning that the FPC would have to regulate natural gas prices.

That case was appealed to the Supreme Court, and in a landmark case, the Court ruled 5–3 that the legislative intent of the National Gas Act was "to give the commission jurisdiction over the rates of all wholesales of natural gas in interstate commerce." This far-reaching decision gave the FPC authority to regulate gas at both ends of interstate pipelines.[27] The outcry by the natural gas industry was swift, and legislation to halt regulation was introduced. Senator J. William Fulbright, a Democrat from Arkansas, charged, "For the first time in our nation's peacetime history, a highly competitive segment of our economy has been wrenched from the free enterprise system and converted into a public utility under the direct domination of the federal government."[28] Shortly before Senate passage of the bill, Senator Francis Case, a Republican from South Dakota, stunned his colleagues by announcing that he would vote against the bill because the industry had offered him a bribe to vote for it. The embarrassing scandal prompted President Dwight Eisenhower to veto the legislation, which he had originally supported.[29]

Even as the political winds were shifting, some New Deal Democrats were fighting back. Illinois senator Paul H. Douglas, elected in 1949, was a poor boy from Maine who had earned graduate degrees from Columbia University and Harvard. He was a practicing Quaker who rejected absolutist pacifism after hearing Benito Mussolini's announcement of a fascist invasion of Ethiopia. He resigned his position as a Chicago alderman to join the Marine Corps as a fifty-year-old private. Severely wounded in World War II, he lost the use of his left arm and was awarded a two Purple Hearts and a Bronze Star.[30]

In 1955 and 1956 Douglas asserted the need for regulation of natural gas, saying there was "irrebuttable proof that the pipeline companies are tied to the giant producers in what amounts to a monopoly situation." Although the twenty largest natural gas producers supplied 90 percent of the fuel, they hid behind the eight thousand other producers, saying regulation would hurt the little guy. Douglas said that six of the ten largest American industrial companies were actually "so-called independent producers of natural gas."[31]

Douglas proved that industry manipulated estimates of gas reserves to make the case against regulation. He showed that producers used creative accounting to diminish tax liabilities, making most of the expense of discovery, development, and production tax deductible. Companies raked in additional financial benefits from deducting interest payments and "intangible drilling and development costs." Douglas said that the consolidation of the industry allowed companies to overcharge, citing Sun Oil's attempt to raise rates 73 percent*—way beyond the cost of production and a reasonable profit.[32]

Unsurprisingly, the industry fell victim to its own arrogant behavior in 1957, when the deregulation legislation failed again. Media coverage of an industry celebration for Joe Martin, a Texas congressman and former chairman of the Republican National Committee—held before the bill's passage—suggested an overly cozy relationship between the industry and its congressional water carriers.[33]

Despite legislative failures, Eisenhower's FPC commissioner appointments from petroleum states had made the agency friendly to the industry. After the 1954 Supreme Court decision freezing gas prices, the agency was deluged with eleven thousand rate filings. But most rate requests were approved.[34] Complaints about regulation were without merit; no evidence exists that rates were set below market levels.[35]

Douglas made progress in his investigation of energy monopolies under presidents John F. Kennedy and later Lyndon Johnson when the FPC commissioners opposed rate hikes on consumers. In 1965 giant petroleum producers and consumer advocates faced off over the price of gas from the Texas–New Mexico Permian Basin region. Transcripts running more than thirty thousand pages reveal that the commission established a two-tier pricing structure. Gas from new wells would be priced at a slightly higher rate than gas already in production, but a price ceiling was set based on the average cost of production, and dry wells would not be reimbursed. The industry immediately challenged the decision in court. The court of appeals refused to overturn the FPC's decision, saying, "A producer has

---

* The fortune accrued by Sun Oil provided the financing for the Pew Charitable Trusts.

no constitutional right to be reimbursed for dry-hole expense." But more hearings on technical points of the FPC ruling were required. In 1968 the Supreme Court upheld the FPC's cost-based pricing procedure by a 7–1 vote.[36]

The stage was set for one of the most vicious public policy battles of the twentieth century.

3

THE NATURAL GAS HEIST

We use 30 percent of all the energy, in the United States. That isn't bad; that is good. That means that we are the richest, strongest people in the world and that we have the highest standard of living. That is why we need so much energy, and may it always be that way.
— President Richard Nixon, November 26, 1973 [1]

On April 5, 1972, petroleum executive Bill Liedtke, president of Pennzoil,* sent his company jet with a suitcase containing $700,000 to the Committee for the Re-election of the President (CREEP). Liedtke was rushing to beat the April 7, 1972, deadline for the new campaign finance law. This was just a fraction of the $20 million that CREEP had raised from corporate supporters on behalf of President Nixon. [2]

Petroleum interests were grateful to Nixon, who had kept his promise to overturn "heavy-handed" regulation of their cartels by appointing John Nassikas as chairman of the Federal Power Commission. According to rumor, Nixon had allowed petroleum lobbyists to interview Nassikas, and the future FPC chairman had vowed to deregulate the price of gas. A Harvard-educated lawyer, Nassikas had been legal counsel to utilities, banks, and insurance companies. Known for dressing in a vest and gold chain and speaking in jargon, the loyal Republican fund-raiser spent his off hours hobnobbing with lobbyists at swanky golf courses. [3]

An article in the November 1, 1969, issue of *Forbes* gushed, "It's hard to see how the troubled natural gas industry could have a regulator more to its taste. . . . He sometimes sounds more like a natural gas executive

---

* Pennzoil merged with its rival Quaker State in 1998 to form Pennzoil–Quaker State. In 2002 the Royal Dutch/Shell Group bought the company.

expounding about how the FPC should regulate his industry than a man burdened with the actual responsibility of regulation."[4]

Nixon also appointed Rush Moody, a corporate lawyer for a large law firm that represented the petroleum industry, and Pinkney Walker, a right-leaning economics professor from the University of Missouri. Walker was known for his consulting gigs with utilities, pipelines, and trade associations.[5]

Walker was determined to have Kenneth Lay, a former student working at Humble Oil, become his deputy technical assistant at the FPC.* Walker knew Lay would do a brilliant job building the case for deregulation.[6] Lay went on to become chairman and CEO of Enron, the energy commodities and services business that was bankrupted by accounting fraud made possible by deregulation.

During Lay's stint at the FPC he effectively became an acting commissioner. Walker said later: "Helen, my then wife, was getting into a very serious Alzheimer's situation, which meant that Kenneth was doing all the work at the office. He thus became a de facto member of the Federal Power Commission." Next Lay moved over to the Interior Department as deputy undersecretary of energy, presiding over federal leases for energy resources.[7] His influence on the FPC had a lasting impact. Over the next several years, the commission presided over large rate increases and forgave massive amounts of industry overcharges. But no matter how obliging the FPC was to the gas industry, it was never enough.

In 1969 critics saw a conspiracy in the making when the industry began to play the scarcity card to argue against regulation. It had played this hand previously when the Supreme Court regulated natural gas at the wellhead in 1954. At that time, the justices found that the argument had no merit and that predictions of shortages had failed to come true. In 1968 the Supreme Court once again ruled against the industry, saying the FPC was authorized to set the price of gas and industry claims of shortages were false.[8]

Senator Phil Hart, a Democrat from Michigan, was suspicious of the monopolized petroleum industry's motivation in declaring a gas shortage. In 1970 he called upon the Federal Trade Commission to investigate the allegations about gas producers withholding accurate information reserves. The commission replied to Hart that "in order that the possibility

* Lay never returned to Humble Oil, which was renamed Exxon in 1971.

of collusion or other unlawful conduct in this field may be more fully explored, we have today directed our staff to commence an investigation which will focus principally on the reporting, estimation, and deployment of reserves."[9]

During his eighteen years in Congress, Hart had become an articulate critic of monopolies and concentration of economic power. Wounded during the D-Day invasion of Normandy, he was elected to office in 1958. He was so well respected that a new Senate office building was named for him as he lay dying in 1976.[10] Known as the "conscience of the Senate," Hart took moral positions, despite the political risk. His support for civil rights issues drew especially heated attacks during the 1970s busing battles that included an attempted recall campaign* during the 1972 election season.[11]

Chair of the Senate Subcommittee on Anti-Trust and Monopoly, he held many hearings in the Senate's eleven-year investigation into concentration in the petroleum industry, where twenty corporations controlled 94 percent of oil and gas reserves and 76 percent of crude oil production.[12] He suspected this control allowed the industry to contrive shortages to increase prices.

When Nassikas appeared before Hart's committee to make the case for deregulation, Hart challenged the idea that the free market was at work in the oil and gas industry. He said that the interdependence of producers precluded competition because they did business through joint operating, bidding, and marketing arrangements. Hart charged they were collectively withholding the true information on reserves.[13]

Haskell Wald, the FPC's chief economist, sent a series of memos in February 1970 to Nassikas saying that the AGA data were based on statistics that the agency had "no way of corroborating." Calling their data unreliable and questionable, he added that it "can hardly be said to match" data published elsewhere by the trade association.[14]

Businessweek reported that the industry wanted a 60 percent increase in gas prices. An August 1, 1970, article stated, "The major oil companies, which control most of the natural gas supplies in the U.S., have made it clear that they are not interested in increasing gas production until it becomes more profitable." On October 2 the *New York Times* agreed: "The major oil companies, which own the lion's share of gas leases, are not averse to an artificially induced gas shortage which would heighten the pressure for a

---

* Federal elected officials cannot be recalled.

hefty increase in gas prices."[15] In congressional testimony, a spokesman for the Consumer Federation of America said, "They have simply announced that there is a shortage. They know that there is a shortage because, they candidly tell us, the industry that is trying so hard to squeeze the consumer for high prices through scare tactics and threats had told them there is a shortage."[16]

If a real crisis had been developing during the 1960s, it is unlikely that the FPC would have endorsed deep discounts to industrial users—the more gas used, the less paid. Real concern would have prompted the Department of the Interior, the agency overseeing leases on federal lands, to have undertaken a detailed survey of natural gas reserves. Instead, it relied on reserve information provided by the major companies to the American Gas Association.

The AGA had no shame about hedging on the truth. A 1971 *Life* magazine ad was typical of its message: "We've been serving you for a hundred years—and we don't intend to stop now. . . . It will take higher prices to keep the gas coming."[17] Meanwhile, industry revenues were surging much faster than consumption. Between 1970 and 1971 wellhead revenue grew by 9 percent largely because of higher prices, as natural gas consumption rose only 3 percent.[18]

In 1974 the General Accounting Office investigated profiteering, finding that between 1970 and 1973 the FPC's ingenious accounting methods had allowed the oil and gas companies to reap an unjustified $3.3 billion on gas sales and that nineteen senior officials at the agency illegally owned stock in the petroleum industry.[19] In response, Shell Oil's full-page ad was representative of the industry response: "How in all conscience can anyone call these excess profits?"[20]

In the meantime, an FTC bureau investigated the collusive under-reporting of natural gas reserves. In 1971 the agency subpoenaed Exxon, Continental Gulf, Mobil, Pennzoil, Shell Standard Oil of California, Standard Oil of Indiana, Tenneco, Texaco, and Union Oil of California. Furious at facing an investigation, all of the companies attempted to quash the subpoenas. By 1975, as the agency fought a court battle for documents, it had received 78,000 documents from four companies and 100,000 from other sources.[21]

The investigation proved that pipeline companies had interlocking boards of directors and they were linked by joint ventures, combined gas and oil leases, and shared ownership of production facilities and pipelines.

And attempts to skirt antitrust laws extended to banks. Dr. John W. Wilson, chief of the FPC's Division of Economic Studies, testified in 1973 that Morgan Guaranty Trust was an example of how interlocking relationships worked between banks and oil companies. There were Morgan employees on the boards of Continental Oil, Cities Service, Atlantic Richfield, Belco Petroleum, Columbia Gas, Louisiana Land and Exploration Company, and Texas Gulf Sulfur. Morgan Guaranty Trust held stock in Texas Eastern Transmission, Panhandle Eastern Pipeline, and many other distribution utilities. Chase Manhattan representatives sat on the boards of Standard Oil of New Jersey (ultimately Exxon) and Standard Oil of Indiana (ultimately Amoco), and the bank was a major shareholder in Panhandle Eastern Pipeline.[22]

By 1975 Senator Hart was seriously ill, but Congressman John E. Moss had taken up his mantle against monopolies. Moss had been shaped by a difficult childhood during the Depression. A self-educated man, he was one of the few legislators who read entire pieces of legislation to study the public policy implications. Moss was a small business owner in the 1930s, but his vocation was political reform. Beginning in 1948 he was elected to the California legislature, and he served in Congress from 1953 until 1978.[23]

In *People's Warrior*, a biography of Moss, Michael Lemov, his former chief counsel, wrote that he had fought for passage of some of the "most notable and far-reaching legislation of the twentieth century, including the Freedom of Information Act, the Consumer Product Safety Act, and major reforms of the capital markets." Decades before recent securities fraud cost investors billions, Moss was warning about the lax oversight of Wall Street.[24] Lemov writes that Moss was key to holding back deregulation of the natural gas industry for several years, saving consumers billions of dollars. Moss often required the heads of the oil and gas industry to raise their right hand and swear under oath to tell the truth—the whole truth.[25]

Ralph Nader remembers that, unlike most congressmen, Moss worked with citizen groups to write legislation and helped develop the strategy to pass it. Once it was law, he "went on to monitor the agency or department tasked with implementing or enforcing the law." He believed in "eternal vigilance."[26]

Moss presided over the Oversight Committee that held hearings on natural gas. He was outraged in 1974 when the oil and gas industry started playing "winter politics" by running ads promoting higher prices to prevent gas shortages. Even the agency's approval of a 100 percent increase in prices for newly drilled natural gas between 1972 and 1974 did not satisfy the industry.[27]

Meanwhile, environmentalists were concerned about industry's use of the shortage message to advocate offshore drilling. Nixon had announced during the waning days of his presidency that the Interior Department would lease 10 million acres for oil and gas drilling in 1975—about twice the size of Massachusetts.[28] While Nixon was faced the Watergate scandal, it became public knowledge that federal land had been leased at absurdly low prices. Senate testimony revealed that the foreign tax credit allowance enabled the five largest petroleum producers to go virtually tax free on profits earned overseas.[29] Yet the entire oil and gas industry was enjoying soaring profits. Exxon saw a 60 percent increase in profits between 1972 and 1973, and the industry averaged profit increases of about 50 percent.[30]

In the fall of 1974 the industry began slowing gas production to bring on a final showdown. Gas drillers delayed production, arbitrarily repairing wells or taking wells offline and pipeline companies cut off supplies. Transcontinental Gas Pipeline Corporation—owned today by Williams Companies—deliberately cut gas supplies to the East Coast, where many members of Congress were opposed to deregulation. With a large pipeline system, Transco was in a good position to punish its opponents. Twenty-five million people and factories employing 1.25 million workers were literally dependent on Transco for natural gas.[31] In the fall of 1974 the company announced that the "shortage" would require a 28 percent curtailment of gas deliveries. Come winter it tightened the screws, announcing an additional system-wide curtailment of up to 35 percent.[32]

Moss and consumer advocates were infuriated by what amounted to outright blackmail. The industry claimed that it needed higher prices and profits to incentivize production to avoid gas shortages, but it appeared that the intermittent cutoffs were more designed to pressure Congress to support deregulation. An internal Getty Oil Company memo revealed the real strategy, saying that deregulation would increase gas prices 400 percent within a year.[33]

In the summer of 1975 Moss began a series of hearings featuring the FTC's investigation of the role of industry collusion in creating shortages. The agency had collected enough evidence from the FPC, pipeline companies, and gas producers to develop a strong case against the AGA. Investigators found that producers kept two sets of books about their proven reserves—one set was their best estimate, and the other was developed for the purpose of misleading the FPC.[34] The estimates destined for the FPC were about a third lower than the AGA's own estimates.[35] An FTC staff's report charged, "The AGA reserve reporting procedures are tantamount to collusive price rigging."[36] The Department of Justice (DOJ) was urged to file an antitrust lawsuit against the trade association and eleven major oil companies. But the DOJ commissioners had no stomach for the battle and failed to take action.[37] Moss discovered that Nixon's appointee to head the FTC, Lewis A. Engman, had met privately with the AGA in 1975 and agreed not to take action.[38]

Meanwhile, in the aftermath of Watergate, the new president, Gerald Ford, continued business as usual at the FPC. In 1976 a Federal Energy Administration (FEA) staffer leaked information about the agency paying an AGA member company to write a pro-deregulation pamphlet, *The Natural Gas Story*. In retribution, the FEA put the leaker on a six-month leave of absence without pay, and cut his salary by 40 percent.[39]

Endgame for Regulation

In 1977, following the election of Jimmy Carter, the last round of gas deregulation began. Carter promoted legislation that consolidated the dozens of energy-related bureaucracies into a pro-fossil-fuel Department of Energy that doomed the conservation and renewables programs he claimed to favor. The long public-relations blitz for deregulation and the artificial gas shortages had scared the public and worn down opponents. The final showdown took place in the Senate, where two young Democratic senators—South Dakotan James Abourezk and Ohioan Howard Metzenbaum—orchestrated a legendary filibuster.[40]

Industry had secured the support of the Senate Energy Committee chair, Democratic senator Henry "Scoop" Jackson from Washington State. A bill that had failed passage two years earlier was reintroduced in committee and sustained a tie vote that normally would have killed it. But against normal procedure, Jackson sent it for a floor vote. Abourezk and Metzenbaum used a parliamentary procedure that has since been eliminated to introduce 508 amendments and conduct a thirteen-day filibuster. Senator Jackson offered compromise legislation giving industry a 2,000 percent increase on gas prices, short of deregulating it.

Although Carter's staff promised Abourezk and Metzenbaum that they were working to stop the deregulation of gas pricing, Carter took the unusual step of sending Vice President Mondale to chair the Senate, breaking the filibuster. The next day deregulation legislation passed 50 to 46—allowing increases in gas pricing and phasing in deregulation over two years. Carter hypocritically called the Senate bill "unfair" and "an injustice to the working people of this country." By 1980, natural gas prices had doubled at the wellhead and gone up by half for residences.[41]

It was a rancorous three months of bickering in the Senate-House conference committee. Not only had Carter caved to industry, but many key conferees also surrendered. The majority of the forty-three original conferees had opposed deregulation, but in the end only seventeen voted against the deal.[42] Beginning in 1978, gas would increase in price steadily every year until the end of 1983, at which time the unregulated market would set prices.[43]

After years of debate on deregulation, it was an anticlimactic ending, portending boom-bust cycles and severe environmental consequences.

4

SEEKING THE ROOTS OF THE FRACKOPOLY

The economy is a wholly owned subsidiary of the environment, not the other way around.
                    —Senator Gaylord Nelson, founder of Earth Day, in 1970[1]

Dubbed "Chairman of the Establishment," Wall Street lawyer John Jay McCloy had a career that spanned five decades, during which he served in interlocking roles as adviser to presidents, director of major corporations, legal counsel to the petroleum industry, and diplomat. McCloy, a Harvard graduate, once famously said, "Why, the Constitution is just a scrap of paper to me."[2]

His legacy includes facilitating the monopoly status of the oil and gas industry that continues today. McCloy advocated successfully for the right of the oil industry to be exempt from regulations governing competition. Virtually unknown today, he was the ultimate power broker—an adviser to nine presidents, from Franklin Roosevelt to Ronald Reagan. But his diplomatic missions on behalf of the petroleum industry often bypassed official channels.

Recruited by Roosevelt's Republican secretary of war, Henry Stimson, McCloy ran the War Department for his elderly boss. McCloy made the decision to "resettle" Japanese Americans in internment camps. He was dogged by criticism for his failure to recommend military action against Nazi death camps. This criticism grew after his appointment as the U.S. high commissioner for Germany, where he commuted the sentences of convicted Nazi war criminals and set them free.[3]

McCloy pursued the welfare of his corporate clients and the national interest as if they were one and the same. He was a mentor and counselor to several generations of Rockefellers. Practiced in law and philanthropy, McCloy promoted the career of a young political scientist named Henry

Kissinger. Serving in a dizzying number of capacities, he also was president of the World Bank, chairman of the Ford Foundation, chairman of the Rockefeller family's Chase Manhattan Bank, an adviser to the Federal Reserve Board, a member of the Warren Commission, and a director of Westinghouse, United Fruit, AT&T, and Metropolitan Life Insurance Company, among other corporations.[4]

McCloy used his influence with President Harry Truman to argue for the "Golden Gimmick," a tax break for oil companies operating in Saudi Arabia that remains in place today. When Saudi Arabia's King Saud demanded an additional payment for oil, the Truman administration agreed to regard the monies paid to the Saudi royalty as a tax that could be subtracted from the companies' income taxes.[5]

But most stunning about McCloy is his advocacy for the petroleum industry when it flouted antitrust laws. Serving as counsel to the "Seven Sisters"—Exxon, Mobil, BP, Texaco, Shell, Gulf, and Chevron—he helped these companies circumvent the laws designed to create a competitive marketplace. McCloy described his role with the Sisters like this: "My job was to keep them out of jail."[6]

the SEVEN SISTERS

In 1975, when British journalist Anthony Sampson wrote *The Seven Sisters: The Great Oil Companies and the World They Shaped*, he popularized the name originally given to the oil cartel in 1952 by Enrico Mattei, an Italian oilman who unsuccessfully attempted to break into the world oil market.

Gulf Oil

Texaco

Royal Dutch
(Shell)

Anglo-Persian Co.
(British Petroleum)

Standard Oil of California
(Chevron)

Standard Oil of New Jersey
(Exxon)

Standard Oil of New York
(Mobil)

John D. Rockefeller's Monopoly

McCloy served as the counselor to a fortune built from America's most famous industrial monopolies, the Rockefeller family's Standard Oil Trust.

None of the titans who made their fortune after the Civil War left a more indelible mark on the modern world than John D. Rockefeller. The empire he built around drilling for oil and refining the oil into kerosene was unique in the history of world affairs. Until electricity became widely available in the twentieth century, most people depended on kerosene lamps for lighting. By 1880 Rockefeller controlled 90 percent of oil sales and had a vast business empire numbering dozens of companies.[7] An adherent of laissez-faire economics—the idea that government should never intervene in business affairs—he felt righteous in circumventing existing laws. Standard Oil dominated all aspects of the petroleum industry, including drilling, transportation, refining, distribution, and sales; it even manufactured the barrels used for transporting oil.[8]

The trust model was devised to circumvent restrictive state laws and to further consolidate Rockefeller's control by streamlining production and logistics. A board of trustees was created to oversee the companies that Rockefeller had a controlling interest in. The forty-one shareholders of the companies constituting the Standard Oil empire transferred their shares to the trustees, giving them a stake in the entire holding. Rockefeller, the trustee with the highest number of shares, maintained control over the multinational corporation. Standard Oil continued to grow in size, expanding its operations around the world.[9] Rockefeller also purchased controlling interests in many other businesses, from iron mines and timberland to different types of manufacturing.[10] The trust was so successful in facilitating the accumulation of wealth that the other large economic interests—finance, meatpacking, mining, transportation, sugar, steel, and tobacco—copied the model.

One tactic that Rockefeller had used in building Standard Oil was predatory pricing. By charging less for a product than it cost to produce, he could undercut the price of other companies, driving them out of business. Because of the volume of business Standard Oil gave the railroad barons, his company was given rebates, providing it another unfair advantage. To get around this problem, Rockefeller's smaller competitors had built pipelines, but as he acquired these competitors the "iron arteries" gave Standard Oil even more monopoly power.[11]

In the first decade of the twentieth century, hundreds of articles were written by muckraking journalists about the abusive tactics of Standard Oil and the other trusts. Ida M. Tarbell, a journalist whose father had been ruined by Rockefeller, became the oil magnate's best-known critic. In 1902 Tarbell's series of articles, later published as *The History of the Standard Oil Company*, inflamed the public with a moving account of the brutal schemes employed by the monopoly.[12]

It was into this highly charged environment that President Theodore Roosevelt was elected to office. Memorialized as a legendary trustbuster, Roosevelt was more inclined to tame monopolistic behavior through punitive legal actions than to fully dismantle Standard Oil or the other trusts.[13] He lobbied Congress to create the Department of Commerce and Labor, an agency that was empowered to investigate and take legal action against the trusts.[14] Among the lawsuits filed by the new department was a massive case against Standard Oil. A special prosecutor accumulated detailed evidence on the workings of the oil industry and how Standard Oil had driven competitors out of business, creating a monopoly with the market power to charge excessive prices. In just twenty-five years, Rockefeller's empire had accumulated almost $1 billion in profits. In 1911, after years of litigation, the U.S. Supreme Court ruled that the company was in fact violating the Sherman Antitrust Act—a law that had passed in 1890 but not been properly enforced. Among the charges lodged by government attorneys against Standard Oil was the use of predatory pricing to eliminate competitors.[15]

The Seven Sisters Emerge from the Baby Standards

In 1911, after a proceeding in which more than 100 witnesses testified for 187 days in 110 towns, creating a record that was 20,000 pages long, Standard Oil was ordered to dissolve.[16] The company developed a plan, approved by the government, that broke it up into thirty-four different companies. John D. Rockefeller and the other Standard Oil owners maintained an interest in these companies. Within months of the breakup, the total value of the pieces was worth $200 million more than before the divestiture, and Rockefeller's holdings jumped by $56 million.[17] These "Baby Standards" were structured to be vertically integrated monopolies, based in different states but coordinating their activities and maintaining their previous commercial relationships. Shares in the new entities were distributed to the trustees according to their original ownership in Standard Oil. The largest of the entities, Jersey Standard (Exxon), began with half of the net value of the parent company.* After a year, the Baby Standards' value had doubled and Rockefeller's net worth had increased to $900 million (the equivalent of about $22 billion in 2015).[18]

In the years following the breakup, under the leadership of Walter Teagle, Exxon grew to be an even larger and most powerful Sister. Teagle had begun working for Standard Oil at the turn of the twentieth century, when Rockefeller bought his family's refinery and put him in charge of it. By 1917, Teagle, who was adept at promoting the company's financial interests in political circles, had become its president. In its role as banker for the other American Sisters, Exxon's wealth and power grew over the next three decades as it bankrolled their exploration and development of oil resources.[19] (See Chapter 16.)

Foreign Rivals Become Sister Co-conspirators

While Rockefeller had been buying up the oil business in the New World, two potential rivals—each of which would become a Sister—began establishing their control of oil in the Old World. The London-based Shell Transport and Trading Company became part of an oil syndicate after the tsar of Russia allowed foreign concerns to prospect for oil in 1873. Shell originally had been founded to sell fashionable boxes made of shells from what was then called the Far East, but it soon began shipping oil from Russia to Europe. Shell's management adopted the same predatory pricing tactics as Standard Oil in an attempt to beat Rockefeller at his own game. Over the ensuing decades, a series of fierce price wars took place globally, ultimately forcing Shell to merge with the upstart oil company Royal Dutch, creating the powerful Royal Dutch Shell in 1906.[20]

Meanwhile, with the discovery of oil in southwestern Persia (present-day Iran) in 1908, the precursor to British Petroleum was born as the Anglo-Persian Oil Company. On the eve of World War I, the First Lord of the Admiralty, Winston Churchill, converted naval operations from coal to oil and persuaded the British government to buy a 51 percent ownership

---

* Standard Oil of New Jersey, which also operated as Humble Oil and Esso, changed its name in the United States to Exxon in 1972. In the rest of this chapter, the modern names of the major oil companies are used for the sake of simplicity.

stake* in British Petroleum.[21] Top officials in Britain and France realized during World War I that access to plentiful supplies of oil would be critical in maintaining future economic and political control, especially of their colonies.[22] This desire for oil was one of the factors considered in their decisions about the breakup of the Ottoman Empire after the bloody war. The redrawn map of the region came to be known as the Middle East.[23]

Antitrust Issues Fade

In 1914, after years of protest by labor and farm groups about antitrust abuses, Congress passed legislation establishing the Federal Trade Commission, an agency that would interpret and enforce antitrust law. That same year, the Clayton Anti-Trust Act also passed in an attempt to define as illegal business practices that led to the creation of monopolies. It clarified and strengthened the Sherman Antitrust Act of 1890. With the hostilities overseas and America's entry into World War I, however, the public pressure for the prosecution of antitrust violations had waned. During the next decade the oil companies were given free reign to stifle competition and maintain high prices.

In the face of new discoveries of large oil reserves, overproduction and lower prices for oil meant lower profits. Teagle believed that federal and state antitrust laws needed to be revised and that cooperation within the industry was necessary to raise the price of oil.[24] The industry also sought new uses for petroleum products, from oil-burning cars to plastic. Exxon executives were key in forming the American Petroleum Institute (API) in 1919 in an attempt to organize producers and refiners to limit production and to lobby for their joint interests. Exxon and other member companies supported API by providing $10,000 annually for its operation.[25]

In 1920 oil interests gained a friend with the election of the Republican Warren G. Harding. His administration suffered the Teapot Dome bribery scandal, when federal oil reserves in Wyoming and California were secretly leased to oil companies by secretary of interior Albert Fall. Harding was beholden to a range of corporate interests, and his well-funded campaign used modern advertising techniques and employed photos (the first

* The British government's shares in BP were sold by Prime Minister Margaret Thatcher in the 1980s.

campaign to use the photo opportunity, or photo op), sound recordings, newsreels, billboards, magazine ads, and other techniques to influence public opinion.[26] Harding regularly played poker with Exxon president Teagle, who once urged the oilman to buy a baseball team.[27]

Teagle was also was very friendly with Calvin Coolidge, who after Harding died in 1923 served out his term and then was elected to a four-year term (1925–29). Harding's speechwriter, who also worked for Coolidge for the first two years of his administration, became the API publicist.[28] At the behest of large oil interests that wanted to limit production and keep prices high, Coolidge created the Federal Oil Conservation Board in 1924 and empowered it to allow API to provide important guidance about production targets and estimates of oil reserves.[29] Coolidge noted, "The future of the oil industry might be left to the simple working of the law of supply and demand but for the patent fact that the oil industry's welfare is so intimately linked with the industrial prosperity and safety of the whole people."[30] Teagle was so confident about Coolidge that he later asked him to head API, a job the former president turned down.[31]

A Cartel Is Born

In July 1928, after the discovery of a huge oil field in Iraq, executives from Exxon, Mobil, BP, Shell, and several smaller oil companies met to discuss the division of oil resources in the Middle East. Drawing a "red line" around the Arab territories—Iraq, Saudi Arabia, Jordan, Syria, and Turkey—the conspirators agreed not to independently seek oil in these countries. Deciding to work together in forming concessions with the host countries, they also consented to exclude Iran and Kuwait from their Red Line Agreement, making it the sole preserve of the British. Exxon negotiated to become a partner in the Iraq oil concession, giving it an important role at the center of future negotiations over the country's reserves.[32]

Just a month later, another secret meeting took place between Teagle and the heads of the two other largest Sisters, Shell chairman Henry Deterding and BP director Sir John Cadman.* Meeting to allegedly shoot grouse at Scotland's remote Achnacarry Castle, they settled upon a set of principles to prevent "excessive" and destructive competition by fixing prices, limiting production increases, and swapping contracts to reduce transportation

---

* The meeting did not come to light until 1952.

The Seven Sisters' Joint Partnerships in the Middle East*

Agreement Dates and Ownership Shares

In the first half of the twentieth century, the Seven Sisters exercised their power to take control of oil production in the Middle East.

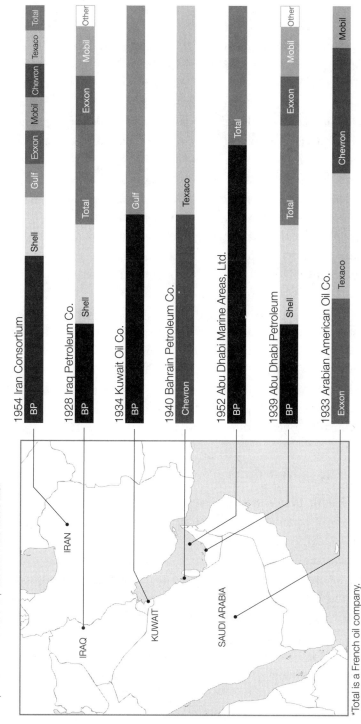

1954 Iran Consortium: BP, Shell, Gulf, Exxon, Mobil, Chevron, Texaco, Total

1928 Iraq Petroleum Co.: BP, Shell, Total, Exxon, Mobil, Other

1934 Kuwait Oil Co.: BP, Gulf

1940 Bahrain Petroleum Co.: Chevron, Texaco

1952 Abu Dhabi Marine Areas, Ltd.: BP, Total

1939 Abu Dhabi Petroleum: BP, Shell, Total, Exxon, Mobil, Other

1933 Arabian American Oil Co.: Exxon, Texaco, Chevron, Mobil

IRAN
IRAQ
KUWAIT
SAUDI ARABIA

*Total is a French oil company.

costs. Their urgency in creating the global oil cartel was the result of a flood of cheap oil from Russia that had created an intense price war. Shortly afterward, Mobil, Chevron, Gulf, Texaco, and eleven smaller companies became party to the conspiracy. In March 1929 API developed a plan to cut oil production that was complementary to the deal made in Scotland. The big companies continued to meet in the early 1930s to discuss their cartel arrangements. In 1934 they met to reformulate the agreement, producing a draft Memorandum of Principles that curtailed competition; companies breaking the agreement would be subject to penalties administered by a special committee of oil industry leaders.[33]

While the oil industry conspired, the United States faced an economic meltdown. The laissez-faire policies of Harding and Coolidge had allowed rampant speculation, leading to a devastating stock market crash in 1929. Newly elected president Herbert Hoover called on Teagle and other corporate heads to voluntarily cooperate in addressing the financial crisis as the Great Depression deepened.[34] Job loss was exacerbated by the failure to enforce antitrust laws during the previous decade, creating a wave of mergers that peaked during the period between 1926 and 1930, when 4,700 independent companies were swallowed up.[35] By the end of the decade, only two hundred firms controlled half of the economy.[36] Between 1929 and 1932, unemployment increased nearly fivefold, with about a quarter of all workers losing their jobs.[37] The situation was so dire that half of the U.S. population lived in poverty.[38]

The Roosevelt Years

President Franklin Roosevelt swept into office in 1933 after a landslide election, promising major public policy reforms. In the first years of the New Deal, Teagle served on the Business Advisory and Planning Council, a body established by the Roosevelt administration to encourage cooperation between business and industry.[39] Teagle sent gifts of salmon and pheasant to the White House until he became hostile to progressive reforms that Roosevelt instituted during the first years of the administration.[40]

Although antitrust matters were not at the top of Roosevelt's agenda, it was a calling for Thurman Arnold, the political appointee who headed the Department of Justice's antitrust division. Arnold, who had a long and varied career, was born on the Wyoming frontier and became a professor at Yale Law School before joining the Roosevelt administration.[41] Launching a major investigation of Exxon that resulted in two lawsuits, he unearthed proof of an Exxon conspiracy to control oil pipeline transportation. The second lawsuit was even more damning and would lead to Teagle's resignation in 1942. Arnold found that Exxon had made a restrictive agreement with the German chemical company I.G. Farben that blocked research on synthetic rubber, a material that was critical for the war effort. Accused of helping the Nazis, Teagle was also forced to testify before Senator Harry Truman's committee investigating national defense. When asked if Teagle's deal with I.G. Farben to restrict synthetic rubber production at a time when the Japanese had seized Malayan rubber plantations was treason, the future president answered, "Why yes, what else is it?"[42]

Just as World War I had impeded antitrust enforcement, however, with the onslaught of hostilities in Europe, the Roosevelt administration and Congress turned their attention away from antitrust violations and other domestic concerns to prepare for entry into World War II. Prosecution of monopolists did not progress until after, during the Truman administration—an investigation that Truman's secretary of state, Dean Acheson, was instrumental in impeding.[43]

DOJ's Investigation Reappears

The Truman administration and McCoy, who had been made the Proconsul of Germany in 1949, were more concerned about fighting communism than stopping the abuses of the petroleum cartel. Nevertheless, when information emerged after the war that the Navy had been overcharged for oil, new life was breathed into the Justice Department's dormant antitrust investigation. Based on the earlier investigation, the Federal Trade Commission wrote an explosive report about secret agreements between the petroleum giants. Senator John Sparkman, chairman of the Senate Select Committee on Small Businesses, released the report, saying that the government endeavored "to hold in check the power of giant organizations." Anthony Sampson, author of *The Seven Sisters: The Great Oil Companies and the World They Made*, describes the findings: "The seven companies controlled all the principal oil-producing areas outside the United States, all foreign refineries, patents and refinery technology . . . divided the world markets between them, and shared pipelines and tankers throughout the world; and . . . maintained artificially high prices for oil."[44]

Acheson was annoyed when the Justice Department launched a grand jury investigation of the American oil cartel at a time when he was enlisting the big American oil companies in foreign policy. In the last days of the Truman administration, the Departments of State and Justice came to an agreement. A civil case was filed rather than the criminal case that the trustbusters in the Roosevelt administration had originally planned. A report written by the Truman State Department and supported by the Departments of Defense and Interior articulated the administration's position: "American oil operations are, for all practical purposes, instruments of our foreign policy."[45]

Under President Eisenhower, oil diplomacy became even more entrenched. The president hosted regular formal (tuxedoes only) men-only (stag) dinner parties at the White House that often included McCloy and Texas oilmen Sid Richardson and W. Alton Jones, who favored promoting business interests when making foreign policy. Eisenhower considered McCloy not only a close friend but a personal adviser on foreign policy.[46]

In the first months after Eisenhower was elected, the civil complaint against Exxon, Mobil, Chevron, Texaco, and Gulf advanced, based on evidence about a conspiracy to divide the market and fix prices. But in 1953, Eisenhower instructed Attorney General Herbert Brownell that enforcement of antitrust laws "may be deemed secondary to the national security interest." Meanwhile, Secretary of State John Foster Dulles weakened the hand of the trustbusters by facilitating the creation of an oil consortium in Iran that could set production levels and thus prices.[47]

Iran would become a thorn in the side of both the oil industry and American foreign policy. The root of the Iranian problem began with the final breakup of the Ottoman Empire in 1922, giving Britain a monopoly on Iranian oil through British Petroleum. Britain's failure to pay a fair price for oil ultimately led to the democratic election of a nationalist prime minister, Mohammad Mosaddeq, who nationalized oil reserves and production facilities.[48]

Eisenhower—under the influence of Dulles and McCloy—allowed the U.S. Central Intelligence Agency to overthrow Mosaddeq and to create a consortium of oil companies to share in the spoils. The attorney general gave his assurances to Eisenhower that this would not constitute a violation of antitrust laws. Unbeknownst to Eisenhower and Brownell, the oil companies had already met in London and made another secret agreement to prevent competition.[49]

Meanwhile, the Golden Gimmick had incentivized American companies to shift to foreign production. This allowed a few independents, including Sunoco, Superior, Pennzoil, and Getty, to become forces in domestic production and refining. The Seven Sisters dominated oil production internationally, with the five American Sisters controlling two-thirds of the Middle East oil.[50]

By the summer of 1960, a glut of oil forced the industry to reduce prices, but companies still enjoyed enormous profits and were able to finance their expansion into new markets. Despite this, Exxon's arrogant chairman, Monroe "Jack" Rathbone, unilaterally cut the price per barrel of oil from the Middle East, creating a cascade of unintended consequences. (See Chapter 16.) The Sisters' interdependency forced them to follow suit, and in September 1960 Iran, Iraq, Kuwait, Saudi Arabia, and Venezuela retaliated, creating the Organization of the Petroleum Exporting Countries.[51]

When President John F. Kennedy took office, McCloy warned that OPEC could withhold oil. Besides advising Kennedy, McCloy was practicing law at Milbank, Tweed, Hadley, and McCloy, a firm representing the Rockefeller family's business interests. He also served as counsel to the Seven Sisters, representing them on antitrust issues and in global business diplomacy.[52]

McCloy told Kennedy that it might be necessary to suspend antitrust laws and allow the companies to bargain collectively with the producing countries. Kennedy arranged for McCloy to speak with Attorney General Robert Kennedy, who told McCloy that he would waive antitrust regulations for the oil giants if necessary. Kennedy provided McCloy with a "business review letter" giving him permission to represent multiple oil companies.[53]

After his initial success with the Kennedy brothers, McCloy met with subsequent attorneys general to reinforce the importance of excluding the industry from antitrust laws when negotiating with OPEC.[54] The companies paid a sizable retainer for his services, which included secret briefings conducted by the CIA and State Department.[55]

Kennedy's Department of Justice did bring forward the languishing civil case, releasing a tough "Statement of Claims" saying that the oil companies had employed "monopoly power" to control prices. Despite its legion of antitrust lawyers, the government was thwarted: Exxon, Texaco, and Gulf signed weakly worded consent decrees, and the cases against Mobil and Chevron were dropped.[56]

Their antitrust problems behind them, the oil barons were as tightly bound as ever through a network of banks, accounting firms, trade associations, and key people. McCloy, in particular, occupied key posts in several intersecting parts of the Rockefeller empire, including looking out for its oil company investments. He was poised to play a starring role in the crisis with OPEC that took place early in the Nixon administration.[57]

President Richard Nixon appointed McCloy to his foreign policy transition team, and he played the role of informal adviser on oil-related issues. He arranged for his oil company clients, many of them donors, along with David Rockefeller, to visit with Nixon and discuss the Middle East.[58]

The Seven Sisters had shortchanged the oil-producing countries for decades. That stingy stubbornness was about to backfire. Muammar Qaddafi, the leader of Libya, demanded a higher price from the twenty-eight American oil companies profiting from Libya's resources. The State Department's chief oil expert, James E. Akins, pointed out that Libya's demands were far from unreasonable, and he warned of a diplomatic and commercial meltdown if the Libyans "concluded they were being cheated."[59]

The indisputably dominant Exxon encouraged the Sisters to reject Akins's advice. Qaddafi responded by seeking to drive a wedge between independent companies and the Sisters. He reduced the production quota for Armand Hammer's Occidental, cutting off the companies supply. Shortly afterward, the independent oil companies agreed to pay more.[60]

The Sisters turned to McCloy, who twice took oil executives to meet with State Department officials during September 1970 in the hopes that the U.S. government would reinforce the companies' demands. They met only disappointment. The State Department admitted that the United States had almost no leverage over Libya.[61]

Texaco and Chevron agreed to renegotiate their contracts. OPEC responded by warning the other companies that if they did not concede that "a concerted and simultaneous action by all Member countries" would follow.[62] McCloy quickly renewed the longstanding agreement that the companies would be indemnified from prosecution for breaking antitrust laws with Nixon's Attorney General John Mitchell.[63]

The top leadership from twenty-three oil companies converged on McCloy's New York offices to jointly draft two documents to address the

crisis. One was a public statement announcing the companies were negotiating with OPEC collectively; the other was a secret agreement between
the companies about sharing in any cutbacks ordered by Libya. While the
energy barons negotiated in the law firm's posh conference room, the Justice Department and State Department representatives passively awaited
McCloy's updates from the industry meeting in a smaller adjoining room.[64]

McCloy advised State that they should send an experienced diplomat
with gravitas to the Middle East to negotiate with OPEC. Undersecretary
of State John N. Irwin II, a political appointee that knew nothing of either
the oil business or the Middle East, was sent to meet with the Shah of Iran,
King Faisal of Saudi Arabia, and the Sheikh of Kuwait. An inexperienced
negotiator, Irwin agreed to negotiations on OPEC's terms. Over a six-week
period, the companies signed agreements conceding to OPEC's demands.[65]

OPEC grew in power as new oil-producing nations joined during
the 1960s and 1970s and as global demand for oil increased.[66] Although
OPEC's power to curtail production took a toll on the economies of the
West, this was a temporary situation. Exxon had initiated a $700 million
exploration program focused on extraction from countries not participating in OPEC. By the 1970s oil crisis, the company was extracting oil from
Australia, Canada, and Alaska. Shell and BP were drilling the vast reserves
in the North Sea.[67]

In retrospect, it was not unreasonable for the oil-producing nations to
have demanded a greater share of the income from their oil. The companies
had paid the OPEC countries only 10 percent of what consumers paid for
oil and gasoline. European countries collected twice as much in oil taxes
as OPEC nations received from the oil companies.[68] The State Department
had allowed a lack of consistency in policies over the course of many administrations. In London, Foreign Office diplomats were ordered not to
"interfere with the commercial policies of the great oil companies," according to Sampson.[69]

This diplomatic house of cards fell apart in October 1973, a casualty of
the Arab-Israeli War. OPEC retaliated against the United States for supporting Israel, initiating a full oil embargo that increased the price of oil
nearly ninefold between 1970 and the end of 1973.[70]

While Americans suffered high energy prices, the companies' profits
skyrocketed. According to an analysis by the Senate Finance Committee,
the oil companies enjoyed sky-high earnings, with stronger returns than at

any time in the preceding decade. In five years the profits of the ten largest oil companies more than doubled, from $4.5 billion in 1970 to $9.5 billion in 1974.[71]

In 1974 Henry Kissinger developed the International Energy Agency as a vehicle for Western energy interests to respond to OPEC. His assistant Thomas Enders said that it was designed to break up OPEC.[72]

Responding to the price gouging, the FTC instigated a lawsuit against the eight largest oil companies, alleging that they had "monopolized the domestic refinery industry in violation of the Federal Trade Commission Act."[73] But ultimately the action failed to exact a real cost from the oil giants, which retained an army of lawyers to challenge the government on every aspect of the suit.[74] The Petroleum Products Antitrust Litigation, a lawsuit combining several cases, took decades of legal wrangling, eventually netting $140 million for four western states and their citizens.[75]

When the price gouging came to light, Senator Philip A. Hart, Congressman John Moss, and other lawmakers tried unsuccessfully to pass legislation addressing price gouging and monopoly power. (See Chapter 5.) Carter appointed consumer advocate Michael Pertschuk to the FTC in 1977 to pursue the antitrust violations. Pertschuk feared that "unrestrained conglomeration could conceivably result in the concentration of an enormous aggregation of economic, social and political power in the hands of a small number of corporate leaders.[76]

Meanwhile, David Rockefeller, McCloy, and Kissinger were working on behalf of the shah of Iran, Mohammed Reza Pahlavi. Rockefeller's bank, Chase Manhattan, held $6 billion in deposits and processed about $2 billion in transactions annually that involved Iran. The threesome hatched a scheme they dubbed "Project Alpha" to pressure Carter to allow the exiled shah (code-named "Eagle" in their spy-novel-like plan) to come to the United States. Carter opposed admitting the shah but ultimately gave the deposed dictator sanctuary, sparking the hostage crisis that led in part to his defeat by Ronald Reagan.[77]

Record amounts of money poured into the 1980 election, and one-third of it came from oil and gas companies. Corporations formed 1,249 political action committees (PACs) that for the first time lavished more cash on the Republicans than on the Democrats. Oil and gas interests targeted longtime congressional opponents. The National Committee for an Effective Congress issued a report on oil and gas PACs that said, "This type of massive expenditure by a selfish special interest poses a real threat to our political process and the well-being of every American."[78]

Unsurprisingly, the Reagan administration would be exceptionally responsive to oil and gas interests and would usher in a new era of attacks on the protections designed to prevent the formation of monopolies.

After leaving office, Pertschuk reflected, "By the early '70s Congress had enacted more than 25 consumer, environmental and other social regulatory laws, and businessmen began to feel real economic pain. When business gets organized, it gets very organized."[79]

5

THE FRACKOPOLY COMES TO POWER

I think they [the Obama administration] genuinely believe that we can go back to medieval times and have windmills. They truly believe we can have windmills, solar energy, and of course, as you know, that will just take us back to a medieval economy.

— Steve Forbes, CEO of Forbes Media [1]

In 1964, a group of wealthy funders instigated a radical insurgency that reshaped the political landscape and weakened democracy. Although their ultraconservative presidential candidate in 1964, Senator Barry Goldwater, was defeated in a historic landslide victory by Lyndon B. Johnson, the election spurred the development of a long-term strategy to take back control of the nation.

Business leaders were revolting over the new laws designed to protect public health and the environment. Angered by the stricter requirements for operating factories, mines, and utilities, many of these leaders were resentful of the social transformation that occurred after World War II.

Despite the bloody war in Vietnam, Johnson advanced many progressive social justice goals. His Great Society programs expanded Roosevelt's New Deal, successfully beginning to address poverty, unemployment, and discrimination. Passage of the Civil Rights Act of 1964 and the Voting Rights Act of 1965 began to reverse long-standing wrongs, while the Supreme Court, under Chief Justice Earl Warren, greatly expanded legal rights for classes of people who had long been excluded. Progressive social changes had become mainstream, with Ralph Nader often appearing on television, inspiring a crusade for consumer rights as young people streamed to Washington, D.C., to join "Nader's Raiders." In 1970, Nixon, reacting to the growing environmental movement, signed both the National

Environmental Policy Act and the Clean Air Act, which had been passed by the majority Democratic Congress. He used an executive order to create the Environmental Protection Agency (EPA), consolidating federal activities around environmental monitoring, standard setting, research, and enforcement, an action that had no impact on the budget. Nixon, who was no environmentalist, also vetoed the Clean Water Act because of its cost. He was caught on tape saying that Ralph Nader and other environmentalists pushing for strict auto pollution standards wanted to "go back and live like a bunch of damned animals."[2] In light of the ascendancy of environmental concerns, however, he was compelled to use pro-environment rhetoric at times and to appear supportive of cleaning up burning rivers and dirty air.

While it is naive to assume that a single event changed history, a 1971 memo to the U.S. Chamber of Commerce from the soon-to-be U.S. Supreme Court justice Lewis Powell was an important marker. A manifesto of sorts, it galvanized corporate interests to revolt. He went on to write the 1978 Supreme Court decision declaring the First Amendment right of corporations to influence elections through contributions.[3]

He advised corporate leaders to organize, saying, "Strength lies in organization, in careful long-range planning and implementation, in consistency of action over an indefinite period of years, in the scale of financing available only through joint effort, and in the political power available only through united action and national organizations." He also wrote, "The most disquieting voices joining the chorus of criticism come from perfectly respectable elements of society: from the college campus, the pulpit, the media, the intellectual and literary journals, the arts and sciences, and from politicians. . . . Much of the media . . . accords unique publicity to these 'attackers,' or at least allows them to exploit the media for their purposes." He singled out one individual: "Perhaps the single most effective antagonist of American business is Ralph Nader, who—thanks largely to the media—has become a legend in his own time and an idol of millions of Americans."[4]

Powell's memo, titled "Attack on American Free Enterprise System," became a call to action among the moneyed leaders of the right-wing insurgency. Cultural studies scholar Dr. Henry Giroux describes it as a "theoretical framework and political blueprint" to attack democracy. Giroux says that wealthy funders Joseph Coors in Denver, Richard Mellon Scaife in Pittsburgh, David and Charles Koch in Wichita, and a handful of other rich dynasty heads became a "formidable alliance" to create an "ultra-conservative re-education machine . . . in which everything tainted with the stamp of liberal origin and the word 'public' would be contested and destroyed."[5]

To this end, an array of right-wing advocacy groups such as the Heritage Foundation and the Cato Institute would go mainstream. Hundreds of right-wing institutes, centers, organizations, and front groups were formed based on Powell's road map to destroy liberalism. Over the next forty years, social, economic, and environmental progress was whittled away. Part of this legacy is the Frackopoly.

In 1966 millionaire ideologues selected former actor Ronald Reagan, known for his communication skills, to run for California's governorship. They included oilman Henry Salvatori; Cy Rubel, head of Union Oil; Holmes P. Tuttle, an owner of Ford dealerships; Justin Dart, heir to the Walgreens drugstore chain; industrialist Jack Hume; Leonard Firestone, of the tire empire; and oil and entertainment magnate Jack Wrather.[6]

After an unsuccessful presidential primary run in 1976, Reagan spent the next four years preparing to oust Carter from the presidency. By 1980 Reagan was recognized as the candidate who could take back America for corporate interests that especially hoped to eliminate antitrust laws. His closest advisers and funders had expanded greatly, with individuals from the oil exploration (Leon Hess, Ed Noble, Norton Simon), construction (J. Robert Fluor), tourism and recreation (Barron Hilton, Walter Knott, J. Willard Marriot), agribusiness and real estate (William Wilson, Charles Wick, Irvine Corporation), supermarkets (Theodore Cummins), textiles (Roger Milliken), and beer (Coors) industries.[7]

Later, Reagan added the spouses of his wife Nancy's closest chums to his "kitchen cabinet." They included Pennzoil heiress Betty Wilson and her husband, oil equipment manufacturer William Wilson; Betsy Bloomingdale, married to Diners Club co-founder Alfred Bloomingdale; and Marion Jorgensen, wife of steel tycoon Earle Jorgensen. Billionaire TV Guide owner Walter Annenberg, and Armand Deutsch, Sears Roebuck heir and retired movie producer, also were closely associated with the Reagans.[8]

But his most important adviser was his lawyer, William French Smith, who served as Reagan's attorney general from 1981 to 1985. Acting as a primary architect of Reagan-era policies, he facilitated the abandonment of antitrust enforcement and civil rights objectives, while promoting secrecy and censorship. A scion of an old New England family, Smith was a member of the Los Angeles law firm Gibson, Dunn, and Crutcher.* His importance to Reagan can be summed up by a remark made by Holmes Tuttle when Reagan was governor. He said that Reagan's closest confidants "never made a move" without first asking, "Has this been cleared with Bill Smith?"[9]

Reagan's administration set about reforming the image of laissez-faire capitalism—the belief that government should play no role in the economy. Rather than recognizing the economy as an institution that operates based on rules created by political decisions, they transformed the marketplace into an omnipotent natural system that is ruined by human interference. To justify their attack on antitrust rules, the reactionaries turned to the Chicago School academics who begun proselytizing against restricting monopolies.

In the 1950s, economist Aaron Director, who was extremely hostile to any efforts to prevent monopolistic behavior, conducted research at the University of Chicago. Director, whose sister married another conservative Chicago School economist, Milton Friedman, influenced many of the people who waged war on antitrust laws. Among his students and protégés were John McGee, Robert Bork, and Richard Posner.[10]

John McGee is not well known to the public, but he is revered by the generations of ideologues who studied his "seminal" article defending John D. Rockefeller's Standard Oil. McGee's article, "Predatory Price Cutting: The Standard Oil (N.J.) Case," used efficiency arguments to buttress his defense of the predatory practices of the oil robber barons.[11] Milton Friedman and the future Federal Reserve chairman Alan Greenspan built on his ideas. A follower of the radical libertarian novelist Ayn Rand, Greenspan attacked antitrust laws as a "jumble of economic irrationality and ignorance."[12]

Conservative jurist Robert Bork took the Chicago School's economic views and created a legal argument for defending the biggest businesses as good for "consumer welfare."[13] While Reagan's nomination of the radical Bork to the U.S. Supreme Court was defeated, his justification for eliminating meaningful antitrust enforcement has left a terrible legacy, including the powerful Frackopoly.

---

* Smith's former law partner, Kenneth Starr, became his counsel at the Justice Department. Smith, who died in 1990, did not live long enough to see Starr become the controversial independent counsel who investigated President Bill Clinton.

Legal scholar Barak Orbach, director of the Business Law Program at the University of Arizona, writes that Bork redefined the Sherman Antitrust Act of 1890—the nation's most important antitrust law. He explains that Bork claimed Congress passed the law with consumer welfare in mind, despite the fact that in 1890 the phrase "consumer welfare" did not exist, nor did the discipline of economics. Rather, Congress was concerned about Standard Oil and protecting small businesses against monopolies. Unfortunately, the U.S. Supreme Court and the nation's antitrust authorities have adopted this rationalization for obliterating the traditional role of antitrust law in protecting small businesses and promoting competition.[14]

The Reagan administration achieved this by adopting Bork's legal theory, weakening the definition of antitrust trust violations and eliminating enforcement. Between 1950 and 1980, the Department of Justice and the Federal Trade Commission had challenged more than a thousand mergers and acquisitions, but under the Reagan regime, there was a virtual freeze on these activities.[15] William F. Baxter, a Stanford University law professor and sharp critic of antitrust law, was appointed to head the antitrust division of the Justice Department. He had once charged that the U.S. Supreme Court had used "wacko economic propositions" and "outmoded, jerry-built, amateur, pseudo-economic propositions" in its antitrust opinions.[16] Baxter pledged to review more than twelve hundred past antitrust agreements that had been forged by government lawyers.[17] He developed a new blueprint for antitrust action that used the same efficiency arguments made by John D. Rockefeller in defending his monopoly.[18]

Sweeping aside rules governing mergers and acquisitions, antitrust proceedings were reduced to a discussion about the price of goods for consumers—not the larger considerations about lack of competition or stopping the domination of every industry by a few politically well-connected individuals. Gone were deliberations over the insidious political impacts of giant corporations buying and selling our democracy.

At the other antitrust agency, the Federal Trade Commission, Reagan appointed James Miller III, the former co-director of the right-wing Center for the Study of Government Regulation at the American Enterprise Institute.[19] He was an even more strident ideologue who drastically cut the commission's budget, eliminated whole departments, jettisoned investigations, and purged staff.[20]

Former FTC commissioner Michael Pertschuk and a Republican colleague on the commission, Patricia P. Baily, wrote a scathing four-hundred-page report to Congress outlining how Miller's actions prohibited the agency from fulfilling its mission. Pertschuk's assessment was that the Reagan administration antitrust and consumer protection appointees surrendered "whole chapters of antitrust laws and [were] engaging in economic frolics and detours around corporate over-reaching and consumer exploitation" that were characterized by "extremism and ideological blindness [and] led to a new era of regulatory nihilism and just plain nuttiness."[21] Pertschuk said that Miller was "opposed to any intervention in corporate misbehavior or enforcement of antitrust law" and was a "very unpleasant individual characterized by the tendency to ingratiate himself with people higher in the hierarchy and to bully those that worked for him."[22] (See Chapter 4.)

Importantly, after the antitrust rules governing mergers and acquisitions were swept away under the Reagan administration, each administration since has followed in its footsteps.

Reagan also gifted the petroleum industry in other ways. During his first month in office, he eliminated the Nixon-era price controls for many petroleum products, leading to immediate increases in energy costs. The frontal attack on antitrust regulation kicked off the merger frenzy in the oil and gas industry. Between 1981 and 1989 oil mergers included Chevron and Gulf, Mobil and Superior Oil, Amoco and Dome Petroleum, Exxon and Texaco Canada, and Occidental's acquisition of Cities Service and MdCon.[23]

Reagan appointed Anne Gorsuch, a far-right Colorado state legislator, to head the U.S. Environmental Protection Agency and to eliminate regulation. She cut the EPA budget by 22 percent and decreased enforcement from regional EPA offices by 79 percent during her first year. Gorsuch, who was found in contempt of Congress for refusing to turn over thousands of pages of documents on hazardous waste, bragged that she reduced the size of clean water regulations from a six-inch book to a half-inch pamphlet.[24]

He appointed former Federal Power Commission member James Watt to oversee the Interior Department. (See Chapter 4.) The Wyoming native was quoted as saying, "If the troubles from environmentalists cannot be solved in the jury box or at the ballot box, perhaps the cartridge box should be used."[25] Watt was a vocal born-again Christian and a "spellbinder" of a fund-raiser for the Republican Party.[26] He championed letting more industries pursue resource extraction on federal land, promising, "We will mine more, drill more, cut more timber."[27] Watt opened more than a billion acres of coastal waters for oil and gas development.[28]

Reagan is reported to have characterized conservation as "easy—it's freezing in the dark." He demonized commonsense energy programs and scoffed at the idea of transitioning from dependence on conventional energy sources to a future of renewable energy. At a time when real progress was being made in developing alternative energy technologies, Reagan gutted Carter-era research and development programs.[29] His administration almost single-handedly killed the burgeoning renewable energy manufacturing industry, which had been dominated by U.S. companies.

In a show of symbolic disdain for renewable energy, Reagan dismantled the White House solar panel installation that had been used to heat water during the Carter years. Ironically, one of the panels ended up in the Solar Science and Technology Museum in Dezhou, China—the country that manufactures 80 percent of the solar water heaters used in the world today.[30]

But among the biggest impacts of the dissolution of antitrust law during the Reagan era was the impact on the media and entertainment industries. During Reagan's first term, fifty corporations controlled most of the media in the United States; today only six firms control 90 percent of the media, with more mergers likely to happen.[31] In 1987 Reagan also killed the Fairness Doctrine, a Federal Communications Commission rule requiring radio broadcasters to offer competing views on the same broadcasts.[32] The elimination of this important rule was another nail in the coffin of fair reporting, giving rise to right-wing talk radio and the rants that so misinform people about fracking and a host of other issues. Falsely charging a liberal bias in the media, the media moguls focused on changing American's core values.

In the following decades, the concentration of the news, communications, and entertainment industry produced a web of complex business relationships and interlocking boards of directors involving energy, banking, agribusiness, and other major industries. While the large number of outlets, especially in the Internet age, give an appearance of diversity, a few media giants that benefit from maintaining the current economic and political structure own print, broadcast, and other communications companies.

Dan Rather, the anchor of the venerable *CBS Evening News* for decades who was fired for covering President George W. Bush's AWOL status during the Vietnam War, observed that the "corporatization, politicization and trivialization of the news" stems directly from the ownership by a few giant corporations.[33] Ben Bagdikian, author of *The Media Monopoly*, says that beyond the unfair advantage in profits and power, "the gravest loss is in the self-serving censorship of political and social ideas, in news, magazine articles, books, broadcasting and movies." He says that the censorship is often not even conscious, but that "subordinates learn by habit to conform to owners' ideas.[34]

Corporate control of the media has facilitated the weakening of our democracy. As corporations grew in size and wealth they used our system of legalized bribery to impact both major political parties while using the media to defend weakening laws, regulations and legal protections. Promoting corporate globalization, they advanced economic, trade, and social policies that dramatically redistributed wealth to the top 1 percent of Americans. Rather than explaining why the middle class is shrinking and the country is suffering from an economic and environmental crisis, the corporate media shifted the blame to environmental regulation, immigrants, and liberal values. The right-wing media and other institutions swung public opinion and encouraged a cultural war based on social issues rather than the root causes of increasing economic stratification.

Just as the Powell memo recommended, college students were targeted, with the nature of higher education changing as large foundations and corporations gifted universities with buildings, research, endowed professorships, paid internships, and underwritten publications. Their echo chamber—policy and research institutes, and lobby, advocacy, and legal organizations—dismissed climate change and renewable energy.

The values and belief system of a large segment of the American public now mirror that of the Koch family and other right-wing funders and business interests. The corporate takeovers of mass media and the deterioration of objective coverage is one of the most challenging problems that we have in stopping the Frackopoly, addressing climate change, and taking back our democracy.

6

THE ROAD TO RUIN

Ken Lay was extraordinarily honorable. . . . He's also been a strong friend of renewable energy, an investor in wind and solar, and a progressive voice on climate issues. On environmental stewardship, our experience is that you can trust Enron.

—Ralph Cavanagh, Natural Resources Defense Council[1]

Enron and its disgraced leader, Ken Lay, have faded from memory, but the policies that Lay advocated—from eliminating federal oversight of natural gas pricing to deregulating interstate gas pipelines and the electric industry—have left a legacy of fracked gas and a threatened climate. With decisions about energy production left to the vagaries of the market, a boom-and-bust cycle has led to increased natural gas use and a lax attitude toward safety and environmental protection.

Rather than viewing electricity as a resource to be used judiciously, the architects of deregulation made the expanded production and use of electricity a new profit center. Production of electricity from natural gas jumped 73 percent between 2003 and 2013.[2] And with the evisceration of antitrust law by the Reagan administration, merger mania ushered in an era of larger and more politically powerful energy companies.

Lay steered the energy industry to the brave new world of speculation by taking a staid pipeline company and turning it into an unregulated financial services empire, trading in commodities that ranged from energy futures to pulp products, from weather derivatives to airport landing rights. Spawned by a merger in 1985, Enron grew in size from $9 billion in sales in 1993 to $103 billion in 2000, becoming the seventh-largest company in the nation before it was bankrupted in 2001.[3] Lay is long gone, but the commodity market where traders gamble and manipulate energy prices prevails. Natural gas—even fracked gas—continues to be viewed as environmentally beneficial; that is Lay's legacy.

Positioning natural gas as a "bridge fuel," a compromise between coal and renewables, Lay forged important relationships with environmentalists.[4] Big green groups—including the Natural Resources Defense Council (NRDC) and the Environmental Defense Fund (EDF)—and their foundation funders eventually hopped on the deregulation bandwagon led by Lay, believing his rhetoric about the potential of electricity deregulation to spark a rapid transition to sustainable energy.[5] He persuaded them that breaking up utilities and opening electricity markets to companies such as Enron would remove the incentives for selling more electricity and building large new electric plants.[6] Market forces could replace the planning process that states traditionally had used in determining if new electricity generation was needed. The Energy Foundation and its grantees embraced this rosy picture and sold it to most environmentalists.[7]

Meanwhile, Enron's unethical practices caused electricity blackouts and soaring energy prices, while the company's demise created a financial tsunami that cost thousands of jobs and destroyed the life savings of millions. After Enron's stunning fall, Lay and more than twenty other Enron executives were convicted of fraud and conspiracy. Politicians, including both Bush presidents, scurried to disavow their relationship with Enron.[8] The elite press rushed to blame the tragedy on a few corrupt executives, leaving the undermining of our democracy unexposed—the decades of influence peddling, the buying and selling of elections, and the revolving door between government and industry.

Tragically, many mainstream environmental leaders did not learn from having been hoodwinked by a convicted felon, and continue to advocate for the use of fracked gas. No consideration is given to the devastating life cycle impacts of fracking or the construction of thousands of miles of pipelines. Many environmental leaders fail to recognize that only aggressive policy changes—won through long-term and strategic grassroots campaigns—can create a transition to renewable energy and conservation. Lack of vision has meant that the shift to a sustainable energy future has not happened quickly enough to halt global climate change. And the deregulatory policies of the late twentieth century have left us with a handful of giant and politically powerful energy companies. Ken Lay's ghost—he died suddenly before he was sentenced in 2006—hovers around the debate on fracked gas.

A Sharp-Witted Scoundrel

Raised in the Ozarks, the child of an itinerant Baptist lay preacher who put food on the table working a series of odd jobs, Lay was greatly affected by the deprivations of his youth. Possessing a winning personality and the desire to please, he thrived in high school and college.[9] He was mentored by his graduate school adviser, University of Missouri economics professor Pinkney Walker, who was a conservative economist. The Nixon-appointed Federal Power Commission member had a profound effect on Lay's philosophy and career. (See Chapter 4.)

Lay was a ready candidate for Walker's "Chicago School" brand of economics, free market fundamentalism. Walker encouraged him to get his master's degree and Lay worked as a teaching assistant, having already taken all of Walker's classes.[10] After Lay's downfall and death, Walker reminisced to the *New York Times* that his former advisee had yearned to make money.[11] After leaving the University of Missouri, Lay headed to Houston for a job as an economist at Humble Oil (Exxon). At night he pursued his doctorate in economics at the University of Houston, developing a mathematical model to predict the economic impacts of reduced military spending. A professor on Lay's doctoral committee in 1970 said that he had "never before or since" seen a PhD candidate "take so confidently independent a stance in front of his entire committee."[12]

Lay ingratiated himself with Humble Oil CEO Mike Wright, writing his speeches during the time Wright served as president of the U.S. Chamber of Commerce.[13] Lay participated in the fight over natural gas regulation and had firsthand knowledge of the benefits that would accrue to the petroleum industry from removing federal pricing oversight.

Lay's strategy for dodging the jungles of Vietnam involved training to become a navy officer. Taking a temporary leave of absence from Humble, he used his connections to fulfill his military duty at the Pentagon as an economist. In exchange for agreeing to return to his position at Humble, Lay received supplemental remuneration from Wright, keeping him at the same salary level he had enjoyed as a petroleum executive.[14] Lay never returned to Wright's staff, however. Instead he accepted an offer from Walker—now the chair of the FPC. As Walker's right-hand man at the agency, he learned the nuts and bolts of the natural gas and electricity businesses, and the best policy levers for removing them from federal oversight.

Lay often stood in for the commissioner when Walker's wife was seriously ill, working to advance the deregulation of gas and pipelines. Soon restless at the FPC, Lay accepted an offer from the Nixon administration to become a deputy undersecretary of energy at the Department of the Interior—a resume-enhancing opportunity with the benefit of creating a network of movers and shakers in the petroleum industry.

Serving under Secretary Rogers C.B. Morton, a well-connected Nixon crony who was chair of the Republican National Committee, Lay's Rolodex grew to include anyone of importance to the GOP. Morton's defense of big oil was legendary. He was reported to have told industry representatives: "Our mission is to serve you, not regulate you. We try to avoid it. . . . I pledge to you that the department is at your service."[15]

Lay supported Morton's expansion plans for drilling on public lands. Testifying at hearings in 1973, Lay advocated drilling along the East Coast from Maine to Florida and in Alaska, promoting President Nixon's plan to triple offshore drilling leases to 3 million acres of the outer continental shelf by 1979.[16]

Lay met his next boss at a hearing in Florida where he was defending Nixon's plan for offshore drilling. He impressed the top executive of the state's major natural gas distributor, Florida Gas Company (FGC). Jack Bowen had brought natural gas to Florida by building a large pipeline. An important figure in the petroleum industry, he held directorships at the Interstate Natural Gas Association, the National Petroleum Council, the World Energy Council, the U.S. Energy Association, the American Gas Association, the All-American Wildcatters, and the American Petroleum Institute.[17]

Lay wrote to Bowen on official Interior Department stationery: "As you know, I have been involved in energy policy making in Washington for the past two and one-half years. I feel it is now time I begin thinking about returning to the private sector and resuming my career in business." In 1973 Bowen offered Lay a new position in the company, managing corporate planning and development. Lay eventually brought Rogers Morton to the FGC board.[18]

Not everyone was a fan of the brash young man. Selby Sullivan, second-in-command at FGC, later commented, "If Ken were to say that I was the most domineering man he worked with, it might be related to the fact that I am probably the only one looking at his career that ever told him 'no.'"

Bowen soon left, becoming chairman of the largest pipeline company in the country, Houston-based Transco Corp, now owned by Williams Companies. Sullivan replaced Bowen, and despite his fiery relationship with Lay, he promoted him to the presidency of a company subsidiary.[19]

In 1979 FGC was purchased by Continental Group, a Fortune 500 conglomerate engaged in multiple businesses. Lay was made president of Continental Resources Company, the new name for FGC. He had become a power broker in the gas industry, acquiring many directorships in energy and finance institutions, including the Gas Research Institute, the American Gas Association, the Interstate Natural Gas Association, the Southern Gas Association, the Slurry Transport Association, and Sun Banks of Florida. Lay was one of the up-and-coming executives who worked with the federal bureaucracy, directing funding for research and developing lobbying strategies for the industry.[20]

In the interim, Lay had embarked on an affair with his secretary, souring his fifteen-year marriage. When salacious gossip ruined his office life, Lay turned to Bowen for a job. In 1981, at almost sixty, Bowen was thinking about retirement. After discussing Lay with Transco's board, Bowen offered him the top job. Lay dumped his devastated wife and moved to Houston, marrying Linda Herrold.[21]

By this time, President Reagan had lifted the price controls on oil, dramatically increasing the price of heating oil and other petroleum products. Large industrial customers had rushed to switch to gas. The resulting increase in energy prices contributed to the first serious recession in decades. Reagan was in a tough spot with his petroleum supporters because he had vowed to decontrol all natural gas prices after taking office.[22] He was urged to do this by issuing an executive order that eliminated the schedule for deregulating different types of gas—a timeline established in the 1978 Natural Gas Policy Act.* (See Chapter 4.)

But with inflation seriously affecting the economy, Reagan's closest advisers feared the political repercussions if he also was directly responsible for price increases. Natural gas was not only a heating and cooking fuel

---

* The Natural Gas Policy Act created two dozen different categories of gas, with a schedule of different dates for deregulation. "New" natural gas, drilled from depths of 10,000 to 15,000 feet, was deregulated immediately and the price was set by the market. The price of "old gas" that had gone through the regulatory process would rise with inflation as it was depleted.

but also a raw material in manufacturing consumer goods, and a sudden price increase would have ramifications across most economic sectors. The Consumer Federation of America charged that deregulating gas would be a "bonanza" for the biggest gas producers but would gouge consumers.[23] Advocates pointed out that producers of unconventional gas also enjoyed an annual tax credit worth billions, a benefit that was not removed until 2002. (See Chapter 1.)

The Reagan administration finally settled on using the Federal Energy Regulatory Commission, the agency that had replaced the FPC, to do the dirty work. The lifting of price controls was cleverly shrouded in technical proceedings at FERC—similar to those used by its predecessor agency. With no fanfare, the agency issued rulings that automatically raised natural gas prices. Public interest critics accused FERC's leadership of deregulating gas prices without congressional approval.[24]

While Reagan dismantled environmental protections and FERC hid deregulation in rulemaking proceedings, chaos ensued. The pipeline companies rushed to sign contracts for long-term supplies of gas, knowing that under deregulation, prices would rise sharply. They made ill-conceived "take or pay" contracts to purchase large supplies of gas at a predetermined fixed price—a binding contract. The recession, made worse by Reagan's policies, reduced demand for gas among industrial customers, leaving the large pipeline companies stuck with contracts for vast amounts of gas at high prices. The pipelines scrambled to escape the contractual agreement that they had agreed to as part of the move to deregulate.[25]

Transco was one of the pipelines on the hook for expensive contracted gas, an embarrassing situation for veteran gas executive Bowen. Lay, who as an FPC bureaucrat understood the obscure and evolving regulatory regime at what was now called FERC, saw a way to manipulate the situation, leading to his legendary reputation in the energy industry.

Lay recognized that the price volatility caused by deregulation and the decreased demand for natural gas had created an emerging spot market, where gas could be purchased at a very low price.* He devised a scheme for using purchases on the spot market to offset the higher costs of the take-or-pay contracts. He facilitated this by using his FERC connections to change the long-established rules that prohibited producers from selling

---

* A spot market allows producers to sell natural gas immediately at an agreed-upon price. Prior to deregulation, most gas was sold via contracts.

directly to large industrial customers. Lay's innovation had made natural gas a tradable commodity, just like pork bellies or corn.[26]

He claimed that one of the first executives he converted to his new strategy was Richard Nelson, manager of natural gas at Royal Dutch Shell's U.S. operation. Lay bragged, "I finally persuaded him that the only way the industry could get through this would be if producers started marketing their gas directly."[27] By expanding spot markets through so-called special marketing programs (SMPs), the gas industry's structure had been fundamentally altered. Companies such as Transco could purchase gas on the spot market and sell it directly to an industrial customer, bypassing the local distribution utility. This amounted to predatory pricing—the practice of stealing a competitor's business. Further, by separating the sale of gas from its transportation, the expense of running pipelines was shifted to local utilities and passed on to smaller gas consumers. In 1985, during litigation over Lay's scheme, SMPs were found to be discriminatory.[28]

The creation of the natural gas spot market coincided with the scheduled deregulatory measures mandated by the Natural Gas Policy Act of 1978. This legislation was focused on increasing the profits of natural gas producers by allowing the price to be set at the wellhead by "market forces." Rather than basing the price on the cost of production and a reasonable profit that was set during a regulatory proceeding, all controls on price eventually would be removed.

With this in mind, FERC established "open access," a euphemism for dividing the natural gas industry into separate businesses for the production, transportation, and distribution of gas—and making similar changes to the electric industry in the future. Traditionally, pipelines had bought gas from producers at the regulated price, which included the fuel and the transportation, and sold it to utilities.

In 1985 FERC deregulated pipelines through Order No. 436, requiring pipelines to give "open access" to companies that wanted to buy gas and sell directly to large industrial customers. The screws were tightened on small gas users in 1987 when FERC issued Order No. 500, empowering interstate pipelines to buy out the costly take-or-pay contracts and to pass the costs on to local distribution companies and their small customers. Deregulation of gas prices at the wellhead was completed in 1989 when Congress passed the Natural Gas Wellhead Decontrol Act, repealing all of the remaining regulated gas prices.[29]

In 1992 FERC issued Order No. 636, finalizing the process of deregulating pipelines by "unbundling" the businesses of transporting, storing, and selling natural gas.[30] By January 1, 1993, after decades of battle, the natural gas producers had finally won—all gas price regulation ended, creating another incentive for a speculative gas market and giving additional economic power to large gas producers.

This sealed the fate of natural gas, spurring its production and use and driving the growth of fracking. Increased natural gas use and the restructuring of pipelines into transportation-only businesses drove the construction of thousands of miles of new pipelines in the following decades.

Enron Is Born

In 1984, Lay was wooed away from Transco by Houston Natural Gas, a company looking for aggressive leadership in the deregulated marketplace.[31] Soon afterward, Houston Natural Gas merged with the Omaha-based natural gas company Internorth, creating an entity with a large amount of high-interest debt. The company was christened Enron.[32]

Its core business was operating 37,500 miles of gas pipeline that stretched across the country, but Lay focused on earnings from the energy trading business that grew out of Enron's oil-trading arm. When it came to light in 1987 that the traders, who had made a fortune for the company, were destroying documents and manipulating accounting records, Lay refused to fire them—that is, until the same traders racked up more than $1 billion in bad trades that almost bankrupted the company, landing one of them in jail. This set the tone for Enron: unethical behavior was tolerated if it was lucrative and went undetected. Enron developed the idea of natural gas futures contracts (which first traded in 1990) and pursued an international power plant construction business and private water services company.[33]

Lay's former classmate at the University of Missouri, Richard Kinder, ran the pipeline business at Enron. When he was passed over for the top job at the company, he left in 1996. Kinder and Bill Morgan, a former Enron executive and also a classmate at the University of Missouri, bought Enron's pipeline assets. Today, after several mergers and acquisitions, Kinder Morgan is the largest energy infrastructure company in North America, with 84,000 miles of pipelines that transport gas, crude oil, and other products.

Meanwhile, Lay's political connections helped create a cozy relationship with the U.S. Securities and Exchange Commission, an agency willing to weaken the accounting rules designed to ensure that companies' assets were properly valued.[34] Enron's financial dealings included the use of derivatives, credit default swaps, and deals financed without equity. Among the clever chicaneries used by Enron were volumetric production payments, a financing deal in which a company sells future production of oil or gas in return for up-front payments. Enron hid debt and losses by using this fast-and-loose accounting, just as Chesapeake Energy's Aubrey McClendon did many times to help keep his debt-ridden company alive as fracking for shale gas boomed.[35] (See Chapter 9.)

Lay and the Enron executives quickly found that speculating on energy futures contracts was more lucrative than producing energy. Because one-third of natural gas was sold to electric generation plants, Lay envisioned selling gas-generated electricity directly to consumers.

Electricity had been regulated as a cost-based service provided by private and public utilities that were licensed to operate as single companies in a service district. Long viewed as a natural monopoly, electric utilities owned transmission lines and power generation facilities, or purchased electricity from another company, and distributed electricity to consumers. State regulatory agencies determined the private utility's profit margin by setting the rate of return on investment in capital expenses. Most states used a planning process to determine the need for new power plants, sometimes considering energy efficiency programs as a substitute for new generating capacity.

Although the electric utilities were politically powerful and used this to their advantage, at least there was a democratic process in place for making decisions. Many nuclear power plants were blocked in the 1970s and 1980s as a result, and the environmental movement increasingly was influencing decisions about electricity production.[36]

But Lay saw the economic potential of speculating on the $15 billion wholesale market for electricity and selling directly to consumers in the $215 billion retail electricity market.[37] He believed that once generation, transmission, and distribution were separated, Enron would be positioned to buy electricity in the newly created market and resell it at a higher price. Lay was among those who successfully pushed FERC to create a bulk wholesale electricity market where companies such as Enron could sell electricity. This change was initiated in 1996 under FERC Order 888, which required transmission owners to offer "open access" for selling electricity, creating a massive incentive to generate and sell more electricity.[38]

Creation of a wholesale market transformed electricity into a speculative commodity.

In 1997 Enron embarked upon a $200 million advertising campaign that launched during the Super Bowl and was designed to make Enron a household name. Speaking on deregulation, Lay told *Businessweek*, "There's no longer a debate on if it'll happen—it's when it happens."[39] He worked with the groups Citizens for a Sound Economy, the Heritage Foundation, and the Cato Institute (all funded by the Koch brothers) and made use of his connections with the Bush dynasty.[40] Already a major player in Republican politics, Lay served as co-chair of George H.W. Bush's reelection campaign in 1992 and as chair of the Republican National Convention in Houston that same year. The Public Integrity Project found that Enron and its employees were the largest campaign contributors to Bush during the period when deregulation was being debated.[41]

Bush had signed the Federal Energy Policy Act of 1992, giving tax credits for producing oil from shale and tar sands, tax credits for independent oil and gas producers, and funding for clean coal research. It also simplified the relicensing of nuclear plants and weakened the Public Utility Holding Company Act. (See Chapter 2.) But Enron reaped perhaps the biggest reward—a key policy component that made it possible to deregulate sales of electricity. In the future, traditional utility companies would be required to open their transmission lines to non-electricity-generating companies such as Enron.

The next year, Lay cronies facilitated an exemption of Enron's energy futures contracts from oversight by the Commodity Futures Trading Commission (CFTC). Tyson Slocum, a senior energy researcher at Public Citizen, wrote a detailed report documenting that Wendy Gramm, chairwoman of the CFTC, had a conflict of interest.* President Reagan had appointed Gramm, the wife of Republican Senator Phil Gramm, to the independent agency, calling her his favorite economist.[42] Shortly before leaving the agency, Gramm exempted Enron from oversight for the trading of energy derivatives; in an apparent quid pro quo, five weeks after stepping down, Gramm was appointed to Enron's board of directors, serving on the board's audit committee. In this capacity she not only was responsible for verifying Enron's accounting procedures but also had knowledge of the company's

---

* I directed the energy program at Public Citizen from 1997 to 2005.

financial information. Wendy Gramm was awarded upwards of $2 million in salary and stock options during her time on the Enron board.[43]

Senator Phil Gramm, the recipient of generous campaign contributions from Enron (Gramm's second-largest donor over the course of his career), pushed the legislation deregulating energy commodity trading through as chairman of the U.S. Senate Committee on Banking, Housing, and Urban Affairs.[44] Slocum reported that Enron took advantage of lax oversight by forming a web of more than 2,800 subsidiaries, more than 30 percent (874) of which were located in officially designated offshore tax havens with weak banking laws.[45]

Gramm also spearheaded passage of legislation in 1999 that removed protective New Deal laws separating the banking, insurance, and broker-age industries.[46] After retiring from the Senate in 2003, Gramm went to work for the Swiss bank UBS—the corporation that took over Enron's energy trading operations after its collapse.[47] This financial deregulation led directly to the financial crisis in 2007–8. *Time* magazine named the former senator one of the chief culprits in the financial meltdown.[48]

Lay promoted the image of Enron as a trendsetter, telling Democrats that futures trading was the economic engine of the future. Enron donated $1.5 million to Democrats between 1990 and 2002, a quarter of what the company contributed to Republicans.[49] President Bill Clinton named Lay to his Council on Sustainable Development, an advisory group that took policy positions that could potentially benefit Enron.[50] Lay used his Clinton relationships to obtain assistance in India with a stalled power plant project. Clinton asked his former chief of staff, Mac McLarty, to keep Lay informed on the project's progress. The White House communicated with the U.S. ambassador to India about the troubled plant. Four days before the project was granted final approval, Enron donated $100,000 to the Democratic National Committee.[51]

During the summer of 1997, President Clinton and Vice President Al Gore met with Lay to discuss a strategy for the Kyoto climate summit to boost natural gas use.[52] Lay favored the carbon trading system for addressing global warming.* Enron lobbyist John Palmaisano wrote from Kyoto:

---

* Carbon trading schemes typically just account for carbon dioxide. Methane, the primary component of natural gas, is another leading driver of global warming. It leaks into the air from sources throughout the oil and gas industry and adds to the carbon footprint of natural gas.

"If implemented, [the Kyoto Protocol] will do more to promote Enron's business than almost any other regulatory initiative outside restructuring of the [electricity] and natural gas industries in Europe and the United States. . . . The endorsement of emissions trading was another victory for us. . . . This agreement will be good for Enron stock!!"[53]

Clinton also helped Enron by promoting Betsy Moler to serve as FERC's chair. Moler had served as senior counsel for the Senate Committee on Energy and Natural Resources from 1976 to 1988, during the battle over deregulating natural gas, and she was Clinton's strategist on pursuing electricity deregulation. First appointed to FERC under Reagan, and later reappointed by George H.W. Bush, she was leading the commission when it required utilities to open their transmission lines to power marketers such as Enron. Clinton later appointed Moler to be deputy energy secretary in 1997.* Soon after her appointment, she met with Secretary of Energy Federico Peña and Ken Lay to discuss electricity deregulation and climate change initiatives.[54]

Lay and Koch-funded groups developed a strategy for deregulating electricity at the state and federal levels, selling it as a cost savings for large industrial customers, which could cut special deals for high volumes of electricity and escape the fixed costs for utility infrastructure. They used their Bush family connections to help grease the wheels for generating electricity from fracked natural gas.

George W. Bush accepted campaign contributions from Lay, whom he called "Kenny boy," throughout his political career. As governor of Texas, he signed the Enron-sanctioned electricity deregulation legislation. He appointed Pat Wood and Nora Mead Brownell to FERC at Lay's request. When Brownell's nomination started to falter, Lay called on Karl Rove to keep the president from wavering. Lay also wrote to George H.W. Bush advocating that he participate in the Kyoto climate talks and support carbon trading. He said, "Among other industries, I am convinced that America's hard-pressed domestic natural gas industry would benefit substantially from a market-based approach to reducing CO_2 emissions."[55]

Lay or Enron representatives met six times with Vice President Dick

---

* Moler was later rewarded with a lucrative job with the Chicago-based electric utility Exelon. Exelon was organized in 2000 with Chicago-based utility Commonwealth Edison at its core. Since that time, it has merged with several other large utilities to become the one of the biggest U.S. power generators, operating in forty-eight states to produce, trade, and distribute electricity.

Cheney and his energy task force, providing Cheney with a memo arguing against price controls on wholesale electricity and advocating that power marketers have open access to the electricity transmission system. Lay argued for removing regulatory obstacles to building new power plants and transmission lines, policies that became part of the Bush energy plan. These recommendations became law with passage of the Energy Policy Act of 2005.[56]

The law exempted the petroleum industry from key provisions of the nation's environmental laws, creating the so-called Halliburton Loophole, which relieved frackers from meeting Safe Drinking Water Act rules on underground injections of fluid. The legislation also granted FERC sweeping new powers to overrule local and state governments in the siting of new pipelines and transmission lines, even when this is contrary to the National Environmental Policy Act. Through its increased power of eminent domain, the agency can seize property for building intrusive and unnecessary infrastructure.

At first the big utilities had been threatened by the state-based deregulation that would open their business to companies like Enron. But soon many large private utilities realized that the political power they enjoyed with state legislatures would allow them to use deregulation to their advantage. Removing merger and service-territory restrictions would allow them to become giant multipronged, even global operations. This triggered a massive lobbying effort to eliminate the Public Utility Holding Company Act, the law that had been passed in 1935 to prevent speculative adventures with ratepayer money and which prohibited utilities' expansion outside of their existing service territories. (See Chapter 2.) Energy corporations, banks, the financial services industry, and other vested interests had been attempting to eliminate PUHCA since its passage. It finally was repealed as part of the Energy Policy Act of 2005.

But most clean energy advocates were not focused on the impacts of corporate power. Lay manipulated thought leaders in the environmental movement to become part of the cacophony voicing support for deregulation. Framing deregulation as "competition," he argued that low-cost efficiency programs and renewable energy would be winners in a free market. He masterminded a diverse nationwide army of deregulation advocates working at the state and federal levels.

Ralph Cavanagh, co-director of NRDC's energy program, floated the idea of repealing PUHCA among environmental groups as part of a deal

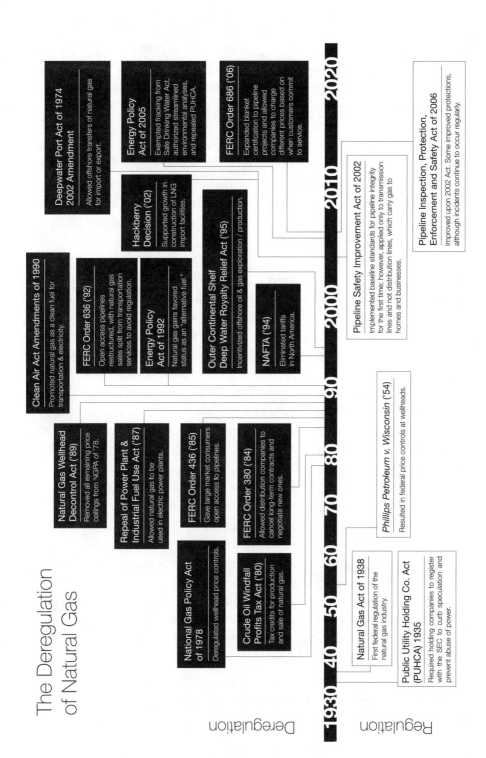

The Deregulation of Natural Gas

Regulation

Public Utility Holding Co. Act (PUHCA) 1935
Required holding companies to register with the SEC to curb speculation and prevent abuse of power.

Natural Gas Act of 1938
First federal regulation of the natural gas industry.

Phillips Petroleum v. Wisconsin ('54)
Resulted in federal price controls at wellheads.

Pipeline Safety Improvement Act of 2002
Implemented baseline standards for pipeline integrity for the first time; however, applied only to transmission lines and not distribution lines, which carry gas to homes and businesses.

Pipeline Inspection, Protection, Enforcement and Safety Act of 2006
Improved upon 2002 Act. Some improved protections, although incidents continue to occur regularly.

Deregulation

National Gas Policy Act of 1978
Deregulated wellhead price controls.

Crude Oil Windfall Profits Tax Act ('80)
Tax credits for production and sale of natural gas.

FERC Order 330 ('84)
Allowed distribution companies to cancel long-term contracts and negotiate new ones.

FERC Order 436 ('85)
Gave large market consumers open access to pipelines.

Repeal of Power Plant & Industrial Fuel Use Act ('87)
Allowed natural gas to be used in electric power plants.

Natural Gas Wellhead Decontrol Act ('89)
Removed all remaining price ceilings from NGPA of '78.

Clean Air Act Amendments of 1990
Promoted natural gas as a clean fuel for transportation & electricity.

FERC Order 636 ('92)
Open access pipelines restructured, with natural gas sales split from transportation services to avoid regulation.

Energy Policy Act of 1992
Natural gas gains favored status as an "alternative fuel."

NAFTA ('94)
Eliminated tariffs in North America.

Outer Continental Shelf Deep Water Royalty Relief Act ('95)
Incentivized offshore oil & gas exploration / production.

Hackberry Decision ('02)
Supported growth in construction of LNG import facilities.

Energy Policy Act of 2005
Exempted fracking from Safe Drinking Water Act, authorized streamlined environmental analyses, and repealed PUHCA.

Deepwater Port Act of 1974 2002 Amendment
Allowed offshore transfers of natural gas for import or export.

FERC Order 686 ('06)
Expanded blanket certification to pipeline projects and allowed companies to charge different prices based on when customers commit to service.

1930 40 50 60 70 80 90 2000 2010 2020

for federal legislation requiring states to deregulate electricity services.[57] Cavanagh, a Yale-educated attorney who has been at NRDC since 1979, was a winner of the Heinz Award for Public Policy in 1993.* He was honored for being "a leader in implementing the notion that environmental solutions should contribute to the bottom line of polluting businesses which traditional regulations prevented."[58]

Cavanagh teamed up with Enron lobbyists in Washington, D.C., and Sacramento, pushing for electricity deregulation at the state and federal levels. He advocated deregulation in exchange for a "systems benefit charge" paid by consumers in their electric bill that could be used for "public goods programs." During the debate in California over deregulation in 1996, NRDC and EDF supported the legislative deal made by Enron and California's large private utilities. This measure ended up empowering Enron and other electricity marketers to manipulate power supplies, driving prices to record heights and creating rolling blackouts. The private utilities convinced NRDC, EDF, and other interests to support a $28 billion bailout for the company's bad investments in nuclear power and expensive power contracts. When the bailout was challenged through a citizen-led initiative, the utilities bankrolled a campaign to confound and confuse ratepayers, defeating the ballot initiative.[59]

In 2014, in a state that should have transitioned to sustainable energy long ago, production of wind and solar energy accounted for only 12.5 percent of total electricity generation.[60] Renewables development happened in California *despite* deregulation, not because of it. Legislation was passed in 2002 establishing the state's renewable portfolio standard (RPS). The amount mandated was accelerated in 2006 and expanded again in 2011. This RPS program requires electric power suppliers to increase procurement from eligible renewable energy resources to 33 percent of total procurement by 2020. California also offers rebates for installing new solar and renewable energy systems.[61]

Cavanagh went further than most environmentalists in promoting deregulation. His prominent standing in the environmental community— enhanced by financial backing from the Energy Foundation and other

---

* Lay was appointed as a trustee of the H. John Heinz III Center for Science, Economy, and the Environment, a philanthropic environmental organization founded by Teresa Heinz Kerry in 1995.

funders—gave him a powerful platform for advancing deregulation. Many regional groups, such as the Chicago-based Environmental Law and Policy Center, were quick to support a "grand bargain" that included deregulation. Forcing their local utilities to restructure had broad appeal to environmentalists who had long fought the policies of the local utility.[62] These well-meaning advocates underestimated the power of the incumbent utilities and independent power producers such as Enron. In 2013, the Environmental Law and Policy Center supported passage of a weak regulatory bill that allows fracking in Illinois.[63]

While first skeptical of deregulation, the Energy Foundation leadership was convinced that it could be tweaked to spur a transition to sustainable energy.[64] Hal Harvey, at the time president of the Energy Foundation,* and Eric Heitz, then a senior program officer (currently the institution's president), wrote in a memo to other foundations: "We now have an emerging vision of how to use more competitive mechanisms to align profits with sound policy. . . . The de-integration of the utility industry opens new opportunities for foundations to support new structures—regulatory or market-based—which will direct tens of billions of dollars to make the energy choices of the future."[65]

Both engineers with little campaign experience, they opted for deal making rather than funding grassroots organizing for real change. Under Heitz's leadership today, the Energy Foundation† still supports the use of fracked natural gas as a transition fuel.[66]

Not only did electricity deregulation spur fracked gas production and use, it raised the price of electricity. According to a study by John Howat, a senior policy analyst at the National Consumer Law Center, the average price for electricity has increased more since 1996 in states that deregulated than in states that never adopted or implemented deregulation or that

---

* Harvey was president of the Energy Foundation from 1990 to 2001 and is now the CEO of Energy Innovation: Policy and Technology LLC. The company's portfolio includes promoting natural gas—"Done carefully, natural gas can be a valuable component of a low carbon future," according to a fact sheet on its website. Harvey is also chairman of the board of MB Financial Corporation, a $10 billion Chicago bank holding company.

† My organization received a small grant from the Energy Foundation in 2013 to educate communities about "clean, affordable energy that protects public health." The grant went toward the successful campaign to ban fracking in New York State.

subsequently suspended it. Howatt found that only fifteen states and the District of Columbia are implementing a deregulated market where consumers choose their electricity supplier, while seven other states deregulated their utilities but eventually suspended it. Since 2001 the weighted average price increase in the active deregulation states was nearly 18 percent higher than in the non-active states.[67]

And, as could have been predicted, the repeal of PUHCA unleashed the formation of extremely large energy companies with outsized influence on our political system. With numerous subsidiaries operating in every aspect of the energy business, their increased size and profits have empowered them to lobby vehemently against taking action on climate change and have spurred the use of fracked natural gas at the expense of renewable energy. Lynn Hargis, a former assistant general counsel at FERC, notes: "Without PUHCA, the potential for gigantic utility/banking failures or abuses, not to mention the impact on utility rates and reliability, is very frightening. It could make the Enron debacle look like just an appetizer [preview] of utility/financial crashes to come."[68]

Utility behemoths have more resources and increased ability to influence public policy. A *Los Angeles Times* exposé in April 2014 disclosed an alliance between front groups funded by the Koch brothers and electric utilities, aimed at reversing state policies promoting renewable energy.[69]

PUHCA's repeal, in concert with energy deregulation, also opened the door for hedge funds and investment banks to own utilities. It has created complex, unregulated energy powerhouses that provide energy services, produce petroleum products, and speculate on the energy market, among other businesses. Deregulating the energy industries has driven the overproduction of petroleum products from fracking, removed the incentives for using less energy, and kept the sustainable energy transition from blossoming.

It is time for a major paradigm shift.

7

MITCHELL MAKES A FORTUNE

God gave me my money. I believe the power to make money is a gift from God.
> —John D. Rockefeller, 1905 interview[1]

In the late summer of 2001, George Mitchell was about to make a fortune cashing in on the sale of his Houston-based company to Devon Energy—a $3.5 billion deal in cash, stock, and debt.[2] He had been in the petroleum business for fifty years, using federally funded research to improve his drilling methods. Along with some real estate development on the side, his gambles on identifying new oil and gas reserves had paid off. Mitchell had always used the tools afforded corporations in the Lone Star state to influence policy, including tame ones such as lobbying and campaign contributions.

Mitchell made sure that the Texas legal system was easy on his drilling operations, making generous donations to judges' electoral campaigns in a state that elects its impartial arbitrators of justice. In 2000, Texans for Public Justice documented that Mitchel had given $16,500 to judges running for office.[3] Commissioners at the Texas Railroad Commission also run for office, and in 1998 it was disclosed that commissioner Carole Keeton Rylander had taken hundreds of thousands of dollars in campaign contributions from oil and gas companies—many with business pending before the commission.[4] Mitchell Energy gave Rylander $6,000 between December 1996 and March 1998, soon after the Railroad Commission pledged an "intensive investigation" into the water pollution from Mitchell's natural gas wells in Wise County.

Plaintiffs in a lawsuit against Mitchell accused the Texas Railroad Commission of a cover-up in the case for trying to settle a $2.24 million penalty

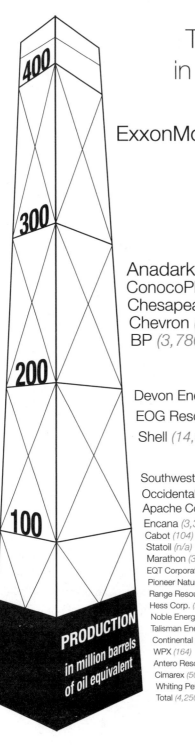

Top Fracking Companies in 2014 by US Production

(2014 international profits in $ millions)

ExxonMobil *(32,520)*

Anadarko *(-1,750)*
ConocoPhillips *(6,869)*
Chesapeake *(1,917)*
Chevron *(19,241)*
BP *(3,780)*

Devon Energy *(1,607)*
EOG Resources *(2,915)*
Shell *(14,874)*

Southwest Energy *(924)*
Occidental Petroleum *(616)*
Apache Corp. *(-5,403)*
Encana *(3,392)*
Cabot *(104)*
Statoil *(n/a)*
Marathon *(3,046)*
EQT Corporation *(387)*
Pioneer Natural Resources *(930)*
Range Resources *(634)*
Hess Corp. *(2,317)*
Noble Energy *(1,214)*
Talisman Energy *(-911)*
Continental *(977)*
WPX *(164)*
Antero Resources *(674)*
Cimarex *(507)*
Whiting Petroleum *(65)*
Total *(4,250)*

PRODUCTION in million barrels of oil equivalent

for $100,000. James and Patricia Bartlett had filed suit against Mitchell Energy for polluting their well water, bringing the original lawsuit in 1987. Seven other families had also filed lawsuits charging that Mitchell wells were involved in polluting their water. After the lawsuits were consolidated, the jury trial had commenced to examine the several ways that Mitchell Energy was at fault. The jury awarded the eight families $204 million after it found that the company had contaminated parts of the Trinity Aquifer with its fracking techniques and had concealed the problem for years.[5]

Mitchell ranted to a reporter that Wise County was a "burned-up, parched, miserable place" before he had started drilling there.[6] He spent more than $20 million to take the case to the Texas Court of Appeals, which overturned the jury's decision. The jury in the original trial had found "that Mitchell Energy's conduct constituted gross negligence and was committed with malice" and awarded large punitive damages. Among the charges were insufficient well surface casings, failing to repair well casing leaks, failing to properly plug a well, and failing to properly cement a well surface casing. At the time of the appeals court decision in 1997, Mitchell had drilled about 3,700 gas wells in Wise and surrounding counties, resulting in about 2,000 active wells, with most having been fracked.[7] Forty-six other plaintiffs for damages of at least $1 million brought similar claims, but the court ruled they could not prove that Mitchell caused the problems that affected their water.[8]

The Texas Railroad Commission had been aware for decades that water was being polluted in Wise County. Russell Gold, a *Wall Street Journal* writer and the author of *The Boom*, used the agency's dockets, interviews and other records to delve into oil and gas industry water pollution in Wise County. He discovered that in 1977, Darwin K. White, a hydraulics engineer living near Mitchell's wells, saw flames come from the three-hundred-foot well that delivered water to his house from the Trinity Aquifer. White wrote to the Texas Railroad Commission to complain about the pollution but never heard back, and he forgot about the well incident after his home was hooked to the city water system. In fact, until Gold contacted him for an interview, he was unaware that the state had investigated. His was the first of many complaints documented by Gold from a review of documents. Eventually a water treatment plant was built to process water from a nearby lake. In 1997 Mitchell Energy paid for most of the cost of a seventy-mile pipeline to bring the lake water to residents—part of a lawsuit settlement.[9]

Gold found that state investigators proposed that Mitchell and other drillers add more cement to surround well casings—metal pipes intended to keep the methane and other hydrocarbons and the wastewater, laden with fracking chemicals, metals, and salts, from leaking out into water supplies as it is all brought up to the surface through the well. When government authorities pushed Mitchell to use casing to a depth of 450 feet, he argued that it would cost $665,000 per well and that it would prevent the company from recovering the steel pipes for reuse. Mitchell prevailed.[10]

It's not surprising that Mitchell knew how to win favors in Texas. He was part of a network of oilmen who knew how to bend the system for their own purposes. They served on the same gas industry and charitable boards and even engaged in a few business deals together. Mitchell Energy did business with other natural gas companies, including Aubrey McClendon's Chesapeake Energy and Ken Lay's Enron. In 1996 the three firms teamed up to build a forty-mile pipeline as well as a forty-mile natural gas gathering network to transport Chesapeake gas in Louisiana to Enron's natural gas processing facility.[11] That same year, Lay and Mitchell joined forces in a Houston business organization aiming to raise up to $75 million to keep the Astros in Houston.[12]

Mitchell saw to it that Enron was part of a case study on sustainability at the 2001 conference he organized and funded, called "Corporate Capabilities and Tools: Making Sustainability Work in the Twenty-first Century." Enron was recognized for participating in the global climate debate and for its emphasis on the environmental benefits of natural gas as a "bridge" fuel. The two industry leaders also shared the honor of the prestigious John Rogers Award from the Center for American and International Law's Institute for Energy Law—Lay in 2001 and Mitchell in 2003—as a reward for service to the petroleum industry.[13]

Both of these men had played a unique role in fighting to deregulate energy prices and in promoting natural gas. Both men served on the influential National Petroleum Council (NPC), a Department of Energy advisory committee that formulated government policy and research priorities. Other notable members of the NPC at this time serving on the subcommittee and promoting natural gas were Dick Cheney of Halliburton, Fred Krupp of the Environmental Defense Fund, John Sawhill of the Nature Conservancy, Larry Nichols of Devon (future owner of Mitchell Energy), and the leadership of many of the largest gas-producing corporations and gas and electric utilities.[14]

The Clinton-appointed secretary of energy, Federico Peña, asked NPC to undertake a comprehensive study on the future of natural gas. Staff members from Enron and Mitchell were among those who worked on issues in the report related to supply, technology, and economics. When requesting the study, the secretary said that "at least two major forces . . . will profoundly affect energy choices in the future—the restructuring of electricity markets and growing concerns about . . . global climate change and regional air quality." [15]

In December 1999, after eighteen months, the NPC study, "Natural Gas: Meeting the Challenges of the Nation's Growing Natural Gas Demand," became the blueprint for making natural gas the favored fuel of the future. Identifying electricity generation as the driver for the "most significant growth in gas demand," the report called for a doubling of the number of oil and gas wells drilled per year to 48,000 by 2015. [16] This was surpassed in 2008, followed by a leveling off of drilling since to just under 40,000 wells each year. [17] According to the EPA, about 25,000 to 30,000 oil and gas wells were fracked annually between 2011 and 2014. [18]

The NPC chair explained, "Demand for natural gas will continue to increase as economic growth, environmental concerns, and the restructuring of the electricity markets encourage the use of natural gas. More than 14 million new customers will be connected to natural gas supply by 2015 and many more will find their growing electricity needs met by gas-fired generators."

In a harbinger of the environmental disasters to come, the report said: "Deeper wells, deeper water, and nonconventional sources will be key to future supply. . . . Future needs include new pipelines to reach supplies in the frontier regions, expansion of existing pipeline systems, new laterals to serve electricity plants." The NPC manifesto called for new cooperation from the secretaries of the Departments of the Interior and Agriculture, saying, "The principles should be used by the appropriate land management and regulatory agencies to establish policies that promote domestic production of natural gas in order to meet national goals." [19]

These policy recommendations were exactly what George Mitchell needed to boost the value of his company. Throughout his career, Mitchell's company had undergone several boom-and-bust cycles. Mitchell had always been a man willing to gamble on very big risks. Jim McAlister, a former vice president of oil and gas evaluation and banking at Mitchell Energy, politely described Mitchell's style of business this way: "George is able to handle the pressure of heavy debt. That's his style." [20]

In 1999, while Ken Lay was fêted for making money on trading schemes, George Mitchell was seventy-nine and his company's stock was losing value—even while he owned thousands of valuable gas leases. He was facing prostate cancer, and Cynthia Mitchell, his wife of more than fifty-five years and the mother of their ten children, suffered from Alzheimer's.[21]

Mitchell was embarrassed by the inability to keep his philanthropic promises: millions in donations were tied to Mitchell Energy Company stock prices, which were now in steep decline, and the contractual obligations to charity organizations were in default. Mitchell Energy had been borrowing millions of dollars to continue its operations, using stock as collateral, and banks were unwilling to make more loans and the Mitchell family was unable to meet its charitable commitments that were backed by Mitchell stock. The company was in trouble, and Mitchell could not attract a buyer.[22]

Rags to Riches

Mitchell's life was the quintessential American rags-to-riches story. His father, Savvas Paraskevopoulos, an illiterate Greek goatherd, had hopped a freighter to Ellis Island in 1901 and taken a job building track as part of a railroad gang. Renamed Mike Mitchell by the railroad paymaster, he made a life for himself in Galveston, Texas, running a pressing shop and shoeshine parlor with his wife, Katina. George Mitchell grew up in the Greek-speaking household with two older brothers and a younger sister. In 1932, when George was thirteen, his mother died, and soon afterward his father was seriously injured, and the younger children were sent to live with different relatives. Mitchell was a brilliant math student and was able to attend Texas A&M University. One summer he worked with his older brother Johnny in the oil fields, sparking his interest in geology and the petroleum industry.[23]

After graduating in 1939 with a degree in petroleum engineering, Mitchell went to work for Amoco in Louisiana, gaining hands-on experience with geology in the field. During World War II he was an officer in the Army Corps of Engineers, overseeing the construction of large projects in the Southwest.

In 1946, Mitchell, along with his brother Johnny and an investor, Merlyn Christie, created a company called Oil Drilling—a wildcatting venture that eventually primarily targeted natural gas. With Mitchell's keen instinct for geology and his partners' talent for schmoozing investors, they funded drilling operations. Mitchell's high-rolling playboy brother Johnny attracted Woolworth heiress Barbara Hutton, oil giant Bob Smith, and gangster Sam Maceo to the business. They hit it big in 1952 in Wise County when they purchased mineral rights on land near Fort Worth based on a bookie's recommendation. The men then formed a subsidiary of Oil Drilling and borrowed money to purchase the drilling rights on more acreage, paying on average $3 per acre. The next year they bought out one of their investors and formed a new company that would eventually morph into Mitchell Energy and Development Corporation. Decades later this investment in the Barnett Shale would make George Mitchell a billionaire.[24]

In 1957 Mitchell and his partners made a major deal, contracting to sell gas to Chicago using the Natural Gas Pipeline Company of America (NGPL)—the very same pipeline that Samuel Insull, the pioneer of giant holding companies, had raised money to build in 1931.[25]

Originally two of the Seven Sisters had been in on the deal. But after the Supreme Court upheld the regulation of natural gas prices at the wellhead, the major oil companies pulled out, refusing to engage in a regulated business. NGPL built the pipeline and advanced Mitchell's company $7 million to drill wells and build reserves. Mitchell Energy received premium prices and a guaranteed market for its North Texas gas production. This pipeline deal continued to be renewed every twenty years until the final contract was bought out by NGPL in 1995.

Toward the end of the 1960s and into the 1970s, Mitchell Energy, a medium-sized independent producer, discovered gas in east central Texas. Needing cash, Mitchell took the company public in 1972, buying out his original partners. Former employee Joyce Gay explained Mitchell's use of public relations: "We did the annual report, the house organ, news releases, press conferences. . . . I later went to securities analysts meetings around the country, setting up the dog-and-pony shows."[26]

In the meantime, Mitchell was drilling in many other locations in Texas and also serving on other gas-industry-related boards, including the NPC. Mitchell wanted higher gas prices and he was among those promoting the deregulation of pricing. Part of this strategy was claiming that regulation was causing gas shortages. (See Chapter 3.) In 1971 the chairman of the Federal Power Commission, John Nassikas, appointed Mitchell to serve on an advisory committee for the agency's Natural Gas Survey, an exercise focused on writing a report to justify this assertion.[27] Mitchell spoke as a panelist in 1975 at a conference sponsored by the New York Society of Security Analysts, "The Impact of Energy Changes on U.S. Industry." He predicted that deregulation would take place soon and that gas would "be an excellent investment for at least the next 15 years."[28]

Mitchell was also most certainly aware of the larger strategy to withhold gas. Evidence of this emerged during a congressional investigation into natural gas industry practices launched by Congressman John Moss, and consequently Mitchell was subpoenaed to testify at oversight hearings in 1975. The company was accused of withholding gas from an offshore Texas field that was to be sold to Transco and transported to Chicago.[29] (See Chapter 3).

Mitchell's mouthpiece at the hearings, Sidney Walker, blamed the gas shortage during the winter of 1974–75 on construction delays and bad weather, but this conflicted with testimony he had presented to the Federal Power Commission about the gas shortage.[30] In February 1976 the House Oversight Subcommittee called Walker's duplicity a "clear-cut case of perjury and obstruction of justice," and chairman John Moss urged the U.S. attorney general under Gerald Ford to take action.[31] The Commerce Committee chairman, Harley Staggers of West Virginia, sent a letter to the attorney general observing that "any individual of average intelligence would conclude that Mr. Walker perjured himself," and although the Justice Department did go through the motions of investigating the case, nothing came of it.[32]

In 1978, Mitchell's insider status paid off in another way when the Department of Energy provided his company with federal funding for a massive hydraulic fracturing experiment in Limestone County, Texas. A million gallons of fluid and 2.8 million pounds of sand were injected into the tight sand formation.[33]

Mitchell continued to advocate for deregulation. A decade after the initial deregulation legislation passed in 1978 and prices had risen dramatically, he still demanded higher prices. In a 1988 newspaper column, he wrote, "America needs to be told the whole truth, and that is that the lunch will not be free, that natural gas can fulfill its many promises but only at a price."[34]

But in fact, the rising price for natural gas that resulted from the FPC's measures in preparation for deregulation provided an important infusion of cash to Mitchell Energy, which in the mid-1970s was loaded with debt from commercial real estate on top of the gas business debt. Over the next few years, Goldman Sachs, Manufacturers Hanover Bank of New York, and other East and West Coast banks became lenders to Mitchell Energy. In 1987 Goldman and First Boston underwrote $250 million in private debt, and two years later First Boston issued another $200 million in corporate debt financing.[35]

The Wall Street loans and corporate bond offerings financed the company's expansion. Revenues from the stronger gas price brought down the interest rates and costs of this borrowing, but in 1993 the company raised $123 million by offering nearly 6 million nonvoting shares in the company. The company's longtime chief financial officer, Philip S. Smith, said, "George has always had a philosophy of primarily growing the company through internal cash flow, and to the extent that cash flow was not sufficient, debt was used."[36]

It appears that Mitchell Energy had short-term economic incentives for scrimping on well casings and other measures that offer some protection to the environment. Even energy writer James Conca admitted in *Forbes* that "cementing is not easy and it takes some time and some money. . . . And for that reason, the cement job is susceptible to the same boneheaded decisions that are made to save a buck but end up losing billions."[37]

Throughout the 1980s and into the mid-1990s—at a time when Mitchell Energy seems to have skimped on well casings and other safety measures—the company spent millions on many failed business ventures. These included a drilling ship on Lake Erie, gas stations, sulfur extraction in Canada and Mexico, lignite mining in Texas, and more real estate, including a handful of Texas destination hotels, commercial developments, and even a ski resort in Colorado. Adding to the uncertainty was the termination of the long-term contract with NGPL after thirty-eight years. The Wise County water pollution case severely shocked the company. The firm responded by streamlining operations, selling investment properties and cutting its staff by a third.[38]

The company's mistakes and misfortunes, combined with sliding oil prices, took a hammer to Mitchell Energy's stock prices, which fell by more than two-thirds from a high of $35 a share to hover at $10 in 1998.[39] Although Mitchell was looking for a buyer, he was still hoping that the government's commitment to unconventional gas would pay off for him. He had been using an early version of fracking since the late 1970s, when the Department of Energy (DOE) had helped fund a frack in Limestone County. In 1986 the DOE had helped pioneer the techniques used in fracking by subsidizing the first productive multifracture horizontal drilling in Wayne County, West Virginia. Five years later, the department helped fund Mitchell Energy's first horizontal well in the Texas Barnett Shale.[40]

Mitchell was using technologies in which the federal government had invested. Companies such as Halliburton, Mobil, Atlantic Richfield, Standard Oil Development Company, and others had received patents for the use of related technologies, many of which the government had helped create—from propping agents like sand holding new fractures open to specialized drill bits and fracking chemical formulations for gels and foams to make fracking cost-effective.[41]

Mitchell's purchase of cheap drilling rights in the Barnett Shale eventually paid off in a huge way—thanks to Nicholas Steinsberger, one of the engineers on his staff. His company had been using an expensive gel for the fracking process—a common practice during this era of drilling. Steinsberger had heard from a friend at Union Pacific Resources about that company's use of a fracking mixture composed of water and lubricants. In 1998 Steinsberger experimented with a similar concoction. Using extra horsepower, they fracked the S.H. Griffin well, injecting more than a million gallons of the fluid they called "slick water," which contained sand and polymers. After three months, it had produced more gas than any other well they had drilled in the Barnett. When Mitchell Energy began using this recipe for fracking in its other wells in the Barnett, gas production went up by 250 percent in only three years. (Steinsberger never received a bonus for his innovation.)[42]

Ironically, the man who is glorified by the gas industry as the father of fracking funded numerous conferences and projects relevant to environmental and economic sustainability. Mitchell openly worried about fracking's cost to the environment, telling *Forbes* in 2012: "They should have very strict controls. The Department of Energy should do it."[43] In an interview with the *Economist* he admitted, "The natural gas industry can no longer simply focus on the benefits of shale gas while failing to address its challenges. We know that there are significant impacts on air quality, water consumption, water contamination, and local communities."[44] This is from the same man who was involved in drilling some ten thousand wells and who battled landowners over water pollution.

The Cynthia and George Mitchell Foundation, a philanthropic organization, promotes natural gas as a bridge fuel and touts "shale sustainability." Now led by Mitchell's children and grandchildren, the foundation "supports the emerging regulatory, industry, environmental and academic efforts to reduce the negative environmental and community impacts of shale formation development and hydraulic fracturing while capturing the energy, environmental, and economic benefits of natural gas," according to its website.[45] In 2008 the foundation partnered with the San Francisco–based Energy Foundation to launch a $6 million initiative "to advance a clean-energy future for Texas . . . to improve air quality and reduce global warming pollution while growing the Texas economy."[46]

Mitchell's son Todd spoke of "the Mitchell paradox": George Mitchell promoted "sustainability" but was a fossil fuel magnate who never invested in renewable energy.[47] Jurgen Schmandt wrote about this inconsistency in *George P. Mitchell and the Idea of Sustainability*: "Mitchell's engagement with sustainability was sometimes as contradictory as it was committed. He was concerned about overpopulation but had ten children. He believed in clean energy but with a businessman's point of view. He promoted natural spaces but with a developer's mindset."[48]

8

DEVON: BIG FISH POLLUTING A SMALL POND

*God's still up there. The arrogance of people to think that we, human be-
ings, would be able to change what He is doing in the climate is to me
outrageous.*

—Oklahoma senator James Inhofe[1]

In 1883 my grandfather rode across the prairie in the far northwestern
Oklahoma Territory during the largest land run ever held. He said in a
memoir that he left Kansas and headed to the frontier in Oklahoma and
"proved a claim" ten miles northwest of Alva in Woods County, on land
referred to as "the Strip." This northwestern area of the Oklahoma Territory was made available to settlers in one of the many episodes in the
long history of the federal government's murderous policies toward Native
Americans—in this case, the Cherokees.

I grew up hearing tales about the difficult life my dad's family had in
their struggle to make a living as homesteaders, especially after his mother's
death from gangrene at the age of thirty-five. My father left Oklahoma on
a freight train during the Depression and never really looked back. But one
of his childhood stories that stuck with me was how he and his siblings
started a fire at an oil seepage—leading to a round of spankings.

You might say that oil greased Oklahoma's way into statehood. In
1897 the discovery of an oil gusher near Bartlesville in the northeastern
Oklahoma Territory inaugurated the oil era. By 1907, after some controversy about the lands that would constitute the new state, the necessary
legislation passed and Oklahoma became the forty-sixth state. Soon after,
it became the largest oil producer in the world. Oil barons J. Paul Getty and
Frank Phillips got their start here, creating vast fortunes during a period
when the oil industry consolidated its power and influence.[2]

My dad also spun tales about the populist movement in Oklahoma and how farmers and ranchers fought back against the moneyed interests. Ironically, today Oklahoma's leaders are promoting policies to criminalize criticism of the petroleum industry's practices.

Recently an attack on First Amendment rights took place when four peaceful protesters were charged in Oklahoma City for a "terrorist hoax."[3] Activists unfurled a banner in the atrium of the office tower owned by Devon Energy, the company that purchased Mitchell Energy in 2001. (See Chapter 6.) Two other activists chained themselves to the building, protesting the company's fracking practices and exploitation of the Canadian tar sands. When the authorities saw that glitter had fallen from the banner, they arrested the protesters. Oklahoman Moriah Stephenson, a graduate student at the University of Oklahoma, said that her concern about Devon's environmental impact had prompted her "to hang a glittery banner that was dramatic."[4]

Kurt Hochenauer, an English professor at the University of Oklahoma who writes the blog *OkieFunk*, says, "Anyone who challenges the prevailing narrative—what's good for oil and gas companies is good for Oklahoma—might find themselves marginalized or ostracized."[5]

Fortunately, a network of grassroots activists is mobilizing people in Oklahoma around the impacts of fracking. They have had great victories here in the past. Earl Hatley was among the activists who successfully campaigned to block the Black Fox nuclear plant in 1982—the only nuclear power plant in the country that was abandoned after construction because of concerted public opposition.[6] Hatley, a Cherokee activist with a master's degree in political science from Oklahoma State University, has organized on many fronts, including documenting the radioactive pollution at Kerr-McGee's plutonium fabrication plant in Oklahoma (which was implicated in the death of plant worker and union activist Karen Silkwood in 1974).[7] He worked on toxics campaigns for several years before moving to northeastern Oklahoma in 1997 to organize the clean-up of Superfund sites. Today Hatley is the Grand Riverkeeper for the upper Grand River watershed.

Ironically, under Oklahoma's draconian law that forces landowners to drill, he now faces having his land fracked. Devon Energy has sent several letters demanding access to his property. The fracking crisis inspired Hatley and other activists to start Clean Energy Future OK. He says, "I've never been afraid to do what's right, and we are going to fight long and hard to stop fracking."[8]

Largest Oil & Gas Companies By Decade

In 1911, the Supreme Court ruled that Standard Oil had violated the Sherman Antitrust Act and the monopoly was split into 38 companies, all of which maintained the same board of directors, which Rockefeller controlled with a quarter of the shares.

Three of the spinoffs, Standard Oil Co. of New Jersey (later known as Exxon), Standard Oil Co. of New York (later known as Mobil), and Standard Oil Co. of California (later known as Chevron) were members of the Western oil cartel called the Seven Sisters.

1940	1950	1960	1970	1980	1990	2000	2010
			Tenneco	Tenneco	Coastal	EOG	Encana
			Coastal	Coastal	Ashland	Chesapeake	EOG
			Ashland	Ashland	TotalFina	Total	Chesapeake
			Petrofina	Fina	Mitchell	Apache	Apache
			Marathon Oil	Mitchell	Marathon	Devon	Devon
			Hess	Marathon Oil	Hess	Marathon Oil	Marathon Oil
			Union Pac	Hess	Union Pac	Hess	Hess
			Kerr McGee	Union Pac	Kerr McGee	Anadarko	Anadarko
		Cities Service	Cities Service	Kerr McGee	Oryx	Occidental	Occidental
		Sunoco	Occidental	Occidental	Anadarko	ConocoPhillips	ConocoPhillips
		Conoco	Sunoco	Sunoco	Occidental	Chevron	Chevron
	Phillips Petroleum	Phillips	Conoco	Conoco	Sunoco	BP Amoco	BP
	Texas Co.	UnoCal	UnoCal	Phillips	Conoco	XTO Energy	ExxonMobil
	Gulf Oil	Texaco	Getty Oil	UnoCal	Phillips	ExxonMobil	Shell
	Standard CA	SoCal	Texaco	Texaco	UnoCal	Shell	
	Standard Indiana	Sinclair	Gulf Oil	Chevron	Texaco		
	Pan American	Atlantic Richfield	SoCal	ARCO	Chevron		
Texas Co.	BP	Standard IN	ARCO	Amoco	BP		
Gulf Oil	Superior Oil	BP	Standard IN	BP	Mobil		
Standard California	Standard New York	Superior Oil	BP	Mobil	Exxon		
Anglo-Persian	Humble Oil	SoconyMobil	Superior Oil	Exxon	Shell		
Standard New York	Standard NJ	Standard NJ	Mobil	Shell			
Standard New Jersey	Shell	Shell	Exxon				
Royal Dutch			Shell				

Fracking Oklahoma

The place where my grandfather homesteaded is underlaid by the Mississippian Lime, a rock formation stretching into Kansas and Nebraska. Dating from 360 million years ago, it was formed when an inland sea left behind the layer of marine limestone. Below the Mississippian Lime is another heavily targeted tight oil formation, the Woodford Shale. Vertical well drilling had declined in the area until fracking changed the outlook for oil recovery. Drilling wells into the Mississippian Lime is less expensive because the oil is found between 3,000 and 6,000 feet below the surface. This is in contrast to the Bakken in North Dakota, where the shale can be up to 10,000 feet down, and to both the Eagle Ford in Texas and the Permian/Delaware Basin in Texas and New Mexico, where the targeted rocks are at depths of at least 3,500 and upwards of 15,000 feet. The closer proximity of the oil to the surface allows the use of lower-cost rigs with less horsepower.[9]

In 2009, lower-cost drilling attracted homegrown companies such as SandRidge that have less capital than larger companies. Periods of high oil prices and a lax regulatory environment made it possible for SandRidge and other smaller companies to take risks and grow. For the capital needed to drill and frack, many companies have established international joint ventures, including with Chinese, South Korean, and Spanish corporations.[10]

More recently, Devon Energy—the largest Oklahoma-based petroleum company and one of the ten largest oil and gas companies in the country—entered into the drilling frenzy in the Mississippian Lime. MineralMarketing.com, a national mineral marketing company based in Alva, Oklahoma, is urging landowners (generally farm families) to sell or lease their mineral rights. Shane Terrel, the company's CEO, says, "We take listings on assets and market them to prospective buyers." He adds, "Devon's presence alone adds credibility to the play."[11]

In 2012 Devon entered into a joint venture with a subsidiary of Sinopec, China's largest petroleum company. Sinopec is investing $2.2 billion, underwriting Devon's costs for drilling, in exchange for 30 percent ownership in Devon's 1.4 million acres of holdings in five plays: the Mississippian Lime, Tuscaloosa Marine Shale, Niobrara, Ohio Utica Shale, and Michigan Basin.[12] With $4.5 billion in annual revenues and nearly 1 million employees, Sinopec operates in all phases of oil and gas production; it ranked second on the Fortune Global 500 list in 2015. By the end of 2015, the 6,600-employee Devon planned to have nearly three hundred wells in production in the Mississippian Lime, where it (and its partners) have invested billions of dollars.[13]

An unexpected consequence of the fracking boom is hundreds of miles of temporary plastic pipes that aggravate residents. In lieu of tanker trucks, pipes are used to deliver water to wells and to remove millions of gallons of salty brine and liquid waste to disposal sites for underground injection. Pitting farmers and landowners against drillers, the stiff plastic pipes are laid without warning, obstructing driveways and damaging property when they are pulled tight against fence posts and mailboxes.[14] Tony Vaughn, Devon's executive vice president of exploration and production, says that the company laid five hundred miles of oil, gas, and water pipelines north of Oklahoma City in 2013.[15]

Farcically, while politicians rant against "takings" of private property, landowners have few rights when they go up against petroleum interests. Individuals own the land adjoining roadways where pipes are laid, but counties have easements along roads for use by public utilities. Based on this, permits are doled out for pipelines—at $250 per mile. A lawsuit by landowners against drilling companies is pending.[16]

Regulators have also failed to grapple with the swarms of earthquakes plaguing Oklahoma thanks to fracking. Frackers have increasingly used underground injection as the disposal method for millions of gallons of waste. As fracked wells increase in number throughout Oklahoma, the industry's disposal problems have grown, especially in the Mississippian Lime. A growing collection of research provides evidence that injection of fracking waste causes earthquakes—human-induced seismic events.[17] When fluid is injected deep underground, the liquid can lubricate fault zones. As the volume of fluid increases, the pressure builds, potentially causing the fault to slip and creating the stress that results in an earthquake.[18]

These quakes used to be rare. Between 1975 and 2008, Oklahoma experienced only one to three earthquakes of 3.0 or greater magnitude annually. Beginning in 2009, the number increased to around forty earthquakes per year.[19] The dramatic rise in the number of earthquakes is associated with rising fracking wastewater injections, which have doubled from 1997 to 2013.[20] In 2014 the Oklahoma Geological Survey found that the state experienced 585 quakes of 3.0 magnitude and greater, more than all the earthquakes in the past thirty years.[21]

In June 2015 the Oklahoma Supreme Court ruled that a woman injured in a quake could sue the two companies that she believes were involved.[22] Stirring the controversy were the more than thirty-five Oklahoma earthquakes of greater than 3.0 magnitude that occurred over one week in mid-June 2015.[23] The fracking industry's earthquake problem is not isolated to Oklahoma. In the eastern and central United States, earthquake activity has also exploded.[24] USGS scientists have found similar seismic activity in other states where this type of wastewater injection is used, such as Arkansas, Colorado, Ohio, and Texas.[25]

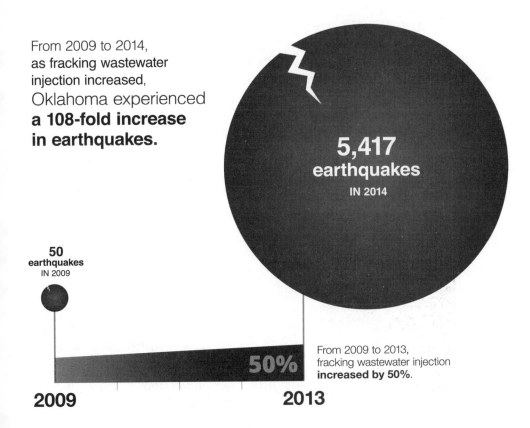

From 2009 to 2014, as fracking wastewater injection increased, Oklahoma experienced **a 108-fold increase in earthquakes.**

5,417 earthquakes IN 2014

50 earthquakes IN 2009

50%

From 2009 to 2013, fracking wastewater injection **increased by 50%.**

2009   **2013**

Petroleum Industry Reigns Supreme

While property owners are prohibited from building a "habitable structure" closer than 125 feet to an active well or 50 feet from related surface equipment, drillers are not prohibited from drilling close to property lines or homes. Although some jurisdictions have zoning laws, the Oklahoma Corporation Commission, the state's regulatory body, offers no such protections to rural residents. An agency official says that "on an unofficial basis," the agency encourages those affected by nearby drilling operations to have a discussion with companies.[26]

Oklahoma state law also gives industry the right to force landowners like Earl Hatley into allowing seismic testing and drilling beneath their property as part of a "pool" of resources.[27]

According to the OCC website in 2015, "if the oil company cannot successfully get all the owners within the unit to agree as to how to develop the unit, the oil company can apply to the Commission to have those people or other oil companies who have not agreed, force pooled into the unit."[28]

Landmen who negotiate the buying and selling of mineral rights also play a big role in Oklahoma politics. The Texas-based American Association of Professional Landmen (AAPL), which has two affiliates in Oklahoma, offers "networking, continuing education, marketing and deal making opportunities."[29] One of its affiliates, the Oklahoma City Association of Professional Landmen, had more than 1,700 members at the end of 2014, one of the largest local landmen affiliates.[30] The AAPL says that it "represented the best interests of our nation's landmen before the public, legislators, and federal administrations and agencies, to advocate for policies and procedures that ensure the continued fulfillment of America's energy needs."[31]

Other powerful players are the Mid-Continent Oil and Gas Association of Oklahoma, the Natural Gas and Energy Association of Oklahoma, and the Oklahoma Independent Petroleum Association (OIPA). OIPA, the largest oil and gas trade group in the state, is the most belligerent and coordinates many lobbying activities, such as the "Rally for the Rigs" held on April 9, 2014, at the state capitol. A thousand people gathered at the statehouse—including busloads from driller Continental Resources with people carrying "Don't be a fracking idiot" signs. The former OIPA chairman thanked the legislature for cutting taxes on horizontal drilling but warned elected officials not to cross the industry, noting, "We're just here to remind our legislative friends, as they take up policies, . . . of how important our industry is."[32]

In 2008 OIPA formed another entity for political giving, Federal PAC, which it proudly says has helped "work with other oil and natural gas associations and companies across the country to defeat proposed industry tax increases and . . . prevent federal regulation of hydraulic fracturing."[33] Oklahoma Republican senator Jim Inhofe introduced a resolution in 2005 in the U.S. Senate "recognizing the 50th anniversary" of OIPA and its members' "vital contribution to the oil and gas industry of the United States."[34]

In the 2014 election, when Republicans took over the U.S. Senate, Inhofe became chairman of the Senate Committee on Environment and Public Works (EPW).[35] Previously, the notorious climate change denier and unabashed champion of the fossil fuel industry had been ranking minority member of the EPW committee's oversight subcommittee. In this role, Inhofe issued an EPW Minority Report in July 2014 subtitled "How a Club of Billionaires and Their Foundations Control the Environmental Movement and Obama's EPA," designed to intimidate and bully environmental groups and public interest funders, and to make the EPA even more timid in pursuing its mandate. Industry advocates crying about conflicts of interest in the political sphere marks a new level of oil and gas chutzpah. My organization, Food & Water Watch, was one of the organizations named in the report.[36]

Months later, in October 2014, the minority EPW staff released another vitriolic report, subtitled "Hydraulic Fracturing and America's Energy Revolution," labeling fracking opponents "extremists." It said, "Far-left environmental groups have teamed up with President Obama's federal bureaucrats and the Hollywood elite in a coordinated effort to distort the truth about hydraulic fracturing."[37] (Of course, the Obama administration's "all of the above" energy approach utterly embraces fracking.)[38]

According to the Center for Responsive Politics, over his Senate career—from the election cycle beginning in 1989 to 2015—Inhofe has received more than $1.7 million from oil and gas companies.[39] Devon Energy's PAC and employees are among his top career donors, giving more than $52,000 between 1989 and 2015.

Political Powerhouse, Oklahoma Style

Devon Energy, founded in 1971 by John Nichols and his son Larry, operates more than 14,500 wells and holds 8.5 million acres of mineral leases across the United States.[40] In 2012, Devon opened its almost $1 billion monument to the company, the Devon Energy Center. At fifty stories high it is the tallest building in Oklahoma City, and was the location of the 2014 banner-hanging protest.[41]

In 1950 John Nichols—the son of an Oklahoma cotton broker with a 1936 accounting degree from the University of Oklahoma—developed the first public oil and gas fund to be registered with the U.S. Securities and Exchange Commission. A large tax shelter, it remained legal until 1986. Investors could deduct 80 percent of their investment in a petroleum fund he created, and retain a stake in the wells that were drilled based on the funding they provided. Wealthy investors received tens of billions of dollars of tax breaks from the fund. Among the investors were actresses Barbara Stanwyck and Ginger Rogers; Willard Rockwell Sr., of Rockwell International; top executives from Chrysler and General Motors; Phillip Armour of Armour Packing Co.; and members of the Pillsbury family.[42]

John Nichols diversified into banks, radio stations, and an oil-field services company in Libya and Nigeria, He had learned the oil and gas business by auditing the books of Kerr-Lynn, the predecessor of Kerr-McGee Corporation. In 1971 he called his lawyer son, who also had an undergraduate degree in geology, home from his job in Washington, D.C. The younger Nichols had clerked for Chief Justice Earl Warren before working at the Justice Department for future chief justice William Rehnquist. After settling an argument about his low salary offer, Larry Nichols went home to work for his father. During its early years the company focused on natural gas production in North America.[43]

After Larry Nichols replaced his father as CEO in 1980, he began to increase the company's size. In 1984 Devon created a master limited partnership—another advantageous corporate tax scheme—to attract investors for funding future acquisitions. Investors buy units in the project that are traded like stock, giving them the flexibility to liquidate their investment quickly if they want access to the monies. Devon maintains a stake in the purchased assets and controls them.[44]

The company went public in 1988, growing steadily through twenty-eight different mergers and acquisitions. Besides the purchase of Mitchell Energy, other major additions came when Devon merged with Pennz-Energy in 1999 and Ocean Energy in 2003.[45]

Devon's 2012 deal with Sinopec raised billions for drilling in the United States. Devon had begun shedding its ownership of foreign concerns, like its interest in the ExxonMobil-operated Zafiro field in Equatorial Guinea. In 2004 Devon was caught up in a bribery and corruption scandal in West Africa that involved ExxonMobil and other petroleum companies.[46] Since then, Devon has sold holdings in Gabon, Côte d'Ivoire, Azerbaijan, the South China Sea, and Brazil.[47]

Although Devon is large for an independent oil company, it is a tenth of the size of ExxonMobil. In keeping with Larry Nichols's focus on acquisitions and corporate expansion, in February 2014 the company made a $6 billion deal to buy assets in Texas's Eagle Ford oil play, forming a partnership with Dallas-based Crosstex Energy, which owns gas processing facilities and rail and barge terminals for oil.[48] Their combined entity, Enlink Midstream Partners, had 8,800 miles of pipelines.[49]

A victim of aggressive overexpansion, Devon is now suffering from low oil and gas prices. In June 2015, a warning about lower earnings from the investment firm Oppenheimer caused its stock prices to drop further. Analysts predicted that the company's profits could continue to fall over the year and its cash flow deficit could widen to $1.9 billion. Other pundits predict that lower stock prices could be offset by potential improvements in its inventory of resources and lower drilling costs.[50]

Public Policy for Sale?

Devon is a major powerhouse at the national level, spending at least $3.78 million lobbying federal officials in 2013 and 2014.[51] A significant campaign donor, it contributes to elected officials at the state and federal levels. Oklahoma state representative Mary Fallin, who received the right-wing American Legislative Exchange Council's (ALEC) "Legislator of the Year" award in 1992, was elected to the U.S. House of Representatives in 2006 on a gusher of oil donations. Between 2005 and 2008 she received $347,000 from oil and gas interests, including $30,650 from Devon Energy. She was elected governor of Oklahoma in 2010. In 2013 Fallin spoke to the ALEC Spring Task Force Summit, that included a workshop on "American energy opportunities," which in Oklahoma, means fracking.[52] In 2014 Fallin supported Devon and other Oklahoma petroleum companies lobbying to maintain a low production tax, and in 2015 she signed legislation preventing local governments from banning oil and gas drilling.[53]

Beyond making donations to Oklahoma's Governor Fallin, Devon Energy and its employees are also large donors in federal elections, contributing over $2 million to federal candidates from 2000 to 2014. Devon's PAC and employees lavished fifteen times more on Republican congressional candidates than on Democratic ones. One of the biggest beneficiaries has been Oklahoma congressman Tom Cole, whose district runs south of Oklahoma City and includes Ada, Norman, and Lawton. Cole received nearly $74,000 from Devon between 2002 and 2014. An important strategist for

Republicans, Cole has served the party in other capacities, including fundraising and serving as the chair of the National Republican Congressional Committee between 2006 and 2008.[54]

In 2015 Cole praised fracking on his congressional website, saying that it is "a technology safely used in Oklahoma for over six decades."[55] In May 2015 he spoke in favor of ending the prohibition on exports of oil.[56] He promoted the creation of tax incentives for the production and use of vehicles that can run on compressed natural gas (CNG), as well as the development of infrastructure for transporting gas.[57]

Devon and other Oklahoma-based energy companies have been at the forefront of promoting the use of natural-gas-fueled vehicles. In response, the Oklahoma legislature created generous tax incentives in 2013 for gas vehicles that are in effect until 2020. Oklahoma also has a private loan program with a 3 percent interest rate for conversion of private fleets to operate on alternative fuels or for purchasing new vehicles.[58]

Similar bills are cropping up in many other states. Likewise, ALEC spread weak, Exxon-recommended legislation on state-level chemical disclosure laws that only requires the companies to share fracking fluid ingredient information on FracFocus, which provides generous trade-secret exemptions that keep information from the public.[59]

Devon has also railed against the EPA's clean air rules, lobbying members of Congress against the EPA's designation of Wise County, Texas, as a "non-attainment" area in 2012 because it does not meet the standards set by the Clean Air Act to protect public health. Wise County, at the heart of the Barnett Shale, is where Devon now operates thousands of wells since acquiring Mitchell Energy's holdings in the region.[60]

A letter from Devon's K Street law firm, Sidley Austin LLP, to the EPA argues that the agency's decision on Wise County was "not supported by sound science, does not have a rational basis in the record . . . and is otherwise arbitrary."[61] Joe Leonard, an environmental, health, and safety engineer at Devon, criticized EPA air pollution regulation in testimony before the U.S. House Committee on Oversight and Government Reform, saying the standards led to "unnecessary and burdensome air quality regulations on the oil and gas industry."[62]

The state of Texas and Devon Energy sued the EPA on its implementation of regulations on ozone emission limits, opposing the agency's designation in forty-six areas; at least ten others, including the state of Tennessee and other gas companies, also brought suits.[63] The battle continued in 2015 with the oil and gas industry pushing for a weaker rule.[64]

Devon has also lobbied on "sue and settle" legislation, designed to hamper the use of litigation by citizen groups to press federal agencies that fail to do their job in protecting public health or the environment. The energy and mining interests have contended that federal officials are involved in a conspiracy with environmental groups that take legal action against government agencies. In 2013 Devon lobbied in favor of the Sunshine for Regulatory Decrees and Settlements Act of 2012, legislation that was approved by the House Judiciary Committee in 2013.[65] In 2014 Oklahoma attorney general Scott Pruitt submitted a letter to the EPA critical of the agency's assessment of pollution from drilling rigs; the text of the letter was merely copied from a Devon memo onto official state letterhead. Devon's government relations director replied in an email to the attorney general's office: "Outstanding! The timing of the letter is great, given our meeting this Friday with both EPA and the White House."[66]

During 2013—according to Devon's own disclosure forms—the company also lobbied in Congress and at the EPA against enforcement of the Endangered Species Act.[67] Devon hopes to prevent the lesser prairie chicken, a colorful type of grouse, from being listed as an endangered species. Destruction of the birds' habitat as a result of drilling is leading to extinction.[68]

Unfortunately, the nonprofit Environmental Defense Fund has actively given cover on this issue to Devon and other energy companies operating in Colorado, Kansas, New Mexico, Oklahoma, and Texas by proposing a scheme that allows "species extinction on the installment plan." The Interior Department has embraced an EDF-sponsored scheme for trading habitat credits. EDF vice president David Festa calls this "pay to endanger" scheme a "stock exchange" where ranchers generate credits to protect habitat and the oil and gas industry buys them.[69] Center for Biological Diversity senior scientist Jay Lininger counters, "It's too little, too late, because it locks chickens into little postage-stamp areas of habitat that aren't big enough to support breeding populations."[70]

Fortunately, although Devon and Oklahoma's energy industry has a dangerous influence on federal and state law, a new generation of brave young activists are organizing to keep fossil fuels in the ground. Hatley praises their goal, saying, "It is in our state's and our country's best interest to first pursue a rigorous conservation strategy combined with renewable energy development."[71]

Longtime activist Barbara VanHanken, another founder of Clean Energy Future OK, is hopeful for the future: "As a native Oklahoman, I am heartened by the growing groundswell of support from many local groups and landowners who are fed up with the treatment they have received from local landmen wanting their property and mineral rights. . . . Collectively, we know that if we don't do it, no one will do it for us!"[72]

9

CHESAPEAKE ENERGY: HIGH-ROLLING FRACKING DRAMA

Be fearful when others are greedy, and greedy when others are fearful.
—Warren Buffett [1]

Aubrey McClendon used Chesapeake Energy as a private piggy bank, funding multimillion-dollar homes, wine cellars with two thousand trophy vintages, and all the trappings of wealth.[2] The company's profits had more to do with flipping leases and ripping off mineral rights owners than with producing gas. Chesapeake's willing board of directors—who enjoyed unusually generous compensation packages—blessed McClendon's virtual Ponzi scheme using leveraged debt to buy mineral acreage and other companies.[3] Relying on an ethically challenged strategy, he made Chesapeake second only to Exxon in natural gas production.[4]

When stock prices were high, the sycophant trade press and Wall Street analysts hyped McClendon. Named by *Forbes* as "America's most reckless billionaire" in 2010, he was glorified for his risk addiction.[5] In 2012 McClendon told *Rolling Stone* journalist Jeff Goodell, over a $400 bottle of French Bordeaux: "We frack all the time. What's the big deal?"[6] That same year Reuters ran a series of articles on McClendon's "lavish and leveraged" lifestyle, sparking investigations that led to his eventual firing.[7]

As a member of a prominent political family in Oklahoma, McClendon knew how to use politicians to Chesapeake's advantage for public policies favorable to the petroleum industry, such as the petroleum depletion allowance. In 2012 Bloomberg disclosed that over its twenty-three-year history, Chesapeake Energy had paid a corporate income tax rate of only 1 percent.[8] Between 1990 and 2014, Chesapeake and its employees donated more than

$6.6 million to federal election efforts and candidates, the vast majority of it going to Republicans, according to the Center for Responsive Politics.[9]

McClendon's wife, Whirlpool heiress Kathleen Upton Byrns, is the first cousin of Republican congressman Fred Upton, the powerful chairman of the House Energy and Commerce Committee.[10] Even though his committee oversees the petroleum industry, Upton has a stake in Chesapeake of between $15,000 and $30,000.[11] Besides the McClendons' personal contribution to Upton of $10,000 in 2014, Chesapeake's PAC and employees contributed $52,100 to Upton from 2001 to 2014 and were among the top contributors in 2014.[12]

McClendon also was a strong supporter of George W. Bush. In the last days before the 2004 election, McClendon gave more than $2 million to several right-wing political committees to influence the outcome of elections, including running slanderous ads on John Kerry's record in Vietnam.[13]

In addition, Chesapeake donated more than $6.4 million to state-level elections between 1999 and 2015.[14] In Pennsylvania, his $450,000 check to a little-known Republican candidate for attorney general, whom he had never met, ushered in an era of policies favorable to unfettered fracking. McClendon's support ultimately helped boost Tom Corbett into the governor's mansion in 2011, leading to the acceleration of fracking in the state.[15]

With little oversight, Chesapeake drilled six hundred wells in heavily fracked Bradford County, located in northeastern Pennsylvania, leaving the once bucolic area scarred.[16] In April 2011, a well that had been fracked with more than a million gallons of fluid failed, causing a massive eruption that spilled tens of thousands of gallons of toxic fluid into Towanda Creek. The blowout took six days to control, threatening drinking water sources.[17] Dr. Tony Ingraffea, a Cornell University engineering professor and a former consultant to the petroleum industry, found that twenty-four of Chesapeake's 141 violations in 2011 involved failures of well integrity.[18] The state issued a $1.1 million fine, with $900 million levied against the company for the well casing failure that contaminated sixteen water wells.[19] As this book goes to press, Chesapeake was the largest violator of oil and gas regulations in Pennsylvania, with 517 violations.[20]

A similar blowout occurred in Wyoming, where Chesapeake also was in a powerful position. In 2012 a blowout caused methane to roar from a well near Douglas, and it took three days to plug the well and stop the spewing gas. Although the company was not fined for the accident, its delayed response to warning signs contributed to the blowout.[21] Chesapeake had failed to properly install the lockdown pin on the wellhead, but the company was not disciplined. Wyoming interim oil and gas supervisor Bob King said: "Accidents will happen. I mean, you can't prevent every accident that is going to happen."[22]

Chesapeake's record of accidents and violations is just one aspect of McClendon's propensity to run the company as if he were accountable to no one. He faced a U.S. Securities and Exchange Commission investigation for shady dealings and dubious perks, such as the Founder Well Participation Program. McClendon was allowed to make millions from the right to purchase a 2.5 percent interest in every well drilled by the company. McClendon borrowed more than $1 billion from a Chesapeake investor, EIG Global Energy Partners, to pay for his share of well drilling.[23] The SEC ended the investigation in 2014 without taking any enforcement action.[24]

The Reuters probe of Chesapeake prompted Michigan attorney general Bill Schuette to examine how Chesapeake and Encana Corporation plotted to maintain low petroleum lease prices. The companies were charged in March 2014 with colluding during the 2010 speculative frenzy in Michigan's Collingwood Shale play.[25] In 2015 Chesapeake paid $25 million to settle these antitrust charges.[26]

ProPublica journalist Abrahm Lustgarten disclosed yet more unethical behavior. Using tactics similar to those of the debt-addicted Samuel Insull (see Chapter 2) in the early twentieth century, McClendon had constructed a vertically integrated corporation with subsidiaries that passed money back and forth by providing services for Chesapeake's core business of drilling. This allowed for lucrative self-dealing as the interlocking companies charged higher prices for services, the cost of which could be passed on to others.[27]

Lustgarten discovered how McClendon used "monopoly power" to "rake in billions of dollars." He created a corporate structure that allowed an affiliate to charge landowners exorbitant fees for gas transportation from the wellhead to interstate pipelines or processing facilities through gathering lines. Landowners were tricked into signing leases that included unlimited fees for this transportation service, sometimes eating 90 percent of their royalty payment. In one case, a landowner was charged thirty times more than the actual cost of moving gas.[28] Chesapeake settled a class-action lawsuit involving royalty skimming in Pennsylvania for $7.5 million in 2013. Lawsuits over underpaying gas royalties have been filed around the country, including in the Texas cities of Fort Worth and Arlington.[29]

Although McClendon spent years touting how fracking would make the United States energy independent, Chesapeake's cash flow nightmare forced McClendon to look to Asian companies to save his company from his profligate spending habits. Early in 2013 Chesapeake announced a sale of a stake in its Oklahoman leases in the Mississippian Lime to China's state-owned oil and gas company, Sinopec. Chesapeake's billion-dollar deal with the Chinese was viewed as a fire sale by investors, and the company's stock price plunged by 7 percent.[30]

As details emerged about McClendon's outrageously expensive lifestyle and his propensity for meshing personal and business affairs, his reputation was sullied. Activist shareholders, angry about low stock prices and his flagrant overspending, forced him to "retire" from Chesapeake on April Fool's Day, 2013.[31]

Energy Dynasty Heir

McClendon is the grandnephew of former Oklahoma governor and U.S. senator Robert S. Kerr, a founder of the energy giant Kerr-McGee (see Chapter 2). Kerr's oil wealth made him a millionaire before he became the purportedly wealthiest senator. As columnist Jack Anderson observed nearly a decade after Kerr's death, he was an "oil millionaire, uranium king, cattle baron and Senator from Oklahoma, who dominated the Senate's backrooms . . . Bob Kerr had three basic beliefs, the Baptist faith, the oil depletion allowance and his divine right to make millions."[32] His petroleum, chemical, and uranium company left a seriously blemished record of environmental pollution that affected nearly the entire country.[33]

One of Chesapeake's fierce competitors, Anadarko, acquired Kerr-McGee for $18 billion in 2006 and moved the company's headquarters from Oklahoma City to Houston.[34] Before the sale, Kerr-McGee shifted its environmental and health liabilities by spinning off its chemical business as Tronox. Some eight thousand people suffer from respiratory illnesses, cancer, and other ailments connected to their chemical exposure to Kerr-McGee's operations. In December 2013 a judge ruled that Anadarko was liable for the life-threatening pollution caused by Kerr-McGee. The Justice Department announced a settlement of $5.1 billion for the cleanup, but the record fine had a much smaller impact than expected. Anadarko's shares soared after the announcement, and the company continued to compete with Chesapeake in the Marcellus, Haynesville, and Eagle Ford shale plays, and in the Rockies.[35]

McClendon, whose father worked for Kerr-McGee for thirty-five years, grew up in Oklahoma City, basking in the reflected glory of the Kerr name.[36] After graduating from Duke University, where he met his wife at a fraternity party, he returned home to Oklahoma City to work for the oil company owned by his uncle Aubrey M. Kerr Jr. Beginning as an accountant at Jaytex, McClendon soon transitioned into what was his calling: becoming a landman.[37] He left the company about the same time his uncle suddenly ran into trouble with the SEC for ill-gotten profits when Jaytex went public.[38]

McClendon took the skills he had learned and went into business for himself, searching courthouse records and buying mineral rights that he then resold to oil companies. In 1983 he joined forces with Tom Ward, an aggressive competitor for leases. In 1989 the partners formed Chesapeake, named for the Chesapeake Bay, an Atlantic Ocean estuary.[39] Their first two wells, drilled in southern Oklahoma, were winners. By 1991 the partners were able to persuade a large West Coast financial institution to loan Chesapeake $25 million in exchange for an equity position in the company.[40] McClendon drove a hard bargain, aggressively seeking low bids for drilling services, demanding rock-bottom prices, and failing to pay bills on time.[41]

When the heavily indebted company was taken public in 1993, a legal battle with Harold Hamm (see Chapter 10) and another wildcatter over money owed for a drilling job cost them dearly. When Chesapeake lost the case on appeal and was forced to pay punitive damages, the company's shares plummeted. Angry shareholders filed lawsuits against Chesapeake for not disclosing the litigation during the IPO process.[42] This failure was followed by a well blowout in Texas in 1995.[43] But the company's luck had turned by 1996, when the price of crude oil rose more than 20 percent and natural gas increased by 47 percent. Chesapeake's stock price soared, and its lucrative leases in Oklahoma and Texas meant that the company was valued at $1 billion.[44]

Chesapeake was still at a disadvantage compared to large, vertically integrated oil companies, however. Volatility in petroleum markets and the cost of drilling made it more difficult for poorly capitalized independents to invest in drilling, the operation of new wells, and the acquisition of new leases. In 1997 and 1998 McClendon borrowed heavily so that Chesapeake could continue growing its acreage and buying additional companies.[45]

He soon ran into trouble when he rushed to buy leases in Louisiana's Austin Chalk but failed to do his homework. Not only was the area expensive to drill, but it produced low volumes of oil.[46] The ensuing economic havoc was intensified by the lower demand for oil—an outcome of the Asian financial crisis. Shareholders brought a class action suit in 1998, charging that company insiders had disposed of 200,000 shares of stock while not disclosing the problem to investors. That year the company lost $881 million primarily from crashing oil prices; the court ruled that Chesapeake did enough to disclose the speculative risks of unproven gas reserves to investors, and so it dismissed the shareholders' suit.[47]

Chesapeake was severely hurt but not fatally wounded. McClendon had bought time by using high-interest debt that would not mature for up to a dozen years.[48] Chesapeake was put on the market, but no buyer appeared.[49] McClendon's next move was to capitalize on the drive to deregulate electricity by becoming an advocate of "clean" natural-gas-generated power. In 2000 he met with Peter Cartwright, founder and CEO of Calpine, a large and aggressive independent power producer that was advocating for electricity deregulation.[50] Cartwright sold McClendon on his vision of merchant power plant operators teaming up with the natural gas industry to dominate the electricity market. Calpine eventually constructed or acquired ninety-three power plants, mostly fueled by natural gas. By 2005, after gas prices had skyrocketed from the price manipulations, the market had dried up for speculative power generators like Calpine, leaving it saddled with $18 billion of debt. Cartwright was fired as Calpine slid into bankruptcy.[51]

McClendon still saw the marketing potential for gas, however, and he knew that the environmental community could help him sell the vision for moving toward gas-fired power plants. In 2008 he informed his board about his relationship with "leading environmental organizations" on issues "where our interests might be aligned." Chesapeake gave the American Lung Association an undisclosed amount of funding for its Fighting for Air campaign.[52] Former Sierra Club president Carl Pope risked the reputation of the venerable environmental organization by accepting $25 million for its Beyond Coal campaign.[53]

McClendon was not discouraged. His inside track on the events surrounding deregulation gave him faith that natural gas would come out on top. McClendon's college buddy Roger Eads had worked for El Paso Corp., a large pipeline, energy services, and trading company that manipulated natural gas prices during the California energy crisis. El Paso Corp. had a virtual pipeline monopoly in the lucrative California markets. Eads wrote a memo to El Paso CEO Bill Wise that described how control of the physical gas market would drive up prices.[54] In 2000 the combination of electricity deregulation and energy market manipulation by firms such as Enron and El Paso turned off the lights for millions of Californians who suffered through intermittent blackouts, brownouts, high energy prices, and unreliable service.[55] The Federal Energy Regulatory Commission approved a $56 million settlement with El Paso to resolve claims related to the jump in gas and electricity prices that caused rolling blackouts.[56]

McClendon convinced his board that a new fleet of gas-fired plants would be the company's salvation. He turned for help to Eads, who was forced to resign from El Paso for his role in the gas price rigging fiasco but was otherwise largely unscathed. Eads had bought a stake in Randall & Dewey, a consulting company that specialized in mergers and acquisitions. In 2004 he began advising McClendon on deals, and soon sold Randall & Dewey to Jefferies Group, a New York investment bank. Eads went on an international road show selling big institutional investors in countries across the globe on the extraordinary returns they would enjoy from fracking. McClendon went on a buying spree with the influx of cash, adding on acres of mineral rights in multiple states. As the economy soured between 2007 and 2011, Eads created a complex web of subsidiaries and joint ventures that brought in $28 billion by selling leases, land, and services, which helped keep Chesapeake afloat.[57]

McClendon also spent heavily building the extensive Chesapeake Energy Campus, a sprawling 111-acre office and retail complex. He directed the purchase of more than one hundred parcels of real estate in Oklahoma City, costing $240 million.[58]

In 2005, Chesapeake acquired Columbia Natural Resources, the fourth-largest natural gas producer, with a reach into the Appalachian Basin from Kentucky all the way to New York. The purchase included 6,500 miles of gathering lines serving producers in the eastern United States.[59] The 3.1 million acres of leased land provided Chesapeake with an estimated 9,400 new drilling locations, making it one of the largest frackers in the country.[60]

West Virginia governor Joe Manchin (elected to the U.S. Senate in 2010) crowed about Chesapeake's entry into the state. McClendon joined Manchin at the state capitol for a welcome ceremony, presenting the governor with a check for $100,000 to provide scholarships at the University of Charleston.[61]

The elation was short-lived. Chesapeake Appalachia, a renamed subsidiary of Chesapeake Energy, was sued in multiple states and found guilty of skimming royalty payments from landowners. Ten thousand plaintiffs benefited from the class-action lawsuit against Chesapeake and the other companies involved in cheating landowners.[62] Before the appeal reached the U.S. Supreme Court, the defendants settled out of court for $380 million.[63] Siding with industry, Manchin, who received $10,900 from Chesapeake for his first Senate run, failed in his attempt to push the legislature to weaken West Virginia's gas royalty law.[64] Chesapeake punished West Virginia by relocating or eliminating 215 of its 255 jobs in the state and canceling the $40 million regional headquarters office complex planned for Charleston.[65]

West Virginia also suffered from Chesapeake's sloppy practice of dumping crushed stone and materials into streams while building roads to drilling sites. In December 2012 the company paid a $600,000 penalty to the federal government for violating the Clean Water Act. A year later the Environmental Protection Agency and the Department of Justice settled with the company for twenty-seven Clean Water Act violations at wetlands and streams. Chesapeake paid $6.5 million for restoration and a $3.2 million penalty.[66]

Trading Schemes

Although McClendon's partner, Tom Ward, left Chesapeake in 2006 to form Sandridge Energy, the two men continued to be involved in business ventures that included ownership in feedlots, the Oklahoma City Thunder basketball team, and speculative ventures on Wall Street.[67] But they had failed to notify the board that they were using the trading desks of Goldman Sachs and other firms to bet on gas futures, which are contractual agreements to buy gas at an agreed-upon price and date in the future. At the same time that the partners were personally betting on future petroleum prices, Chesapeake was using futures contracts to hedge the company's risks from volatility in the price of gas.[68]

The 2012 Reuters investigation found that the men continued their partnership in a hedge fund that they had formed in 2004. Started with $40 million of their own cash and housed at Chesapeake's Oklahoma headquarters, Heritage Management Company traded in petroleum and other commodities. In 2011, when Reuters asked McClendon if he traded for himself in energy markets, he lied, saying: "No, no, no. I'm part of Chesapeake's hedging committee."[69]

Throughout the four years of its operation, Heritage enjoyed returns of between 15 and 25 percent a year. Because Heritage shared an accountant with Chesapeake, the arrangement raised many questions about the intermingling of personal and company business. McClendon and Ward recruited investors, providing additional earnings for themselves with management fees and a percentage of their investors' profits.[70]

In the months before the financial crisis, when oil and gas prices peaked, questions remained about the fund's speculative activities. Carl Holland, a trading compliance official at the former U.S. oil company Texaco,* told Reuters, "An executive's first responsibility is to shareholders." He continued: "Personal trading in the commodity around which the CEO's business is based would be a clear no. We would never have tolerated that, ever."[71]

Using records from the U.S. Commodities Futures Trading Commission obtained by Senator Bernie Sanders, Reuters calculated that in 2008 McClendon and Ward each bought $2.3 billion in natural gas derivatives; in addition McClendon purchased $240 million in oil contracts. Reuters wrote that of the "300 banks, hedge funds, energy companies and other traders . . . only four held larger bullish bets [than McClendon and Ward] in natural gas." In the last six months of that year the partners lost big as oil plunged by 75 percent and gas by 60 percent.[72]

McClendon's financial woes multiplied when the value of his investments declined precipitously and his brokers required a deposit of cash or the sale of assets to cover losses. McClendon was forced to sell more than 90 percent of his shares in Chesapeake, bearing a $2 billion loss on paper, and Chesapeake's share price dropped by 88 percent. Although Chesapeake's board restricted the amount of money that its executives could borrow to trade its shares, the board helped McClendon through the crisis with a $112 million compensation package at the end of 2008.[73]

Cost-Cutting Puts Workers' Lives at Risk

The petroleum industry is one of the most dangerous places to work.[74] Those risks are compounded by the Wild West business culture of the fracking

---

* Texaco merged into Chevron Corporation in 2001, and some of its gas station franchises were sold to Shell Oil Company.

industry, where operators can easily boost profits by cutting costs. A *Houston Chronicle* exposé on worker safety in the Texas oil and gas industry found that sixty-five workers were killed and eighteen thousand were seriously injured in 2013 alone. It found that Chesapeake Energy had sixty-six worker injury claims between 2008 and 2013 that cost the company only about $1.6 million—some $24,000 per claim.[75]

These problems are not isolated to Texas. A 2013 *EnergyWire* investigation found that there were 6,500 "serious" violations of workplace safety regulations in the oil and gas industry between 2003 and 2011.[76] Not only are fines rare or insignificant compared to profits, but companies simply view them as the cost of doing business. This is especially true in the petroleum industry, where shortcuts save time and money.

Companies also use legal proceedings and out-of-court settlements, where they refuse to accept blame as a condition for providing compensation, as a strategy for addressing worker injuries. The *Houston Chronicle* uncovered an accident at a Chesapeake Energy well and its now defunct subcontractor, Goober Drilling. A worker was severely injured when Chesapeake hired Goober to yank out a drilling pipe that had become lodged in a borehole rather than disassembling the pipe, considered the best practice. The heavy hoist cable unraveled under the tension and broke loose, striking a worker and leaving him in a coma with multiple skull fractures, a broken jaw, a severed ear, and permanent hearing loss. His lawsuit was settled out of court for an undisclosed amount. Chesapeake blamed Goober Drilling, which was sold to a larger company and now operates under a different name. The injured worker's compensation benefits ran out in 2010, and he was forced to return to the oil industry, working offshore.[77]

One former Chesapeake subsidiary, Nomac, was marked by accidents and fatalities.[78] Between 2010 and 2013 the Occupational Safety and Health Administration inspected Nomac sites thirty-five times, giving citations at sixteen of the drilling sites and proposing penalties of $65,300 for safety violations.[79] In June 2014 Chesapeake spun Nomac off as a stand-alone company called Seventy Seven Energy.[80]

Meanwhile, Chesapeake Energy continues to suffer from the mess that McClendon left behind. In 2015 its stock was performing poorly as petroleum prices continued to slide.[81] Chesapeake's new CEO, Doug Lawler, slashed spending and sold more than $5 billion worth of assets in 2014. The previous year, twelve hundred employees were laid off or left Chesapeake, leaving it with a workforce of eleven thousand.[82]

Up to His Old Tricks

Six months after being ousted from Chesapeake, McClendon launched American Energy Partners with John Raymond, CEO of the private equity firm Energy and Minerals Group and the son of former Exxon CEO Lee Raymond. McClendon soon purchased 600,000 acres of mineral rights in Ohio, Oklahoma, Texas, and West Virginia, using two-thirds equity and one-third debt. The compensation package that McClendon has with the company incentivizes him to constantly make deals, increasing his chances of getting a big payoff when the investors finally see a return on their investment.[83]

Before long, Chesapeake had McClendon in court, suing him for stealing proprietary information from maps of the Ohio Utica shale formation. McClendon had already snatched up $1.5 billion of properties in this area. His problems multiplied when crashing petroleum prices rendered the partnership's assets much less valuable.

According to Chris Helman of *Forbes*, in 2015, Raymond removed McClendon as CEO of the partnership's Appalachian affiliate, filling the position with a former top manager from Chesapeake. Without involving McClendon in negotiations, Raymond settled with Chesapeake over the information that McClendon had stolen, paying Chesapeake up to $25 million and giving the company six thousand acres of mineral leases in Ohio.[84]

With oil prices low and his ability to profit curtailed at American Energy, the incorrigible McClendon formed Avondale Acquisition Corp., a company without property or operations that uses stock to acquire assets. He also is attempting to access billions from two private investment funds that he has initiated. But controversy continues to swirl around him at American Energy concerning his high management fees and a flurry of lawsuits over his biggest deal for the company, an acquisition of sixty thousand acres in Texas. But in the deregulated environment of the petroleum industry, where profits trump all else, McClendon continues to be allowed to operate as if there is no tomorrow. Helman reports that the former Chesapeake CEO is now seeking 16 million acres in Australia's MacArthur Basin, where shale gas is just waiting to be liquefied and sent to Asia.[85]

10

WHEN WILL THE BAKKEN BOOM
GO BUST FOR GOOD?

It's like my worst nightmare come true. We've been invaded.
—Don Kalil, former Williams County
Commissioner and farmer[1]

North Dakota, a place of breathtaking vistas and rich cultural and historical resources, is at the epicenter of a twenty-first-century melodrama. Sparked by the underground sea of oil and gas that stretches two hundred thousand square miles, it has driven a new boom-and-bust cycle in oil production.

The Bakken formation, locked in the subsurface of the northern Great Plains in the Williston Basin, lies deep within a geological deposit marked by 365 million years of history. Over eons, pressure and heat broke down the remnants of carbon-based organisms that had thrived from the sun's energy. This energy is still held in the chemical bonds of the molecules—the hydrocarbons—that make up what we call oil and gas.

About thirty layers of gravel, sandstone, limestone, and other rock formations—like a multitiered cake—lie as far as thirteen thousand feet below parts of the Dakotas, Montana, Saskatchewan, and Manitoba.[2] Fracking brings to the surface a mixture of liquids and gases, including crude oil, natural gas, and natural gas liquids, together with ancient brines full of salts, metals, and radioactive material.[3]

Long one of the country's agricultural powerhouses, North Dakota has been an important part of the American "breadbasket" zone that has exported wheat and other products around the world for more than a century. But in a state that takes pride in its heritage, it remains increasingly difficult to make a living on all but the largest North Dakotan farms. The agricultural economy, like oil and gas, is marked by booms and busts. The same federal policies that have allowed massive mergers in the oil and gas industry also have facilitated monopolized agribusiness and food-related corporations that have enormous influence on federal food and farm policy. These powerful economic interests—grain traders, meat corporations, and food processors—desire low-priced commodities for higher margins on their products.

In 1996 a coalition of corporate interests fought successfully to pass legislation that would drive down the price of grain and shift food production overseas. Among the so-called free-market-oriented policy changes that were finalized in the 1996 Farm Bill—legislation passed every five years to govern farm policy—was the elimination of the U.S. Department of Agriculture's role in supply management of commodities and the abolition of the federal grain reserve. Overproduction, low prices, and destabilization of grain markets were the predictable result.[4] Consequently, between 1997 and 2012, North Dakota lost about half (more than nine thousand) of the farms producing wheat, the state's top agricultural crop.[5]

More recently, crop prices have risen and many farmers have shifted to corn production for ethanol. Although the average net cash farm income in North Dakota has doubled, this is a deceptive measure of the economic viability of the state's farms. A closer look at the USDA's most recent data—the most accurate economic information available—shows that even with high prices, all but the very largest North Dakota farmers are struggling. Fully a quarter of North Dakota farms experienced net farm losses, meaning that their farm expenses were greater than the money they received from their crops and federal subsidies.[6]

No wonder that many hardworking North Dakota farmers—hoping to save their farms—listened to the assurances that fracking was perfectly safe when the landmen came knocking. Low and undulating grain prices made the prospect of steady earnings from petroleum attractive to many farmers and landowners. When Hess, Continental Resources, Whiting, EOG, and dozens of other companies sent the salesmen out to cut deals in sleepy rural areas, landowners leased tens of thousands of acres to the fortune-hunting corporations, without a full understanding of the technologies used or the impacts fracking would bring.

Fracking is reshaping the landscape, irrevocably polluting the environment and damaging historical sites. An enormous industrial undertaking has extracted almost a million barrels of oil from the ancient geological deposit. Billions of gallons of water have been sucked from rivers, lakes, and aquifers for fracking in North Dakota. Under state law, water sources belong to the state, and any individual or corporation with an interest in a piece of land—ownership, a mineral lease, or surface occupancy—can apply for a permit to use water resources. This has sparked acrimonious battles about "mining" the state's precious underground water resources and taking water from Lake Sakakawea.[7]

Until recently, wastes from fracking wells were placed on-site in reserve pits. But this changed when forty-seven reserve pits overflowed after the spring thaw of 2011, leaving a toxic trail of waste. When the state Department of Mineral Resources essentially eliminated these pits, hazardous waste began appearing at landfills. But following a spate of fires, chemical burns, and other problems at landfills, operators have rejected loads of waste, especially those exceeding legal radiation levels. Kurt Rhea, the owner of Next Generation Solutions, a company that collects radioactive drilling waste at thirty sites in the Bakken—to be disposed of out of state—estimated in 2013 that only 20 percent of the waste is being discarded legally.[8]

Beyond the harm to the environment, quality-of-life and safety issues plague the communities near the oil fields. As waves of hopeful workers seeking jobs descended on sparsely populated western counties, the population has surged, with close-knit communities such as Williston more than doubling in size since 2000. North Dakota became the fastest-growing state, with the population expanding almost as much recently as in the previous sixty years. By 2014 the state's overall population had surged over 14 percent to almost 740,000 from just over 642,000 in 2000, although many temporary workers are not included in these figures.[9]

Before fracking, people left their doors unlocked and women walked the streets without fear. Now a range of problems—crime, civic disturbances, and traffic accidents—mar life for old and new residents alike. In this Wild West atmosphere, lonely roustabouts working long hours in a notoriously dangerous industry seek entertainment and respite. Alcohol and drugs lead some in the overwhelmingly male workforce to engage in risky and irresponsible behaviors, from substance abuse and drunken brawls to soliciting prostitutes and rape. A few of the thousands of itinerant workers—a ratio estimated to be ten men to one woman in some areas—have made the oil patch dangerous for women.[10]

Women are twice as likely to get raped in Williston as in the rest of North Dakota. There are more than 105 rapes per 100,000 residents in

Williston, double the statewide rate and nearly triple the national figures. The number of rapes in Williston is stark in comparison to America's largest cities. A woman is nearly four times more likely to be raped in the small city of Williston than in Los Angeles, nearly three times more likely than in New York, and twice as likely as in Baltimore.[11]

In fracked counties, traffic deaths have increased 350 percent, from fourteen in 2003 to sixty-three in 2013, with roads twice as deadly per mile driven as the rest of North Dakota. Each fracked well requires more than two thousand truckloads of machinery, water, sand, and other materials, greatly increasing traffic on narrow roads at all times of day.[12] Trips by oversized and overweight trucks more than doubled between 2010 and 2013, damaging narrow streets and country roads that now require millions of dollars to repair.[13]

In the first years of the fracking frenzy, rustic "man camps" cropped up for roughnecks and other workers. Hundreds of men camped out or parked their RVs in open areas, seeking safety and sociability in the lonely boomtown. In the wake of the 2008 economic meltdown and the recession that followed, unemployed financial refugees poured into North Dakota. The aspiring roughnecks had little money to afford housing, and many resorted to living in their cars or motor homes.[14]

As the boom expanded, a new business emerged: acres of professionally run dormitory-style living for men only. Sited haphazardly, these industrial-sized man camps have rows of low-slung modular buildings that offer differing levels of comfort and services, depending on the price. Companies sometimes include this temporary housing as a perk in employment contracts to attract skilled workers. Even "luxury" facilities popped up, advertising chef-prepared meals, saunas, and swimming pools.[15]

Target Logistics, the largest man-camp operator in the nation, bragged that it would house 1 percent of the state's population. Tioga Lodge, a facility that it operates in Williston, has nearly 1,250 beds in a complex with a heated central corridor, twenty-four-hour dining options, a fast-food restaurant, a convenience store, and a barbershop.[16] Algeco Scotsman—a multinational with subsidiaries specializing in modular space, portable storage facilities, and temporary housing for corporations to house transient workforces—purchased the man-camp operator for $625 million in 2013.[17] But by 2015, as oil and gas prices retreated, oil companies are cutting back on expenses such as paid housing, and the man-camp firms are losing money. Now some workers are scrounging to find space in RV parks.[18]

A jumble of development is sprawled along damaged and traffic-laden roads, featuring seedy trailer parks, convenience stores, strip clubs, and dive bars. Long-term residents are hit hard by rising inflation as the price of food, housing, goods, and services soars. Many retirees have insufficient resources to live near the boom, while younger families face crowded schools and rents that can be $3,400 for three bedrooms. Even workers making high wages find their income counterbalanced by rising living expenses, and some people never find work because they lack the necessary skills.[19]

Still, the oil boom has brought wealth to some. Mountrail County is now one of the one hundred richest counties in the nation. Income per person doubled between 2005 and 2010 and then rose another 23 percent by 2013, as the boom continued.[20] Despite the newfound wealth, complaints about the oil industry cheating on royalty payments abound, and not all farmers or landowners have benefited equally. Other residents live with the serious impacts of fracking but do not enjoy income from it.

The latest boom is not the first in oil-rich North Dakota. Natural gas was first discovered in 1892 and commercialized in the early part of the twentieth century.[21] In 1912 a young geology graduate student found fossil coral along the bank of the Cannonball River, indicating that oil had formed from the ancient sea. A monument near Tioga marks the beginning of the gold rush on April 4, 1951, at Clarence Iverson's farm, where oil surged from thousands of feet below his farm. Amerada Petroleum had prospected for oil using dynamite, perforating the well casing and enabling oil to flow for the next twenty-eight years.[22] Iverson's son, Cliff Iverson, reminisced that his father had been upset when Amerada used explosives, saying, "He worried a lot about his water wells."[23]

Within a few months 30 million acres of land was leased and the area was transformed by the hasty arrival of oilfield service companies. Standard Oil of Indiana (part of BP today) began construction of a thirty-thousand-barrel-per-day oil refinery in the region, while its large pipeline arm, Service Pipeline Company, began construction of a pipeline.[24]

Five miles from Iverson's property, Amerada drilled at Henry O. Bakken's farm. After months of drilling, oil flowed from a natural fracture in the rock formation that eventually came to bear his name.[25] Today it takes about a month to drill and frack a well in North Dakota, and Amerada's successor, Hess Corporation, has become one of the largest frackers in the state. Hess acquired Amerada in 1969, but at a price that activist shareholders said undervalued the company. Years of rancorous litigation followed, with a federal court ruling that Leon Hess had not fairly valued assets in the merger negotiations. But the judge refused to go as far as to void the deal.[26]

A master at branding, Leon Hess sold generations of American children Hess-model gas trucks that were cherished. Politically astute, he had a close relationship with interior secretary Stewart Udall, who served under Presidents Kennedy and Johnson. Udall granted Hess an important exemption from federal law that allowed the company to build the world's largest oil refinery, located in the U.S. Virgin Islands. Hess Corporation enjoyed special tax benefits and received federal subsidies for its domestic operations while employing low-cost foreign-flag vessels for shipping oil to the East Coast.[27] The refinery's closure in 2012 caused an economic shock, and the plant left a legacy of industrial contamination.[28]

In 1995 Leon Hess's son took over management of the company and pursued international foreign oil and gas exploration across the globe. In 2001 he acquired Triton Energy Limited for $3.2 billion—a multinational company that had been charged by the U.S. Securities and Exchange Commission with violating the Foreign Corrupt Practices Act for bribing foreign officials and falsifying records.[29] *Forbes* called the Triton purchase "largely a bust."[30] An investigative report by the magazine also uncovered the company's relationship with a racketeering operation in Russia. The mafia-like group made $40 million annually in illegal profits stealing oil from pipelines owned by a state-controlled crude producer in Russia. Subcontractors for the Hess subsidiary, Samara-Nafta, were the conduit for the operation, and a top executive at the subsidiary was one of the masterminds. After the *Forbes* story was published, Hess fired the executive with mob ties and later sold Samara-Nafta to Lukoil, Russia's second-largest oil company, in 2013.[31]

The drama and poor performance instigated more shareholder activism, triggering a proxy fight organized by billionaire Paul Singer of Elliot Management, focused on a long list of management missteps made by John Hess. A loss of $800 million in the company's fracking adventure in the Eagle Ford play undoubtedly was one of these.[32] Just hours before the vote, Elliot cut a deal with the Hess faction, giving them three board seats in exchange for the hedge fund's support of the company's slate of five directors.[33]

Hess was the second-largest oil and gas producer in the Bakken, holding leases on 645,000 acres in 2013.[34] In 2014 Hess opened its expanded natural gas processing plant in Tioga, hoping to process 250 million cubic feet of gas per day as part of its plan to become more profitable.[35]

Many other companies have a similar strategy to collect natural gas (and gas liquids) in the Bakken; they include Whiting Petroleum Corporation, Kodiak Oil and Gas Corporation, and EOG. But by far the largest is Oklahoma City–based Continental Resources, the largest fracker in the state. The company owns more than 1.17 million acres of mineral leases in the Bakken, most of it in North Dakota.[36]

Continental's founder and CEO, Harold Hamm, is a billionaire oilman with a big personality and a rags-to-riches story. He was the thirteenth child of cotton sharecroppers in Oklahoma, and successful wildcatters were his role model growing up. He saved enough money to drill for himself, starting on acreage Royal Dutch Shell had abandoned, and later lucked out, finding a million barrels of oil in a meteor crater not far from his hometown. He kept up with new drilling technologies, pursuing horizontal drilling in the Rockies.[37]

A pilot with his own plane, Hamm sought leases in North Dakota, where they were cheap in the 1990s. News travels fast in an industry where gossip thrives, because of the many subcontractors and roughnecks working at multiple well sites for different companies. When he heard rumors about the success of Houston-based Burlington Resources, Hamm traveled incognito to a hearing before the North Dakota Industrial Commission, the agency that oversees the oil industry, about Burlington's horizontal drilling operations. He liked what he heard and quickly began leasing land.[38]

But as is so often the case in the expansion-and-contraction cycle of the petroleum industry, oil prices collapsed in 1998, leading to losses of $18 million for Hamm. Unlike McClendon, Hamm had not borrowed recklessly, allowing Continental to weather the price drop. When prices rose two years later, he began leasing land at $50 and $300 per acre—a fraction of today's cost.[39]

Although share prices were modest during the initial public offering in 2007, peaking at $15, Continental soon adopted multistage fracking at its horizontal wells, dramatically increasing production.[40] By continuing to improve fracking techniques, the company enjoyed a hefty profit from high oil prices that more than doubled in 2009 and held steady until the drop in 2014.[41]

Hamm began using his fortune and prominence to promote Continental's agenda. In 2012 he was named chairman of presidential candidate Mitt Romney's Energy Policy Advisory Group, followed by *Time* magazine naming him one of the hundred most influential people in the world that year. Invited to appear before the U.S. House Energy and Commerce Committee, he testified against regulating fracking.[42] "There has not been one instance of contamination to ground water attributed to hydraulic fracturing in the 60-year history of this common-place procedure," he told the committee. Unabashedly he argued for maintaining tax breaks, saying that "tax policies that let us keep our own money to drill" are needed for energy independence.[43]

According to Citizens for Tax Justice, Hamm's assertion that Continental paid an effective tax rate of 38 percent was false, as the company paid a tax rate averaging only 2.2 percent over five years.[44] Using figures from the SEC, the watchdog group documented that oil companies and the American Petroleum Institute obfuscate the truth by counting taxes that are deferred, not paid. This tax loophole allows petroleum companies to often get away with never paying the full amount that was originally owed. Companies also can deduct expenses such as designing and building the oil rigs used for drilling.[45]

Continental Resources produced more than 130,000 barrels per day from its Bakken wells in 2014.[46] Hamm said in an interview in 2014 that the company hoped to triple production to three hundred thousand barrels per day.[47] This is possible because of new designs that allow multiple wells per pad, a technology pioneered by Continental and now used by 90 percent of frackers in the Bakken.[48] Continental's giant rig "walks" on hydraulic legs to drill the different sections of each well in succession, a technology called "batch" drilling. The rig is called the ECO-Pad, where "eco" stands for "efficient," "economical," and "ecological."[49]

Continental sometimes uses this well pad to drill some wells into the Bakken while drilling others into the deeper Three Forks formation. The company first drills the top portions of all the wells, followed by drilling the intermediate sections, and ending with the long horizontal sections, which are fracked in thirty stages. Continental's use of a single rig on a giant pad cuts 10 percent of the cost of production.[50]

North Dakota facilitated use of the large well pads strategy by creating an industry-friendly grid system for spacing wells. State officials maintain that well pads on standardized north-south 1,280-acre spacing units, one by two miles in size, minimize surface impacts and truck trips. Many nearby residents who must live with the excessive traffic, noise, and land impacts disagree. And Continental has even larger pads with sixteen wells on one site.[51]

Bust

Between 2007 and 2014 Bakken oil production grew by 700 percent. In July 2015 the U.S. Energy Information Administration reported that crude oil production in the Bakken during June 2015 was up 5 percent over the previous year, to 1.22 million barrels per day. Production is beginning to slide in the Bakken, however, declining every month since the April 2015 high point of 1.25 million barrels per day. Each rig is producing more than 650 barrels of crude per day—more than twice as much as in 2012—primarily because they are drilling further horizontally than ever. This glut of oil is contributing to the slump in oil prices.[52]

Many people in North Dakota are concerned about when and how the Bakken boom will bust. As this book goes to press, oil prices have sunk below half of what they were during the heady days before they dropped precipitously in 2014.[53] Past experience shows that when oil prices drop, a boom can quickly go bust. North Dakota has suffered several painful economic crashes in the past—in energy and agriculture—that have followed periods of high profits and big hopes for energy production and farming.

Clay Jenkinson, a North Dakota columnist and university lecturer and the director of the Dakota Institute, worries about what will happen when the current boom ends. Although Jenkinson has been a big supporter of oil exploration, he knows that when prices collapse or a big oil discovery is made somewhere else, it will bring a rapid end to North Dakota's boom. He says: "Other places go through minor booms and minor busts along with the business cycles of the industry, but this is different. . . . The minute it's over, people are going to get the hell out."[54]

Gene Veeder, who directs job development for McKenzie County, says that towns make decisions about development and infrastructure based on a boom of up to ten years and hope that after the drilling rush subsides, a quarter of the workforce will remain to operate the wells. But Jenkinson is not optimistic about this. He estimates that less than 1 percent of the influx of new workers will stay in North Dakota, virtually turning Williston into a ghost town.[55]

Harold Hamm has no worries about the future. He says, "We're just getting started." He predicts that technology could boost production in the Bakken to 45 billion barrels before the resource is completely tapped.[56]

David Hughes, president of Global Sustainability Research—who spent thirty-two years with the Geological Survey of Canada as a geoscientist and research manager—is skeptical about the long-term productivity of the Bakken. Hughes compiled sixty-six months of production data, ending in May 2012. He found that the production of wells on average dropped 69 percent in the first year of drilling and, at the end of five years, declined by 94 percent.[57]

Hamm's most famous well, the Robert Heuer 1-17R, is an example of this. When it started producing in May 2004, it gushed 2,358 barrels per day. But production declined quickly. Hughes compares this situation to the Red Queen telling Alice, in *Through the Looking-Glass*, "It takes all the running you can do, to keep in the same place."[58]

Oil companies in the Bakken are on an accelerating treadmill to maintain production, not just increase it. Companies tapped the best spots early on, and wells drilled today are not as productive as those drilled in the first years of the bonanza. Predicting that production will peak in 2017, Hughes says, "The Red Queen syndrome just gets worse and worse and worse."[59] He says production is stagnant or declining almost everywhere around the world.

Art Berman, a petroleum geologist who spent twenty years with Amoco and now runs Labyrinth Consulting Services in Sugar Land, Texas, mirrors these concerns, saying that it's "more of a retirement party than a revolution." He goes on to say, "It's the last gasp."[60]

Fighting Back

While the industry experts debate the boom and bust, the movement against the ongoing drilling and fracking in the state continues. Dakota Resource Council (DRC) is helping give a political voice to its members—farmers, ranchers, and other concerned citizens—on the devastating impact of the oil and gas industry on people's lives and on the environment. Don Morrison, the organization's executive director, says that the history of North Dakota has been one of booms and busts and that oil prices will rise again.[61]

DRC member Cedar Gillette speaks eloquently about the role of Chippewa women as water keepers who look ahead for the needs of future

generations. Gillette's concerns about water impacts and quality-of-life issues on the reservation led her to become one of the leaders of No Fracking
Way, the grassroots Chippewa group that pushed for the first resolution in
the nation to ban fracking on tribal lands.[62] This important and inspira-
tional resolution reflects the value that the Chippewa traditionally place on
protecting natural resources. The Tribal Council of the Turtle Mountain
Band of Chippewa voted unanimously in favor of the preemptive ban at a
meeting in November 2011.[63]

Since then, DRC members throughout the state have continued working to protect their communities. Rosella Person, a farmer and rancher,
sums it all up when she describes her experiences in stopping a polluting oil
waste facility from being built at the top of their valley. She says that they
have been able "to change a lot of things because of the fight they put up."
Person declares, "Good does come from fighting back."[64]

Theodora Bird Bear, a longtime DRC member from western North Dakota, says that her state has lots of potential for people to have a voice, but it
takes courage. She wants people to fight back, "no matter the odds."[65]

11

POISONOUS LEGACY IN WYOMING

The EPA has been on a witch hunt to shut down hydraulic fracturing, but yet again the evidence has determined it is safe.
—David Vitter, Louisiana senator and ranking Republican on the Senate Environment and Public Works committee in 2013 [1]

John Fenton has an easy smile that belies the fact that he has lived for over a decade with water and air poisoned by fracking—and, making matters worse, was betrayed by the Environmental Protection Agency. The Fentons and their neighbors in Pavillion, Wyoming, a town of two hundred people, have suffered seizures, loss of taste and smell, ringing ears, and nerve damage that they suspect were caused by Encana Corporation's operations.

When the U.S. EPA confirmed in December 2011 that their water was polluted, the political outcry from the industry, Wyoming's public officials, and Oklahoma senator Jim Inhofe created a mighty furor just as President Obama's reelection battle was heating up. It is an ugly story that is not over yet, because Fenton and other community leaders in fracking sacrifice zones are speaking out, and a national movement has coalesced to ban fracking. [2]

Fenton still farms in Pavillion, but he worries about the impact of fracking on the hundreds of acres of hay that he sells to beef cattle operations and on the calves he raises. Running his ranch means dawn-to-dusk workdays of often backbreaking labor at a time when market vagaries and an increasingly unstable climate make agriculture a tough business.

But these days, rather than loading bales of hay, Fenton is just as likely to be at a meeting of Pavillion Area Concerned Citizens, a group he helped form, or speaking at an international conference on fracking. A tall man who wears a wide-brimmed ten-gallon cowboy hat, Fenton stands out in a crowd, and he is a born orator who holds his audiences spellbound. In the winter of 2014 Fenton was invited to Australia by the Lock the Gate Alliance, a coalition working to stop extreme energy, and in December 2015 he spoke in Paris on panels organized around the United Nations climate change conference, COP21.

Growing up in the small town of Hudson, Wyoming, Fenton never imagined in his wildest dreams that he would become an internationally known environmental leader. His dad was a horse trainer, and he and his brothers grew up working as unpaid stock hands, breaking horses, mending fences, and shoveling manure. As he came of age in Wyoming, the big sky, magnificent views, and wide-open space spoke to him. So even though Wyoming is a hard place to make a living, Fenton stayed after high school, working as a mechanic and welding in the gas fields.

The ranch that he, his wife, Catherine, and their youngest son live on in western Wyoming is situated in Fremont, a county roughly the size of Vermont. Ironically, it is named after the famous explorer John Charles Frémont, who visited as the first presidential candidate of the newly organized Republican Party. Fenton is outraged that the Republican-dominated Wyoming state legislature has blocked new science standards for public schools because they might lead students to believe in climate change.

Natural gas was discovered in Wyoming in 1936 when California Oil Company—later renamed Chevron—found more of it than oil while drilling near Pinedale, located in western Wyoming. At the time, no market for the gas existed in the area, however, and pipelines for transporting gas were nonexistent. The wells were plugged until El Paso Gas Company bought the leases and drilled wells in the 1940s and 1950s, but it found the gas was too tightly held in sandstone to flow.[3]

Although magnificent western Wyoming was a target for drilling from the 1950s onward, it wasn't until the 1970s that exploration accelerated. President Richard Nixon blessed the use of "nuclear stimulation technology" for gas production. In 1967 the Atomic Energy Commission (AEC) hatched a scheme with the U.S. Department of the Interior and the El Paso Natural Gas Company to explode five nuclear devices underground in western Wyoming to fracture sandstone and release gas.[4] Known as Project Wagon Wheel, the nuclear fracking experiment was to be conducted deep below the surface of Sublette County.[5] The scenario envisioned by El Paso was to wait from four to six months so the "short-lived isotopes" could decay before flaring the well for a year to release any remaining radiation.[6]

Nuclear fracking had already been tried in 1967 by El Paso and the government in northwestern New Mexico, as part of Project Gasbuggy. The Associated Press reported that the scientists behind Gasbuggy "estimate the nation's natural gas reserves will be doubled if nuclear blasts are found to be a feasible way to free gas from underground rock formations."[7] The twenty-nine-kiloton blast blew the AEC scientists and El Paso energy observers out of their chairs two and a half miles away. El Paso gas customers were unwilling to buy the radioactive gas from the New Mexico test, so the gas was all flared off.[8]

Although the AEC admitted that the New Mexico blast released a significant volume of contaminated gas, in 1969 the AEC detonated a second nuclear device near Rifle, Colorado, to stimulate gas production.[9] Claude Hayward was offered $100 a month for the rest of his life in exchange for the use of his 292-acre potato patch. Hayward declined the offer until "the AEC came back around with a whiskey bottle and got him good and juiced up and said they would pay him $200 a month for the rest of his life."[10] But he never received a dime, because the small print in his contract specified that he "got paid only if the well made money for the energy companies."[11] A third test with three bombs in Colorado's Piceance Creek Basin also produced gas that was too radioactive to sell.[12]

In 1972 citizens organized a straw poll during the presidential election to demonstrate local opposition to the test blast; 71 percent of the people polled opposed the test.[13] In Wyoming citizens formed the Wagon Wheel Information Committee to stop nuclear fracking experiments.[14] One of the committee's leaders spoke on the *Today* show, and they held public meetings, generated letters to the editor, collected petitions, and urged local, state, and federal officials to listen to their constituents and oppose Project Wagon Wheel.[15] Their organizing efforts won the day and Project Wagon Wheel was relegated to history.[16]

While the U.S. Bureau of Land Management encouraged gas drilling in western Wyoming, no headway was made in drilling tight sandstone until the 1990s. Casper-based McMurry Oil bought leases on 25,000 acres of public land in the Pinedale Anticline and Jonah Fields, located in Sublette County.[17]

In 1993 Halliburton fracked McMurry Oil's first well, seventy-six miles southwest of Pavillion as the crow flies. McMurry Oil's investment was enhanced by state tax dollars that helped finance a nine-hundred-mile pipeline from Wyoming's gas fields to Bakersfield, California.[18]

In 1993 McMurry Oil began experimenting with nitrogen-foam-based fracking fluid that was more effective in cracking rock. Soon Snyder Oil and Amoco Corporation began using seismic survey equipment to frack, allowing the companies to identify natural faults where gas was located.[19] In June 2000 Alberta Energy Company bought McMurry Oil, one of the companies that would become Encana, the largest natural gas corporation in Canada.[20]

Wyoming's water, land, forests, and air were to suffer greatly from fracking. Injecting millions of gallons of toxic fracking fluid deep underground threatens aquifers, while the wastewater that spews from the well pollutes rivers and streams. Fracking seriously pollutes the air with benzene and other lethal substances, making people and wildlife ill and harming vegetation. Building wells sites, roads, condenser stations, waste pits, and pipelines destroys wildlife habitat and adversely affects land and forests.

Tests revealed that the large aquifer underlying the gas fields was contaminated with the dangerous chemicals benzene, toluene, and xylene, which are found in petroleum products. The BTEX chemicals are highly flammable and have a strong odor. More than a third of the drinking water wells tested were contaminated with cancer-causing chemicals, and the Bureau of Land Management (BLM), which has jurisdiction over the vast majority of the fracking wells on public lands, has done no definitive assessment on groundwater impacts.[21] Well testing of groundwater has shown high levels of fluoride—a chemical used by Halliburton, which began fracking in the area in 1993.[22]

The once remote area, covering one of the longest big-game migration routes in the nation, is home to birds of prey, wild horses, sage grouse, pygmy rabbits, pronghorn antelope, and mule deer. But the area has been compromised by drilling operations. The mule deer herd—one of the most affected species—winters in the northern portion of the Pinedale Anticline gas field. Although the BLM had restricted drilling during winter in 2008, Obama bowed to industry pressure, allowing year-round drilling.[23] A 2010 BLM report shows that the population of deer has declined by 60 percent because of well pad and road development.[24]

Pinedale's ground-level smog rivals that of Los Angeles.[25] Air quality in the region began declining in 2000, despite the fact that the nearest urban area, Salt Lake City, is 180 miles away. Smog is created by chemical reactions between sunlight and emissions from leaky wells and fracking equipment, which include nitrogen oxides, methane, and other volatile organic compounds. Snow, which reflects sunlight, intensifies the chemical reactions, and low-wind conditions in the area exacerbate smog creation.[26] In 2008 the Wyoming Department of Environmental Quality began issuing "ozone alerts" to notify the public about the unhealthy and potentially toxic air pollution levels.[27]

The drilling frenzy has changed the character of an area once graced with wilderness and a few small towns and ranches. Between 2000 and 2007 the population grew 34 percent, causing many of the same problems seen in North Dakota's oil boom. A 2008 survey of long-term residents found that their overall satisfaction with the community had decreased and their social relationships had declined. Local officials were left to grapple with the acute infrastructure problems, socioeconomic concerns, traffic, and pollution, Housing, schools, and services such as law enforcement and health care were strained.[28]

Because of falling gas prices, the boom was short lived. In the spring of 2013, residents of Pinedale, the county's largest town, saw their fears about the growing economic hardship confirmed in the Casper Star-Tribune's headline, "Gas drilling slowdown means quiet bust for Pinedale." Encana's fifteen hundred employees have dwindled to one hundred in Sublette County. Hotel rooms have been left empty and restaurants are without customers because the roughnecks have gone north to the Bakken. The general manager of the grocery store sums it up: "It's widespread through the community. Everyone feels the pinch."[29]

John and Catherine Fenton were not opposed to gas drilling when they moved to her family's farm in 1995, even though they did not own the mineral rights.[30] This was long before Wyoming allowed the gas industry to trample their rights, make them sick, and ruin their property values. They moved to Pavillion to farm, supplementing their income with a gas-field welding business. When their health problems became obvious, the Fentons shuttered the welding business. While they receive a small fee for use of their property for gas extraction, they have no legal recourse under Wyoming's split-estate law, which provides for the separate ownership of surface and mineral rights. John Fenton did attempt to negotiate the location of well pads on their property, but Wyoming does not give the surface owner leverage over the company. If an agreement cannot be reached, the driller can circumvent the surface owner by posting $2,000 with state authorities.[31] This means that when Fenton plants and mows alfalfa, he must dodge the well pads and pipelines that crisscross the property. The small amount they receive for use of their property does not pay for the damage or compensate for the well pads located only one hundred yards from their home.

Two wells on the Fentons' property are conventional and predate the mid-1980s, but the other twenty-two were fracked between the late 1990s and 2007, when Encana finished drilling and began the gas production phase. The Fentons were never informed about the composition of the fracking fluid. Up to fourteen times a day methane is flared, leaving smoke and toxins in the air, an increasing concern as the Fentons' youngest son—who was two at the onset of drilling—began having seizures and neurological problems.

Farms in the area were originally located near good water sources, and the water on the Fentons' farm had been excellent before the drilling. Likewise, Louis and Donna Meeks had clear, sweet well water on their forty-acre alfalfa farm until 2005, three months after Encana laid a gathering line to a fracked well five hundred feet from their home. Smelling like fuel, the once-pure water now glistened with the characteristic rainbow-colored swirls of floating hydrocarbons.[32]

Meeks contracted for a new water well to be drilled into the top layers of the thirty different formations containing fresh water in Pavillion. When the contractor reached 540 feet, a powerful rumbling shook the earth, building until a tower of gas erupted from the well and gushed for seventy-two hours. Encana was ordered by a judge to take action, giving Meeks enough leverage to make Encana agree to deliver water costing $3,000 each month. The Meekses soon discovered that they were not alone. Jeff and Rhonda Locker, neighbors down the road, had suffered from polluted water that resulted from drilling. Rhonda had such serious nerve damage that the pain felt like knives piercing her skin and jabbing her bones. Contamination was so severe that Encana paid for a water filtration system for their home.[33]

The Fentons, the Meekses, and several other affected families formed Pavillion Area Concerned Citizens, demanding that the state take action. They began working with Deb Thomas, a ranch owner from near Yellowstone National Park whose groundwater had been polluted by a 2006 Windsor Energy well blowout. Thomas works for the Powder River Basin Resource Council, a watchdog group that is an affiliate of the Western Organization of Resource Councils. (See Chapter 11.) The activists began compiling data about the effects of fracking on their community.

In April 2009 filmmaker Josh Fox, who was facing fracking near his family's property in Pennsylvania, visited Pavillion to interview community members. Fox's 2010 documentary *Gasland* featured heart-wrenching interviews with John Fenton, Louis Meeks, and Jeff Locker about the impact of fracking on their lives. As proof of the impacts of fracking mounted, the Academy Award–nominated film helped jump-start a movement to ban fracking around the world.

The EPA began investigating the water pollution in 2008, eventually conducting four rounds of sampling. They tested water from forty residences and dug two deep wells that reached below the layers contaminated by agricultural chemicals or old drilling operations. Shallow well tests revealed the presence of methane, oil, arsenic, copper, vanadium, and traces of a fracking chemical called 2-butoxyethanol phosphate. Tests from the deeper wells contained thirteen chemicals associated with fracking, including acetone, toluene, naphthalene, diesel fuel, and the carcinogens benzene and phenols. These chemicals, which do not occur in nature, offered proof that human activities caused the pollution.[34]

In March 2010 EPA administrator Lisa Jackson announced a major national study on the risks posed by fracking to water resources. Prompted by Congressman Maurice Hinchey, who had slipped a request into 2009 environmental appropriations legislation directing the EPA to conduct the study, the agency was to use "a credible approach that relies on the best available science."[35] The long-awaited study, released on June 4, 2015, turned out to be compromised, but even with its poor design and industry meddling, it showed that fracking adversely impacts water resources. (See Introduction.)

This 2015 report replaces the 2004 Bush-era one that had declared fracking safe. Weston Wilson, an environmental engineer with the EPA for thirty-seven years, sought whistle-blower protection for informing Congress that he questioned the 2004 findings. He charged that the findings were "scientifically unsound" and that the conclusions were "unsupportable." Five of the seven members of the peer review panel had been or were industry employees.[36] *ProPublica** reported in 2008 that Bush EPA officials negotiated with Halliburton to soften the 2004 report.[37]

---

* The local newspapers at the epicenter of the fracking boom and the national media that have bought into natural gas as a "bridge fuel" have largely ignored the risks associated with fracking. The independent, nonprofit, Pulitzer Prize–winning *ProPublica* has done the best investigative reporting into the environmental, human health and economic downsides of fracking. See www.propublica.org/series /fracking.

Around the same time that the EPA announced the new national study, the agency initiated more water sampling in Pavillion, in coordination with the Agency for Toxic Substances and Disease Registry, a division of the federal Centers for Disease Control and Prevention. The report concluded that fracking was likely responsible for the contamination in Pavillion. Noting an "explosive hazard" posed by light hydrocarbons—methane, ethane, propane, butane, pentanes, and hexanes—it cautioned residents against drinking their water and advised, "Residents should ventilate their bathroom during showering."[38]

In December 2011 the EPA wrote up its findings in a dramatic draft report that was unusual in its clarity about the impacts of fracking. The EPA report concluded, "When considered together with other lines of evidence, the data indicates likely impact to groundwater that can be explained by hydraulic fracturing."[39]

EPA's investigation elicited an intense industry campaign denying that fracking pollutes groundwater. Petroleum industry complaints poured into the Obama White House, and their trade associations barraged the media with attacks on the agency. Oklahoma senator Jim Inhofe launched a full-force attack on the investigation; as his spokesman noted, "the leading advocate for hydraulic fracturing" in the Senate has "concerns about the Obama administration's war on natural gas."[40] A typical response came from the director of government affairs for the Independent Petroleum Association of Mountain States, who said, "[Fracking's] got an exemplary safety record and it's vital to ensuring an American energy source. Keep in mind that it has been regulated by the states for the last 60 years."[41]

Pavillion community members were hopeful that EPA's report would make a difference. Louis Meeks said, "Encana ruined my well and now . . . they can't fix it. That's why we need federal oversight."[42] In what was clear retaliation for the media statement, Encana punished Meeks by discontinuing his water deliveries. Unable to afford the $3,000-per-month expense, Meeks started hauling drinking water himself to supply his home and livestock. But he had to use the poisonous water for bathing. With few choices, he was forced to settle with Encana for an undisclosed amount.

Encana spokesman Doug Hock charged, "What we have here is not a conclusion, but a probability—and based on the facts, not a good probability."[43] As to finding methane and benzene in the two deep test wells, he said, "Yeah, they found benzene. We're not disputing that. That is there, naturally occurring, because they're in a gas-bearing zone."[44] Wyoming governor Matt Mead accused the EPA of "scientifically questionable" conclusions.[45] Senator Inhofe claimed, "EPA's conclusions are not based on sound science but rather on political science. . . . [The EPA's report] is part of President Obama's war on fossil fuels and his determination to shut down natural gas production."[46]

John Fenton was elated by the EPA's conclusions, however, saying, "This investigation proves the importance of having a federal agency that can protect people and the environment." He continued, "Those of us who suffer the impacts from the unchecked development in our community are extremely happy the contamination source is being identified."[47]

The battle lines had been drawn as the country moved into the run-up to the 2012 presidential election. Millions of dollars of industry money poured into political coffers, while the EPA became a constant target of abuse by industry representatives and elected officials. And millions were being spent in an Orwellian media campaign designed to curb criticisms about the environmental damage linked to fracking.

12

POLITICS, BETRAYAL,
AND BROKEN COMMUNITIES

Whether we and our politicians know it or not, Nature is party to all our deals and decisions, and she has more votes, a longer memory, and a sterner sense of justice than we do.

—Wendell Berry[1]

When Steve Lipsky made a fortune in banking and built a mansion in Parker County, Texas, he knew nothing about the impacts of fracking the Barnett Shale. In 2005 he had a well drilled into the Trinity Aquifer, a groundwater source that furnished clean water.[2] Five years later, after months of experiencing nausea and fatigue, he called the county fire marshal, Shawn Scott, about the methane leaking from his water wellhead. Scott told the *Dallas Observer* that placing a lit match at the wellhead caused an "uncontrolled flame."[3] Lipsky contends his well became polluted after Range Resources drilled a gas well in 2009.[4] The fire marshal replied, "We really can't touch those guys at all."[5]

Soon afterward Lipsky filed a complaint with the Texas Railroad Commission, the state's energy regulatory body. He also hired Alisa Rich, an environmental consultant, to sample the water. When the sample showed high levels of methane, Rich warned the Lipskys that their home was at risk of exploding. She also contacted the U.S. Environmental Protection Agency's Region Six office to report her findings. Soon afterward the EPA tested Lipsky's water and took samples from two fracked gas wells that Range Resources had drilled horizontally and which stretched nearly to the ground beneath the Lipsky home.[6] The EPA found that the well water contained methane, benzene, toluene, ethane, propane, and hexane, some in concentrations that could "endanger the health" of the Lipskys.

Furthermore, the agency made an "isotopic fingerprint" match showing that the well's methane contamination came from the Range Resources gas drilling. In December 2010 it concluded that the contamination "may present an imminent and substantial endangerment" from methane explosions or benzene exposure, and it issued a rare emergency order giving Range Resources forty-eight hours to install a meter to detect methane levels and to begin providing drinking water to the Lipskys and other affected families.[7]

Range Resources had been fracking aggressively in several counties in northeastern Texas. In 2006 the company had acquired Stroud Energy, including its Barnett Shale acreage. By 2009 it owned nearly 132,000 acres in the Barnett and nearly three hundred operating or planned drilling locations.[8] By the end of 2010, Range had increased its production every fiscal quarter for eight straight years.[9]

The Lipskys received no sympathy from the three Texas Railroad Commissioners, who are elected and blamed the EPA for causing trouble. Commissioner Michael L. Williams claimed, "This is Washington politics of the worst kind."[10] The commissioners announced a January 2010 hearing that would clearly be biased in favor of Range. The EPA and the Lipskys declined to participate in this show trial.

Clearly distraught, Steve Lipsky said in a deposition, "My water lights on fire. I want to know why. . . . I just want to know what happened. I want to know if we have to leave. I want to know if we can stay. I want to know if it's coming through the ground. We want our lives back."[11] The day before the hearing, the Department of Justice filed a lawsuit to enforce Range Resources' compliance with the emergency order.[12]

Range Resources spent $3 million on lawyers and experts for the two-day Railroad Commission trial.[13] Evidence regarding methane contamination and the high benzene levels found in water samples were ignored. The commission ruled that Range's two gas wells had "not contributed to contamination of any domestic waterwells."[14]

Range Resources abruptly announced in February 2011 that it planned to sell the Barnett acreage and shift operations to the Marcellus.[15] The same month, Senator Inhofe sent a letter to the EPA inspector general demanding that the agency preserve all communications and records concerning the emergency order, and he began to personalize the attack, targeting Region Six administrator Dr. Al Armendariz as the enemy.[16]

Facing continuing health threats, the Lipskys sued Range Resources and hired petroleum engineer and former Texas Railroad Commission hearing examiner Thomas H. Richter to investigate. He found that the failure to properly cement the wells and/or to make them ready for fracking (well completion) "was a cause or contributor to the contamination of the Lipskys' wells.[17] When Range had drilled down though other gas-bearing formations to reach the Barnett shale, methane had likely seeped into the aquifer, contaminating the Lipskys' well.[18]

Water Pollution Crisis in Pennsylvania

In Dimock Township on New Year's Day in 2009, Norma Fiorentino's methane-contaminated water well exploded, blowing the concrete slab off the well house. The well near Fiorentino's trailer—located a few hundred yards from Cabot Oil and Gas Corporation's fracking operation—was just one of nineteen homes with tainted water sources in one corner of heavily fracked northeastern Pennsylvania.[19] Cabot had begun fracking in Dimock in 2006, eventually drilling almost five hundred wells in the region. In the summer of 2015 the company was second only to Chesapeake Energy in violating Pennsylvania's petroleum-related laws, with 494 violations— more than one violation for every gas well.[20]

Later in 2009, after much public pressure, Pennsylvania's Department of Environmental Protection (DEP) issued violation notices to Cabot for allowing gas to pollute groundwater.[21] After three spills at one Cabot well in Dimock in a single week released nearly 7,000 gallons of Halliburton-manufactured fracking fluid containing possible carcinogens, DEP issued Cabot a stop-work order on all its wells in Susquehanna County.[22] The agency ordered Cabot to pay for drinking water deliveries and indicated support for a municipal water pipeline to the community that would replace the contaminated water wells. The agency said that Cabot was "presumed to be responsible for the pollution."[23]

Over the next year, Democratic governor Ed Rendell's administration lost its resolve to be tough with Cabot. DEP signed a final agreement with Cabot in December 2010 that obliged the company to install filtration systems in the homes with contaminated water but effectively did not require any water testing be done once the methane filters were in place and did not require testing for any other contaminants.[24] When Republican Tom Corbett took office in 2011, Cabot was granted permission to end water deliveries in December 2011, leaving affected families to drink poisoned water that stank of contaminants.[25] Activists in Pennsylvania and New York rallied to raise money for water deliveries, with artists Mark Ruffalo and Josh Fox lending support to the efforts.[26]

Proof of the Corbett administration's complicity with the industry emerged several years later from a deposition of the technical director of DEP's Bureau of Laboratories. DEP had intentionally failed to provide testing results to impacted residents on sixteen of twenty-four metals— including metals such as copper, nickel, zinc, and titanium, which can harm human health and are known contaminants from fracking.[27]

Meanwhile, evidence was mounting that fracking impacted water resources. *ProPublica* had documented more than one thousand cases of water contamination in six states that were linked to the practice.[28] In March 2010 the EPA announced what it promised would be a comprehensive national research project on fracking.[29] It would replace the EPA's discredited Bush-era study concluding that fracking did not impact water resources.[30] Weston Wilson, who had been an environmental engineer at the EPA for thirty-seven years, was forced to seek whistleblower protection after he questioned the report's conclusions. Wilson, who subsequently left the agency, warned Congress in 2004 that the study's conclusions were "scientifically unsound and contrary to the purposes of the law."[31] *ProPublica* later obtained documents proving that Bush's EPA worked with the petroleum industry in writing the 2004 report's conclusions.[32] In 2011, a former Bush administration official stated that they had "never intended for the report to be interpreted as a perpetual clean bill of health for fracking or to justify a broad statutory exemption from any future regulation."[33]

Dimock's impacted families were excited that the research would include a case study of their township. The EPA had announced that it would include seven case studies in the research project, including two prospective ones that would start with baseline water testing before fracking commenced. Five case studies, including Dimock's, would be retrospective, examining the impacts on water resources where fracking had occurred.[34]

In December 2011 EPA Region 3 finally took action by asking the Agency for Toxic Substances and Disease Registry (ATSDR) to conduct an evaluation of Dimock water well data, as had been done in Pavillion. Referring to the Dimock families' exposure to toxic chemicals, the EPA Region 3 office stated that "residents are potentially in contact through dermal, inhalation and ingestion pathways" and requested that "if you should identify any potential health threats please notify us as soon as possible."

The ATSDR complied, saying in a December 28, 2011, Record of Activity/Technical Assist that based on home visits and a preliminary review of data, it was concerned. Among the agency's cited concerns were "the reliability of methane removal systems" and "the presence of other contaminants besides methane (metals, volatile organics and non-naturally occurring organics) for which the well treatment systems are not designed or in place to address."[35]

In January 2012, months after Cabot had ended water deliveries, the EPA announced that it would begin delivering water to four homes, and that it would test water in sixty homes in Dimock. The ATSDR had found arsenic, barium, and other toxic chemicals in the well water. Concerned citizens—believing that this move signaled that the EPA was becoming more serious about looking into fracking—cheered Region 3 administrator Shawn M. Garvin's announcement. Garvin declared: "We believe that the information provided to us by the residents deserves further review, and conducting our own sampling will help us fill information gaps. . . . We will work to help get a more complete picture of water quality for these homes in Dimock."[36]

In a letter to Garvin, Pennsylvania DEP secretary Michael Krancer told him that the agency did not know what it was doing. "EPA's understanding of the facts and science behind this activity is rudimentary," he wrote. "Fortunately, Pennsylvania is not new to all of this and we have a long history of experience at overseeing and regulating oil and natural gas extraction activities in our state, including fracking."[37] Krancer went on to question the EPA's motivation for the investigation of water contamination in Pavillion, calling it a "rush to conclusions."

Industry Pressure Mounts

As the election loomed, EPA had become a favorite whipping boy of presidential candidate Mitt Romney. He said in a Republican candidates' debate that the agency was "a tool in the hands of the president to crush the private enterprise system, to crush our ability to have energy. . . . And I look at the effort on the EPA for instance to—to stop—step in the way of fracking . . . this is all an effort to just say let's go solar and wind."[38]

The impacted families from around the country were hopeful that the investigations would continue, but they wondered if EPA would buckle under the intense political pressure on President Obama during a tough reelection campaign. In his 2012 State of the Union address, without explicitly mentioning fracking, Obama signaled his support for natural gas development, saying, "We have a supply of natural gas that can last America nearly 100 years. And my administration will take every possible action to safely develop this energy."[39]

The next day the EPA officially extended the public comment period for the draft report on water contamination in Pavillion, moving the comment deadline from late January to March 12, 2012. (See Chapter 11). Doug Hock, a spokesperson for Encana, enthused over the extension, "This will allow time for them [EPA] to provide the additional data we have requested and allow us the opportunity to provide more thorough and detailed comments on the draft report."[40]

In mid-March 2012 the EPA announced that water in Dimock was safe to drink, despite the tests showing dangerous levels of methane as well as the presence of other contaminants that can pose threats to human health.[41] The EPA's final report, delivered later in July, simply stated that "the residents have now or will have their own treatment systems that can reduce concentrations of those hazardous substances to acceptable levels at the tap."[42]

Scott Ely, a Dimock resident whose drinking water was contaminated with three times the state limit for methane and also with lithium—a chemical that can cause kidney and thyroid disease—said he was "flabbergasted." Ron Bishop, a chemist at the State University of New York's College at Oneonta, told *ProPublica*, "Any suggestion that water from these wells is safe for domestic use would be preliminary or inappropriate."[43]

EPA Chickens Out in Parker County

Meanwhile, the Lipskys' situation was worsening. In January 2012, state district judge Trey Loftin refused to hear their $6.5 million lawsuit against Range Resources, ruling that the couple was not allowed to sue since the Texas Railroad Commission had already exonerated the company. When Range Resources countersued the couple and their environmental consultant for damaging the driller's reputation, Loftin refused to dismiss the spurious case against the Lipskys, saying their efforts to highlight the risks of fracking were deceptive and "calculated to alarm the public."[44] Judge Loftin's pro-petroleum bias became public during his reelection campaign that year, contributing to his defeat. Loftin had distributed campaign reelection materials promoting his role in the fracking case with the line "Why is Rush Limbaugh congratulating Parker County's own Trey Loftin?"[45]

In March 2012 the EPA also pulled the plug on its investigation of Range's contamination of drinking water. The agency retracted the emergency order without notifying the Lipskys. In exchange, Range Resources agreed to participate in EPA's national study on fracking. Nearly a year later, the Associated Press revealed the details of the negotiations, having obtained documents showing that although EPA had evidence that Range was to blame for the contamination, it failed to pursue legal action.[46] EPA had contracted with an independent scientist to analyze water from thirty-two water wells. The tests had revealed that the wells contained gas with a chemical footprint very similar to that of the gas from the Range Resources operations.

One of the primary reasons that the agency withdrew its emergency order against Range Resources was that the company agreed to participate in the national study. An investigation by Environment & Energy Publishing's *EnergyWire* found that it was former Pennsylvania governor Ed Rendell, a past chairman of the Democratic National Committee, who had lobbied the Obama administration on behalf of Range Resources. His behind-the-scenes intervention was brought to light in the more than one thousand pages of emails obtained by *EnergyWire* from a Freedom of Information Act (FOIA) request to EPA Region 6.[47]

One of the email exchanges disclosed that Scott McDonald, chief of the Water Enforcement Branch in the EPA's Office of Regional Counsel, had told Region 6 administrator Al Armendariz that Rendell had "proposed certain terms to the Administrator" and that he was acting as "a spokesman for Range." Armendariz had attempted to do his job. He wanted Range to deliver water to two affected families in Parker County until the results from the water testing were completed, and he wanted the testing data to be made public. He had also asked the EPA's lawyers to impress upon Range the need to behave less aggressively in Texas-based litigation.[48] But when the EPA dropped its case, Range immediately noted that the EPA's capitulation would help in the multimillion dollar defamation against the Lipskys.[49]

The EPA was also stalling on the Pavillion situation. The day before the EPA withdrew the emergency order in Parker County, it extended the public comment period for the draft report a second time, until October 16, 2012.[50]

At the end of April, Rush Limbaugh viciously attacked Armendariz, saying on a broadcast that "Senator James Inhofe took to the Senate floor today to draw attention to a video of a top EPA official saying the EPA's 'philosophy' is to 'crucify' and 'make examples' of oil and gas companies." Included in Limbaugh's vitriolic monologue was a defense of oil, which he called "the fuel of the engine of freedom." [51]

Inhofe had ignited this controversy after his staffers located a 2010 video of Armendariz discussing EPA enforcement in Dish, Texas—a community that had suffered from the consequences of fracking the Barnett. He had said, "Find people who are not complying with the law and you hit them as hard as you can and make examples of them." [52] Using an ill-chosen metaphor, Armendariz said that cracking down on polluters was "like when the Romans conquered villages in the Mediterranean. They'd go into Turkish towns and they'd find the first five guys they saw and crucify them." [53] Armendariz's comments, taken out of context, had meant that if the agency punished the worst polluters, it would deter other petroleum companies from taking shortcuts with safety.

Within days of Inhofe's release of the video, Armendariz resigned, saying in his letter to Administrator Jackson, "I have come to the conclusion that my continued service will distract you and the agency from its important work." [54]

FOIA requests by *ProPublica* netted numerous communications from Inhofe and his staff demanding repeated briefings on the EPA water pollution studies. The agency was swamped with questions surrounding every detail of its budget for the Pavillion study, even asking for dollar figures spent at labs testing water samples. In a thinly veiled political maneuver, Inhofe wrote to EPA administrator Jackson, calling the draft report on Pavillion "unsubstantiated." He went on to deride the report as part of an "administration-wide effort to hinder and unnecessarily regulate hydraulic fracturing at the federal level." [55]

President Obama's key adviser on energy and climate was actually very sympathetic to the gas industry, however, and she had been watchdogging the EPA's pursuit of the case. Based on information that has become public, it is clear that Heather Zichal saw championing natural gas as a strategy to blunt the Republicans' criticism of the Obama administration's energy policy.

Zichal had cut her teeth on political tussles, having worked in Congress as a legislative director for Democratic New Jersey congressmen Frank

Pallone and Rush Holt. She had managed energy and environmental issues for John Kerry in his failed presidential campaign as well as serving
as Kerry's legislative director when he was in the Senate. She moved on to
become energy policy director for the Obama campaign, crafting the 2008
energy platform and serving on the Obama-Biden transition team.[56]

In April 2012, the thirty-six-year-old White House energy adviser
gushed about natural gas in a blog she wrote about the Obama administration's new interagency working group on natural gas: "The president has
made clear that he believes this important, abundant domestic resource
holds unique promise to fuel our energy sector, fuel our vehicles, as well
as fuel job growth—all while reducing harmful emissions."[57] President
Obama had issued an executive order forming an interagency working
group composed of more than a dozen agencies that would "facilitate
coordinated administration policy efforts to support safe and responsible
unconventional domestic natural gas development."[58]

The emails obtained by *EnergyWire* showed that Zichal had been briefed
by top EPA officials and was designated to manage the attacks. When the
EPA was accused in early January 2012 of having used a flawed process in
acquiring water samples in Pavillion, Zichal wrote to deputy EPA administrator Bob Perciasepe, "Can we get some talking points on this asap?"
EnergyWire's investigation also showed that Zichal e-mailed with then
EPA administrator Lisa Jackson on the Pavillion investigation.[59] The e-
mails revealed that Zichal played an important role in the administration's
handling of proposed regulations for fracking on public lands—weak rules
that were finalized in 2015. The news organization's review of White House
visitor records from 2012 revealed more than twenty meetings that Zichal
had with industry groups and company executives on the rules. She met
with representatives from a who's who of oil and gas companies and trade
groups, including the American Petroleum Institute, the Independent Petroleum Association of America, BP, Devon Energy, and ExxonMobil. In
comparison, environmental groups had four meetings with Zichal.[60]

By the early summer of 2012, Zichal was gaining the upper hand in
guiding EPA about the development of the rules for disclosing fracking
chemicals under the Toxic Substances Control Act. She advocated voluntary
disclosure and use of the industry-sponsored website FracFocus. Speaking
at the Natural Gas Roundtable on June 21, 2012, she said the administration was focused on "existing platforms like FracFocus, so that so we're not
creating new regulatory hurdles that make your job impossible."[61] Dave

McCurdy, chief executive officer of the American Gas Association, the Washington-based trade group of gas utilities and a former congressman from the gas heartland of Oklahoma, later commented that the industry could count on Zichal to make sure that the federal agencies would not push unnecessary rules.[62]

Zichal left the Obama administration in 2013, the next year accepting a directorship on the board of Cheniere Energy, a company leading the push to export liquefied natural gas overseas. She received more than $400,000 worth of Cheniere stock her first year with the company.[63] (See Chapter 16.)

The EPA Capitulates

In July 2012 the EPA announced that the investigation in Dimock was over and that water deliveries to the families would cease.[64] An internal EPA PowerPoint presentation, later leaked to the *Los Angeles Times*, showed that Region 3 staff had warned their bosses about water well contamination. It concluded, "Methane is at significantly higher concentrations in the aquifers after gas drilling and perhaps as a result of fracking [hydraulic fracturing] and other gas well work."[65] A Duke University study demonstrated that the methane contaminating the shallower water wells had the same chemical fingerprint as the methane from the Marcellus Shale formation.[66]

Robert B. Jackson, a professor of environmental science at Duke University, reviewed the EPA PowerPoint presentation and said, "What's surprising is to see this data set and then to see EPA walk away from Dimock." He continued, "The issue here is, why wasn't EPA interested in following up on this to understand it better?"[67]

In August the DEP allowed Cabot to begin fracking the seven wells that had been the subject of the EPA stop-work order in 2010.[68] That same month Cabot reached an agreement with thirty-two Dimock-area households who had sued the company for poisoned water.[69] Almost all of the affected residents joined the ranks of individuals silenced by the oil and gas industry. The industry forced impacted residents to sign a nondisclosure agreement in exchange for compensation for the harm and trauma that they suffered.[70]

Ray Kemble, whose water was badly contaminated, refused to be gagged by the industry. Kemble was advised by his attorney to accept the settlement with Cabot or expect to receive a bill of $80,000 for legal services and other fees. Kemble—an outspoken opponent of Cabot and a man not used to being threatened—says he was able to outsmart Cabot by negotiating a specially worded settlement that does not gag him. Kemble's willingness to speak out has made him a leader in the movement to stop fracking. He says that he has nothing to lose because Cabot has polluted his water, ruined his property values, and destroyed his business.[71]

Shale Gas Review blogger Tom Wilbur reported that several of the residents who agreed to Cabot's terms were "conflicted, battle weary, and resigned to accept the deal on the advice of their attorney."[72] According to Wilbur, one-third of the settlement will go to attorney's fees, and an undetermined amount to expenses. Cabot's offer did not include filtration systems.

As election day loomed, pressure mounted on the Obama administration to cave in on the Pavillion investigation. In September 2012 the U.S. Geological Survey released two reports criticizing the EPA's testing program in Pavilion.[73] In October the EPA extended the public comment period for the Pavillion draft research report a third time, to January 15, 2013.[74]

Emboldened and seeing another opportunity to go on the offensive, Inhofe released a Senate Energy and Public Works Committee Minority Report titled "A Look Ahead to EPA Regulations for 2013: Numerous Obama EPA Rules Placed on Hold Until After the Election." The report claimed the testing in Pavillion and other actions by Obama's EPA would "inevitably result in the elimination of millions of American jobs, drive up the price of gas at the pump even more . . . and essentially shut down American oil, natural gas, and coal production."[75]

In December, after enduring four years of attacks, EPA administrator Lisa Jackson announced her resignation.[76] Former EPA chiefs have observed that the vicious treatment of Jackson, the first African American woman to hold the post, was worse than any other agency administrator had faced, and she had experienced the most aggressive assault on the agency to date.[77]

As rumors swirled about the fate of the Pavillion study, in mid-January 2013 the EPA extended the public comment period a fourth time, until September 30—twenty months after the original comment period was supposed to have ended. Shortly afterward, President Obama pledged in his State of the Union to "keep cutting red tape and speeding up new oil and gas permits."[78]

President Obama made two energy-related nominations in March 2013. Gina McCarthy, a former top state environmental official in Massachusetts during Mitt Romney's tenure as governor there, would become EPA administrator. At the time of her nomination, the career public official was the EPA's assistant administrator for air and radiation—a position she had had no trouble being confirmed for during Obama's first term. The other nominee was Ernest Moniz, a pro-fracking physicist at the Massachusetts Institute of Technology, who would replace energy secretary Steven Chu.[79]

Inhofe and other petroleum-industry allies did not oppose Moniz's appointment, but they were hostile to McCarthy. Republican senators boycotted the committee vote on her nomination, which was to be held in early May.[80] McCarthy had suffered much verbal abuse and answered more than a thousand questions in the contentious lead-up to the vote. On the day Inhofe boycotted the vote, lobbyists from Fierce, Isakowitz and Blalock—a firm that works for a who's who of industry that includes BP, Noble Energy, and Edison International—hosted a fund-raiser for the senator at Charlie Palmer Steak House. The price of admission was a $1,000 donation for a political action committee and $500 for an individual.[81]

As the outrageous obstruction of McCarthy's confirmation continued, the Obama administration grew more timid. In June 2013 the EPA officially backed down on the Pavillion investigation, announcing that it would turn the investigation over to the state of Wyoming.* The study would be funded in part by $1.5 million from Encana—the corporation that affected residents believe caused their poisoned water.[82] John Fenton and the other affected community members were stunned. They had been kept completely in the dark about the negotiations between the EPA and Wyoming, and they had no faith in the outcome of a Wyoming-led investigation.[83] As this book goes to print, Wyoming has not released a final report on Pavillion. In 2014 a preliminary report was released saying that wells were properly drilled and maintained but that more study was needed.[84]

The impacted families in Parker County, Dimock, and Pavillion had been betrayed by Washington politics and the timidity of the Obama administration. In off-the-record conversations with investigative journalist Abrahm Lustgarten, high-ranking EPA officials conceded that the Pavillion investigation and other environmental initiatives were stymied under tremendous pressure from the drilling industry and its powerful allies in Congress. These insiders also reported the investigations were the victim of

---

* The EPA officially discontinued the public comment period for the Pavillion draft report on September 11, 2013—a busy news cycle day twelve years after 9/11.

"financial constraints" and "a delicate policy balance sought by the White House."[85]

Some of us also wondered if a deal had been cut between the Obama administration and congressional Republicans to dump the Pavillion investigation in exchange for Gina McCarthy's confirmation. Republicans dropped their filibuster, and the vote—59 to 40—finally took place 151 days after she was nominated, less than a month after President Obama handed the Pavillion investigation back to Wyoming.[86]

Fracking activists across the country continue to demand that EPA reopen the investigations. At a congressional briefing sponsored by Pennsylvania congressman Matt Cartwright in 2014, Ray Kemble spoke, summing up the EPA's blatant betrayal: "EPA officials literally told us officially that our water was safe to drink but then told us off-the-record not to drink it. Now the truth is out and we want justice."[87]

13

SACRIFICE ZONES IN THE KEYSTONE STATE

*If large numbers of people believe in freedom of speech, there will be free-
dom of speech, even if the law forbids it; if public opinion is sluggish, in-
convenient minorities will be persecuted, even if laws exist to protect them.*
— George Orwell [1]

Craig Stevens says he's "an accidental activist," explaining that his philosophy in the past was "Drill, baby, drill," but now it is "Drink, baby,
drink." Stevens—whose family helped found heavily fracked Susquehanna
County—promised his dying father that he would do everything he could
to stop the frackers from destroying the place he loved. [2]

Three months after Steve Stevens, Craig's father, died in 2007, Steve's
siblings arranged for a Chesapeake Energy landman to go to the nursing
home where their mother—Craig's grandmother—lived to sign a lease
for fracking on their jointly owned property. Craig and his two siblings,
who had inherited a one-third stake in the house, were never contacted by
Chesapeake. The chronically cash-poor company had formed a partnership with the Norwegian government's state-owned oil company, Statoil,
making it more difficult for landowners to determine and collect a fair
percentage of the royalties. The two companies pay leaseholders separately
and account for expenses differently, an arrangement that can be used to
skim profits. [3]

Stevens is bitter that acreage in Salt Springs Park, where his grandmother was born decades before it became a park, has been leased to Talisman Energy. [4] The company has a sketchy record, listed as third in the
number of fracking-related violations in Pennsylvania from 2009 to 2013. [5]
In 2012 the EPA levied a $62,000 fine against the company for failure to
provide health and safety information to emergency response agencies

about chemicals used at their fifty-two natural gas wells and compressor stations, creating a potential public safety crisis.[6]

Living in a frack zone has changed Stevens's life, focusing him on a mission to stop fracking. The onetime Tea Party activist has become a leader in the national movement to ban fracking, traveling around the country telling the story of how Pennsylvania became a "state-sponsored sacrifice zone." With his Republican credentials, Stevens is working to convince Republican lawmakers that fracking is too dangerous to pursue.

Sacrifice Zones

In Butler County, residents of Woodlands have suffered from polluted water ever since Rex Energy began drilling in 2010. Many people began noting dark sediment floating in their discolored drinking water, which smelled like "rotten eggs." People became sick, vomiting and experiencing rashes, while their animals refused to drink the visibly contaminated water.[7]

Janet and Fred McIntyre were among the residents impacted. Janet first noticed the water one night after suffering a powerful headache and vomiting; her husband went to get her a glass of water, but only foul-smelling foam came out of the tap.[8] The couple complained to the DEP, and the agency's lab found that the McIntyres' water contained detectable levels of chemicals known to be used in fracking fluids, including tert-butyl alcohol, acetone, chloromethane, toluene, and 1,3,5-trimethylbenzene. But the DEP refused to follow up, saying that low-level chemical contamination was not a health risk. The DEP spokesman, Kevin Sunday, proposed that the contamination could have happened at the agency's lab or have come from abandoned vehicles near the couple's property.[9]

Kim McEvoy, another affected resident, was told by DEP staff that the unpleasant change in odor in the water from her three-hundred-foot well was from garden slugs rotting. She says, "They just insult your intelligence. I don't trust the DEP."[10] She wrote a letter to Governor Corbett, saying that her "water turned black and had a foul, smelly odor."[11] She went on to describe how she and her fiancé had become "sick with headaches, fatigue and painful sinuses." The letter was delivered to the governor in September 2011 when a thousand people marched to Governor Corbett's office during the Shale Gas Outrage, a two-day event in Philadelphia organized by the group Protecting Our Waters.[12]

For a short time Rex Energy delivered water to the affected families in Butler County, but in the winter of 2012 the company removed the water tanks.[13] Marcellus Outreach Butler organized a water delivery and a rally to demonstrate support for the families. Speaking at the event, Janet McIntyre said she saw "a grown man cry" when Rex workers removed a water tank from a neighbor's home, pouring hundreds of gallons of water onto the ground.[14] In 2013 the McIntyres became the lead plaintiffs in a lawsuit against Rex Energy, joined by eight other families. They charged that the company polluted their water, negatively impacted their health, and destroyed their quality of life.[15]

In 2014 microbiologist John Stolz, director of the Pittsburgh-based Duquesne University Center for Environmental Research and Education, finished a three-year study of the water contamination in Woodlands. He found, based on testing and surveys, that the water in 56 of the 143 households studied had diminished quality, taking on an odor and/or changing color. Stolz concluded that it was "quite plausible" that the drilling and fracking of sixty-five wells in the area was responsible.[16]

Thirty-five families from Woodlands rely on drinking water provided from the "water bank" set up by nearby White Oak Springs Presbyterian Church. Reverend Lee Dreyer has been a leading force in creating the nonprofit Water for Woodlands, which spends $400 each week to provide water. He and volunteers such as Janet McIntyre and Rosemary Smith are providing this public service since federal and state governments have looked the other way.[17]

Anything Goes

The residents of Woodlands represent a few of the many victims of the unrelenting drilling and fracking in Pennsylvania that began in 2003 when Range Resources drilled the first new Marcellus well.[18] Over the next six years, the number of new fracking wells drilled each year increased nearly 250 times, from eight wells in 2005 to almost two thousand in 2011. Of the nearly five thousand new shale gas wells drilled between 2005 and 2011, nearly four out of five were located in rural counties.[19]

Oil and gas drilling in Pennsylvania is marked by a history of lax oversight. The industry was unregulated until legislation was passed in 1956 requiring companies to obtain a permit when drilling near a coal mine. In 1963 all drillers were required to obtain permits, but the state had no authority to refuse permitting. It is estimated that the state has five hundred thousand abandoned wells, but no one knows for sure, since there are no records before the mid-1950s.[20]

In 1984 the Oil and Gas Act was passed to address concerns about oil and gas drilling. Under the law, minimum requirements were developed and enforced by the DEP. All new wells were to be permitted by the agency before drilling could begin, and old wells were to be registered if they had not been permitted in the past. Minimum safety rules were developed for disposing of the brine—a salty and contaminant-laden waste product that surges up from wells during drilling operations. Some parameters were set for cementing and casing of wells and for plugging wells before they are abandoned.[21] The regulations required that drilling waste be hauled to a processing plant or injected into a deep disposal well, but it allowed the use of the brine, which is sometimes radioactive, to be used on roads for deicing or to suppress dust.[22]

In the first few years of shale gas extraction, the Pennsylvania legislature took no action to protect the environment or landowners. With the long record of mining and drilling in Pennsylvania, mineral rights on pieces of property have been divided, bequeathed, and gifted in many ways over the decades, meaning that many owners cannot be identified. In 2006 the General Assembly passed the Dormant Oil and Gas Act in 2006, allowing companies to extract oil and gas from beneath properties even if not all of the owners of the mineral rights could be located.[23]

Six years later, the passage of Act 13 took away communities' local control powers, thus preventing municipal governments from using local zoning laws to regulate or ban fracking within their borders. This particular provision was designed to supersede a Pennsylvania Supreme Court ruling that upheld municipal governments' right to pass zoning laws that would exclude drilling.[24] This provision of the legislation appears to have been based on a model bill prepared by the American Legislative Exchange Council (funded by the Koch brothers) and endorsed during a meeting of ALEC's Energy, Environment, and Agriculture Task Force in 2010.[25]

Several Pennsylvania townships and the Delaware Riverkeeper Network litigated over Act 13's attack on local control, resulting in a July 2012 decision by the state's Commonwealth Court to throw out the part of the act restricting local zoning decisions for oil and gas development. In December 2013 the state supreme court upheld the lower court's decision, 4–2, ruling that a restriction on a municipal government's ability to zone for drilling was unconstitutional.[26] The court sent some parts of the law back to the lower Commonwealth Court, however. In July 2014 this lower court ruled that local governments, not the state, have the authority to zone the industry. Pennsylvania's Public Utility Commission has appealed this decision, which has not yet been heard by the higher court.[27]

Act 13 also requires frackers to pay a small impact fee for active wells; the fee declines over the wells' lifetime and can change each year based on the price of natural gas.[28] The fees are a small fraction of the billions of dollars in profits generated by drilling and fracking in Pennsylvania. Localities with wells receive 60 percent of the monies collected; in 2014 the five counties with the most drilling each received between $4.5 million and $6.5 million.[29]

Forty percent of the fees go to state agencies overseeing drilling and to the Marcellus Legacy Fund.[30] This fund provides grants to counties and municipalities, some of which can be used to fund "planning, acquisition, development, rehabilitation and repair of greenways, recreational trails, open space, parks and beautification projects."[31] In 2014 only $915,000 of the fund's spending went to environmental programs—less than 0.5 percent of the $221 million the fund disbursed.[32]

Sam Bernhardt, a Food & Water Watch senior organizer, says that Corbett presented Act 13 as a boon for conservation funding and then gutted alternative funding sources in that year's budget, leaving conservation programs severely impaired. This dangerous move meant that conservation programs now rely on the continuation of fracking for funding.[33]

Act 13 has had a chilling impact on public health advocacy. Buried in the bill, which ran for more than a thousand pages, was a provision designed to muzzle doctors and nurses, preventing them from warning sick patients that their illness may be related to fracking. Health care professionals who request information about proprietary chemicals must sign a nondisclosure agreement that prohibits them from sharing any information about those chemicals with their patients.[34] At the same time, funding was cut for the registry that tracks respiratory problems, skin conditions, stomach ailments, and other illnesses potentially related to gas drilling.[35]

Pennsylvania state senator Daylin Leach said that legislators were unaware of the proprietary fracking chemical provisions in the law and that the secrecy provisions were misguided. He said, "The importance of keeping it as proprietary secret seems minimal when compared to letting the public know what chemicals they and their children are being exposed to."[36]

The University of Washington School of Public Health dean, Howard

Frumkin, put it bluntly to WHYY radio in Philadelphia: "In more than two decades of practicing occupational medicine, I'll tell you how often I was able to make the right diagnosis and plan the right treatment when I didn't know what the patients were exposed to—zero times."[37]

In June 2014, two retirees from the Pennsylvania Department of Health came forward and revealed that they had been silenced in a blatantly political attempt to sweep fracking's impacts under the rug. Tammi Stuck, a community health nurse in Fayette County for almost thirty-six years, disclosed that she had been told not to return phone calls from residents who were concerned about the health effects of natural gas drilling. She said, "We were absolutely not allowed to talk to them." Stuck said they were given a list of "buzzwords." She went on: "There were some obvious ones like fracking, gas, soil contamination. There were probably 15 to 20 words and short phrases that were on this list. If anybody from the public called in and that was part of the conversation, we were not allowed to talk to them."[38]

Marshall P. Deasy III, who spent more than twenty years at the Bureau of Epidemiology, said that during the time he worked at the department, "community health wasn't told to be silent on any other topic that I can think of" besides fracking.[39]

Former Pittsburgh city council member Doug Shields, who early on recognized the dangers posed by fracking, was infuriated at the Corbett administration's spin on the buzzword scandal. Shields and his wife, Bridget Shields, were the principal organizers for Pittsburgh's fracking ban in 2010. When the scandalous policy was uncovered, Doug Shields said, Corbett dodged the question and "rolled out the press spokesperson to utter the usual nonsensical blather."[40]

In light of Pennsylvania's failure to track the health impacts of fracking, in 2011 several foundations funded the establishment of the Southwest Pennsylvania Environmental Health Project.[41] Employing more than a dozen health professionals, the project surveyed people who came to them for help in 2012 and 2013. Among the symptoms they reported were rashes, breathing difficulties, eye and throat irritations, nausea, abdominal pain, headaches, nosebleeds, and anxiety.[42]

Dr. Poune Saberi, a University of Pennsylvania physician and public health expert who has treated many people exposed to fracking, believes the impacts on human health are real. She says that this is borne out by the similar symptoms seen in sick patients who live near drilling sites.[43]

In the fall of 2012, Earthworks' Oil and Gas Accountability Project, which was founded in 1999, published a report based on air and water testing that detailed chemicals those living near fracking sites are exposed to, and surveyed the symptoms experienced by people living near drilling sites. Of the hundreds of different fracking fluid chemicals known, sixty-five are listed as hazardous by the federal government. The tests revealed that nineteen dangerous volatile organic compounds were found in air samples, including acetone, toluene, and benzene. Water samples also found chemicals associated with fracking, including methane, barium, bromide, and strontium. There are no federal safe drinking water standards for some of the contaminants found.[44]

They found that the residents in drilling communities developed new health problems after fracking began and that those who lived closest to drilling or gas facilities have the highest rates of illness. The researchers discovered that the children living near gas production sites have symptoms and illnesses including throat irritation, nasal irritation, skin rashes, eye burning, nosebleeds, sleep disturbances, frequent nausea and shortness of breath, and even several conditions that are unusual in young people, including severe headaches, joint pain, and back pain.[45]

Jenny Lisak of the Pennsylvania Alliance for Clean Water and Air started tracking the human health, animal health, and economic impacts in the List of the Harmed, which has more than twelve hundred entries from around the nation.[46] She wonders how long the list will become before something is done.

Failure to Protect the Public

In July 2014, Pennsylvania auditor general Eugene DePasquale released a report critical of the DEP's effectiveness in regulating shale gas development, saying that the agency was "unprepared" for the industry's expansion. Evaluating the DEP's regulatory track record between 2009 and 2012, the report noted serious deficiencies in regulating fracking, including the failure to issue administrative orders requiring drilling operators to take action after a water resource had been found to be contaminated.[47]

In July 2014 the *Pittsburgh-Post Gazette* found from a DEP records request that between 2007 and the time of the article, drilling and fracking had contaminated or diminished water flow 209 times, with incidents occurring in nearly every part of the state where drilling was occurring.[48] The companies responsible for the problems were not listed in the records, making it difficult to track the worst offenders. Initially the agency fought record requests from news organizations, but after a court order requiring disclosure of the information, the DEP complied.

As this book goes to print, the controversy over Act 13 continues. In August 2015, under Democratic governor Tom Wolf's watch, DEP was taking comments on the final version of oil and gas regulations. Thirty thousand public comments have already been submitted during the four-year process, which began before the current DEP secretary, John Quigley, was appointed. Tracy Carluccio of the Delaware Riverkeeper Network is especially critical of the regulations governing drilling waste, saying that the wastewater impoundments will continue to be open to the environment.[49] At the same time, the industry is fighting the rule requiring centralized wastewater impoundments to close in three years if they are not upgraded and re-permitted.[50]

Other Impacts

Meanwhile, policy makers have largely ignored the social impacts of fracking. Residents in the heavily fracked areas of the state have observed an influx of transient workers and a rise in alcohol-related crimes, traffic accidents, emergency room visits, and sexually transmitted infections.[51] The increase in crime from the influx of natural gas workers has put a burden on state and local police departments.[52] The police chief in Wellsboro, Pennsylvania, attributed significant increases in alcohol-related crime—including public intoxication, barroom brawls, and drunk driving—to shale gas industry workers.[53] The most-fracked Pennsylvania communities have also seen steep upticks in drunk driving, traffic violations, and bar fights. On average, disorderly conduct arrests rose about 30 percent faster in heavily fracked rural counties after fracking began than in unfracked rural counties over the same period. The average annual increase in disorderly conduct arrests was three times higher in heavily fracked rural Pennsylvania counties after fracking began than it was in unfracked rural counties.[54]

Likewise, an increase in the average number of cases of sexually transmitted infections was greater in heavily fracked rural counties than in those without fracking. The average annual number of gonorrhea and chlamydia cases increased by about 32 percent in the most heavily fracked rural Pennsylvania counties once fracking began, compared to the 20 percent increase observed in rural unfracked counties.[55]

The energy boom in Pennsylvania also increased road congestion and heavy-truck traffic. Accidents have soared as trucks drive on narrow roads not designed for industrial-sized vehicles. Many roads in rural fracked areas have no marked speed limits, allowing traffic to travel at fifty-five miles per hour, which increases the risk of accidents. Nationally, the number of automobile accidents has been declining steadily since 2005, and in Pennsylvania, the number of heavy-truck crashes has generally declined since 2000.[56] In rural Pennsylvania counties where fracking is pursued, however, this trend is reversed. Counties with the most fracking have experienced the largest increase in heavy-truck crashes. While in unfracked rural counties crashes decreased by 12.4 percent, in heavily fracked counties they rose by 7.2 percent.[57]

Heavy truck traffic also causes enormous damage to roadways. Researchers from the RAND Corporation and Carnegie Mellon University examined the impacts on roadways in the Marcellus Shale region and found that local roads, which are designed for passenger vehicles, would require road repairs much sooner and that "the useful life of a roadway is directly related to the frequency and weight of truck traffic using the roadway."[58]

In terms of road impacts, the study estimated that one horizontally drilled and fracked well costs the state about $13,000 to $23,000. They estimate that by 2011 heavy truck traffic from fracking had cost $8.5 million to $17 million per year in road damage.[59]

Fighting Back

In 2014, Berks Gas Truth, Food & Water Watch, and many other organizations organized a diverse coalition—Pennsylvanians Against Fracking—to fight for a ban on fracking. Its short-term goals are to stop new wells and fracking-related infrastructure and to support research on the impacts of fracking in the state.

Karen Feridun was one of the primary organizers of the effort. She is a co-founder of Berks Gas Truth and the chair of her local Democratic Club. In 2013 Feridun was one of the party activists involved in a team effort to change the Democratic Party's platform to support banning fracking. They obtained a list of all of the Democratic committee members who could vote and lobbied them during the Pennsylvania State Committee meeting, handing out buttons with slogans like "Stop Fracking Now" and "The

Planet Doesn't Get a Vote, You Do." The resolution passed in July 2013 by a vote of 115 to 81.[60]

As this book goes to press, the coalition has a membership of a hundred organizations. Focused on changing the pro-fracking policies of Governor Wolf and the agencies he oversees, the activists are determined to create a new energy future for Pennsylvania.

Feridun believes that the Democratic Party should be accountable to its base. She says, "We're going to be in Wolf's face everywhere he goes, to make our message heard and make him respond."[61]

14

NOT A DROP LEFT TO DRINK

In an age when man has forgotten his origins and is blind even to his most essential needs for survival, water along with other resources has become the victim of his indifference.

—Rachel Carson[1]

Stifling heat and the fumes spewing from the bumper-to-bumper SUVs and large luxury vehicles hit me in the face as I walked out of the airport in Dubai. Back in 2012 I was visiting one of the least sustainable cities on earth, attending the industry-sponsored Global Water: Oil and Gas Summit, which featured representatives from Shell, Saudi Aramco and Conoco-Phillips as speakers.[2] Dubai was a fitting location for the bizarre grouping of polluters, resource extractors, and opportunists to meet and discuss the best way to divvy up and profit from using the world's water for oil and gas development.

I was eavesdropping on a discussion about how the oil and water industries plan to coordinate profit-making activities in the future, taking advantage of a rare chance to hear a candid discussion about the long-term plans of the industry. Not hiding my identity, I quietly sat in the back, furiously typing notes, as I heard a frightening scenario for the future. Representatives from some of the most powerful companies in the world (Shell, Dow, GE, Veolia, CH2M Hill, and AES) as well as many smaller companies (such as Aquatech and Fountain Qual) were consummating an alliance focused on profiting from the overuse and pollution of water resources.

Even in Dubai, where solar energy should power the future, natural gas is the fuel of choice. Saeed Mohammad Al-Tayer, head of the government-run power and water provider and vice chairman of the Supreme Council of Energy, said at the conference that the sheikhdom currently generates

90 percent of its electricity from gas. Future plans call for reducing the gas use to 70 percent by using a mixture of coal, nuclear energy, and renewable sources to supplement it.[3]

At the meeting, all pretensions of advancing beyond fossil fuels to an economy based on renewable energy were dropped. Never once did anyone mention gas as a bridge to the future. No ethical debate took place about using dwindling water resources to extract the fossil fuels that are ruining the stability of our planet's climate. It was obvious that the meeting participants understood the consequences of fossil fuels and how the petroleum industry's use of water contributes to the world water crisis. But overriding these concerns is their focus on short-term profit; they are willing to use as much water as it takes to drill for every last drop of fossil fuels.

Corporations such as the giant private water firm Veolia already have a reputation for ruthlessness.[4] Many of the water companies pursuing a relationship with the oil and gas industry are the same ones that privatized water services, in countless cases allowing the poor to go thirsty. The privatization of water has met with forceful resistance across the world, even in the United States, and many privatization ventures have failed. But that has not prevented the industry from turning to another controversial business: providing water for fracking, and feeding off the oil and gas industry's need to dispose of its polluted wastewater.

And it's no wonder, considering that the oil and gas industry is using and polluting more water, and bringing more waste to the surface, than ever before in its history. Foreshadowing the overuse and contamination of water, industry representatives at the meeting enthused about the enormous volume of water required to frack at the scale necessary to recover oil and gas. They rarely mention that most of water injected underground is lost forever. Depending on the rock formation, between 5 and 50 percent returns to the surface in the initial days and weeks after fracking. In the Marcellus region, about 90 percent of the volume injected stays belowground.[5]

A representative from Aquatech BV, a water technology company specializing in desalination and water reuse, spoke of the business opportunity presented by the large amounts of petroleum-generated wastewater. The latest figures seem to bear this out: every day U.S. oil and gas wells generate 2.4 billion gallons of wastewater, with another 8.1 billion gallons brought to the surface in the rest of the world, for a total daily volume of 10.5 billion gallons of polluted water.[6] This is enough poison liquid to cover the entire country at a depth as thick as a penny. And according to a representative from GE Power, who spoke at the meeting, the volume of oil-and-gas-industry wastewater produced each year is increasing at a rate of 8 percent.

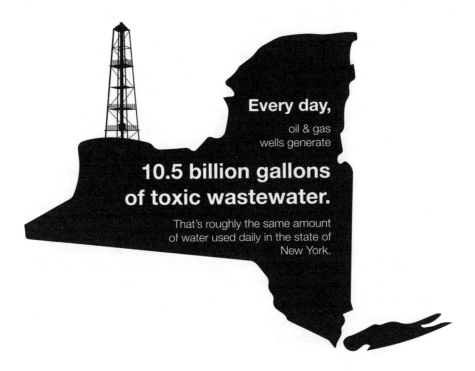

Every day,
oil & gas
wells generate

10.5 billion gallons
of toxic wastewater.

That's roughly the same amount
of water used daily in the state of
New York.

Wastewater is expensive to treat, and the higher the level of contamination, the more expensive the process. Processing wastewater requires sophisticated equipment, adding a significant cost to production of each well, depending how much contamination is removed.[7] The likelihood that cost-sensitive operators will be willing to pay for this decontamination is remote. The petroleum industry has a long history of evading environmental and safety regulations to boost profits. It is much cheaper for industry to simply inject its wastes underground, despite the fact that this causes earthquake swarms.

This issue of cost explains why one of the main focuses of this summit was figuring out how to make the public recognize "reused" water as a valuable resource that consumers should be willing to pay for. Speakers at the summit spoke about how they must "educate" policy makers and the public about its worth. Among the solutions suggested for making waste-water more "valuable" was instituting freshwater pricing. They believe that monetizing the value of water would give even wastewater higher worth in an era of water scarcity.

Using ocean water for oil and gas development was another hot topic at the summit. Desalination has become the holy grail for many industrial water users and other economic interests that want to profit from it.[8] Proponents of this expensive and energy-intensive technology rarely talk about the high concentrations of chemicals and salt dumped into the ocean during the process. At the summit, proponents discussed the additives needed for desalination—disinfection agents, coagulants, flocculants, anti-scalants, surfactants, acid-based cleaning agents, and corrosion inhibitors. No matter how sophisticated the desalination equipment may be, the "dispersion technology" to eliminate the remaining waste uses the same old, failed approach: the solution to pollution is dilution.

Many of the senior engineers attending the meeting were well intentioned, but they were so narrowly focused on their area of expertise that they had lost sight of the big picture. Yet executives from the water technology and petroleum industry seemed to view water scarcity with delight—a source of future profits. To someone truly rapacious, scarcity will not only make water more precious but also make the technologies for removing contaminants or creating new sources of water much more valuable. It is good for the corporate water business.

A New Water Ethic

By 2025, the United Nations says, 1.8 billion people will be forced to survive under acute water scarcity and two-thirds of the world's population will live under water stress.[9]

Author and activist Maude Barlow has been warning about water scarcity and pollution for more than two decades, helping to spur a global water justice movement. In Barlow's newest book, *Blue Future*, she advocates for a new water ethic that puts water protection at the heart of all policy decisions—economic, trade, agriculture, and energy policy.

Beginning in the 1990s, Barlow sounded the alarm about the threat that trade pacts such as the North American Free Trade Agreement posed to water resources, putting corporate profits above public health and the environment. After years of fighting for water justice, in 2008 she was asked to serve as the senior adviser on water to Miguel d'Escoto Brockmann, the sixty-third president of the United Nations General Assembly, to work for enshrining the human right to water.[10] Together they assembled a team committed to moving this important aspiration forward inside the UN. They coordinated with the international water movement to push nations around the world to vote in favor of the resolution. In 2010 the General Assembly adopted the resolution.[11]

Barlow says, "It was the high point of my working life!" She continued, "It means that whether a country voted for the resolution or not, it is legally required to accept and recognize the right to water." But Barlow fears that the level of water extraction needed for fracking is one more threat to clean water availability.[12]

On average, each fracked well uses upward of 5.7 million gallons of water to drill and operate the well, about fifty times the amount used for conventional oil and gas wells.[13] Half of the shale gas and tight oil being targeted by industry lies beneath regions marked by high water stress, meaning that the amount of water withdrawn for fracking in those regions makes up a very large and unsustainable percentage of the total amount of water available for use.[14] The competition for water between the oil and gas industry and agriculture will only increase as unconventional oil and gas development expands.

A team of hydrologists studied crop-specific water usage and recharge rates to create a model of groundwater depletion.* Groundwater use doubled between 1960 and 2000, and global groundwater stores are vanishing, particularly across the American West.[15]

In Colorado, authorities estimate that the oil and gas industry consumes more than 6 billion gallons of water a year for fracking operations,[16] while total water usage for all stages of oil and gas development is estimated to be as much as 12.8 billion gallons a year.[17] Water law in Colorado treats the resource as a commodity to be sold to the highest bidder.[18] In 2012, fracking companies outbid farmers at the state's major water auction from the Colorado River Basin, water that was not yet allocated to water rights owners in the state.[19]

Water from the Colorado River Basin is chronically overallocated

---

* Recharge is the flow of water into an aquifer, ultimately from precipitation, and the amount of water in an aquifer declines when withdrawal rates exceed the rate of recharge.

because it is based on a very wet period for the region, and its unsustainable use threatens the entire Southwest. Water used for fracking in Utah and on both sides of the Continental Divide in Colorado fails to flow across the Colorado Plateau, through Canyonlands and Grand Canyon national parks, never reaching the chronically drought-stricken Lake Mead on the Arizona-Nevada line. Most years since 1960, the mouth of the Colorado River has been completely dry.[20]

The problem extends beyond overuse of surface water to unsustainable use of groundwater. For ten years Jim Davis has been selling water from five wells near the Black River in New Mexico, a tributary of the Pecos River. Water is pumped into holding tanks and piped directly to the fracking sites. He says the venture provides "substantially more" money than farming in the arid climate.[21] He asserts that some well owners are not playing by the rules, which is "grossly unfair" to those who do. Overpumping in the area has caused some water wells to go dry.[22]

A report by Ceres, a nonprofit organization that provides information on environmental risks to institutional investors, found a significant relationship between groundwater depletion and groundwater use by the petroleum industry. Using information from FracFocus, the industry-sponsored database, Ceres found that almost half of oil and gas wells fracked since 2011 were using water in regions with high or extremely high levels of water stress; more than half were in areas suffering from drought. More than one-third of the wells were in areas with depleted groundwater resources. The petroleum industry consumed 97 billion gallons of water between January 2011 and May 2014, almost half of it in Texas. Chesapeake, EOG Resources, Exxon, and Anadarko were the biggest users, while Halliburton handled the most fracking wastewater at 25 billion gallons, followed by the other two major oil and gas field contractors, Schlumberger and Baker Hughes. Anadarko had the most operations where water scarcity is a problem, with 90 percent of its wells operating in regions with water stress. Apache, Encana, and Pioneer also have fracking operations in water-stressed regions.[23]

The shrinking Ogallala Aquifer—the source of drinking water for four out of the five residents living in the states above it—now faces more depletion from fracking. Overused by agribusiness, it provides water to at least one-fifth of irrigated lands in the nation and is a water source for many of the largest beef feedlots. Stretching 174,000 square miles from South Dakota to northwest Texas, agribusinesses are withdrawing water from the aquifer at a pace more than ten times its recharge rate, meaning that the aquifer will be sucked dry in a matter of decades at current rates.[24]

The Center for Geospatial Technology at Texas Tech has mapped the Ogallala's depletion and estimates that large portions of four counties in the Texas panhandle have fewer than fifteen years of usable water left. Lucia Barbato, associate director of the center, says, "When anybody tells me it's going to last for 50 years, I just laugh."[25]

In the Texas Panhandle, water rights owners can dig a well, suck up water from the Ogallala, and use it for oil and gas extraction, irrespective of drought or the impact on other landowners. Some landowners lease their rights to oil and gas operators or sell water to the service companies that are fracking nearby.[26] Water is drawn from the ground and piped into manmade reservoirs for use by the petroleum industry.

Energy billionaire T. Boone Pickens, a onetime owner of Mesa Water, bought water rights to the Ogallala in several counties in the northeastern part of the Texas Panhandle. Intending to pump it, pipe it, and market it to the highest bidder, Pickens eventually sold most of his water rights to the water authority serving several jurisdictions in West Texas.[27] More recently he has been using water from the Ogallala to frack on the large ranch he owns in the Panhandle. Pickens, like other water rights owners in Texas, faces few restrictions on how much he pumps from the aquifer. Most counties do not require a permit for water withdrawal, because oil and gas drillers are considered in most cases to be an exempt class of water users. Only a few jurisdictions require water wells and usage to be reported.[28]

Oil and gas advocates claim that their water use is low relative to overall water use, but sweeping statistics on water use—averaged over large areas or long periods of time—are deceptive. But if individual counties are examined, as opposed to statewide averages, a different story emerges: intensive fracking creates local water scarcity.[29] For instance, in 2011 water use by the mining sector (almost entirely the petroleum industry) in Wise County, Texas, was estimated to be larger than consumption for municipal, irrigation, and livestock purposes combined.[30] Fracking hundreds of new wells in a concentrated area of a state can add up to a large fraction of the total water consumption.

While the industry claims it recycles water, a report by University of Texas researchers found that only one-fifth of the water for fracking came from recycled or brackish water. They found that the volume of water used for fracking in Texas more than doubled between 2008 and 2011, and they expect it to continue to increase until it levels off in the 2020s.[31]

Not only water-stressed regions are affected by overuse. Researchers studying the Fayetteville and Marcellus Shale formations found that stream flows are adversely affected when water is dammed to create holding ponds or is extracted in large quantities for fracking. They concluded that this concentrated use could cause regional water shortages during droughts and could degrade critical habitat for aquatic species. Reducing stream flows can also concentrate contaminants and negatively affect downstream water quality as less becomes available to dilute pollution.[32]

In 2013 Earthworks analyzed the use of water during the life cycle of fracked wells in Pennsylvania and West Virginia, finding disturbing evidence of the impact of fracking on water resources. Using publicly available data to examine the amount of water pumped from lakes, rivers, and streams for fracking, the researchers found that in West Virginia, 80 percent of the water used for the process comes from surface water. Five million gallons of liquid are injected into each well, with 92 percent remaining underground—removed from the hydrologic cycle.[33]

An earlier assessment of the Monongahela River watershed, conducted in 2011 by the U.S. Army Corps of Engineers, determined that there were "major water resource problems" in northern West Virginia, southwestern Pennsylvania, and the sliver of western Maryland that drains into the river. The report noted that the quantity of water resources, as well as their quality, is a problem in the region. The Corps concluded, "Water in the basin is 'fully tapped' but new sources of pollution such as gas drilling are rapidly growing."[34]

Another example of the excessive pressure on water resources is Encana's operations in Rapid River Township in Kalkaska County, Michigan. Within a span of just days, the company used more than 11 million gallons of water to frack a single well—a scale of intensive industrial water use never seen before in Michigan. When Encana's water wells located not far from Lake Michigan did not produce enough water for the frack job, 3 million more gallons were hauled from the Kalkaska municipal water system.[35]

The same overuse of water is also happening in drought-stricken California, the fruit and vegetable basket of the United States. Democratic governor Jerry Brown signed Senate Bill 4, giving the green light to fracking in the chronically water-stressed state.[36] Brown declared a state of emergency in January 2014 and begged Californians to voluntarily conserve water. By mid-July 2014 the statewide drought had become so serious that restrictions on the outdoor use of water were made mandatory, with fines for offenders.[37] By April 2015, the governor ordered more extensive mandatory water restrictions, requiring that urban demand be slashed by 25 percent—but the oil industry's use of water was left untouched.[38] Further, the Brown administration has refused to close exemptions that are allowing the oil industry to inject wastewater into potentially usable underground sources of drinking water—sources that would require treatment, but which may soon be needed.[39] More alarming, during the drought some companies were selling treated fracking wastewater—which still has been found to contain contaminants in some cases—as irrigation water for farms in California's Central Valley, although no one knows whether this wastewater is potentially contaminating the food that is grown there.[40]

A New Profit Center

Private water companies view water supply and treatment for the petroleum industry as a multibillion-dollar market.[41] Among the most aggressive companies pursuing this strategy are American Water and Aqua America. These publicly traded corporations are dues-paying members of the fracking industry lobby group, the Marcellus Shale Coalition.[42] American Water's retired CEO Jeff Sterba said in 2011, "We're continuing to expand service in the Marcellus Shale region where we have 29 points of interconnection, serving 12 different drilling companies."[43]

Aqua America, the second-largest publicly traded U.S. water utility, is also pursuing the fracking wastewater business. Former CEO Nick De-Benedictis, who retired in July 2014, said, "We're looking at probably the biggest thing to happen to Pennsylvania in the past 30 years, which is the natural gas in the Marcellus Shale. Drilling firms need water to push down the hole to get the gas out. We make some money for our shareholders."[44] DeBenedictis told stockholders, "We are currently pursuing the growth opportunities provided by the shale drilling industry, especially in Pennsylvania's Marcellus Shale, and focusing on the 'clean water' aspects of the drilling business."[45]

Although projections vary, one industry analyst predicted that the total market for treating shale gas wastewater would likely exceed $100 billion over the next forty to fifty years.[46] An anonymous water treatment company executive discussing the immensity of the market off the record told the trade journal *Global Water Intelligence*, "GE is involved, Veolia is involved, Siemens is involved. Most of the people who are major players in the water industry are focused on that market."[47] According to an article in the *Wall Street Journal*, "The growing volume of dirty water produced in shale-gas drilling has triggered a gold rush among water-treatment companies."[48]

Tracking what actually happens to the wastewater is becoming more difficult. Besides the large private water companies, dozens of new start-ups have gotten into the business of treating wastewater in a regulatory environment that is lax.[49] Downstream Strategies attempted to track the eventual disposal of wastewater for a study prepared for Earthworks' Oil & Gas Accountability Project on Pennsylvania and West Virginia. They found it to be impossible, citing lack of accurate data and the various methods of disposal. Staff scientist Meghan Betcher said, "We just couldn't do it."[50]

In February 2011 the *New York Times* reported that radioactive waste-water had been processed in municipal wastewater plants that were not equipped to deal with radiation. The *Times* reviewed more than thirty thousand pages of federal, state, and company records, much of which was obtained from drilling reports accessed by visiting regional offices and from documents obtained by records requests from state and federal regulators. Using "never-reported studies by the E.P.A. and a confidential study by the drilling industry," the *Times* disclosed that wastewater treatment plants had dumped partially treated waste into waterways and that the radioactivity could not be "fully diluted in rivers and other waterways." The *Times* found that 1.3 billion gallons of wastewater were produced by Pennsylvania wells over a three-year period—enough to cover Manhattan three inches deep.[51]

Among the waterways where partially processed fracking waste was dumped were the Monongahela River, which provides drinking water to more than 800,000 people in the western part of Pennsylvania, and the Susquehanna River, which flows into the Chesapeake Bay and provides drinking water to more than 6 million people. Discharges into the Dela-ware River, which provides drinking water for more than 15 million people in Philadelphia and eastern Pennsylvania, were lower than in the other riv-ers. Two wastewater facilities in New York also discharged fracking waste-water into waterways, and at least one plant in West Virginia disposed of partially treated wastewater into the Ohio River.[52]

In April 2015 the EPA released proposed rules on the pretreatment of shale gas wastewater that would ban municipal wastewater treatment plants from receiving untreated wastewater from fracked wells.[53] The EPA said that since frackers have largely stopped sending fracking wastewater to municipal water treatment plants, the proposed rule would not impose costs on the industry, but it also would not generate measurable environmental benefits.[54]

Since the *New York Times* revealed wastewater treatment plants' complicity in fracking pollution, most investor-owned utilities are more tight-lipped about wastewater disposal and business plans. But according to Lux Research, wastewater management continues to be lucrative. Even with the slump in petroleum prices and less fracking, the market is still worth $1.9 billion "for companies that know how to play the opportunity."[55]

Lack of meaningful federal oversight means that wastewater disposal and treatment will remain at the state level. As an intergovernmental panel on the issue put it, "The federal government has largely and deliberately cut itself out of the regulatory picture."[56] And with disposal via deep well injection now proven to cause earthquakes, more wastewater is likely to be disposed of through other means. The result will be that as the water industry pursues more profit, overuse, accidents, and water pollution will threaten water resources into the future.

15

THE REAL COST OF FRACKING INFRASTRUCTURE

I am proud that the U.S. Department of Energy has heeded my calls to
speed its approval of pending liquefied-natural-gas export terminals.
    —Mark Udall, former Democratic senator from Colorado[1]

It was a brutally hot Sunday in the summer of 2014 as I stood on the stage in front of the reflecting pool at the U.S. Capitol looking out at the sea of people voicing opposition to the Federal Energy Regulatory Commission's approval of a proposed liquefied natural gas (LNG) facility in nearby Maryland. Activists from forty different national, state, and local organizations, along with residents of Lusby, Maryland, had convened in the shadow of the Capitol to call out the Obama administration for approving the export of gas to foreign nations and for exposing the neighbors of the Cove Point LNG terminal to untold dangers. Approval of more LNG export facilities will also spur fracking, turning more communities into sacrifice zones. Building these energy-intensive facilities and the necessary infrastructure will generate more greenhouse gas emissions, increasing the carbon footprint of natural gas and amplifying the threat to the global climate.

In the 1990s, most people had never heard of the Federal Energy Regulatory Commission, an independent agency under the Department of Energy. FERC authorizes interstate natural gas pipelines, as well as the connection of liquefied natural gas terminals to these pipelines, while the Department of Energy separately authorizes actual LNG export amounts.[2] FERC faces widespread opposition from around the country for facilitating the export of fracked gas.

By December 2015 the DOE had approved sixteen plans to export gas to countries that do not have free trade agreements with the United States, amounting to more than 5 trillion cubic feet per year (about 20 percent of domestic demand in 2014).[3] Total approved exports to all countries would amount to the equivalent of exporting 60 percent of U.S. production in 2014.[4] The export authorizations are a major reversal of public policy and are designed to give energy companies the right to sell gas into lucrative markets in Asia and Europe. Exports to countries with which the United States has signed a free trade agreement are rubber-stamped, and by law assumed to be in the interest of the public.[5]

Import facilities such as the one at Cove Point have been mostly dormant in recent years, but the overproduction of natural gas has prompted the fracking industry to promote natural gas exports to prop up prices.[6] Because transporting natural gas is difficult, the fuel is liquefied into a form that takes up less space than traditional gas. This involves cooling it to –162 degrees Celsius (–260 degrees Fahrenheit) until the gas turns into a clear, colorless, and cold liquid that, if released, is extremely volatile. It takes a large amount of refrigeration, and thus energy, to make and keep the natural gas in this form.[7]

Upgrading this technology and building storage capacity means that billions of dollars have been sunk into upgrading Cove Point for exports.[8] Over the next three decades, investors expect to enjoy handsome returns on their investments in LNG plants, compressor stations, pipelines, and the other infrastructure that supports the continued exploitation of fracked fossil fuels into the future.

Promotion of exports has changed industry rhetoric from touting energy independence to advocating the consumer benefits of stabilizing prices. Writing in *Forbes*, the directors of a global consulting firm argued that "LNG exports will help to provide better balance between supply and demand in the market, dampening price volatility in North America, and providing circumstances in which industrial gas investments and feedstock natural gas purchases can be made with greater confidence in long-term natural gas pricing. . . . In this sense, it would seem that industrial-community opposition to exports based on perception of price impacts is short sighted."[9] The Center for Liquefied Natural Gas, an industry advocacy group, claims that LNG exports will help with "the U.S. trade balance, U.S. foreign policy and the energy security of our trading partners around the world."[10]

A DOE study on the economic impact of exports qualifies the economic benefits contrary to industry claims, however. The report says, "Impacts will not be positive for all groups in the economy. Households with income solely from wages or government transfers, in particular, might not participate in these benefits."[11] The implication is that the investor class, especially those with income from investments in the oil and gas industry, will benefit, while those who pay for gas, especially wage earners and the working poor, will face higher prices.

Energy Policy Left to the Vagaries of the Market

Originally built in the 1970s to import LNG from Algeria, Cove Point was obsolete by the time it was completed in 1978.[12] Deregulation of natural gas pricing had caused overproduction, and domestic prices were low. The two gas companies that originally built the facility disappeared into a morass of mergers and bankruptcy.[13] In 2002 Cove Point was purchased by Williams, the giant natural gas processing and transportation company, and two years later Dominion Resources paid $217 million for the facility. Reopening in 2003, Cove Point was used for imports, hosting about eighty LNG cargo ships annually.[14] When the fracking boom made imports obsolete, Dominion began retrofitting the facility for exports; it is slated for completion in 2017. Dozens of other export facilities may also be under construction.[15] History shows that this huge expansion in capacity may lead to another boom-and-bust cycle.

Dominion is typical of the giant utility that was created as a result of deregulatory measures and the repeal of the Public Utility Holding Company Act in 2005. (See Introduction.) Owning 24,600 megawatts of electricity generation, it operates nearly 11,000 miles of natural gas pipelines and 6,400 miles of electric transmission lines. Dominion also owns one of the nation's largest natural gas storage systems and serves utility and retail energy customers in ten states.[16] A political and economic powerhouse, the company is also one of the nation's largest polluters of water and air.[17]

Dominion Resources has used its political influence to override local citizens' concerns about Cove Point, which is located fifty miles from the nation's capital and three miles from the Calvert Cliffs nuclear power plant. FERC's environmental review did not adequately address the threat posed by a LNG-related accident involving a nuclear power plant. Stockpiles of highly volatile and toxic chemicals will be located at the export facility.[18]

The Congressional Research Service wrote that LNG facilities present "serious hazards . . . since LNG is inherently volatile and is usually shipped and stored in large quantities." Its report remarked that super-hot fires above LNG spills "cannot be extinguished" and produce flammable vapor

Dominion Resources

Growth of one of the largest energy companies in America

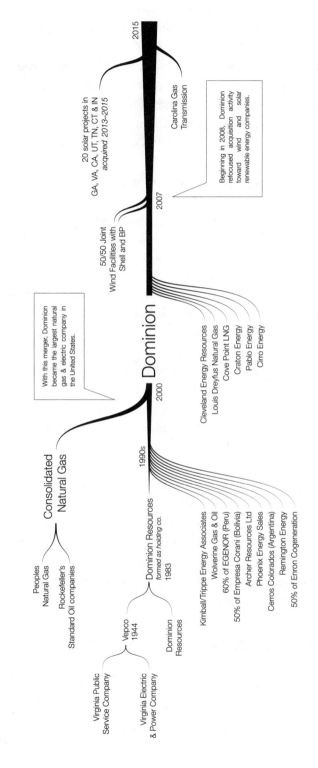

Virginia Public Service Company

Virginia Electric & Power Company

Vepco 1944

Dominion Resources

Dominion Resources
formed as holding co.
1983

Kimball/Trippe Energy Associates
Wolverine Gas & Oil
60% of EGENOR (Peru)
50% of Empresa Corani (Bolivia)
Archer Resources Ltd
Phoenix Energy Sales
Cerros Colorados (Argentina)
Remington Energy
50% of Enron Cogeneration

1990s

Peoples Natural Gas
Rockefeller's Standard Oil companies

Consolidated Natural Gas

Dominion

2000

With this merger, Dominion became the largest natural gas & electric company in the United States.

Cleveland Energy Resources
Louis Dreyfus Natural Gas
Cove Point LNG
Craton Energy
Pablo Energy
Cirro Energy

50/50 Joint Wind Facilities with Shell and BP

2007

Beginning in 2008, Dominion refocused acquisition activity toward wind and solar renewable energy companies.

20 solar projects in GA, VA, CA, UT, TN, CT & IN
acquired 2013–2015

2015

Carolina Gas Transmission

clouds that could cause "considerable damage."[19] An accident at Cove Point involving the explosive fuels and chemicals could trigger a fireball, with calamitous results for the more than 830 people who live within a mile and a quarter of the facility.[20] A catastrophic accident at Cove Point would also have adverse effects on the Chesapeake Bay, the largest estuary in the United States. "FERC has put blinders on in failing to look at the true impacts of this project," said Betsy Nicholas, executive director of Waterkeepers Chesapeake.[21]

A recent accident points to the potential danger. In March 2014 five workers were seriously injured and a thousand people had to be evacuated in a two-mile radius near Plymouth, Washington, after an accident occurred at the Williams LNG terminal. A pipeline exploded within the facility, sending shrapnel flying into a 14.6-million-gallon storage tank, cracking it and causing the LNG leak.[22]

LNG export facilities also require thousands of miles of new and often larger pipelines. Maya van Rossum, a Delaware Riverkeeper, says that pipeline development is "destroying forests, cutting through creeks, irreparably transforming wetlands, causing more polluted runoff, and decimating habitat critical to creatures in our region."[23]

To keep the piped gas moving to Cove Point, compressor stations must be built along pipelines in communities near Baltimore and Washington, D.C. This battle over compressor stations is heated in Frederick County, Maryland, where Dominion Resources plans to build a large compressor station to pump natural gas, compounding local air pollution problems.[24] Already more than 450 natural gas compressor stations and processing plants have been built in Pennsylvania since 2008.[25] While the impact of each facility is considered in isolation, the aggregate emissions from these facilities have caused additional tonnage of pollutants to be released into the air, including formaldehyde, volatile organic chemicals, nitrogen oxide, and other greenhouse gases. To those living in close proximity to compressor stations, the air emissions present a severe health hazard.

Knowing the Right People Pays

While Cove Point is a retrofit project by a major utility, Sabine Pass on Louisiana's Gulf coast is owned by Cheniere Energy Partners, a business venture with no track record in running large energy projects. In 2011, after a review lasting only nine months, the DOE authorized Sabine Pass to be the first terminal in the lower forty-eight states approved for exporting gas to non-free-trade-agreement countries.* In 2012 it became the first to clear FERC's environmental review.[26]

The company's flamboyant former CEO, Charif Souki, an Egyptian-born businessman who grew up in Beirut speaking Arabic and French, was the most highly rewarded executive in 2013, enjoying a $142 million compensation package. Souki was fired by the company's board in December 2015.

The oversized financial rewards that Cheniere executives have garnered prompted a large shareholder to sue the company. Kent Hughes, a managing director of the shareholder advisory firm Egan-Jones Proxy Services, says Souki's compensation is "just over the top."[27]

The son of a correspondent for *Newsweek* in the 1950s and 1960s, Souki describes his younger self as "fairly restless and rambunctious." After graduating from Columbia University's business school, he used his language skills and Ivy League credentials to land a job with an investment banking firm, pitching investments to Middle Eastern oil barons and socializing with Saudi royal family members.[28]

Souki and his second wife, *Sports Illustrated* swimsuit model Rita Tellone, moved to Aspen, Colorado. He opened Mezzaluna, a watering spot in downtown Aspen patronized by the likes of Jack Nicholson and Hunter S. Thompson. Souki and his brother opened a chain of restaurants and bars, eventually moving his family to Los Angeles.[29] In the Brentwood area of the city, his second Mezzaluna location was frequented by well-known Hollywood figures, becoming notorious in the aftermath of the double murder of Souki's employee Ron Goldman and Nicole Brown Simpson, who were at the restaurant on the night of the murders.[30]

Souki began a third career in 1996, starting a small offshore petroleum exploration company that he named Cheniere. Only marginally successful as a wildcatter, he relied on his network of Wall Street and Middle Eastern business cronies to raise cash for the company, planning to use new seismic data to prospect for petroleum in the Gulf of Mexico. Moving his family to Houston, he was in the right spot to benefit from the election of President George W. Bush in 2000.[31] Bush pushed to jump-start development of LNG storage and import terminals along the Gulf Coast, which aligned neatly with Souki's planned import facility, Sabine Pass.[32]

---

* The DOE took thirty months to approve the next LNG facility, Freeport LNG, located in Freeport, Texas.

Souki developed mutually beneficial economic relationships with powerful people. This cast of characters included Neil Bush, President George W. Bush's younger brother, and Spencer Abraham, the former Bush energy secretary who lobbied for Cheniere.[33] The board has included John Deutch, who was director of the CIA from 1995 to 1996 and served as chair of a DOE advisory committee on natural gas. Deutch was an author of the MIT study "The Future of Natural Gas," which was led by President Obama's current energy secretary, Ernest Moniz.[34] Vicky Bailey, another board member, was an assistant secretary in the Office of Policy and International Affairs at DOE from 2001 to 2004 and a former FERC commissioner from 1993 to 2000. Former Obama point person on energy and climate, Heather Zichal, is also a board member.[35] (See Chapter 12.)

By 2008, when Sabine Pass was ready to import, it had accrued $2 billion in debt and was obsolete because of fracked gas. On the day that Sabine Pass had its grand opening, the company's management learned that Moody's was about to downgrade its stock. So while the guests ate Cajun food and fought off mosquitoes, the company lost 36 percent of its value in just one day. Half of the company's 360 employees were soon laid off, losing their jobs in the midst of the nation's subprime mortgage crisis, and as fracking for shale gas boomed.[36]

Souki quickly changed course, transforming Sabine Pass into an export facility. Jetting around the world, he enticed investors to spend more than $7 billion on the export facility. Most remarkably, he influenced the Obama administration's approval process.[37]

Cheniere will have a virtual monopoly on U.S. LNG exports until other companies build their facilities. Slated for completion in 2016, Sabine has five massive storage tanks with a capacity of 17 billion cubic feet of natural gas—about one-quarter of the amount used each day in the entire United States.[38]

Pressure has been growing to allow export facilities to be built on the West Coast, with demand for LNG across the Pacific growing every year. Increased demand for LNG is not just coming from China and the developing economies in the region; Japan's turn to gas generation in the wake of the country's 2011 Fukushima nuclear disaster only added to this demand, creating premium prices for LNG exported to Asia.[39] Two of the proposed LNG terminals in Oregon that have already been given approval are especially well positioned to sell into markets in Japan, China, India, and other countries.[40]

The Ruby Pipeline, and Beyond

Pipelines foisted on the public to transport natural gas from remote wells to LNG terminals, power plants, and urban markets are increasingly controversial. Buried at variable depths, carrying volatile and hazardous hydrocarbons, the systems experience leaks, failures, and accidents. The U.S. Department of Transportation reports a total of 10,991 reported pipeline incidents with varying degrees of seriousness from 1994 to August 2014. There have been 370 deaths and 1,424 injuries associated with pipeline accidents involving the transport of gas, oil, and other hazardous materials between 1994 and 2013, and a total cost of $6.1 billion in damages.[41] More recently, a 2015 investigative piece by *Politico* found that in 2014 alone "more than 700 pipeline failures killed 19 people, injured 97 and caused more than $300 million in damage."[42]

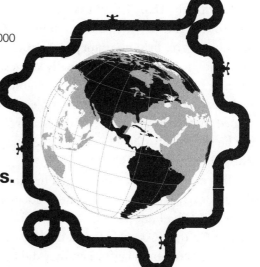

Between 1984 and 2014, gas companies added at least 936,000 miles of pipeline in the United States—about 85 miles every day.

There are now at least 2.5 million miles of natural gas pipelines nationwide.

**That's enough to circle Earth
more than 100 times.**

Pipeline construction was accelerated by natural gas deregulation in the early 1980s and 1990s.[43] And although the gas industry has had booms and busts on top of deregulation, pipeline construction has been growing steadily. Between 1984 and 2014 gas companies added at least 936,000 miles of pipeline—about 85 miles every day—and there are now 2.5 million miles

of transmission, distribution, and gathering lines.[44] This is likely a significant undercount of new pipelines because many states do not regulate or
track the construction of gathering pipelines. And hundreds of thousands
of miles of rural gathering lines are necessary for connecting the thousands
of fracked wells to larger pipelines.[45]

The almost 680-mile-long Ruby Pipeline, owned and operated by
Kinder Morgan (see Chapter 6), running between Wyoming and Oregon, exemplifies the destructive and expensive infrastructure that moves
fracked gas to urban or overseas markets. Crossing more than a thousand
rivers and streams in some of the most remote and unspoiled wilderness
in the nation, the Ruby Pipeline has impacted crucial habitat for several
endangered species and wreaked havoc on private and public lands.[46] The
lengthy battle over the controversial pipeline provides more evidence of
FERC's poor track record on assessing the impacts of infrastructure. FERC
based its July 2010 approval of the pipeline on an inadequate assessment of
the risks by the Department of the Interior.

In 2008 the U.S. Fish and Wildlife Service, which is part of the Department of the Interior, sent a letter to FERC raising concerns about the serious impacts on fish, migratory birds and other natural resources. Several
mitigation measures were originally suggested by the service, but with the
ensuing political pressure in favor of building the pipeline, these were not
included in the final review of the project.[47] Most glaringly, the service concluded that a rupture at one of the hundreds of waterways crossed "would
not be reasonably likely to occur," and as a result "the Service will not address pipeline ruptures."[48]

This conclusion was challenged in a long legal battle to block the pipeline's construction based on the inadequate environmental assessment.
After FERC had allowed the construction of the pipeline, the Ninth U.S.
Circuit Court of Appeals found that federal agencies had violated the nation's environmental laws when they did their initial assessment.[49]

Noah Greenwald, endangered species director at the Center for Biological Diversity, the organization that brought the original lawsuit along with
Defenders of Wildlife and the Summit Lake Paiute Tribe, said, "We wish
the Ruby pipeline had never been built, but since it was, it's crucial that
everything possible is done to minimize harm to the endangered fish that
live along its route."[50] Unfortunately, this was not to be the case.

In November 2013, based on the court-ordered biological assessment,
which was equally as inadequate as the original one, the Bureau of Land

Management (BLM) reauthorized the illegally built pipeline and refused to mitigate environmental damage. Amy Atwood, senior attorney for the Center for Biological Diversity, charged, "This pipeline destroyed thousands of acres of diminishing sage grouse habitat . . . and there's no excuse for BLM's arbitrary decision not to mitigate that."[51]

The Ruby Pipeline moves gas from southwestern Wyoming to the Malin Market Center in southern Oregon, where it interconnects with other pipelines, such as the Williams Northwest Pipeline. Natural gas deregulation spurred the development of a system of hubs, where pipelines interconnect.* In the 1990s, after FERC separated the sale of gas from its transportation, the hubs became profit-generating trading platforms, with administrative services for the companies that were buying, selling, and trading gas. The twenty-eight market centers† located across the country play a central role both in physically moving gas and in setting spot market prices for it, as well as in futures trading.[52]

Opal Hub serves as the market center for Wyoming's Jonah and Anticline fields, among others, and sets the price for the spot market in the region.[53] The Rocky Mountain gas is slated to go through Wyoming's Opal Hub and be piped west to the Malin Center in Oregon. From here, it would be piped to the proposed LNG terminal, Jordan Cove, on Oregon's Coos Bay.[54] The contentious $7.5 billion project would include an LNG terminal, the 230-mile Pacific Connector, and a natural-gas-fired power plant. It is being developed through a partnership between Canadian-based Veresen and Williams.[55]

The Pacific Connector poses significant threats to the communities along its route.[56] Crossing public and private land, it would require a 230-mile-long, 95-foot-wide swath of land to be clear-cut, fragmenting forests and impacting four hundred streams and rivers at the expense of

---

* "Market center," "market hub," and "hub" are sometimes used interchangeably. But technically a hub is where gas pipelines converge and gas is moved forward to markets; processing facilities are also often located on site. Today, market centers and market hubs generally offer the same services. They have facilities for buying, selling, storing, and transporting gas and offer information and electronic trading services. They can loan gas and carry out intra-hub transfers of gas.

† Henry Hub, located in Erath, Louisiana, serves as the primary pricing point for natural gas futures contracts traded on the NYMEX. It interconnects nine interstate and four intrastate pipelines.

salmon habitat. At each crossing, the pipe would be elevated or a tunnel would be drilled for it.[57]

Building the pipeline would subject nearly seven hundred landowners to eminent domain, forcing them to sell an easement for the pipeline even if they object.[58] Landowners accuse Williams of using hardball tactics to seize land and trample on property rights. Complaints include offering "insultingly low" prices for easements and threatening property owners by saying they would not even recover attorneys' fees if they go to court.[59] Rogue Riverkeeper has been challenging the project's impacts on salmon populations and the potential for pipeline ruptures.

Two LNG terminal projects are also garnering stiff opposition. Citizens Against LNG, a volunteer citizens organization on Oregon's South Coast, has mobilized hundreds of people to comment on FERC proposals and attend public hearings. Jody McCaffree calls the Jordan Cove project "total insanity" for proposing to build an LNG import-export terminal "on a sand spit, across from an airport, in the flight path of the runway in a tsunami inundation zone and earthquake subduction zone."[60]

Geologists say that a serious quake takes place in the Coos Bay area every 240 years, and they calculate that there is a 40 percent chance of a "mega-thrust quake" in the next fifty years. The fault line that would cause the catastrophic accident runs parallel to the coast of Oregon, eight miles from where the terminal and a power plant are to be located. The geology of the area mirrors the site of Japan's devastating 9.1 earthquake and tsunami.[61]

The other liquefied gas project, Oregon LNG, is proposed for the mouth of the Columbia River near the coastal tourist town Astoria. Leucadia, a large financial holding company with $52.6 billion in assets, is planning the facility.[62] If built, the Oregon LNG project would threaten fragile wetlands at the mouth of the Columbia River, destroy critical habitat for endangered salmon, and significantly increase shipping traffic.[63] The company says in documents filed at FERC that the terminal will bring 127 additional ships to the river each year.[64] Many of the newer LNG tanker carriers are massive in size, up to twenty stories high and three football fields long.[65]

Community leaders are confident about galvanizing opposition to the project. Several organizations in the Northwest were victorious in a David-and-Goliath battle that culminated in 2010 when the proposed Bradwood LNG terminal was not built.[66] Brett VandenHeuvel, executive director of Columbia Riverkeeper, called the battle his organization helped lead "a tremendous victory for family farmers, fishermen, and Columbia River salmon."[67]

The organization has also been among the groups working in a cross-state border coalition to stop the 140-mile Williams Washington Expansion pipeline project, which would add to Williams's already extensive Northwest Pipeline system. If all parts of the Northwest Pipeline are allowed to move forward, it would include nearly four thousand miles of pipe, transporting fracked gas from Canada, Wyoming, Utah, and Colorado to the Pacific Northwest.[68]

The Pacific Northwest has had several serious pipeline accidents over the past sixteen years. A dangerous accident occurred near Auburn, Washington when a section of Williams Northwest Pipeline ruptured in 2003, causing an explosion that shot rock and debris hundreds of feet, forcing nearby residents to evacuate.[69] In 1999 Williams Northwest exploded in rural Umatilla County, Oregon, leaving ten thousand customers without heat for several days.[70]

Fighting Back

Landowners and fracking activists are having some success in fighting pipelines, especially when permitting can be stopped locally. In Kentucky, local resistance was key to stopping the Bluegrass Pipeline, in which Williams owned a 50 percent stake.[71] It would have transported natural gas liquids from fracked-gas processing facilities in the Northeast to petrochemical factories along the Gulf Coast.[72] FERC grants natural gas pipeline companies eminent domain if it determines that construction would serve the public interest.[73] But granting eminent domain for a natural gas liquids pipeline, rather than a natural gas pipeline, is a state-by-state issue. In Kentucky, landowner resistance and a groundswell of libertarian fervor was key in stopping the project.[74] But other proposed pipelines threaten the region.

Another big pipeline project is garnering major opposition from its threat to the Big Bend region of Texas. Three and a half feet in diameter—even bigger than the Keystone XL—the Trans-Pecos Pipeline would cut through the heart of an area renowned for its rugged beauty, sweeping landscapes, dark nighttime skies, and unique flora and fauna. It would require new roads and infrastructure that would harm one of the last wilderness areas in the United States. The Big Bend Conservation Alliance is coordinating efforts to keep the project from being approved.[75]

Although sometimes activists cannot stop the undemocratic process at FERC, the mobilization to halt these projects is part of building a movement with the political power to bring about the major legislative changes necessary to reform the FERC process, including taking away their right to declare eminent domain.

The fight over Spectra's $1.2 billion pipeline in New York City is one example. The company faced fierce opposition from the Sane Energy Project as it dug under the Hudson River, laying a pipeline from New Jersey to Manhattan's densely populated West Village. Transporting 800 million barrels of fracked gas from the Marcellus into the city every day, the large-diameter, highly pressurized pipeline could cause a devastating explosion.[76] The high radon content of fracked gas from the Marcellus poses a health threat to New Yorkers living in poorly ventilated apartments.*

Since the Spectra pipeline battle, Sane Energy has increased its opposition to fracked gas, helping to organize against the 124 infrastructure projects in the state that it has identified. Claire Donahue, co-founder of the Sane Energy Project, sums up the sentiments of the thousands of activists around the nation working on these issues: "They built a pipeline, we built a movement."[77]

---

* Radon is a colorless, odorless, and tasteless radioactive gas that is the second-leading cause of lung cancer in the United States. While radon is present outdoors in most areas of the country, it is dangerous to human health when trapped indoors. It is a product of the radioactive decay of radium, which is present in the Marcellus formation, and in the ancient brines brought to the surface along with shale gas in Pennsylvania.

16

EXXON: MORE POWERFUL THAN EVER

The consequences of a misstep in a [fracked shale gas] well, while large to the immediate people that live around that well, in the great scheme of things are pretty small, and even to the immediate people around the well, they could be mitigated. These are not life-threatening, they're not long-lasting, and they're not new.

—Rex Tillerson, chairman and CEO, ExxonMobil,
at a presentation to the U.S. Council on Foreign Relations in 2012[1]

When future historians give their verdict on the twenty-first century, Exxon will be a top contender for committing the worst crimes against the earth. In recent years the behemoth's attempts to derail action on climate change, while becoming the largest producer of fracked gas, have added to its record of secrecy, intimidation, and lies. And even with the decline in natural gas and oil prices, Exxon's profits were $32.5 billion in 2014.[2]

At the national headquarters, nicknamed the "Death Star," a culture of arrogance prevails. Exxon, with operations in fifty countries, has been the most profitable publicly traded company in the world for decades.[3]

Exxon—originally Standard Oil of New Jersey—has always been the largest of the Baby Standards. Created from the 1911 breakup of John D. Rockefeller's Standard Oil, the company historically has followed an aggressive strategy of growth through acquisition. In 1959 it jumped in size when its notoriously arrogant CEO, Monroe "Jack" Rathbone, finalized a buyout of Humble Oil Company, itself one of the largest petroleum corporations at the time. Within six years of the merger, the much larger company's profits had nearly doubled.[4] A chemical engineer, "Mr. Jack" spent forty-four years with the company he called "Jersey." Credited with revolutionizing the refining process for oil during World War II, Rathbone

Reconsolidation of Big Oil: Seven Sisters Through the 20th Century

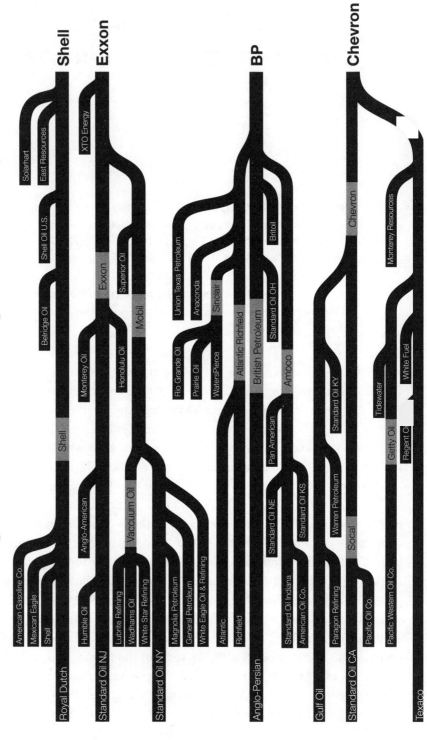

increased the company's international reach dramatically, raising its profits to more than $1 billion in 1964.[5]

Known for his overconfidence and unwillingness to listen to his colleagues or staff, Rathbone, a West Virginia native and a descendant of Confederate Civil War general Stonewall Jackson, played a major role in prompting the formation of the Organization of the Petroleum Exporting Countries (OPEC).[6] In 1960 he unilaterally reduced the posted price of oil, a move that lowered the monies paid to the oil-producing nations.* Taking this action against the advice of the company's Middle East negotiator and the other members of the Seven Sisters, he also failed to comply with his board's direction on the matter.[7] In 1972 Humble merged with its parent, Standard Oil of New Jersey, absorbing its long-standing "independent" subsidiaries such as Humble and Esso to become Exxon.[8]

Lee Raymond, president and chairman of Exxon during some of the company's most turbulent times, spent more than forty years at the oil giant, beginning as a young chemical engineer. Promoted to president in 1987, he became chairman in 1993, retiring in 2005. Upon his departure, the man who terrified everyone—from his employees to Wall Street analysts—received a $398 million compensation package, one of the largest on record. Exxon picked up his country club fees, financial planning costs, and even a personal driver for two years.[9]

Raymond succeeded Lawrence Rawl, a petroleum engineer who came to Exxon with the Humble merger.[10] Rawl's career took a nosedive following his mishandling of the 1989 *Exxon Valdez* accident in Alaska's Prince William Sound. The grounding of the loaded tanker ship caused the worst oil-related catastrophe up to that time, spilling almost 11 million gallons of oil and despoiling more than 1,100 miles of coastline.[11] Even a quarter century later, the aftereffects of the spill are still lingering: only a third of the monitored wildlife populations have recovered, and tens of thousands of gallons of oil still taint the shores.[12]

A formidable opponent, Raymond played hardball in the litigation over the *Exxon Valdez* accident, defending the company's actions after the spill.[13] Stubbornly refusing to pay punitive fines but willing to pay $400 million to its corporate defense attorneys, Raymond dragged litigation on for decades.

* The posted price was the basis for splitting revenues with oil-producing countries. The OPEC nations were already angry that the major oil companies did not fairly compensate them for oil.

The company's appeal, which reached the U.S. Supreme Court, established a legal precedent regarding environmental damages that benefits polluters.[14]

More powerful than the leaders of most countries, Raymond worked from a suite known as the "God Pod" in the company's fortress-like headquarters in Irving, Texas. Despite Exxon's many requests to the United States for help on various matters—and the taxpayer subsidies it enjoys—Raymond was quoted as saying, "I'm not a U.S. company, and I don't make decisions based on what's good for the U.S."[15] Exxon stands apart in the magnitude of its profits and in the political and economic power it has wielded over the past century.

Under Raymond, Exxon launched a disinformation campaign to cast doubt on the science around global warming, while bullying climate scientists.[16] An unapologetic climate-change denier, his strategy went beyond traditional lobbying to stop U.S. ratification of the Kyoto Protocol, the international climate agreement with binding targets for emissions reductions.[17] In 1998 a memo was leaked from a meeting Raymond attended at the American Petroleum Institute. He was quoted as describing a strategy of giving "logistical and moral support" to climate change skeptics, "thereby raising questions about and undercutting the 'prevailing scientific wisdom.' "[18]

Greenpeace has documented that from 1998 to 2006 Exxon spent at least $25 million funding climate denial efforts.[19] Although the company pledged in 2007 to stop this funding, in 2015 researchers revealed that Exxon continued to fund Harvard climate skeptic Dr. Willie Soon through 2010.[20] As this book goes to press, Exxon is under investigation by New York's attorney general, Eric T. Schneiderman, for lying to the public about the risks proposed by climate change.

Exxon also spends heavily to influence public policy in the United States and worldwide. Exxon spent $208 million lobbying the U.S. Congress and federal agencies between 2008 and 2015, according to figures from political watchdog group the Center for Responsive Politics, making it one of the top five corporate lobbying spenders for more than a decade and a half.[21] The company was also the largest spender in lobbying the European Union in 2014, along with Microsoft and Shell, spending more than €4.7 million ($5.3 million) lobbying on energy and environmental issues, including specifically promoting fracking and "natural gas policy including shale gas" in the EU.[22]

Exxon is a member of BusinessEurope, the largest corporate lobby organization in the EU, similar to the U.S. Chamber of Commerce. Claiming that shale gas can be produced sustainably, the trade association regularly lobbies against protective actions on fracking. A member of the influential International Oil and Gas Producers Association, Exxon has benefited from the impact the powerful trade association has had with the European Commission.[23]

Raymond's worldview is similar to that of his longtime friend, former U.S. vice president Dick Cheney. Former neighbors in Dallas, the men and their wives began socializing when Cheney was CEO of Halliburton, the oil and gas services company. The two couples also met at retreats and meetings of the Koch-funded American Enterprise Institute, where Raymond was on the board and Lynne Cheney was a senior fellow. During the Bush presidency, Raymond met two or three times a year with Cheney on energy policy.[24]

Raymond summed up his attitude about Washington this way: "Presidents come and go; Exxon doesn't come and go." And his easy access to Cheney and the White House was nothing new. Raymond also had access when Democrats were in the White House. He said that Exxon's access to the Clinton administration was similar to what the company enjoyed in the Reagan years.[25]

Raymond successfully merged Exxon with Mobil, then the third-largest petroleum company. At the time BP, the second-largest company, had already merged with Amoco and was pursuing a merger with Atlantic Richfield (ARCO). President Clinton's Federal Trade Commission had barely blinked in approving the reunion of these various offspring of Standard Oil. The merged entity ExxonMobil had assets of $135 billion, becoming twice as large as the merged BP/Amoco/ARCO.[26]

Although the petroleum industry has changed with the rising dominance of several large, state-owned companies, Exxon's power and influence have not diminished. While Saudi Arabia's Aramco, Russia's Gazprom, and Iran's National Iranian Oil Company surpassed Exxon in output during 2014, Exxon is still the largest and most profitable publicly traded oil company in the world, and among the largest corporations worldwide.[27] State-owned oil companies often depend on Exxon to provide assistance with new technologies, such as those used for fracking. Exxon invests in the operations of these companies, partnering in joint ventures and strategic alliances.[28]

Since Rex Tillerson replaced Lee Raymond in 2006, Exxon has continued to use its political muscle not only domestically but also internationally. For instance, in 2010, ExxonMobil and Halliburton were among the twenty companies lobbying to stop tightened sanctions against Iran, a move that they said would cost the United States $25 billion in lost exports.[29] In 2013 the oil minister of Iran named Exxon as one of the companies that Iran would like to engage with in the future.[30] Exxon bridled at limitations on investment and business with Iran because that country has the fourth-largest reserves of oil and the second-largest reserves of natural gas.[31] On January 20, 2014, after some sanctions were eased, Bloomberg reported that shipments of crude oil and condensate from Iran increased 28 percent.[32]

Exxon's management has opposed sanctions on Russia, spending $12.6 million lobbying the White House, State Department, and Congress on Russian sanctions, among other issues, in 2014.[33] Russian president Vladimir Putin honored the Exxon chief with the Order of Friendship during an economic forum in St. Petersburg.[34] In their first joint venture, costing $3.2 billion, Exxon and its Russian state-owned partner found oil and gas in the Kara Sea, but the project reached this milestone just a week before the sanctions took effect in September 2014. Under the new sanctions, Exxon was forced to wind down its role in the exploration.[35] Exxon hired Mike Solon, a well-connected lobbyist who formerly worked for Republican senators Phil Gramm, Trent Lott, and Mitch McConnell, to lobby against the sanctions.[36]

Exxon wants the ability to partner with Russia's state-owned oil companies, giving it access to its vast petroleum reserves.[37] Future joint ventures include drilling in the Black Sea and fracking in Siberia, the location of enormous petroleum resources. Exxon will be able to count these reserves on its books, covering its ongoing problem of proving to regulators and Wall Street that the company has enough oil and gas reserves to replace the amount that it produced during the previous year.[38]

The actual estimation of reserves is controversial, leaving regulators and investors guessing about the accuracy. Both Raymond and Tillerson have misrepresented Exxon's actual proven reserves to Wall Street, at times by not using the approved accounting methods in reporting to the Securities and Exchange Commission.[39]

Exxon Under Tillerson's Watch

Tillerson has continued on the path of his predecessors, gambling on big deals, giant acquisitions, and big engineering projects. In 2010 Exxon announced that 10,000 of its nearly 84,000 employees would be consolidated at a new headquarters, the largest corporate complex in the world, featuring twenty office buildings, child care facilities, and a wellness center on 385 acres in a community near Houston that was developed by George Mitchell.[40]

Tillerson also has approached fracking in a big way, having had experience with the technology after joining Exxon in 1976 as a production engineer.[41] Tillerson was assigned to follow natural gas drilling rigs around East Texas that were experimenting with fracking methods. He designed experimental fracking programs by using punch cards in a computer. Tillerson reminisced about the bitter temperatures: "I would stand between those big fracking tanks to stay warm, because the water's heated. I'd stay there until they were ready to crank those babies up, and then I'd have to go out into the weather."[42]

More than three decades later he decided that with public policies favoring natural gas, it was time to expand Exxon's position. Exxon's internal forecasts showed that gas demand would rise significantly over the next twenty years. Tillerson was compelled "to do something about natural gas."[43]

In 2009 he began merger discussions with Bob Simpson, the founder of XTO, a large oil and gas company. Simpson had grown XTO by gambling on the futures and derivatives market and then purchasing oil and gas properties at the bottom of the market.[44] The company fracked the conventional wells on these properties, becoming extremely profitable. Hoping to operate in every major U.S. shale play, Simpson went on an $11 billion shopping spree that included paying top dollar for Hunt Petroleum Corporation and other properties. In October 2008, when the economy crashed, a margin call forced him to sell 30 percent of his XTO holdings.[45]

Soon Tillerson came calling. XTO was merged into Exxon in a stock transfer worth $24.7 billion, becoming a subsidiary.[46] One of the drivers for the massive deal went back to Exxon's ongoing challenge of having sufficient resources to replace annual production. The 2009 weakening of the rules by the SEC to allow unconventional oil and gas resources to more easily meet the requirements for proven reserves meant that Exxon could count XTO's large shale gas holdings.[47] Eight million acres of land sat above the XTO holdings, about the size of Massachusetts and Connecticut combined.[48]

Exxon Fracks the World

Exxon's website touts operations in almost twenty European countries, and its fracking efforts originally were focused on Poland, Hungary, Germany, Ukraine, and Turkey.[49] It since has pulled out of Poland and Hungry and has had only preliminary talks about a joint venture with a state-owned company in Turkey. In Ukraine Exxon signed a deal with the state-owned company Naftogaz, but the political upheaval there has made the country less attractive for development.[50]

In Poland, the government and industry were enthusiastic about pursuing fracked gas, but farmers and rural communities opposed fracking. ExxonMobil halted exploration after completing testing at two wells, and sold its concessions to state-owned PKN Orlen. Multiple reasons were suggested for the hasty exit, including the fact that the Polish government considered taxing profits at rates up to 40 percent.[51]

Exxon has pursued fracking in Germany much more aggressively than in other European countries. The company acquired leases on 750,000 acres in Lower Saxony, located in the far northwest. The largest country in the European Union, Germany has a strong industrial base and is also the largest natural gas user in the EU.[52] Awareness about fracking has changed dramatically since 2006, when ExxonMobil fracked a new gas reservoir and received a high-profile Germany—Land of Ideas award and was celebrated by local politicians for what was viewed as an engineering feat.[53]

When news spread that some residents living near the coalbed methane fracking operations in Lower Saxony had developed cancer, opposition to fracking intensified. Locals learned about benzene leaking from ExxonMobil plastic wastewater pipes—three years after Exxon notified the German regulators of the potential leak. Farmers purportedly found concentrations of benzene many times higher than what is considered dangerous. Residents were concerned about the potential contamination of their water supplies by the known carcinogen benzene, especially following a spike in cancer cases in at least one nearby town.[54]

German fracking activist Andy Gheorghiu says that Exxon's accident in Lower Saxony, which he calls "the Texas of Germany," woke people up to the dangers of fracking. Gheorghiu left his job at the building permits department where he lives in Korbach, Hessen, to work full-time stopping fracking.[55] Local grassroots groups have taken the lead in alerting people about the dangers, according to Gheorghiu. In the region where he lives, in central Germany, forty thousand people have joined the campaign to stop fracking. Knowledge about the environmental damage also grew with the 2010 release of Josh Fox's movie *Gasland*, further helping to galvanize German opposition. The organizing efforts have resulted in Hessen denying exploration licenses and in North Rhine–Westphalia, a state to the west that includes the large cities of Cologne and Dusseldorf, an official moratorium was adopted.

Meanwhile, Germany's Green Party has been politically powerful enough to begin moving the country away from polluting energy sources and investing in renewable energy—an effort known as the *Energiewende* (energy transition). While also topping the world in energy efficiency measures, Germany's economy continues to show steady growth.[56] Ironically, the country's plans to phase out nuclear power by 2022 and to achieve zero carbon emissions in the electricity sector by 2050 are being used as an argument for fracking.[57] Despite public support for the shift away from conventional fuels, many industrial leaders are pressing for more natural gas development.[58]

Exxon has expended enormous resources in Germany to change public opinion, funding an expensive propaganda campaign with full-page ads in leading newspapers and magazines and running thirty-second TV spots before the most popular nightly news program. Featuring testimonials from Exxon engineers about safety, the ads use phrases that translate to "environmental friendliness," "safe," and "responsible." The company spent liberally in an effort to show that it was a good corporate citizen. To address safety concerns, staff were sent around the country to citizen forums, hearings, and local meetings.[59]

In 2011 Exxon spent €1 million ($1.4 million) on an initiative that was advertised as a "participatory stakeholder consultation process" and a "neutral" risk assessment of hydraulic fracturing. The results of the expert panel were presented at online "info-dialogues" where participants were told that there was no reason to ban fracking and that, while there were major and minor risks, the risks are manageable, echoing the opinion of the U.S. Department of Energy secretary Ernest Moniz, the chief fracking advocate in the Obama administration.

The Berlin national daily newspaper *Tageszeitung* criticized the Exxon process as a "pseudo-dialogue" that was "cosmetic" and "manipulative" in the effort to give legitimacy to its fracking operations. The paper pointed out that the company had attempted to give the "illusion" of a dialogue of equals: on one side were farmers and small-town officials and on the other were distinguished researchers and powerful corporate executives. By limiting the discussion topics, Exxon had prevented a meaningful debate on future energy policies and on the long-term environmental devastation associated with continued reliance on fossil fuels.[60]

In the summer of 2014 German chancellor Angela Merkel's energy ministry announced a plan to move forward with fracking regulations that would allow drilling for shale gas, a step that the industry believed could help open Europe to fracking.[61] To counteract the widespread opposition to allowing the no-holds-barred fracking boom of the United States to migrate to Germany, fracking advocates attempted to confuse the public by claiming that German regulations would ban shale fracking and allow fracking only of tight sand formations.[62] Activists decried this move, pointing out that the same dangers of fracking shale apply to its use in producing tight gas.

In February 2015 the German government released a draft law allowing commercial shale gas fracking at depths exceeding three thousand meters (almost ten thousand feet), putting an end to the de facto moratorium in the country. An expert panel would be created to review fracking projects at shallower depths on a case-by-case basis. Maria Krautzberger, president of the country's federal environment agency, told the *Guardian*: "It is important to have a legal framework for hydraulic fracturing. . . . We have had a voluntary agreement with the big companies that there would be no fracking, but if a company like Exxon wanted, they might do it anyway as there is no way to forbid it."[63] If the draft law is finalized, the expert panel would be formed by 2018, and fracking could begin in 2019.

Sascha Müller-Kraenner, federal managing director of the German environmental group Deutsche Umwelthilfe, expressed the concern of many environmentalists, saying, "Allowing [fracking] now is incomprehensible from an environmental and energy policy point of view."[64]

Germany is serious about beer, and brewmasters are among those on the front lines of opposing the fracking law. Beer is protected in Germany by the world's oldest food safety regulation dating to 1516, the *Reinheitsgebot* or "purity law," which mandated that only malted barley, hops, and water may be used in making beer. After the discovery of yeast as a desirable ingredient, the law was updated to allow its use.[65] Friederike Borchert, whose family owns a brewery in Lünne, Lower Saxony, says, "Fracking could spell the end of our existence." Explaining that water used for brewing must be even cleaner than drinking water, Borchert declares Germany to be a "beer nation" where politicians respond when brewers voice their concerns.[66]

The Bavarian Brewers Association has won assurances from Merkel's government that the spring waters needed for beer making will be protected from fracking. Brewmasters were assured that the federal states could determine where their springs were located and prevent fracking in those areas.[67] While this seems like a clear admission by the government that fracking can pollute water, it also represents a strategic move to divide the foes of fracking. But the decision-making process on fracking is not over yet, and German activists will continue to be a countervailing force to Exxon's influence on the Merkel government. They understand that allowing production of fracked gas runs against the spirit of the *Energiewende*, a program that remains popular with the German public not just for its environmental common sense but for its democratization of how the country produces and uses energy.

The reason that Exxon has targeted Germany for fracking may in fact have little to do with future profits from gas and everything to do with co-opting—if not disrupting—the successful model of a major industrial nation shifting to a sustainable energy future. In addition to its plans to phase out nuclear energy by 2022, Germany aims to cut greenhouse gas emissions by at least 80 percent by 2050. Dirk Jansen, director of the BUND Friends of the Earth office in North Rhine–Westphalia, explains: "Part of the *Energiewende* is that by the middle of the century, we want to decrease energy consumption in Germany by at least 50 percent. We want to decrease our use of energy from fossil fuels and invest more in energy-efficient technology. That means the need for fossil fuels is going to drop massively."[68]

Viewing this as a battle for its very existence, Exxon will do everything it can to drill for every last drop of fossil fuels, from the Arctic to the Everglades. That includes pursuing every avenue to discredit and destroy renewable energy, energy efficiency, and the political careers of those advocating slashing fossil fuel demand. Exxon's vice president J.S. Simpson was honest about the company's view of renewables. Testifying before a U.S. House Select Committee on Energy Independence and Global Warming, he said, "The pursuit of alternative fuels must not detract from the development of oil and gas."[69]

Percentage of Average Annual
Electric Power Generation
1990–2014

	1990–94	1995–99	2000–04	2005–09	2010–14

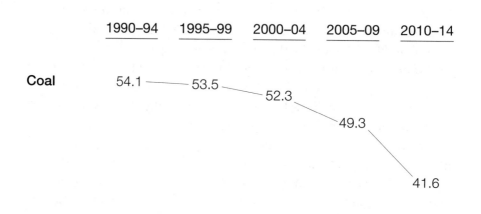

Coal 54.1 — 53.5 — 52.3 — 49.3 — 41.6

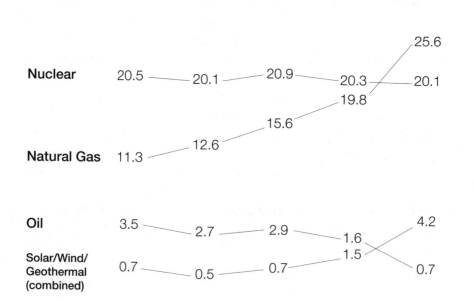

Nuclear 20.5 — 20.1 — 20.9 — 20.3 — 20.1

25.6

19.8

Natural Gas 11.3 — 12.6 — 15.6

Oil 3.5 — 2.7 — 2.9 — 1.6 — 4.2

1.5

Solar/Wind/Geothermal (combined) 0.7 — 0.5 — 0.7 — 0.7

17

THE CLIMATE CHANGE HEIST

Fidelity purchased with money, money can destroy.
—Lucius Annaeus Seneca[1]

In August 2015 President Obama announced the final regulations for the Clean Power Plan, his administration's program for reducing the carbon footprint of the largest emitter in the nation: the electricity industry. Aimed at closing coal-fired power plants, the rules incentivize natural-gas-fired generation, which emits less carbon pollution than coal-based generation.[2] As noted in *Fortune* magazine, the natural gas industry is poised to be a "major beneficiary" of the president's plan, as states will "inevitably turn to cleaner burning natural gas plants over coal plants."[3]

The plan sets targets for each state to lower emissions, but it fails to stipulate the method for achieving the reduction. Even if the targets are met, they fall far short of the economy-wide goals set by the Intergovernmental Panel on Climate Change (IPCC), a United Nations body in which hundreds of scientists and other experts participate. Each state is left to decide on its energy mix, leaving officials able to select non-sustainable sources of energy. If a state fails to submit a plan, the EPA will seek to impose a federal solution, almost certain to involve pollution trading schemes.[4]

When EPA secretary Gina McCarthy discussed the draft Clean Power Plan in June 2014, she described it as an "all-of-the-above strategy that paves a more certain path for conventional fuels in a carbon-constrained world." She said: "We know that coal and natural gas play a significant role in a diverse national energy mix. This Plan does not change that—it recognizes the opportunity to modernize aging plants, increase efficiency, and lower pollution."[5]

States are free to use renewable resources to meet the goal, but they are not required to do so. Some states actually allow dirty energy projects to qualify as renewable energy, counting "clean" coal, "advanced"-technology nuclear plants, and burning trash as part of their standard for renewable energy.[6]

The EPA admits that this is far from a "fundamental redirection of the energy sector" and states that "under this rule, the trends for . . . natural gas-fired generation, nuclear generation and renewable generation will remain generally consistent with what their trends would be in the absence of this rule."[7] In its formal analysis of the impact of the final rule on U.S. electricity production, the EPA actually projects that over the next ten years more power would be generated from renewables without the rule than with it.[8]

Critics of fracking have long pointed out that the use of fracked natural gas will lead to an even more dangerous rise in methane emissions.

Methane: The Achilles's Heel of Natural Gas

Since the late 1980s, many environmental groups have followed the lead of the Environmental Defense Fund and the Natural Resources Defense Council in promoting the use of natural gas as a transition fuel to renewable energy. The environmental community's support for using gas as a "climate friendly" bridge fuel has greened its image. Until recently, little attention has been given to the fact that natural gas is composed mainly of methane. Methane is a potent greenhouse gas, pound for pound trapping more atmospheric heat than carbon dioxide. The IPPC estimates that methane is eighty-seven times more potent than carbon dioxide over a twenty-year period, and thirty-six times more potent over a hundred-year time frame.[9]

In 2011, as concerns about the many impacts of fracked gas mounted, two well-respected Cornell University professors, Robert Howarth and Anthony Ingraffea, collaborated on an important study challenging the potential of natural gas to address climate change. Published in the journal *Climatic Change*, the study examined the difference in methane emissions between fracked shale gas and conventionally produced gas. Their data refuted the long-held assumption that switching from coal to natural gas would reduce the risk to the global climate.[10]

Noting that methane emissions from fracked gas were much greater than and "perhaps more than twice as great as those from conventional gas," the Cornell researchers found fracked gas to be even worse for global warming than coal. Howarth and Ingraffea looked at the implications of such high emissions, relying on the latest science about the global warming potential of methane, and concluded that neither fracked gas nor conventional gas presents a real alternative to coal in terms of greenhouse gas emissions. The scientists say they did not intend for their research study to justify continued use of coal, but that substituting shale gas for coal "may not have the desired effect of mitigating climate warming."[11]

Their collaboration began when Howarth, a professor in Cornell's Department of Ecology and Evolutionary Biology, returned from a year-long sabbatical in Paris in 2009 to find that fracking had become a huge controversy in the local community. Ingraffea, a professor in the School of Civil and Environmental Engineering, had been examining the impacts of fracking and was concerned about how it would affect New York. The two scholars met over a glass of wine and decided to use their different areas of expertise to look at the potential of natural gas to mitigate climate change.[12]

Dr. Howarth—trained as an earth scientist, ecosystem biologist, and biogeochemist—became concerned about the environment at a young age and was an organizer of the first Earth Day in 1970. In 1979 he worked as a staff scientist at the Woods Hole Research Center in Massachusetts with his mentor, legendary ecologist George M. Woodwell, who was one of the first scientists to sound the alarm on climate change. In 1985 Howarth went to Cornell, where he and his wife, Dr. Roxanne Marino, now run the Howarth-Marino Lab, conducting research on biogeochemistry and ecosystem science.

Specializing in the impacts of global climate change and the interaction of energy systems and the environment, Howarth is an expert on sulfur, nitrogen, phosphorus, and carbon cycles. He was the founding editor of the journal *Biogeochemistry* and served as its editor in chief for twenty-one years. Among the many prestigious national and international scientific collaborations he has been involved in are co-chairing the International SCOPE Nitrogen Project, chairing the National Academy of Sciences Committee on Causes and Management of Coastal Eutrophication, and serving as president of the Coastal & Estuarine Research Federation.

Based on his experience as a chief consultant to the state of Alaska during oil and gas litigation in the 1980s, Howarth became a skeptic about the petroleum industry's practices and honesty. Native groups had been told by Amoco—a company now owned by BP—that the white foam surfacing in Norton Sound, south of the Seward Peninsula, was "whale snot." Later, evidence emerged about the company's failure to report environmental violations and toxic discharges to the U.S. EPA.[13] Howarth says that his contribution to this case was "one of the proudest moments of my career." He laments that information about the case was never made public because of the settlement agreement, but he learned firsthand how the oil and gas industry suppresses information and fails to follow regulations.[14]

Dr. Ingraffea says that he never meant to be a "rock mechanic." In fact, he laughingly discloses that he wanted to be an astronaut, but the Vietnam War intervened. While he was a student at the University of California at Berkeley in 1973, during the energy crisis, a professor of mechanical engineering—one of the greats in the discipline—told him to go into rock mechanics. He pointed his finger at Ingraffea and said, "Why don't you go read about fracture as it pertains to rock, geothermal energy, and oil shale?"

And that's exactly what Ingraffea did. After spending two years as a structural engineer with the Grumman Aerospace Corporation and two years as an engineer with the Peace Corps in Venezuela, he earned a doctorate in engineering from the University of Colorado at Boulder on the physics of rock fracturing. Since 1977 he has taught fracture mechanics as well as numerical methods for using computers to simulate fractures.

In this capacity, Ingraffea has collaborated frequently with the U.S. Department of Energy and the oil industry, and had a two-decade-long consulting relationship with the oil services company Schlumberger. He created software that the company now owns that models the fracturing taking place during the fracking process. An author of over two hundred studies, Ingraffea has worked with his graduate students in developing pioneering research using computational simulations, interactive computer graphics, and in-lab testing to understand precisely how rocks and other materials fracture under stress.[15]

As the principal investigator on more than $35 million worth of research and development projects, Ingraffea has had his work funded by the Gas Research Institute, Sandia National Laboratories, the Association of Iron and Steel Engineers, General Dynamics, Boeing, the Caterpillar National Science Foundation, the National Aeronautics and Space Administration, the Air Force Office of Scientific Research, Kodak, the Federal Aviation Administration, IBM, and many others.

Howarth and Ingraffea's comprehensive examination of the entire life cycle of methane emissions from natural gas—from preproduction to combustion—showed that the data on methane emissions were seriously incomplete. Unlike the comparison between coal and natural gas when burned, a full life cycle accounting for methane showed that leaks occur throughout the supply chain. Although emissions during transport, storage, and distribution are the same for both conventional and fracked gas, the process of fracking for shale gas causes significantly more methane emissions then conventional drilling. According to the researchers, it could be nearly two hundred times more.[16]

Methane leaks after each stage of fracking, as plugs used to isolate different stretches of the well are removed. Leakage also occurs from the flowback fluids, in which gases mix with the millions of gallons of fracking water and chemicals and then surge out of the well during the fracking process.[17] These pollution-intense phases of well completion are unique to fracked wells.

Because methane remains in the atmosphere for a shorter period then carbon dioxide, a comparison of the greenhouse gas potency, or global warming potential, of methane and carbon dioxide requires use of a specific time frame. Howarth and Ingraffea used a twenty-year horizon, in addition to the more commonly used hundred-year period. They did so because reducing potent greenhouse gas emissions is critical in the short term if the worst impacts of climate change are to be averted. Howarth and Ingraffea conclude that up to 7.9 percent of the total lifetime production of methane from fracked wells leaks into the atmosphere, resulting in fracked gas emissions that are at least 30 percent higher—and potentially more than double—those from conventional gas production.[18]

The study received widespread media coverage, including recognition from *Time* magazine, where Howarth and Ingraffea were included in the "People Who Mattered" section of the December 2011 issue.[19] Unsurprisingly, the industry's response to the study was quick and predictably nasty. Energy in Depth, a particularly aggressive oil industry front group, dismissed the study by claiming that Howarth had prejudged the findings because he is opposed to fracking. Mark Whitley, of the fracking company Range Resources, claimed that Howarth's findings don't "make any sense."[20]

Melanie Kenderdine, executive director of the MIT Energy Initiative, attacked the study for focusing on the twenty-year time frame. She claimed, "There are major scientific organizations that think we should actually extend that hundred-year period, not shorten it."[21] Founded by

Obama's secretary of energy, Ernest Moniz, the MIT initiative is funded by energy companies, including BP Amoco, ExxonMobil, Shell, Chevron USA, Hess, and Constellation, as well as by the nonprofit Environmental Defense Fund.[22]

The first academic pushback against the Howarth-Ingraffea study came from their Cornell colleague Lawrence Cathles, who attacked their use of the twenty-year time frame.[23] This attack was no surprise, considering that Cathles has been a climate change denier. He signed on to the Global Warming Petition Project, which stated, "There is no convincing scientific evidence that human release of carbon dioxide, methane or other greenhouse gases is causing . . . catastrophic heating of the Earth's atmosphere and disruption of the Earth's climate."[24]

Howarth and Ingraffea refined their research in a second study, published in 2012, responding to criticism about their use of the twenty-year time frame. They argued for the importance of using a shorter time frame to avoid reaching a "tipping point" beyond which changes in the climate are irreversible.[25]

Evidence on Methane Emissions Mounts

Research on methane emissions has continued to validate Howarth and Ingraffea's findings and to show that the EPA has underestimated the amount of leakage from natural gas production and infrastructure. A study published in *Science*, in which researchers from Stanford University, the University of Michigan, the National Oceanic and Atmospheric Administration (NOAA), and several other institutions participated, found that the EPA's inventory of methane leaks is inadequate and that "measurements at all scales show that the official inventories consistently underestimate actual methane emissions, with the natural gas and oil sectors as important contributors."[26] The agency's measurement data are skewed because they only come from locations where the natural gas industry has granted the EPA permission to conduct research. Researchers are now able to use new technologies to obtain measurements without the consent of the industry. Measurements can be taken from the air and from stationary equipment, giving a much more accurate picture of emissions.[27]

Scientists from the Cooperative Institute for Research in Environmental Studies at the University of Colorado and from NOAA used air samples taken from towers located on Colorado's front range to measure methane, finding that emissions have been underestimated in current inventories.[28] Following up on this earlier research, scientists from these institutions used methane monitors on aircraft to fly over gas fields in Utah's Uintah County. Measurements taken in February 2012 showed that between 6 and 12 percent of the methane produced during the day on which the measurements were taken had leaked into the atmosphere.[29]

In 2014 a groundbreaking study found that methane emissions during the drilling of some wells were a hundred times higher than previously believed.[30] In the study, Purdue University atmospheric chemistry scientist Dana Caulton and colleagues reported the results of real-time methane measurements observed by aircraft in southwestern Pennsylvania during June 2012. Their findings included a significant amount of methane spewing from industry sites, including high levels of methane associated with well pads, fluctuating over a large swath of the fracked area. Significantly, the shale gas pads were identified as being in preproduction during the drilling stage, before fracking had even begun or the well had produced flowback fluids (previously associated with high methane levels). The levels of emissions measured were in some cases higher than those identified in the original Howarth-Ingraffea study, suggesting that the Cornell researchers' estimates were accurate, and perhaps low.

Ingraffea also published a paper in the *Proceedings of the National Academy of Science* in 2014 that examined the impact on methane leakage from failed cement casings in natural gas wells. Up to 12 percent of fracked gas wells drilled in Pennsylvania since 2009 have had some loss of structural integrity.[31] Casing failures allow methane and other toxic chemicals such as benzene to leak into the air and potentially into water resources. Ingraffea explained, "From a climate point of view, when you've got thousands of wells all emitting [methane] during drilling, it's not inconsequential anymore."[32]

After the IPCC raised its estimate of methane's global warming potential in 2013, Howarth revisited the earlier findings of his 2011 paper with Ingraffea. The new paper, published in *Energy Science and Engineering* in 2014, used the "best available data and a 20-year time period for comparing the warming potential of methane to carbon dioxide." Howarth concluded that fracked shale gas and conventionally produced gas have a larger impact on the global climate than coal or oil, and that the adverse effect of gas is greatest when it is used for residential and commercial heating.[33]

Environmental Defense Fund's Research Initiative

In light of the growing criticism of methane emissions from fracked gas, the Environmental Defense Fund has been at the center of the controversy about environmental groups promoting natural gas as a climate-friendly fuel. Contending that methane leaks can be reduced through regulation, the group embarked on a multiple-study research project in 2012 to look at where methane is leaking and in what quantities. The organization hopes to use the information in its efforts to work with what it calls "stakeholders" in developing policies to lower emissions.

EDF's natural gas guru, Mark Brownstein, promoted the effort, explaining that for "natural gas to be an accepted part of a strategy for improving energy security and moving to a clean energy future, it is critical for all of us to work together to quantify and reduce methane emissions."[34] Funded by millions of dollars of support from foundations and industry, the research has been conducted by various universities and a long list of researchers. Brownstein said the study should short-circuit the debate over fracking's methane emissions so that we can "fix the leaks and move on."[35]

EDF formed a partnership with many of the largest oil and gas companies to gain access to data and well sites.[36] Although the industry hoped that reduction of methane leaks could be accomplished on a voluntary basis, many of the companies involved in the research saw the writing on the wall: methane leaks would have to be curtailed if natural gas was to maintain its "green" reputation among some environmentalists.

The EDF-sponsored research has at times favored the industry's low-balling of methane emissions, but it also has led to results that expose the industry's problems with methane leaks. The very first study that was published—conducted by the University of Texas—was quickly embraced by the industry, at least in part, while other research has shown that methane emissions are higher than previously reported. A problem that has flummoxed EDF, as well as the EPA, is that the industry controls the data as well as access to sites. This means that most data are skewed toward understating how much natural gas is ultimately dumped into the atmosphere.

The University of Texas study involved an EDF partnership with a handful of energy companies: Anadarko Petroleum Corporation, BG Group, Chevron, Encana Oil & Gas (USA) Inc., Pioneer Natural Resources Company, Shell, Southwestern Energy, Talisman Energy, and ExxonMobil.[37] Measurements from well sites selected by the fracking companies were taken during twenty-seven hydraulic fracturing events that were also selected by the companies. Only well sites using "green" completion—a system designed to capture methane gas at the wellhead—were selected and analyzed. This skewing of data meant that emissions appeared to be much lower overall than they really were, and thus were hardly representative of fossil fuel production at the tens of thousands of oil and gas wells around the country each year.* [38] The industry had cherry-picked the data, while EDF lent the research credibility, and the elite media cheered the news. The *Wall Street Journal* was typical, its headline proclaiming, "US Overstates Leaks by Gas-Drillers, Says Study." [39]

In contrast, an EDF-sponsored study released in August 2015 took a more honest look at emissions. [40] The study, by Colorado State University researchers and colleagues at several other institutions, found that methane emissions at gathering facilities are eight times greater than the EPA had estimated. Researchers compiled emissions data from gathering lines and other infrastructure used to combine gas from multiple wells and to transport it to processing facilities or larger pipelines. These emissions are not tracked and collected for the EPA's inventory of emissions. [41]

Publication of the study was planned to coincide with the release of the administration's draft methane rules in late August 2015, shortly after the carbon rule was finalized. EDF has worked closely with the White House, both in supporting fracked gas and in advocating for more regulation of methane.

The White House Acts to Reduce Methane

Responding to the growing evidence about out-of-control methane emissions, President Obama announced in January 2015 that his administration intended to develop draft rules to reduce methane emissions over the next decade by up to 45 percent from 2012 levels. [42] To the dismay of clean-energy activists, although Obama indicated that the EPA planned to use the Clean Air Act to regulate future wells and infrastructure, the

---

* As of 2015, the EPA requires that new fracked gas (but not oil) wells require green completions. The study presented the ideal world of what might be achieved (barring the occurrence of a 1-in-1,000 event) if the industry spent the necessary funds and paid complete and undivided attention to detail during drilling, a very unlikely scenario based on the history of the industry.

agency would depend on voluntary guidelines for existing wells and infra-structure. Close adviser to Obama and perennial Washington insider John Podesta wrote on the White House blog that oil and gas companies had the option of reducing methane emissions by adopting voluntary efforts that "could realize significant reductions in a quick, flexible, cost-effective way."[43]

Months later, in August 2015, the draft regulations were released shortly after the carbon regulations were finalized. Even with the mount-ing evidence of methane leaking from all phases of natural gas production and use, including the embarrassing findings from the Colorado State Uni-versity study, the EPA proposal exempted thousands of wells and the sup-porting infrastructure from compliance, making it unlikely that methane emissions can be reduced significantly in the short term.[44]

Meanwhile, Cornell University professor Robert Howarth has con-cluded that, despite a decrease in carbon emissions (mostly from the reces-sion, but in part from the closing of coal plants), the threat to the global climate has increased. He writes, "Significant quantities of methane are emitted to the atmosphere from shale gas development: an estimated 12% of total production considered over the entire lifecycle from well to delivery to consumers, based on recent satellite data."[45] He projects that with the continued expansion of shale gas production, emissions will continue to increase through 2040.

Considering the history of the oil industry in cutting costs at the ex-pense of the environment, it is unlikely that companies would follow even the most commonsense regulations, especially when natural gas prices are low. Past experience shows that the industry will skirt making the invest-ments necessary to reduce emissions to a point where natural gas is even marginally better for the global climate. Without a dramatic change in energy policy, the outlook for the global climate is bleak.

18

POLLUTION TRADING: A SHELL GAME

Being reasonable is exactly the way to save the planet.
— Fred Krupp[1]

At the heart of the debate in the environmental community over fracking is the belief that the use of natural gas—a fuel with lower carbon emissions when burned—will lower carbon emissions overall. Touting it as a "bridge" to renewable energy, the Environmental Defense Fund and other environmental organizations advocate the use of natural gas in tandem with pollution trading to tackle the climate crisis. Fred Krupp, EDF's executive director, has been so enthusiastic about gas-generated electricity that he has even promoted new technologies that gasify coal and convert it into methane. He and co-author Miriam Horn, who works on special projects at EDF, wrote in their book *Earth: The Sequel*, "Rapid emergence of these technologies [coal gasification] will make it possible in the near term for utilities to substitute new natural gas plants for previously planned conventional coal-fired facilities, providing a valuable bridge to still cleaner options."[2]

EDF has been at the forefront of advocating market-based solutions such as cap and trade, an emissions program that they claim is a win-win for industry and the environment. Having largely abandoned the idea that polluting industries should be prohibited from poisoning the environment, they back the adoption of complex and technical policy mechanisms that are supposed to incentivize a reduction of pollution while allowing industry to make a profit. In contrast to actually requiring that fossil fuel use be phased out or that fracking be prohibited, EDF has aggressively supported cap and trade, the policy instrument that it calls the "most environmentally and economically sensible approach to controlling green-house gas emissions."[3]

Krupp writes: "This is the beauty of a cap-and-trade system. . . . It would be up to the market—not the government—to find the best ways forward. Instead of forcing utilities to make certain decisions or to back certain technologies, a cap-and-trade system sets a limit and lets the market figure out the cheapest and most efficient means of getting there."[4]

The Clean Power Plan released by the EPA in 2015 both promotes switching to natural gas and encourages states to meet their emissions targets using cap-and-trade programs that are similar to California's. Methane emissions are included in the definition of tradable greenhouse gases in the California cap-and-trade program.[5] Viewed as a model program, it puts an economy-wide cap on greenhouse gas emissions from power plants, gasoline refineries, industrial facilities, and transportation fuels, and lowers the cap about 3 percent per year until 2020.[6] The program is geared toward reducing California's emissions in 2020 to the 1990 level, and if it is successful, emissions will be 28 percent less than they are expected to be without the program.

In Maryland, during the last days of Democratic governor Martin O'Malley's administration, he proposed regulations that required lowering fugitive methane leaks from fracking-related activities and infrastructure but allowed the industry to use cap and trade to lower emissions. The O'Malley administration claimed that this would result in a "net zero" amount of methane emissions.[7]

As evidence continues to mount about the large amount of methane emissions escaping from fracking operations and natural gas infrastructure, we can expect to see cap-and-trade programs promoted as the solution, especially if this is embraced by the environmental community.

The Cap-and-Trade Shell Game: Who Really Benefits?

In June 2015, in an encyclical on the environment, Pope Francis issued a bold and honest statement on carbon emissions trading, saying that it simply creates a new type of financial speculation but does not bring about the changes necessary for avoiding catastrophic climate change.[8]

The Pope's clear assessment puts him well ahead of many in the mainstream environmental movement, who support cap-and-trade programs that allow polluters to pay for the right to pollute rather than prohibiting emissions in the first place. These schemes involve a governmental body or central authority setting an overall limit on emissions and then either selling at auction or gifting polluters with credits that represent the amount of the pollutant they have the right to discharge into the environment. Depending on the program, credits also are called pollution allowances or permits. Credits or their derivatives can then be traded within a single market, between linked markets, or on Wall Street.

Companies must maintain enough of these credits to match the amount of pollution they are allowed to emit. If they reduce emissions below their limit, they can sell or trade the remaining credits that represent emissions not discharged. A polluter that buys these excess credits gains the right to discharge the amount of the pollutant that the credits represent. To get buy-in from industry and Wall Street, the overall cap is set to reduce only a part of overall emissions. So even if the trading system worked, the emissions reductions would be too low and too late. Champions of these schemes claim that the lower cost of purchasing credits instead of direct reductions or technology upgrades, as well as the ability to make money from selling the credits, makes it the cheapest and most efficient way of reducing emissions.

While cap-and-trade programs provide higher profits for utilities, environmental justice advocates point out that emissions trading allows the dirtiest plants to continue spewing hazardous pollutants in the places where they are located, often in low income and people of color communities. Mike Ewall, executive director of the Energy Justice Network, says the cap-and-trade schemes concentrate pollution in vulnerable communities that lack political clout. Dr. Nicky Sheats, director of the Center for the Urban Environment at Thomas Edison State College in Trenton, opposes trading programs, emphasizing that particulate matter from power plants should be reduced along with carbon.

Many large energy companies support cap and trade, a concept originally developed by Republicans and supported in the past by prominent members of the party, from former Massachusetts governor Mitt Romney to Senator Lindsay Graham. Anthony J. Alexander, president and chief executive of FirstEnergy, a large utility utilizing coal-fired generation, praised cap and trade in 2014, saying, "By trading on carbon credits, we'll be able to achieve significantly more cuts at a lower cost." John McManus, a vice president at American Electric Power, one of the largest coal utilities in the country, concurred, "We view cap and trade as having a lot of benefits."[9]

Shell, a giant gas producer with a large trading arm, also has spoken in favor of cap and trade.[10]

But perhaps the most enthusiastic proponent of emissions trading is the financial services industry. The largest investment banks pushed for federal cap-and-trade legislation between 2008 and 2010. Goldman Sachs spent $3.5 million lobbying for legislation in 2008, an effort that ultimately failed two years later.[11] The *New York Times* notes that pollution credits have become the newest commodity, saying: "Thousands of people—in small offices in San Francisco, on trading floors in Houston, at power stations all over Europe—now buy and sell the permits every day. They are not all representing polluters; some are simply speculators placing bets on what will happen to carbon prices over time." [12]

Calling cap and trade "a virtual repeat of the commodities-market casino," financial writer Matt Taibbi explains that Goldman Sachs and other investment banks stand to make a fortune in a market that could generate "upwards of a trillion dollars annually." [13] Steve Horn, a research fellow at *DeSmogBlog*, notes: "Cap and trade is, was, and always will be a giveaway to the biggest polluters and Wall Street financiers. It is a shame some environmental groups went along for the ride . . . and we're all better off ultimately that it didn't pass." [14]

California's program—cited by the Obama White House and the EPA as a model for other states to follow in enacting the Clean Power Plan—is already rife with speculation. The economy-wide program directs electricity companies, food manufacturers, cement producers, oil refineries, and other manufacturers to buy pollution allowances from the California Air Resources Board—the agency charged with overseeing the carbon market—to reduce the impact of the greenhouse gases they emit. An analysis in the fall of 2014 of the actions of pollution allowances to date showed that of the 240 million allowances purchased, 20 million were purchased by "financial intermediaries and speculators" for resale at a profit.[15] The program's integrity was further compromised by the board giving away $10 billion worth of free pollution credits through 2020. Other than capitulating to the demands of these politically powerful corporations, it is difficult to see how the California Air Resources Board justified compensating polluting corporations for their "compliance costs." [16]

Stanford University Law School policy experts have documented another way that the system can be rigged, called "resource shuffling." This happens when a coal-fired plant participating in California's cap-and-trade program swaps its contract for electricity with a gas-fired power plant in a state not participating in the cap-and-trade program. The California plant gets a credit for lowering pollution, but no real reduction in emissions has occurred, because both plants continue to operate.[17]

Considering that speculators have recently caused the biggest economic crisis since the Great Depression—an economic disaster that also was caused by Wall Street—it is difficult to understand how so many smart and well-meaning people have faith in a system that so easily can be scammed and that ultimately is under the control of Wall Street gamblers.

Gambling on the Global Climate in the EU

The European Union's highly volatile Emissions Trading System, covering eleven thousand power plants and industrial facilities in thirty-one countries, has required significant intervention from the European parliament to even stay afloat.[18] Riddled with fraud and corruption since it was initiated in 2005, the program has shown little meaningful success in reducing emissions. In the first years of its existence, emissions actually rose 2.1 percent under the trading regime.[19] Only in the wake of the 2008 global financial crisis did emissions fall, but this was due to the economy crashing, not to the trading program.

From the start of the program, an excess of emissions credits was offered for free, as the EU allowed the largest polluters to grandfather in emissions levels. Sandburg, an organization that monitors the trading program, says that the proliferation of credits resulted in windfall profits for some players. The problem was intensified by the use of offsets, with up to half of emissions reductions coming from the developing world. Because oversight is lacking, and because of the close relationships between the organizations validating projects and the companies profiting from them, the Emissions Trading System is further compromised.[20]

Besides selling fake carbon offsets or stealing credits from national carbon emission registries, tax fraud has besieged the program in Europe. In January 2011, computer hackers managed to steal more than 3 million carbon credits with a combined value of $62 million. In December 2010, Italian authorities announced that they were investigating a €500 million ($570 million) tax fraud scheme in which value-added taxes were collected by sellers but never paid to a national government.[21] Corruption and a failure of the carbon market to function as promised means that it has failed to deliver real emissions reductions.

Myles R. Allen, a prominent U.K. climate scientist, has criticized the EU's program, telling the *New York Times*: "The reason I don't support what we're doing is not that I don't think something needs to be done. I just don't think it's effective, and I don't see it ever being effective."[22]

Offsets: A Con Job

Cap-and-trade programs also use "offsets," the creation of pollution credits from an activity that is supposed to reduce carbon emissions from a polluter by compensating with an activity elsewhere. Based on the theory that a ton of emissions in one place is equivalent to a ton of emissions in another place, offsets programs lend themselves to deception and scamming. Critics of offsets question whether pollution emitted during a moment of time can be equal to emissions reduction over a long period of time or if emissions from burning fossil fuels can really be equivalent to those from planting trees in a deforested area. Assertions that carbon emissions from energy production can be compensated for by planting trees or by reducing methane pollution on industrial animal farms seem far-fetched, or at the very least difficult to verify.[23]

The U.S. Government Accountability Office (GAO) found in 2008 that it is nearly impossible to verify whether offsets actually represent real emissions reductions. Not only are these greenhouse gas emissions difficult to substantiate, but often the credits come from projects that would have been undertaken even without payment for the offset. The GAO notes that more than six hundred different entities develop, market, or sell offsets in the United States, and the market involves a wide range of participants, prices, transaction types, and projects.[24]

Problems also have arisen in California over the offsets program. An investigation of offsets by the California Air Resources Board questioned the legitimacy of 4.3 million carbon-offset credits issued for the cap-and-trade market. The offsets came from the Clean Harbors Incineration facility in El Dorado, Arkansas, a facility that has been charged with violating environmental laws. The EPA settled a lawsuit with the company, which will pay a penalty of almost $600,000 for "improperly identifying and disposing of hazardous waste, improper storage of hazardous waste, and failure to comply with air emissions standards." This noncompliance with the nation's environmental laws brings into question the offsets generated by the facility. These types of shenanigans show how offsets can create a shell game, rather than truly addressing climate pollution.[25]

It is important to note that the "net zero" emissions program proposed in Maryland for dealing with methane emissions from fracking operations is based on the theory of offsets. Polluters would be required to measure methane emissions—a controversial and uncertain endeavor—and then buy carbon offsets to compensate for the escaping methane.[26]

Did Cap and Trade Really Reduce Acid Rain?

Advocates of emissions trading usually point to the Acid Rain Program mandated in Title IV of the Clean Air Act Amendments of 1990 as proof that this market mechanism can reduce global warming emissions.* Reductions in sulfur dioxide (SO_2) emissions from coal power plants, one of the chief causes of acid rain, have been touted by trading advocates as proof that emissions trading can work to reduce global warming emissions.[27] The goal was to reduce annual SO_2 emissions to about 8 million tons by 2010, down from the 15.7 million tons emitted in 1990.[28] The program incentivized polluters to seek the lowest-cost short-term solution for old and out-of-date power plants and factories, rather than advocating the elimination of polluting technologies through upgrades.

Research indicates that SO_2 reductions were achieved, but it is unclear that the emissions trading mandated in 1990 was responsible for the success. Brian Tokar, who teaches in the Environment Program at the University of Vermont, says, "State utility regulators, in this instance, played a far more crucial role in the successes of the acid rain program than the permit trading system, as did unrelated incentives that reduced the cost of low-sulfur coal."[29] In fact, despite the orthodoxy that has been created about the success of the trading regime in reducing sulfur emissions, it is just as likely that the reductions were achieved *in spite of* pollution trading.

---

* These pollutants undergo chemical transformations when they are dissolved in precipitation, greatly damaging water quality and vegetation. Two-thirds of SO_2 and one-fourth of nitrogen oxides (NO_X) are emitted by power plants. While the main pollutant trading program was for SO_2, eventually some smaller regional trading programs were created for NO_X.

Prior to the enactment of Title IV, an assessment projection indicated that reductions in sulfur dioxide as great as those achieved under a market-based program could be attained if older coal-fired power plants simply had complied with the Clean Air Act's technology-retrofitting requirements. But with the introduction of trading, those technological modifications fell by the wayside. Research shows that polluting electricity plants have managed to avoid triggering requirements for installing upgrades, meaning that older plants continued to operate without adopting new pollution control technologies.[30]

While we may never know the exact impact of substituting trading mechanisms for requiring upgrades on U.S. power plants, the results from Europe's acid rain approach suggest that we would have done much better simply by requiring utilities to upgrade. A 2004 comparison of the U.S. program for reducing sulfur with regulatory systems in the European Union and Japan show a much greater reduction when energy companies were made to comply with the law, rather than engaging in trading. The United States reduced emissions by 39 percent, but in the EU sulfur emissions were reduced by 78 percent, and Japan's emissions fell by 82 percent.[31] We also know that the EPA now attributes at least 1 million tons of sulfur reductions during the Acid Rain Program to factors unrelated to trading, namely, the increased availability of and switch to low-sulfur coal sources from the Powder River Basin in the early 1990s.[32]

C. Boyden Gray Recruits EDF's Fred Krupp

The radical idea of replacing laws preventing pollution with an unproven economic abstraction such as emissions trading can be traced to the Chicago School of Economics. Right-leaning economists adopted part of a theory that had been written about by British economist Arthur Cecil Pigou, who conceptualized the idea of "internalizing the externalities" and applied it to lethal chemicals that pollute the air or water during the manufacturing of goods.[33]

Brian Tokar, at the University of Vermont, notes that Chicago School economist Ronald Coase believed that the economic losses from regulating pollution were equivalent to harm from pollution. Coase argued that "the right to do something which has a harmful effect is also a factor of production" and that market forces should always establish the best allocation of resources.[34] John H. Dales, an economist at the University of Toronto, took the concept further, writing the seminal work on creating a market for pollution rights in 1968.[35] Dales suggested that a market based on the right to pollute would be cheaper and administratively simpler than regulation. He justified the concept by saying, "The pollution rights scheme, it seems clear, would require far less policing than any of the others."[36]

As we have seen, when the backlash against environmental regulation and social progress deepened in the 1980s, pressure grew to embrace the Chicago School's brand of economics. The EPA began experimenting with small-scale trading deals in 1974, allowing polluters to "offset" pollution from new industrial facilities by reducing existing emissions at another facility.[37] The agency brokered individual agreements with DuPont, US Steel, and 3M, allowing the corporations to offset pollution from one facility by reducing emissions at another industrial site.[38] Future Supreme Court justice Stephen Breyer boosted the concept in a 1979 *Harvard Law Review* article while teaching at Harvard Law School. Writing that "marketable rights to pollute" were a viable substitute for regulation, he suggested that regulation is appropriate only when it replicates the market conditions of a "hypothetically competitive world."[39]

The election of Ronald Reagan unleashed a powerful attack on the nation's environmental laws, setting the stage for an ugly showdown over the Clean Air Act. Last amended in 1977, the law had not addressed acid rain, which had not been well recognized or fully understood at the time. In the deregulatory fervor of the Reagan years, the electric utilities claimed that there was not sufficient science to justify regulating the SO_2 spewing from coal-fired power plants. Richard Ayres, chairman of the National Clean Air Coalition, an alliance of environmental groups and consumer groups, put his finger on the reason that no action was taken on acid rain during the 1980s. As he told the *New York Times*, "The main reason we have not had an acid rain bill is clear: the Reagan Administration opposed it and permitted the utility and coal interests that opposed it to have full sway in Congress."[40]

C. Boyden Gray, a lawyer in the Reagan White House, developed the political strategy for substituting pollution trading for a law requiring electric utilities to reduce emissions. Gray had been a partner at the lobby shop and corporate law firm Wilmer, Cutler and Pickering (today known as Wilmer-Hale) before joining the Reagan administration as counsel to Vice President George H.W. Bush. Gray—a multimillionaire heir to the R.J. Reynolds tobacco fortune and other family wealth acquired from banking, publishing, cable, and radio—had a background similar to Bush's.[41] Both men grew up in affluent families, attended prestigious boarding schools in Massachusetts, and went to Ivy League universities.

Growing up, Gray lived in a white-columned mansion on the campus of the University of North Carolina, where his father was president. He had attended Harvard as an undergraduate and had gone home to the University of North Carolina for law school.[42] As an attorney, he represented energy companies that ran afoul of pollution rules under the Clinton administration and lobbied to block other clean air standards during the George W. Bush administration.[43] While a diplomat in Europe, he tried to block the EU's enactment of rules that would require manufacturers to test industrial chemicals and make the health data available to the public.[44]

Gray served as counsel to Reagan's Presidential Task Force on Regulatory Relief, the anti-regulatory committee chaired by Vice President Bush. Termed the "wrecking crew" by Bush's Democratic opponent for president in 1988, Michael Dukakis, the task force was responsible for abandoning, delaying, and weakening the nation's environmental protections.[45] Although Gray is better known today for his involvement in the Tea Party and other initiatives funded by the Koch brothers, he was key to supporting emissions trading.* Alluding to the task force's work in this area, Reagan sent his proposal in a 1987 "Quest for Excellence" message to Congress: "We are also developing proposals that make use of market incentives to control air pollution caused by sulfur dioxide and nitrogen oxide emissions and the causes of acid rain."[46]

It was in Reagan's second term—a time when the idea of emissions trading was still unfamiliar in most policy-making and environmentalism circles—that Boyden decided it would be critical to have an environmental organization give a green seal of approval to emissions trading. Boyden recruited EDF's Krupp to be a partner on using emissions trading as a substitute for regulating sulfur under the Clean Air Act.[47] As the Bush team prepared for the coming election, Gray brought EDF staff into the Reagan White House to discuss the language that later would be incorporated in the Clean Air Act amendments of 1990.[48]

In the wake of Reagan's successful bid for a second term in office, another strange alliance came together to push market mechanisms as a

---

* Gray has his own lobby shop today, but he served on the board of Koch-funded Freedom Works until resigning in 2013 during a spate of infighting.

replacement for traditional environmental regulation. Strident Republican think tanks, centrist Democrats, and the public relations arms of polluting corporations coalesced to put their stamp on an update to the Clean Air Act and on future actions to protect the environment. Trading pollution rights began to be supported by seemingly divergent political forces—from the right-wing American Enterprise Institute to the centrist Democratic Leadership Council, which recruited Bill Clinton in 1989.[49]

Another major player in promoting emissions trading was economist Robert N. Stavins, who directed a bipartisan effort called Project 88 that brought together academics, government officials, and environmentalists, along with corporations that included Chevron, ARCO, and Monsanto, to advocate for the use of "market forces" to improve the environment.[50] Stavins was a staff economist at EDF from 1982 to 1983 and later a professor at Harvard; he has written hundreds of articles on emissions trading, cap and trade, and the use of market mechanisms, and also has served on a long list of advisory committees and boards. He served as the chairman of the EPA's Environmental Economics Advisory Board under Presidents Bill Clinton and George W. Bush and was a lead author in two rounds of climate change assessments from the IPCC.[51]

Stavins has noted that in the battle over the Clean Air Act in the late 1980s, with the exception of EDF, environmentalists were hostile to the notion of trading "rights to pollute."[52] Project 88, co-chaired by former Colorado Democratic senator Timothy Wirth and the late Pennsylvania Republican senator John Heinz, played an important role in promoting emissions trading. Senator Wirth called it "an attempt to put a green thumb on Adam Smith's invisible hand." The late Senator Heinz's wife, Teresa Heinz Kerry, and Senator Wirth's wife, Wren Winslow Wirth, both have served on the EDF board.* Senator Wirth unveiled Round II of Project 88 in 1991, after Senator Heinz's death in a plane crash, detailing the use of emissions trading to fight global warming.[53]

Fred Krupp explains that EDF also was involved in working with Wirth and Heinz on Project 88 after C. Boyden Gray contacted him in 1986. Krupp says: "I wrote an op-ed in the *Wall Street Journal* announcing the arrival of a 'third wave' of environmentalism. . . . The op-ed ended with

---

* Teresa Heinz Kerry is married to the Obama administration's current secretary of state, John Kerry, and is president of the Heinz Foundation. Wren Winslow Wirth is president of the Winslow Foundation.

a brief reference to using 'market-oriented incentives' to achieve 'greater environmental and economic benefits at a lower social and economic cost.' Those few words would ultimately open many doors. On the day of publication, I got a call from [Gray] . . . and began working with a young Harvard professor named Rob Stavins, who had been an EDF intern in California. . . . We wrote a report called 'Project 88.' "[54]

After George H.W. Bush was elected president in 1988, Gray continued as his legal counsel, working with key advocates of emissions trading to help broker a deal with energy interests. Meanwhile, a heated battle raged internally in the White House, where advisers such as Chief of Staff John Sununu opposed supporting clean air legislation at all. In Congress, the debate over the legislation continued for another year. Eventually, the Bush White House decided to support legislation if emissions trading was substituted for a regulatory requirement.[55] Gray, using EDF as environmental cover, brokered the deal that resulted in passage of the Clean Air Act Amendments of 1990—triggering the acid rain emissions trading system— and also helped shape the Energy Policy Act of 1992, which paved the way for electric utility deregulation and the incentivizing of natural gas.[56]

Enron's Ken Lay, a major funder of George H.W. Bush's presidential campaign, took the opportunity to promote emissions trading, writing to Bush and copying Gray about the benefits to natural gas of using emissions trading to address climate change. He said: "I am convinced that America's hard-pressed domestic natural gas industry would benefit substantially from a market-based approach to reducing CO_2 emissions. Natural gas is our cleanest fossil fuel and through its increased use in electric power generation could play a major role in reducing CO_2 emissions."[57]

Paving the Way for Cap and Trade

Al Gore popularized the idea of pollution trading in his 1992 book *Earth in the Balance*, saying that it should be part of a "global Marshall Plan." He wrote, "Governments should develop an international treaty establishing limits on CO_2 emissions by country and a market for the trading of emission rights among countries that need more and countries that have an excess amount."[58]

In 1997 Gore, then vice president, arrived in Kyoto, Japan, toward the end of a tense round of climate negotiations going on around the clock, joining two thousand delegates from more than 160 nations. Upon his arrival, he was briefed by EDF economist Dan Dudek on the ongoing talks, and together they strategized on pushing through the cap-and-trade system that eventually became part of the Kyoto Protocol. At the time, some European leaders were unconvinced that emissions trading was the answer, and many European environmental groups were angry about a plan designed to benefit polluters.[59]

Gray continued to promote trading, even writing a position paper advocating an "aggressive emissions trading" system for greenhouse gases together with Wirth and John Podesta, who served as chief of staff for President Clinton, counselor to President Obama, and adviser to Democratic presidential candidate Hillary Clinton.[60] Gray, like many figures from the first Bush administration, went on to serve under George W. Bush, becoming ambassador to the European Union in 2006–7 and special envoy for European Union affairs in 2008–9.[61] He defended the second Bush administration's handling of climate change negotiations, saying toward the end of his tenure as EU ambassador: "Recall that the Senate voted 95–0 against the Kyoto protocol during the Clinton administration. It was Republican administrations that produced clean fuels, lead phase-down, the Montreal protocol and the emissions trading model for the European Union's emissions trading system."[62]

EDF's strong endorsement of emissions trading paved the way for the mainstream environmental community to embrace "market mechanisms," making this a legitimate strategy for addressing pollution. Millions of dollars in support from environmental funders became available to environmental organizations that embraced an emissions trading system for stabilizing the global climate. New generations of environmentalists have accepted this strategy as genuinely the best method for lowering greenhouse gases.

Today EDF is playing a similar role by taking the most extreme position in the environmental community: promoting fracking and incentivizing natural gas through a cap-and-trade system. Although many grassroots activists feel betrayed by EDF's propensity for deal making and negotiating with industry, EDF began as a local environmental group.

A Web of Relationships

Inspired by the work of Rachel Carson, the Brookhaven Town Natural Resources Coalition was created by community activists, students from the

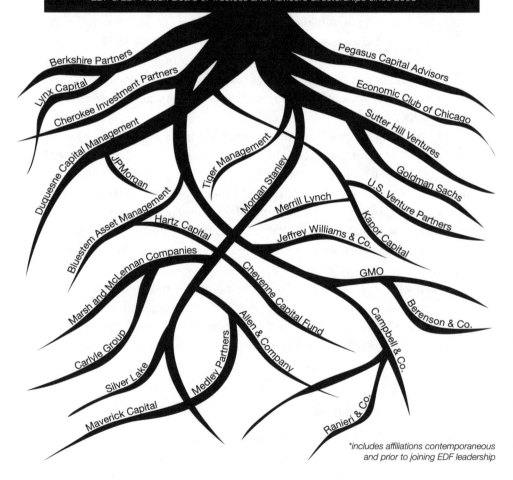

Environmental
Defense Fund

The Wall Street Roots of Corporate Environmentalism
*EDF & EDF Action Board of Trustees and Advisors directorships since 2006**

Berkshire Partners

Lynx Capital

Cherokee Investment Partners

Duquesne Capital Management

JPMorgan

Tiger Management

Morgan Stanley

Merrill Lynch

Bluestem Asset Management

Hartz Capital

Jeffrey Williams & Co.

Kapor Capital

Marsh and McLennan Companies

Cheyenne Capital Fund

GMO

Carlyle Group

Allen & Company

Campbell & Co.

Berenson & Co.

Silver Lake

Medley Partners

Maverick Capital

Ranieri & Co.

Pegasus Capital Advisors

Economic Club of Chicago

Sutter Hill Ventures

Goldman Sachs

U.S. Venture Partners

*includes affiliations contemporaneous
and prior to joining EDF leadership*

State University of New York at Stony Brook, and scientists from Brookhaven National Laboratory. Opposed to Suffolk County's high-profile spraying of DDT, the group joined forces with a local lawyer, Victor Yannacone, to successfully sue over the use of the dangerous pesticide. Yannacone and his wife, Carol, along with scientists Art Cooley, Charlie Wurster, and Dennis Puleston, expanded the mission of the original group, co-founding EDF in 1967 along with several of the other trustees.[63]

After the group sought financial support from the Audubon Society and failed—because, at the time, some trustees had ties to chemical companies and other industries—the group began seeking funding elsewhere. Robert Gottlieb, editor of the *New Yorker* from 1987 to 1992, commented on the history of EDF in his 1992 book *Forcing the Spring: The Transformation of the American Environmental Movement*: "In its first years, the organization was dominated by Yannacone through his forceful personality, effective use of cross-examination, willingness to go public and mobilize people as part of his legal strategy, and irreverent adversarial stance that linked him in some ways to the protest culture of the period."[64]

At the first Earth Day celebration, held in Washington, D.C., in 1970, Yannacone gave a rally speech titled "Sue the Bastards." Reportedly Yannacone soon was forced out of the organization, as key figures in its leadership sought to temper EDF's approach. New trustees with corporate ties were added in the early 1970s, and the organization's tone and goals were moderated. This opened up an opportunity for significant funding from the Ford Foundation. In exchange for a $285,000 grant—half of the EDF budget at the time—its leadership agreed to an oversight group, called the "Gurus," that comprised five past presidents of the American Bar Association. EDF also was required to create the Litigation Review Committee—comprising prominent members of both political parties—that would have veto power over litigation.

Amyas Ames, a partner in the powerful investment banking firm of Kidder, Peabody and a major underwriter of investor-owned utilities, was added to the EDF board. Ames, who served as chairman of the Investment Bankers Association from 1962 to 1969, later said that he joined the board because of "EDF's very early policy of working in cooperation with business and industry."[65] Gottlieb writes:

> The group kept its distance from grassroots activities and movements, continuing to emphasize its professional character. . . . During the late 1970s the organization began to more systematically pursue the idea that

Kidder, Peabody's Amyas Ames had first raised on joining the EDF board: cooperation with industry through the search for what the organization called "win-win" strategies. . . . This focus on a potential economic common ground between industry and environmentalists, encouraged by the growing number of staff economists within the organization, evolved during the Reagan and Bush years into an overarching EDF strategy to promote market incentives, replacing regulation as a primary tool for reshaping environmental policy.[66]

By the 1980s, NRDC had overtaken EDF as the most prominent environmental litigator and, according to Gottlieb, "had come to symbolize the ascendency of professionalism among the mainstream groups." NRDC also had been funded by the Ford Foundation and was subject to the same litigation review process as EDF, and the organization benefited financially from having wealthy and powerful board members such as Laurance Rockefeller. In 1984, as EDF's litigation efforts were overshadowed by NRDC's, EDF was not only searching for a new president but also struggling to raise money for its litigation agenda.[67]

Frank Loy, chairman of EDF's board of trustees, was in charge of the search for a new president, a grueling process. Loy reminisced that a headhunter introduced Krupp to the hiring committee late in the game, after the board had already selected another candidate. The thirty-year-old Krupp, a graduate of the University of Michigan Law School and a former EDF and NRDC legal intern, had been working for the statewide advocacy group that he had co-founded, Connecticut Fund for the Environment. Ten years younger than the other candidates, he was a long shot for the job of president, in an organization staffed by more seasoned attorneys. Krupp acknowledges that most of the staff at the time did not accept his "approach" because they hoped to evolve the organization into one "built around first-class litigators."[68]

Krupp was amenable to the corporate-friendly views of Loy, a trustee of EDF since 1981, with an emeritus status today. Loy acknowledges that even before Krupp was hired, EDF staff members "were Wall Street tree-huggers rather than California tree-huggers." He says the place was "very Main Street, which made it distinct from Greenpeace, Sierra Club, Friends of the Earth, even NRDC. Back then a very large fraction of the environmental movement was hostile to business. Environmental Defense, even before Fred, was not."[69]

At the time that he hired Krupp, Loy was serving as president of the German Marshall Fund (GMF), an American foundation established during the Cold War to promote U.S. economic and political policies in Western Europe. Loy, a German-born American, has played a role in public policy debates similar to that of John McCloy, the power broker dubbed "Chairman of the Establishment," and their professional lives had some overlap. Both men received law degrees from Harvard, practiced financial law in prestigious law firms, and established close relationships with investment banks and other powerful corporate interests. Emblematic of the revolving door between corporations, business-oriented nonprofits, and government, McCloy and Loy also served on many corporate and nonprofit boards. McCloy, an honorary trustee of the GMF at its inception in 1972, was instrumental in its founding and continued to be involved with the foundation until his death in 1989.[70] He had extremely close ties with its founder, Guido Goldman, and trustee David Rockefeller.[71]

While Loy was president of the German Marshall Fund from 1981 to 1995, he facilitated the funding of communication efforts in Germany that reflected a corporate-friendly, free-market economic and trade agenda. The GMF provided training and scholarships for the next generation of German policy makers in a way designed to shape their belief system and values, making them sympathetic to a laissez-faire economic system.[72] When the Berlin Wall fell in 1989, the GMF was one of the first organizations to establish an operation in what had been East Berlin, expanding its work in Central and Eastern Europe, where it promoted this economic agenda under the rubric of "democracy." The GMF funded and deployed nonprofits that supported adopting an economic system that would benefit U.S. corporate interests.[73]

Under Loy's leadership, the GMF also supported a program on acid rain through an initiative at the National Governors Association. In 2001, after years of pressure to weaken the Clean Air Act by replacing regulation with emissions trading, the National Governors Association passed a unanimous resolution supporting "a flexible, market-based program" that "should provide regulatory certainty . . . by providing market-based incentives such as emissions-trading credits to help achieve the required reductions."[74]

Appointed by President Clinton in 1998 to be undersecretary of state for global affairs, Loy took the opportunity to talk about his association with EDF at his confirmation hearing before the U.S. Senate Committee on Foreign Relations. He said: "I joined the board of the Environmental Defense Fund because it was interested in assessing the economic implications of various environmental programs, and was willing and anxious to work with the business community and other parts of American society. I served as chairman of its board from 1983 to 1990. In that period the organization developed and launched what was called the "third wave of environmentalism," i.e., solving environmental problems by relying on economic incentives and market-based mechanisms.[75]

While serving in this State Department position from 1998 to 2001, Loy was the lead on climate issues, serving as chief negotiator at The Hague Climate Conference during this period. Talks broke down because of the intransigence on the use of carbon offsets, a centerpiece of the U.S. policy on cap and trade. European negotiators had grave concerns about the United States refusing to cut emissions from power plants, factories, and cars and insisting on the right to use carbon sequestration* in forests and cropland to offset emissions.[76]

In 2008, Loy served as key environmental and energy policy adviser to the Obama campaign as well as part of the campaign's official fund-raising committee. When Obama appointed Loy as alternate U.S. representative to the 66th Session of the UN General Assembly in 2011, his was the fourth administration to appoint Loy to a senior position at the Department of State.[77] Loy continues to serve on the EDF board, where more than a quarter of the trustees are closely associated with the financial and investment industry, a sector that benefits from speculating on natural resources and market mechanisms such as cap and trade. *Fortune* magazine called EDF's board one of the most influential in the country.[78]

Today Loy, Stavins, and Gray continue to work in the same policy circles, promoting emissions trading and other corporate-friendly mechanisms for solving environmental problems. The three men serve on the board of Resources for the Future (RFF), another organization that is advancing "environmental economics" and "market mechanisms." The group's director, Phil Sharp, was a Democratic congressman from Indiana from 1983 to 1995. He was chairman of the House Energy and Power Subcommittee,

---

* Rather than cutting climate pollution emissions, some advocates of cap and trade argue that polluters should be able to buy credits "sequestered" in carbon sinks—the carbon dioxide absorbed from the atmosphere by forests, the ocean, or other natural resources.

playing a key role in passage of the 1990 Clean Air Act amendments and the 1992 Energy Policy Act, which led to the deregulation of the wholesale electricity market. Sharp serves on the board of the Energy Foundation and also was co-chair of the Energy Board at the Keystone Center, a pro-fracking policy group.[79] The Energy Foundation gave more than $900,000 to RFF between 2000 and 2013, including grants for carbon markets and energy policy.[80] With additional support from the Sloan Foundation, RFF is engaged in a study to determine the "pathway toward responsible development" of fracking and how to manage the risks of the practice.[81]

Politically powerful elites from both major political parties have used their prestige and position to promote both cap and trade and fracking, at the expense of the global climate, the environment, and public health. The current crisis demands much more than experiments with emissions trading and reliance on fracked gas. It is past time to demand what we really want and need: an end to fracking, keeping fossil fuels in the ground, and truly addressing the climate emergency.

Photo courtesy of Food & Water Watch

19

HARD-FOUGHT VICTORY IN NEW YORK

I've never had anyone say to me, "I believe fracking is great."
—New York governor Andrew Cuomo[1]

"Ban fracking now!" was the powerful rally cry of the tens of thousands of activists who won a historic victory in New York in 2014. After years of relentless grassroots opposition to fracking, Democratic governor Andrew Cuomo's administration banned fracking, citing "significant public health risks."[2] The victory in New York was possible because the large movement of fracking opponents called for what they really wanted—a ban on fracking—instead of what was deemed politically feasible.

Going up against the powerful oil and gas industry, the tenacious New York anti-fracking movement redefined fracking as a serious threat to human health and built the political power to ultimately influence the governor's decision. Shifting public opinion, which has been documented by regular polling on the issue, was largely a result of the years of campaigning by the "ban fracking" movement. By December 2014, 55 percent of New Yorkers approved of a ban, while only 25 percent disapproved.[3] This contrasts sharply with a poll in August 2011, in which 47 percent of New Yorkers supported fracking while only 42 percent were opposed.[4]

The Battle for the Ban

In 2008, when news began spreading that the oil and gas industry was buying leases in the counties sitting atop the Marcellus Shale, a small group of grassroots activists began sounding the alarm. At the same time, leaders in New York's mainstream environmental community called for the state to regulate fracking, an option that they felt was most realistic. In response to concerns about fracking, New York's Department of Environmental Conservation (DEC) instituted an environmental review.[5] Opposition continued to mount as anecdotal evidence emerged in other states about fracking's devastating impacts on drinking water and air. In response, the Onondaga Nation and many frontline grassroots activists began calling for a ban on fracking—a goal that mainstream environmentalists felt was unachievable.

By 2009, when the DEC released its draft environmental assessment, the agency had received thirteen thousand comments on whether to allow fracking in New York.[6] The following year, as pressure mounted regarding the inadequacy of the review, Governor David Paterson vetoed legislation that put a moratorium on fracking and on more conventional drilling. At the same time, he signed an executive order prohibiting fracking until the DEC completed its comprehensive environmental review.[7]

In the meantime, Josh Fox, whose family had been approached by a natural gas company interested in leasing their land in Pennsylvania, had been making a movie about the impacts of fracking. Fox and other concerned grassroots activists organized screenings of the Oscar-nominated film *Gasland* around the state prior to its release at Sundance in 2010. The film served as a catalyst for the rapidly growing number of deeply committed people opposed to fracking in New York.[8]

Actor Mark Ruffalo, a resident of upstate Sullivan County, became so concerned about the dangers posed by fracking that he committed to using his popularity to inform the public about the potential risk to water resources. On a fact-finding trip to Dimock, Pennsylvania, organized by Catskill Mountainkeeper, Ruffalo saw firsthand the devastating impacts that residents of fracked communities faced. It became one of many trips that he would take to support affected families.[9] Wes Gillingham, program director at the organization, teamed up with photographer J. Henry Fair to take aerial photos of the scars left by fracking in Pennsylvania, which he and others used in presentations around the state. Ramsey Adams, Catskill Mountainkeeper's executive director, committed resources to publicizing the industry's attempts to gain a foothold in New York.

During these early years of the movement, news spread quickly about the risks associated with fracking. Grassroots environmental activists began holding forums and conducting outreach to a broad base of people. Dozens of local grassroots groups formed, meeting around kitchen tables and in coffee shops and church basements.

As this wave of activism intensified, former corporate attorneys Helen and David Slottje pioneered a legal approach that towns could use to ban fracking within their borders. Although some of the most prominent environmental attorneys in the state had given up on using the legal system to stop fracking, the two lawyers developed a legal theory based on a clause in the state constitution that gives municipalities the right to make local land-use decisions. The Slottjes worked with scores of communities over the next several years, and by 2014 more than 170 jurisdictions in New York had used the language that the couple had developed to enact local prohibitions. On behalf of their work, Helen was awarded the Goldman Environmental Prize in 2014.[10] When challenged in New York's highest court, the Slottjes' legal theory proved to be sound. Helen says that they wanted to "get people involved in their local politics and use that as an entry point where you can begin to effect some change, despite the dysfunction at higher levels of government."[11]

While the Slottjes were plugging away on local bans, Julia Walsh was forming Frack Action, a grassroots powerhouse that would be central in the fight to ban fracking. Bringing hundreds of young people into the grassroots movement, Frack Action's leadership team began a statewide organizing effort focused on coordinating and building the movement in all regions of the state. In the months before contentious elections in 2010, Walsh, who had been elected to the New Paltz town council in 2003 at the age of twenty-three, focused on communicating the dangers posed by fracking.

By emphasizing the similarities with the BP Gulf of Mexico oil disaster, Walsh worked to successfully garner support for passing a moratorium on fracking in the state's legislature. In an effort to attract media attention, she organized one of the dozens of press conferences that would be held on the issue of fracking over the next several years. At an event featuring folksinger Pete Seeger, Ruffalo, and Ulster County legislator Susan Zimet, Seeger roused the crowd, poignantly singing: "When 'drill, baby, drill' turns to 'spill, baby, spill' / God's countin' on me." Ruffalo, holding a jar of contaminated water from Dimock, Pennsylvania, told lawmakers to "get off your butts and lead."[12]

On the last possible day that the New York Senate could meet before the 2010 election, activists from Frack Action, Catskill Mountainkeeper, and a small group of concerned residents arrived at the state capitol ready to drag every Democrat to the floor for the vote on the moratorium. After an extremely chaotic day of arm-twisting, the bill passed, 48–9. In November, the more environmentally minded State Assembly voted 93–43 in favor of a similar bill.[13] Outgoing governor David Paterson vetoed the legislation, however, replacing it with an executive order placing a moratorium on horizontal fracking until the state could complete an environmental review.[14] The moratorium would remain in place for several years as the movement built the political power to win the ban.

News about the dangers related to fracking was spreading rapidly, prompting gutsy United for Action activists David Braun and Ling Tsou to launch a mighty organizing effort in the Big Apple. Braun explains, "We knew that it would take guts to fight for a ban, but that it was the only responsible option."[15] Notes Tsou, "The mainstream environmental organizations thought the best we could get were good regulations and thought we were crazy."[16] United for Action turned out large numbers of people for events in New York City and for buses to Albany.

In January 2011, Andrew Cuomo was sworn in as governor of New York. He had already signaled his willingness to accept fracking during the campaign, saying, "The economic potential from the Marcellus Shale could provide a badly needed boost to the economy of the Southern Tier and even many environmentalists agree we want to produce more domestic natural gas that reduces the need for environmentally damaging fuel sources such as coal."[17]

New York's power structure—in bed with the frackers—had another blow coming. Cornell University professors Bob Howarth and Tony Ingraffea shook the industry and its allies a few months later with the release of their peer-reviewed study on the global warming footprint of shale gas. (See Chapter 17.) But the research seemed to have made no impression on Governor Cuomo, who continued moving the state toward the legalization of fracking, ordering New York's DEC to complete its latest draft of the fracking environmental review.[18]

Yet the evidence about the dangers of fracking continued to grow. Food & Water Watch became the first national organization to call for a ban on fracking, releasing a widely circulated report in June 2011 called "The Case for a Ban on Fracking." Outlining research by scientists, Congress, and investigative journalists documenting the serious health and environmental impacts associated with fracking, the report made the case that regulating fracking (as opposed to banning it) could not prevent the serious threats that it posed.

Despite the growing body of scientific evidence, the Cuomo administration sought to divide and conquer the expanding anti-fracking movement by announcing later in the summer an outright ban on fracking within the New York City and Syracuse watersheds, thus protecting drinking water sources for the state's largest urban areas.[19] The response by the grassroots fracking movement was swift.

Braun recalls that Frack Action began planning a rally in Albany to say no to this contentious plan, and United for Action started filling buses with activists for the three-hour ride from New York City to Albany, a ride that they would take many times in the coming years. Fracking activists made clear that they would not support creating a fracking "sacrifice zone" anywhere in New York, and the growing coalition of fracking opponents called on the governor to ban fracking.[20]

In the fall of 2011 the DEC released the proposed fracking regulations for comment. Under fire from activists who were regularly protesting in Albany, Cuomo said that the rule making was "fair, intelligent and open, and I am letting the process proceed."[21] The movement began a massive organizing effort to get people out to hearings in different parts of the state and to send in comments.

By January 2012 the DEC had received a record 67,000 comments, with the majority against fracking.[22] The large grassroots effort had made this outpouring possible.

New Yorkers Against Fracking

Frack Action, Food & Water Watch, Catskill Mountainkeeper, Water Defense (Mark Ruffalo's organization), Citizen Action of New York, and the Working Families Party initiated a series of meetings about forming a coalition. Uniting under New Yorkers Against Fracking (NYAF), an alliance with a formalized decision-making structure, the coalition's leadership developed a strategy that focused on Cuomo—the ultimate decision maker.

Ecologist Sandra Steingraber, Distinguished Scholar in Residence at Ithaca College and a recipient of the Heinz Award for her life's work—a prize that comes with a $100,000 check—was excited about the coalition. Donating some of the seed money to help get NYAF off the ground, she said, "There is no more important investment that I could make right now than to support the fight for the integrity of the ecological system that makes their lives possible." Joining Steingraber on the advisory committee were singer Natalie Merchant; Ruffalo; and Lois Gibbs, a Niagara native, former Love Canal resident, and the founder of the Center for Health, Environment and Justice.[23] Coordinated through a steering committee of the founding organizations, regular communications with grassroots members were a key component of success. One method of giving and receiving information was regularly sponsored conference calls conducted by Braun and other coalition leadership.

NYAF helped unify and amplify the efforts of the more than 250 organizations that eventually joined in campaigning for the ban. Alex Beauchamp, Northeast Region director for Food & Water Watch, explained the philosophy behind the alliance: "Too often, organizations try to win these battles in the halls of the capitol, but we put our resources into building and mobilizing power where it could have the greatest impact—at the grassroots."[24]

The coalition strengthened grassroots efforts by hiring regional organizers to help coordinate activities in different parts of the state. The coalition's structure made it possible to synchronize tactics—petition drives, letters to the editor, call-in days, rallies, and other strategic activities focused on the governor. NYAF members and other grassroots activists were unrelenting in "bird-dogging" Cuomo wherever he appeared, sometimes by the hundreds or thousands, always demanding a ban on fracking. Karen Scharff, executive director of Citizen Action of New York, notes, "It was really important that the coalition adopted tactics that were energizing and inspiring for the grassroots, enabling them to have their voices heard and feel the movement growing."[25]

Cuomo Moves Ahead

On June 12, 2012, the *New York Times* floated the Cuomo administration's plan to allow fracking to commence in five Southern Tier counties that adjoin Pennsylvania.[26] NYAF immediately jumped into action, organizing rallies around the state and a press conference that included mainstream environmental groups. The solidarity between NYAF groups and big environmental groups on a refusal to permit sacrifice zones meant that the Cuomo administration had no cover from green groups for moving ahead with this plan.[27] Steingraber reflected: "Partitioning our state into frack and no-frack zones based on economic desperation is a shameful idea. . . . There are no children and counties in our beloved state that we are willing to sacrifice."[28]

Responding to the threat, the coalition began organizing different constituencies into a political force demanding a ban on fracking. During the summer of 2012 NYAF announced that more than a thousand businesses had signed on in support of a statewide ban on fracking. "The gas industry makes a lot of claims about jobs," said Larry Bennett of Brewery Ommegang, near Cooperstown. "But we have actually been creating jobs in upstate New York and know that fracking will make it harder for us to grow our business."[29]

Activists began uniting around a powerful new "Pledge to Resist Fracking in New York." Major rallies were held around the state encouraging people to take and sign the pledge, agreeing to do everything they could to stop fracking if Governor Cuomo permitted it in any part of New York State. At a massive rally in Albany at the end of August, more than twelve hundred people marched through the streets to demonstrate that New Yorkers would not accept a single fracked well in their state.[30]

It was clear that the governor, an ambitious politician, was weighing how his position on fracking would affect his political future. So in September 2012, when he flew into Charlotte, North Carolina, to attend the Democratic National Convention, he was greeted by an ad calling on him to be a leader. More than a hundred organizations from across the nation co-signed the full-page advertisement in the *Charlotte Observer* that he encountered when he exited the airport.[31] Also that month, in response to mounting concerns from health professionals, Cuomo's environmental chief announced that New York's health commissioner would undertake a health review of the state's draft fracking guidelines.

At the end of November 2012, after it had come to light that fracking waste from the Marcellus region was significantly more radioactive than had been recognized in the past, the DEC released the draft fracking rules. Cuomo's top environmental chief did not schedule any public hearings and gave only thirty days for public comment—a time that stretched over the busy holiday season.[32]

The regulations offered little in the way of protections for land and water resources or public health. The coalition jumped into action over the next several months, organizing an outpouring of opposition. New Yorkers sent more than two hundred thousand comments to the DEC opposing fracking. More than fifteen hundred New Yorkers descended on the state capitol in January 2013 as the governor gave his State of the State address.[33] Activists arranged dozens of screenings of Jon Bowermaster's film *Dear*

Governor Cuomo, which documented the reasons that such a diverse number of constituencies—from musicians to scientists—were fighting to ban. In the meantime, the governor's staff began to keep his schedule under wraps, attempting to prevent the nonstop bird-dogging.

At the end of January 2013, as the deadline for the release of the final fracking rules passed, NYAF brought impacted residents of Pennsylvania to an Albany press event. NYAF marked the occasion by running television ads highlighting the emerging stories of sick families, dead cows, and poisoned water. Later in the winter, when the chief of the DEC testified at a budget hearing, hundreds of New Yorkers filled the hearing room to capacity, emboldened by the latest statewide public opinion poll that showed an even division between those for and against fracking, but with opponents much more passionate than supporters.[34]

In the next several months, NYAF continued to push back. Dozens of faith leaders traveled to Albany to lead a multidenominational prayer against fracking in front of the governor's office. More than three hundred faith leaders and institutions across the state had joined in the call for a ban on fracking.[35] When Cuomo, a future presidential hopeful, traveled to Iowa, NYAF organized a full-page ad in the *Des Moines Register*, co-signed by 135 environmental, public health, faith, and labor organizations.[36] New York health professionals released a letter from health and environmental leaders, advocating for a New York–specific health impact assessment that would include public participation before making a decision on fracking.[37]

Cuomo was swamped with calls for a ban during the spring and summer of 2013. NYAF made public the fact that ExxonMobil had spent $2 million in New York touting fracking in ads, making it the second-biggest vested interest in the state in 2012.[38] It was revealed that a consulting firm that the DEC had contracted with to provide research on the economic and seismologic impacts of fracking had a conflict of interest, having signed a letter to Governor Cuomo, organized by the Independent Oil and Gas Association, urging that New York move forward with fracking.[39] More than two thousand New Yorkers traveled to Albany in June 2013, calling on the governor to reject fracking and to adopt policies that would lead to a renewable energy future.[40]

Next, the celebrity-conscious Cuomo learned that Yoko Ono and Sean Lennon had organized Artists Against Fracking, a new network announced on *Late Night with Jimmy Fallon*. One hundred and thirty artists strong, the group included Leonardo DiCaprio, Julianne Moore, Alec Baldwin, Lady Gaga, Josh Fox, the Beastie Boys, and many others.[41] A few weeks later NYAF organized rallies to greet President Obama in Buffalo, Syracuse, and Binghamton, telling him to reject fracking as a false solution to climate change.[42] In the late fall, with the governor beginning to run for reelection, NYAF members rallied a Cuomo fund-raiser in Buffalo, urging him to listen to the science and ban fracking.

Growing Evidence of Harm

Paralleling the growth of the movement was an increasing body of scientific evidence about the public health threats from fracking. Early on, Larysa Dyrszka, a retired pediatrician from Sullivan County, had used the handful of peer-reviewed studies to raise awareness about potential threats. In 2012 she and Sandra Steingraber were two of a number of doctors, scientists, and others in the medical profession to form Concerned Health Professionals of New York, a group that would play an important role in bringing the facts to light and demanding that science be used in the decision-making process.

By 2013 an avalanche of research had come forward, with almost two hundred studies showing risks and adverse health effects. By the end of December 2014 Concerned Health Professionals had produced an updated compendium of research that included four hundred peer-reviewed studies on the different impacts of fracking. PSE Healthy Energy, a multidisciplinary research and policy institute, conducted a statistical analysis of the research, finding that 96 percent of all the papers published on health impacts indicated potential risks or adverse health outcomes.[43]

2014: Another Year of Organizing

Thousands of New Yorkers once again descended on Cuomo's State of the State address, demanding a ban on fracking.[44] As exhausted as the ban-fracking activists were, they realized that it was critical to keep the momentum going, organizing events, traveling to Albany for hearings, and bird-dogging the governor.

During the spring of 2014 the American Petroleum Institute spent millions of dollars on a new national ad campaign focused on New York. NYAF drew reporters' attention to a Gallup Poll showing that Americans have less confidence in the oil and gas industry than in any other business.[45] NYAF helped organize the response to New York's draft state energy plan, sending fifty thousand comments to the governor.

At the end of May, with the election growing closer, Zephyr Teachout, a Fordham University Law professor, declared her candidacy in the Democratic primary for governor. Teachout, who advocated for a ban on fracking, declared, "The system is rigged, and Andrew Cuomo is part of the broken system."[46] While Teachout took the state by storm, giving Cuomo a run for his money, NYAF continued its signature tactic of bird-dogging the governor day in and day out by scouring the media for information on his public appearances. All told, the coalition organized rallies outside more than thirty of the governor's public events in 2014.

On primary day in September, Food & Water Watch campaigner Eric Weltman and a band of protesters greeted the governor as he went into the polling station to vote, calling out to him, "Ban fracking now." Inside the polling location, Cuomo told reporters that the anti-fracking movement was "literally the most prevalent protest group in the state by far." He told reporters inside that when they had arrived at an event and not been greeted by anti-fracking demonstrators, his daughter had joked, "We must be in the wrong place. There's no fracking protesters."[47]

Teachout took one-third of the vote in the primary, the greatest challenge to an incumbent governor since primaries were initiated in New York in 1970. She won counties across the state, from those bordering Canada to the suburbs of New York City.[48] On Election Day in November Cuomo beat his Republican opponent, Rob Astorino, but he won with what was likely the lowest number of votes since Franklin Roosevelt was reelected governor in 1930—even though there had been 6 million fewer New Yorkers back in FDR's day.[49]

After the election, fracking activists held their breath, wondering what Cuomo would do now that this milestone was past. Southern Tier residents rallied in Binghamton on the day before the Cuomo administration was to make its decision. NYAF member groups had joined with mainstream environmental organizations in the campaign calling for "Not One Well" in the Southern Tier. Although the large environmental organizations had never joined NYAF in calling for a ban, the big greens did not undermine NYAF's work and were an important force in elevating the visibility of the health and environmental risks. Unlike in states such as Illinois, where mainstream groups signed off on weak regulatory deals, in New York NYAF and the mainstream environmental community had good communication and a respectful relationship.

In addition to the work of NYAF and the other groups discussed in this chapter, many additional nonprofit organizations, grassroots groups, and activists played an important role in winning the campaign. The success came both from having a clear strategy and from the selfless work of the people committed to the same goal: protecting New York from fracking.

Winning!

On Wednesday, December 17, 2014, after working diligently for more than seven years to maintain the fracking moratorium former governor David Paterson had declared, fracking activists gathered in front of their computer monitors to watch the televised cabinet meeting where the Cuomo administration's final verdict on fracking would be revealed.

Acting health commissioner Howard Zucker summarized the Cuomo administration's decision to ban fracking: "We cannot afford to make a mistake," he said. "The potential risks are too great. In fact, they are not even fully known." [50] Besides serious health threats, the 184-page report documented a whole host of dangers: earthquakes, soil contamination, noise pollution, and air pollution. [51] After years of investigation, deliberation, and organized grassroots power, the public health argument won the day.

In an unusual twist, the jubilant NYAF groups and other allies hastily organized a victory rally outside the governor's midtown Manhattan office. The mood was joyful, with activists returning to the site where they'd yelled "Ban fracking now!" countless times. Governor Cuomo showed up to welcome the crowd. He was all smiles as he congratulated the fracking activists for "making your voices heard." The crowd had signed an oversized thank-you card. Cuomo took the card and with a grin said, "This one, I'm going to keep."

Julia Walsh from the grassroots organization Frack Action, which had long campaigned for a fracking ban in New York State, issued a statement that read in part: "This decision will affect New York for generations to come. We now look forward to making New York the renewable energy capital of the United States, leading the nation to a better, brighter future." [52]

Photo courtesy of Food & Water Watch

20

THE BAN MOVEMENT GROWS,
STRETCHING COAST TO COAST

And my friends, in this story you have a history of this entire movement.
First they ignore you. Then they ridicule you. And then they attack you
and want to burn you. And then they build monuments to you.

—Nicholas Klein,
Amalgamated Clothing Workers of America, 1918[1]

As enormous pressure was growing in New York to ban fracking, a second front in the battle opened when Pennsylvania's former governor, Tom Corbett, schemed to allow fracking in the Delaware River Basin. Rain, snow, and icy water flow from the mountains and rolling hills into the basin's two hundred tributaries, eventually reaching the 330-mile Delaware River and providing drinking water for more than 15 million people in New York, New Jersey, Delaware, and Pennsylvania. The fate of the watershed depends on an obscure interstate agency, the Delaware River Basin Commission (DRBC), a body formed during the Kennedy administration and directed by the governors of the four states.[2]

When Corbett's fracking plans surfaced in 2010, the Delaware Riverkeeper Network sounded the alarm and a network of groups came together to develop a strategy for halting the governor's plot. At this early period little research was available on the threats posed by fracking, and Food & Water Watch teamed up with Barbara Arrindell from Damascus Citizens for Sustainability to write the report "Not So Fast, Natural Gas." In a testament to coalition work, Delaware Riverkeeper Network helped organize a large rally and press conference before the commission hearing in July 2010, where the report was released. Word spread quickly about the threats, so each time the commission met, increasing numbers of people came to voice their opposition. In each of the four Delaware basin states, activists' efforts focused on the governors, the ultimate decision makers at the DRBC.

In early 2011 the commission announced six hearings on its draft fracking regulation. By this time the anti-fracking coalition had grown to over sixty organizations, which included many local groups, such as the Franciscan Response to Fracking and the Industrial Union Council. Tens of thousands of people signed petitions supporting bans on fracking in each state, which were delivered to the governors, and hundreds of people attended the hearings. But none of the governors or their representatives attended these meetings.

In the meantime, Food & Water Watch's New Jersey office led a campaign to ban fracking in that state, succeeding in getting legislation passed in June 2011. Governor Chris Christie vetoed the bill and, in its place, declared a one-year moratorium on drilling.[3] Greatly disappointed by the veto, activists were hopeful that the pressure that Christie felt would discourage him from supporting fracking at the DRBC.

Also responding to public sentiments, New York State attorney general Eric Schneiderman sued the U.S. Army Corps of Engineers, the federal representative on the commission, as well as the DRBC itself and several other federal agencies, for failing to conduct an environmental impact review of fracking, as required by the National Environmental Policy Act. Although the lawsuit was thrown out of court, it embroiled the DRBC decision in more controversy.[4] Pressure also mounted on Delaware governor Jack Markel, whose state has no shale resources and has little to gain from supporting fracking.

A final vote on the rules was scheduled for September 2011. Thousands of people signed up in advance to travel by bus to the meeting where the vote would take place, and hundreds vowed to engage in civil disobedience. This tremendous mobilization caused the commission to push the vote off until October.[5]

Pressure continued to build on the DRBC when it received a letter signed by more than 170 environmental, consumer, and faith groups. Jim Walsh, a regional director at Food & Water Watch, urged the DRBC "to stop working to figure out how to drill in the Delaware River and start moving towards a permanent ban in that critical watershed to make sure this drinking water is protected."[6]

Tracy Carluccio, deputy director of Delaware Riverkeeper Network, declared, "People fought very hard to put that moratorium in place. . . .

[Fracking] is destroying our streams and waterways and there is no way we can allow that to happen at the Delaware watershed."[7]

In a blatant attempt to depress turnout, the vote was rescheduled again, this time for the Monday before Thanksgiving. But the strategy failed. Just days before the vote, simultaneous rallies opposing drilling were held throughout the region, and Delaware governor Markel released a letter stating his opposition to drilling in the Delaware River Basin. The following day the DRBC announced that it would cancel the vote planed for the following week and table plans to allow fracking in the basin.[8] Despite the cancellation of the vote, more than a thousand people traveled to Trenton, New Jersey, the site of the canceled meeting, to celebrate the victory.

As of this writing, the DRBC regulations are still officially tabled, although a vote can be scheduled with as little as ten days' notice. Pennsylvania's new governor, Tom Wolf, elected in 2014, is a fracking proponent but has pledged to maintain the Delaware River Basin moratorium,[9] and New Jersey governor Christie is unlikely to want to deal with the controversy while running for president. So, for now, the basin is safe.

The victory in the Delaware River Basin spurred further organizing throughout the region. Buoyed by the victory, the Vermont Public Interest Research Group led a campaign in 2012 that resulted in passage of an indefinite moratorium on fracking in that state—a de facto ban. While some states have or had broader laws that prevented the practice, Vermont was the first state to pass a measure specifically outlawing high-volume hydraulic fracking in response to the recent boom. Even though there is little shale in Vermont, this effort still drew significant opposition from the oil and gas industry.[10]

In New Jersey, communities have continued to push for a ban on fracking and on the disposal of fracking waste being brought into the state from neighboring Pennsylvania. Dozens of communities have passed measures supporting statewide legislation and prohibiting fracking and frack waste, and the legislature overwhelmingly passed a ban on both fracking and frack waste, only to have these measures vetoed by Governor Christie.[11] Still, as of this writing, there is no fracking in the Garden State.

Coloradans Fight Back

More than fifteen hundred miles away, in Colorado, activists faced Democratic governor John Hickenlooper, who, like Corbett, had eagerly embraced fracking. With its long history of fossil fuel development, Colorado is one of the most fracked states in the country and has more than 52,000 active wells.[12]

In 2014, there were two oil or gas spills every day in Colorado—and local residents were typically kept in the dark, even though one-fifth of the spills contaminated groundwater or local streams.[13] There were more than two thousand spills between 2008 and 2012, 17 percent of which contaminated groundwater, including with cancer-causing chemicals such as benzene.[14] Researchers from the University of Missouri reported that hormone-disrupting chemicals have been found in the Colorado River near concentrated drilling sites.[15] Coloradans have discussed the terrible health impacts they experienced from living near wells, while a recent study showed that close proximity to oil and gas drilling, including fracking, was associated with a greater incidence of birth defects in rural parts of the state.[16]

Also, unlike New York, where courts have upheld the long-established rights of local communities to enact local land-use controls on industrial activities such as fracking, the Colorado legislature and its courts have spent the last several decades actively handing the state over to the oil and gas industry, with little regard for the rights of citizens and for the health and safety of local communities. Two state court cases from the 1990s held that it is the state that determines oil and gas land use restrictions such as setbacks, noise abatement, and visual impacts, not local governments, which are preempted from enacting more protective standards.[17] Coloradans are living with a fracking fiasco that New York will never see.

It is against this oppressive setting that the citizens of Longmont, Colorado—including Kaye Fissinger, president of Our Health, Our Future, Our Longmont—and other local communities have been fighting their ongoing battle to save their homes. "People are getting tired of powerful interests coming in and telling us how to live," Fissinger said.[18] Led by these grassroots activists and assisted by Food & Water Watch, the people of the city of Longmont overwhelmingly passed a fracking ban in their community in a November 2012 election, after deciding that they did not want to live their lives and raise their children under the ongoing threats to health and the environment posed by this irresponsible method of energy extraction.

The Longmont win was even more remarkable given the spending by the oil and gas industry. In a community of just 87,000 residents, the industry spent $440,000, bombarding voters with misleading radio and television ads, multiple mailers, and full-page newspaper ads. Despite being outspent nearly twenty to one, almost 60 percent of Longmont's voters elected to protect their community from fracking.[19] Longmont's citizens voted for the ban knowing full well the uphill battle they would face in Colorado's courts.

It was not unexpected that the lower court decided against the people of Longmont in July 2014, with the judge declaring Longmont's fracking ban illegal. In a decision that served to further galvanize the push for local control of fracking in Colorado, the court held that a democratically enacted ban was invalid because it conflicted with the state's interests in promoting mineral development. "It's tragic that the judge views the current law in Colorado as one in which fracking is more important than public health; reversing that backward priority is a long-term battle that we're determined to continue," Fissinger commented.[20]

In its finding, the court stated: "Longmont and the environmental groups, the Defendant-Intervenors, are essentially asking this Court to establish a public policy that favors protection from health, safety, and environmental risks over the development of mineral resources. Whether public policy *should* be changed in that manner is a question for the legislature or a different court."[21] Although the court ultimately disagreed with the residents of Longmont, its open invitation to appeal while maintaining the ban leaves Longmont positioned to reverse the misguided state policy of placing industry's financial interests over citizens' health. As of August 2015 the Longmont case is still on appeal, and nearly three years after its passage, the ban remains in effect, protecting Longmont—for the time being—from fracking.

The passage of the ban helped spur the anti-fracking fight across the state, in no small part because it was achieved in the face of incredible odds. In November 2013 four communities placed measures to halt or ban fracking on the ballot, and all passed.[22] The *Denver Post* estimated that statewide the oil and gas industry outspent the grassroots fracking opponents by nearly thirty-four to one, with the Colorado Oil and Gas Association spending nearly $880,000.[23] Voters in Broomfield, led by the community group Our Health, Our Future, Our Broomfield, passed a five-year moratorium. In Fort Collins, voters approved a five-year moratorium organized by Citizens for a Healthy Fort Collins, in spite of industry spending. Frack

Free Colorado led a successful effort to pass a five-year moratorium in Boulder. In Lafayette, voters approved a community bill of rights to ban fracking, led by East Boulder County United.

Some in the environmental arena have suggested that Longmont may have reached too far in banning fracking, and that more-conservative land use approaches would have been an easier fight. But the fact is, when it comes to stopping fracking in Colorado, there is no easy fight. Longmont's fracking ban is a reach, but it is a reach for the stars; advocates who are fighting for their very futures should never reach any lower. Thanks to the people of Longmont, including Kaye Fissinger, and the other community leaders throughout the state, the Longmont case is moving into higher courts, and anti-fracking activists statewide are rallying to fight for additional local bans and moratoriums, statewide ballot initiatives, and constitutional amendments. There is now a chance to bring to Colorado what New Yorkers and some others across the country have enjoyed for years: the opportunity to determine the rights and futures of their communities and to live free from contamination caused by reckless oil and gas extraction. It's a fight that we should all be applauding.

Further, the local ban movement has translated to wins at the state level. Several industry-friendly pieces of legislation have been blocked in the face of this growing citizens' movement, including one bill that would have given pipeline companies the ability to use eminent domain to take residents' land for their projects. Groups have joined together to form a statewide coalition called Coloradans Against Fracking, with the goal of protecting the community wins and ultimately stopping fracking in the state. The coalition is led by many of the community groups that spearheaded the successful local ballot fights, as well as by Food & Water Watch, the Colorado People's Alliance, Our Loveland, and 350 Colorado. Building on the statewide efforts, a diverse group of racial justice groups, labor unions, craft breweries, faith leaders, and public interest groups launched the Don't Frack Denver campaign in 2015 to stop fracking next to homes and in the watershed that supplies nearly 40 percent of the drinking water for Colorado's most populous city.

Organizing at the National Level

In light of the movement's growing momentum, Food & Water Watch began discussing with close allies the benefits of a large coalition to shift the national debate on fracking and to demonstrate the broad-based support for a ban. Until then, most national discussion—at least in the halls of Congress and in the mainstream press—was over how fracking could be regulated, not whether it was inherently dangerous. A national coalition with regular strategy meetings and calls also could provide a mechanism for national organizations to support key state fights. The Center for Biological Diversity, Credo Action, 350.org, and Democracy for America were enthusiastic, and many local, state, and regional groups—such as Illinois People's Action, Berks Gas Truth, Our Longmont, and Frack Action—saw a real value in working together for the shared long-term goal of banning fracking.

Launched in December 2012 with a hundred groups, the nationwide coalition Americans Against Fracking has now grown to over three hundred organizations, including many leading national organizations, such as Breast Cancer Action, National Nurses United, MoveOn, Environmental Action, Progressive Democrats of America, Friends of the Earth, Greenpeace, and hundreds of leading grassroots groups. Since it was formed, the coalition has placed a national focus on the EPA's failure to protect communities from water contamination, targeting the agency with actions and petitions featuring more than 250,000 signatures. This was followed by the joint delivery of more than 650,000 petition signatures critical of the Bureau of Land Management's proposed rules for fracking on public lands.

Also formed in 2012 at a people's forum convvened by Earthworks, Stop the Frack Attack has organized several conferences of impacted people. The network is committed to elevating the leadership of impacted people in addressing the abuses of the oil and gas industry. Coordinated by Robby Diesu and Liz Butler, Stop the Frack Attack brings resources to communities to tackle health impacts and other injustices. Among the many strong leaders in the network are Shane Davis, John Fenton, Jenny Lisak, Robert Nehman, Deb Thomas, Calvin Tilman, Jill Weiner, and Sharon Wilson.

Coalition groups also have worked together to block federal legislation that would have significantly fast-tracked exports of liquefied natural gas. In 2014, Colorado senator Mark Udall and Representative Cory Gardner (who is now the junior senator from Colorado) introduced legislation in their respective houses that would have bypassed Department of Energy review. Although efforts to speed up LNG exports remain a significant threat, the worst provisions were stripped from the legislation, in a major win for the movement.[24]

Water Wars in California

In the spring of 2015, the *Los Angeles Times* revealed that recycled fracking wastewater was being used to water crops in California's Central Valley. Scott Smith, chief scientist at Mark Ruffalo's group Water Defense, had carried out testing in Kern County over a two-year period, revealing the presence of acetone and methylene chloride. The energy giant Chevron, which recycles 21 million gallons of water a day from its oil drilling operations and sells it to the Cawelo irrigation district for use by farmers, would not reveal the chemicals that it uses in drilling, while denying it used either of these dangerous pollutants.[25] According to a researcher from the Lawrence Livermore National Lab, fracking wastewater sold to Cawelo has been used for irrigating crops.[26] Food & Water Watch filed a public records request to garner the names of companies irrigating produce with recycled wastewater. They include Halos; Bee Sweet; Sunview; Trinchero Family Estates, the maker of Sutter Wines; and others.[27] The use of drilling wastewater began another chapter in the controversy over fracking in California and its detrimental effect on water resources in the drought-stricken state.

California is the third-largest oil-producing state in the country, and Kern County has four of the largest oil fields in the nation, producing 6.4 percent of the U.S. crude oil supply. Other major oil-producing regions include Los Angeles, Ventura, and Santa Barbara Counties. (The infamous Union Oil spill of 1969 occurred offshore, near the city of Santa Barbara, helping to spur the modern environmental movement). Over the past few decades, California oil production has been slowly declining, but the oil and gas industry has set its sights on ramping up production via fracking as well as other enhanced recovery techniques that use hydrochloric acid and steam.[28]

In response to the growing threat, Food & Water Watch, the Center for Biological Diversity, and Environment California formed Californians Against Fracking in 2013, a statewide coalition that now has more than two hundred member organizations across the state. Its membership includes environmental, environmental justice, social justice, agricultural, and community organizations, including 350.org; CREDO; the Center on Race, Poverty, and the Environment; California State Grange; and Courage Campaign. Since its launch, the coalition has gathered more than 250,000 petitions calling on Governor Jerry Brown to ban fracking statewide, and has organized large demonstrations.

In 2013 and 2014 Holly Mitchell, a state senator from Los Angeles, introduced the first piece of legislation to place a moratorium on fracking, helping to build and legitimize the ban movement at a time when conventional wisdom called for a regulatory approach. Although the bill ultimately did not pass amid a barrage of spending and lobbying by the Western States Petroleum Association, the *Los Angeles Times* editorial board endorsed Mitchell's bill as a commonsense approach that would have given Californians time to evaluate the risks before more harm could be done.[29]

In 2014 Californians Against Fracking organized the first major anti-fracking action in the state, bringing four thousand people to Sacramento to call on Governor Brown to ban fracking. In early 2015 double that number came to the group's second major action, this one held in Brown's hometown, Oakland. Although the state-level activity has been significant, major victories are being won at the local level. In 2013, communities living on the front lines of oil and gas extraction in Los Angeles came together to discuss the negative health impacts of this activity in their neighborhoods, including headaches, nosebleeds, and respiratory problems. In early 2014, the Los Angeles City Council, led by council members Paul Koretz and Mike Bonin, voted unanimously to direct the city attorney to draft an ordinance to ban fracking and other production techniques.[30] The city attorney and planning department never prepared the draft and recommended other regulatory options that would continue to leave many communities unprotected. During this time residents continued to share stories and find common ground for collaboration, eventually uniting in the coalition Stand Together Against Neighborhood Drilling, Los Angeles (STAND-L.A.). It persists in pushing for a broader ordinance that would prohibit oil drilling and injection wells where they pose the greatest threat to human health: within fifteen hundred feet of sensitive receptors, such as residences, schools, daycares, or hospitals.

Photo by Michael Woolsey

In the spring of 2014 the Santa Cruz County Board of Supervisors passed an ordinance introduced by Supervisor John Leopold to ban fracking and all oil and gas development in the county, making it the first county in California to do so. Community activist Lauren Steiner and Mayor John Mirsch were among the activists working in Beverly Hills, the first city in California to ban fracking.[31]

In Carson, where the Carson Coalition had been working for years to stop a two-hundred-well project proposed by Occidental Petroleum, the city enacted a forty-five-day moratorium on oil development. Under tremendous pressure from some labor groups and from Governor Brown himself, the city declined to extend the moratorium. The Carson Coalition and regional allies were undeterred and continued to organize, and in early 2015 Occidental announced that it was withdrawing the project.[32]

In November 2014 California saw its first major wins at the ballot, when voters in San Benito County passed a measure to ban fracking and other dangerous forms of oil extraction. The measure won with 60 percent of the vote, despite the industry spending close to $2 million to defeat it.[33] Led by the community group San Benito Rising, with support from Food & Water Watch and the Center for Biological Diversity, community members waged an impressive grassroots campaign, supported by farmers and vintners throughout the county.

Also in November, Mendocino County passed a community rights measure to ban fracking, another important win for the movement. In February 2015 Hermosa Beach had its turn at the ballot, overwhelmingly rejecting an industry measure that would have lifted a ban on drilling to construct new oil and wastewater injection wells.[34] The campaign was led by Hermosa Beach Oil Watch, Keep Hermosa Hermosa, and South Bay 350, and was supported by a wide range of environmental and community groups.

Not every ballot measure results in a win, and strong community efforts in Santa Barbara County and the small Los Angeles County community of La Habra Heights were defeated after massive industry spending—nearly $7 million in Santa Barbara's case—overwhelmed community efforts.[35] But even in those cases, communities came out of the efforts stronger and more organized than before, and active campaigns continue in those places. At the same time, work is escalating in other counties, including Butte, Monterey, Orange, Ventura, and Kern, the last of which accounts for approximately 70 percent of California's oil production.

Meanwhile, in the summer of 2015, it was revealed that state agencies in California had allowed the industry to inject toxic wastewater directly into aquifers while the state was in the midst of an extreme drought. Water and water shortages have been major issues in the anti-fracking campaign, in addition to health, earthquakes, and climate. The impacts of fracking have led prominent chefs, celebrities, farmers, vintners, health professionals, businesses, and faith leaders to mobilize across California, calling on Governor Brown to protect the Golden State.

Despite this scandal and the fact that recycled fracking wastewater was being used to water crops, the Brown administration finalized regulations on fracking and other dangerous oil extraction techniques.[36] But as the evidence grows about the industry's careless accidents and dangerous practices, members of Californians Against Fracking are confident that they can turn the tide and make Governor Brown lay out a plan to quickly get California off fossil fuels and rapidly move the state to 100 percent renewable energy.

Moratorium in Maryland

On the other side of the country, in Maryland, where the oil and gas industry has no drilling operations, the fight to stop drilling and fracking has been intense. In 2011, former Governor Martin O'Malley, a supporter of fracking, issued an executive order establishing a commission to develop best management practices for the industry, without adequately analyzing the essential public health, economic, and environmental risks. Then in November 2014, in what was a shock to many in Maryland, Republican candidate Larry Hogan defeated O'Malley's lieutenant governor, Anthony Brown, in the gubernatorial election. As a candidate, Hogan had referred to the natural gas in the Marcellus Shale as "an economic gold mine."[37] Just a few weeks after the election, O'Malley announced that fracking could be done safely and released regulations, based on his commission's report on best management practices.[38] The O'Malley administration pitched these regulations as the "gold standard" for the country.

At this point, some groups in the state believed that the only possible way forward was to legislate O'Malley's regulations so that they would become law before Hogan took office. Food & Water Watch, Chesapeake Physicians for Social Responsibility, and many grassroots leaders from western Maryland, where the fracking would take place, read the changing political dynamics as the perfect opportunity to push for a moratorium on fracking in Maryland. Although it was clear that passing a moratorium bill was an uphill battle and many environmental allies were skeptical of its success, in a matter of weeks the Don't Frack Maryland Campaign was launched, with more than one hundred organizations signing on in support of a long-term moratorium.

Delegate David Fraser-Hidalgo in the House and Karen Montgomery in the Senate introduced a bill that would institute an eight-year moratorium and require a panel to review the scientific evidence on fracking and then make a recommendation to the legislature. During the ninety-day legislative session, the coalition worked feverishly. Letters from more than a hundred western Maryland business owners were delivered to legislators, while more than a hundred health professionals and more than fifty restaurant owners, chefs, vintners, and farmers signed on to support the moratorium bill. The campaign held multiple press conferences and rallies in Annapolis, garnering significant media attention, and newspapers from across the state, especially western Maryland, received a steady stream of letters to the editor from residents who oppose fracking. The Don't Frack Maryland campaign sent more than twenty-five thousand messages to legislators supporting a moratorium, with a steady stream of phone calls in key legislative districts.

As the session progressed, the bill was amended several times, which weakened it. But Environment and Transportation Chairman Kumar

Barve, moved by the powerful statewide support to stop fracking, championed the bill and a three-year moratorium passed through the House by a veto-proof vote of 93–45. That same day the *Baltimore Sun* editorialized in favor of the bill. The Senate amended the bill further, removing the requirement for a panel to review the health literature, but eventually passed a bill calling for a two-and-a-half-year moratorium.[39] After the bill passed through the legislature, the coalition worked to pressure Hogan not to veto the bill. Even actor and Maryland native Edward Norton helped the effort, providing a radio ad appealing to the governor to sign the bill. To the joy of activists, who are now organizing for a state ban on fracking, the moratorium became law in late May 2015 without Hogan's signature because he did not veto the legislation.[40]

Keeping Florida Frack Free

A movement is also growing to stop fracking in Florida—a state that is a sunny tourist destination. More than a thousand new wells could be drilled in Florida in the next decade, some near the state's iconic Everglades National Park and Big Cypress National Preserve. Thus far twenty-six permits have been issued, but the prospect of more on the horizon has spurred people to fight back. A coalition of anti-fracking groups persuaded state agencies to hold an oil company accountable for illegal drilling near the Everglades. After several rallies, thousands of letters, and lots of media stories on the threat organized by a community group named Stone Crab Alliance with the support of Food & Water Watch, the Florida Department of Environmental Protection sued the Texas company. Not too long after, the company left the state and abandoned its drilling operations.[41]

At the state level, in 2013 and 2014 legislation was defeated that would have facilitated increased fracking in Florida. Superactivist Craig Stevens traveled around Florida speaking to policy makers about the impacts in his home state, Pennsylvania. In late 2014 Florida's campaign for a ban took off in earnest when legislation to ban fracking was introduced by state senator Darren Soto and state representative Evan Jenne; by the summer of 2015 thirteen counties, including Miami-Dade, and three cities had passed resolutions calling for a statewide ban.[42] An emerging coalition that includes Food & Water Watch, Our Santa Fe River, ReThink Florida, and Stone Crab Alliance is mobilizing Floridians for more victories against fracking in the future.

Facing Down the Frackers in Texas

Fracking also has raised considerable controversy in fossil-fuel-dominated Texas. As the impacts of fracking are felt in highly populated areas, the movement to protect communities has begun to have success at the local level. In 2013, FracDallas–Citizens for Safe Drilling, a community group headed up by tireless activist Marc McCord, successfully passed a setback measure in Dallas, which amounts to a de facto ban on fracking in Texas's third-largest city.[43] Since that time, McCord has been watchdogging state legislation designed to benefit the frackers and coordinating lobbying activities.

In 2014 Frack Free Denton passed the first local ban in Texas at the ballot box—a ban that was later repealed when the Texas Legislature passed a bill that took away the ability of communities to have local control over oil and gas operations. McCord called the legislation "the most blatant assault on home rule authority in Texas's history."[44]

Fortunately, Texas activists are not giving up. A new coalition is in the process of forming, with their eyes on the long-term goal of building a statewide movement to hold their elected officials accountable on energy issues. They hope to repeal the undemocratic legislation that takes away their ability to ban fracking at the local level.

Stopping Fracking Madness in the Midwest

As in other states, the emergence of fracking in Michigan has engendered significant community backlash. Starting in 2011, Food & Water Watch began working with local communities to ban fracking. Detroit became the first city in the state to call for a statewide ban and was quickly followed by Wayne County. Since that time, community activists have passed twenty municipal resolutions against fracking, and in January 2015 Cannon Township became the first township in Michigan to pass an ordinance to regulate fracking.[45]

Across Michigan, protests around mineral-rights auctions by the state's Department of Natural Resources were organized by Don't Frack Michigan, Citizens Against Drilling on Public Land, and others bringing additional attention to the process. In 2014 Michigan's attorney general, Bill Schuette, charged Chesapeake Energy and Encana with colluding to keep the prices gas companies paid landowners low during a 2010 auction. In 2015 Chesapeake settled the charges, pleading no contest to an antitrust violation without admitting wrongdoing, and paying $25 million into a fund to compensate landowners who were shortchanged.[46]

Many strategies are being employed in the state, where public opinion still favors fracking. The Committee to Ban Fracking in Michigan has been working to pass a ballot measure to ban fracking since 2012 and is collecting signatures to put this measure on the ballot in 2016.

Extensive campaigns are also under way to stop new pipeline construction and to shut down Line 5, a sixty-two-year-old twin oil and gas pipeline that runs through the worst possible place in the Great Lakes for an oil spill.[47] Food & Water Watch has been working with its allies in the Oil and Water Don't Mix campaign, including FLOW, the Michigan Land Use Institute, Michigan Citizens for Water Conservation, and the Sierra Club.

Fortunately, the fracking wells that have been drilled in northern Michigan have not been as productive as the oil and gas companies expected, and so the rush to drilling that was anticipated has not occurred (this may also be due to the overproduction of natural gas in other parts of the country). Unfortunately, however, the oil and gas companies are now moving farther south, closer to the larger population centers.

Meanwhile, Illinois has faced heavy lobbying by fossil fuel interests, becoming a prime example of how deal making by green groups backfires. Legislative leaders, industry representatives, and the Environmental Law and Policy Center negotiated a weak legislative regulatory package that was then supported by the Natural Resources Defense Council, the Illinois Environmental Council, and the Sierra Club.[48] They had failed to recognize the large grassroots mobilization for a moratorium—led by Illinois People's Action and Southern Illinoisans Against Fracturing Our Environment—and supported by wide range of organizations, including Food & Water Watch, Breast Cancer Action, 350.org, and others. The legislation passed and was signed by Governor Pat Quinn. Many of the mainstream greens later regretted their support for the weak legislation and admitted that if they had supported a moratorium, it could have passed.

The proposed rules were so weak that more than thirty-five thousand comments were submitted highlighting the inadequacy of the rules, under the leadership of Illinois People's Action. The loophole-ridden rules were ultimately finalized in 2014, but the grassroots coalition is continuing to work to make sure that this is not the end of the story.[49]

Elsewhere in the Midwest, Ohio communities are mobilizing against fracking and fracking waste disposal, despite industry dominance of all three branches of government. Ohio has received much of the fracking waste from Pennsylvania and West Virginia, and it uses injection wells to dispose of the bulk of it, causing swarms of earthquakes.[50] Communities are organizing to pass local ordinances to stop fracking and frack waste disposal. The grassroots movement—led by groups such as Athens County Fracking Action Network, Frack Free Ohio, Ohio Student Environmental Coalition, Mothers Against Drilling in Our Neighborhoods, and Southwest Ohio No Frack Forum—have passed fracking-related measures in Athens, Broadview Heights, Cincinnati, Mansfield, and Oberlin.[51] At the state level, groups such as Food & Water Watch, Buckeye Forest Council, and Center for Health, Environment and Justice have supported these efforts, while working to introduce legislation to ban fracking and injection wells.

The depth of the industry's stranglehold on Ohio politics was evident in early 2015, when the State Supreme Court in a 4–3 decision ruled that local communities do not have the authority to use home-rule powers to regulate the oil and gas industry, invalidating the zoning restrictions on fracking imposed by the city of Munroe Falls. In his dissent, Justice William O'Neill called out industry influence for what it was: "Let's be clear here, the Ohio General Assembly has created a zookeeper to feed the elephant in the living room. What the drilling industry has bought and paid for in campaign contributions they shall receive."[52] The oil and gas industry has gotten its way, and local control of drilling-location decisions has been unceremoniously taken away from the citizens of Ohio. Despite this setback, communities are continuing to mobilize, and fracking and its impacts in Ohio are sure to be front and center heading into 2016, when the Republican Party holds its national convention in Cleveland.

Regrouping in North Carolina

Oil and gas interests also met incredible resistance in North Carolina, where the General Assembly introduced a bill to allow fracking. Laws dating from the 1940s prohibited directional drilling and anything but water from being injected underground, creating a de facto ban. But two basins in the central part of the state caught the attention of the industry, and it pressured leaders in North Carolina's General Assembly to allow fracking.[53] In 2012 legislation was introduced calling for the legalization of fracking, while instituting a moratorium until the regulatory framework was in place. The bill also created a commission to develop the rules and prohibited local officials from taking protective measures.[54]

Frack Free NC, an alliance of dozens of groups, generated thousands of comments and phone calls to the legislature opposing fracking. More than a thousand people attended the three public hearings held by the Department of Environment and Natural Resources, the majority commenting against fracking. When the final vote came, the General Assembly passed the bill legalizing fracking. Yet the unprecedented pressure from organizations and citizens led Governor Beverly Perdue to veto the bill. Her staff acknowledged that the more than ten thousand comments she received were overwhelmingly in opposition to fracking.[55]

A few short days later, the General Assembly reconvened in an effort to overturn the veto, which needed a supermajority to be sustained. The last person to vote had consistently voted against fracking in the past. But she claimed that in her rush to vote, she pushed the wrong button, overturning the veto. Within seconds, realizing her mistake, she raised her hand to change her vote. The Speaker ignored her, however, and the fracking veto was overturned.[56]

In 2014, after legislation was passed lifting the moratorium regardless of the quality of the final regulations, the alliance delivered fifty thousand petitions to Governor Pat McCrory calling for a ban. More significantly, activists targeted several of the legislators who voted for fracking, making it a campaign issue, and in the November 2014 election three of these lawmakers were defeated.[57] Although fracking is now legal in North Carolina, as of the fall of 2015 no companies have applied for permits, and the organizing efforts have turned to stopping gas pipelines, offshore drilling, and other energy related issues. In August 2015 Chatham County passed a two-year moratorium on fracking. The chairman of the county's Board of Commissioners, Jim Crawford, said, "It's all about the water."[58]

The Battle over Frac Sand

In other states, large mining operations for silica sand—the hard, perfectly round grains of sand needed for fracking—are impacting communities. Iowa, Minnesota, and Wisconsin have become ground zero in the battle against the mining of this known carcinogen. Fine particles of silica exacerbate respiratory and cardiovascular problems, disrupt the landscape, and destroy farmland and important habitat. Dozens of new mines and processing facilities have opened with little oversight, and in some jurisdictions officials have left their positions to join frac sand mining companies.[59] In Iowa, Minnesota, and Wisconsin, a strong fight is taking place as activists hold rallies, pack meeting halls, and organize for measures to stop the mining.

In Minnesota, a fierce battle has been waged against frac mining. In the southeast—the region of the state that is most threatened—council meetings have overflowed with opponents demanding an end to mining. Although a few sand mines were operating in the south-central region of the state, industry players have proposed many new, large mines since fracking has increased the demand for silica sand. Many groups across the state, including the Land Stewardship Project, Citizens Against Silica Mining, Save the Bluffs, and the Catholic Worker Movement, have been engaging in efforts to oppose frac sand mining. Among their victories are moratoriums on sand mining passed in five southeast counties.[60] Permanent measures prohibiting or limiting the industry also have been put in place by various townships and cities.[61]

In response to the grassroots organizing campaign, the legislature took up the issue in 2013, resulting in legislation prohibiting frac sand mining within a mile of trout streams in the southeast without a special permit. State agencies were also directed to develop new rules governing mine reclamation, air quality, and environmental review for frac sand proposals, which in 2015 were still in development.[62]

In the interim, some frac sand mine proposals for the southeastern region remain on the table, and new ones continue to come forward. Some frac sand processing and shipment facilities—primarily for handling sand mined in Wisconsin—have been established in southeast Minnesota in the Mississippi River towns of Winona and Wabasha, with harmful impacts on residents there.

Johanna Rupprecht, a policy organizer at the Land Stewardship Project, says: "Only a few small frac sand mines have been permitted in southeast Minnesota out of at least twenty that have been proposed. Citizen organizing has either defeated or continues to hold off the rest. A proposed frac sand plant that would have become a major regional hub for mining in southeast Minnesota was voted down by the city of St. Charles after local opposition in 2013."[63] Corporate players continue to operate without transparency, but the grassroots movement will do everything possible to protect public health and the environment.

In Wisconsin, an ordinance against non-metallic mining that was passed in 2008 by Cooks Valley, a small town in Chippewa County, became the center of a legal controversy. Although the frac sand industry sued to take away local control, the ordinance was upheld by the Wisconsin Supreme Court.[64] This ruling has inspired organizing around the state, as frac sand mines and processing facilities have increased from five in 2010 to more than sixty mining sites and forty-five processing plants since then. Ken Schmitt, a resident of the town of Howard, is typical of farmers and other residents who oppose frac sand mining. He says: "As a farmer, land should be better for the next generation than how you received it. This doesn't pass that test in my opinion."[65]

In 2013 Mary Logue and other residents were able to pass a ban on frac sand mining in a sensitive area: a ten-mile strip of land along Lake Pepin. Logue said: "This is fabulous because it really protects all of the area of Lake Pepin in Pepin County. It's a huge victory for us."[66] In 2014 the Wisconsin Network for Peace and Justice issued a resolution to ban fracking that was endorsed by more than seventy-five civic and environmental organizations, including forty-nine Wisconsin groups and twenty-nine groups from seven other states where Wisconsin sand is used for fracking.[67] Activists are continuing to organize for local bans and to prevent the state legislature from further weakening Wisconsin's protections against these large, destructive mining operations.

In Iowa, the local community organization Winneshiek County Protectors mobilized to pass eighteen-month moratoriums on frac sand mining. In 2014 Allamakee County Protectors, under Robert Nehman's leadership, passed a strong regulatory ordinance in the county that amounts to a de facto ban on mining in the county.[68] These local wins continue to be protected thanks to organizing at the state level by Iowa Citizens for Community Improvement, Food & Water Watch, and the Iowa Chapter of the Sierra Club, which joined with community groups to prevent state legislation that would have undermined local control of frac sand mining.

"We need local control over frac sand mines, and we need local control over factory farms," said Brenda Brink, an Iowa Citizens for Community Improvement Action Fund member from Huxley, Iowa. "Local people should have a say in whether these industries, which damage our natural resources and quality of life, can come into our communities."[69]

Defeating Infrastructure Projects

From coast to coast, communities also have been organizing to stop many kinds of fracking infrastructure: the vast networks of pipelines, compressor stations, and export facilities used to move natural gas around the country and export it to foreign markets. (See Chapter 16.)

Activists organized an amazing victory when the six-hundred-mile Bluegrass Pipeline was stopped. After fierce resistance, the project's owners, Williams Companies and Boardwalk Pipeline Partners, announced that they were abandoning the construction project, which would have piped natural gas liquids (ethane, propane, butane, and other gases) from West Virginia, Pennsylvania, and Ohio through Kentucky, where it would connect in western Kentucky with the Texas Gas Transmission Pipeline that ends in Louisiana. While it was announced that the project would be canceled because of a lack of firm commitments for the gas, it is clear that the significant citizens' movement against the pipeline was a major factor.

All across the proposed pipeline route, citizens rallied together to oppose the project. In Kentucky, Kentuckians for the Commonwealth, the Kentucky Resources Council, the Sisters of Loretto, and numerous other citizens' groups came together to form the Bluegrass Pipeline Blockade, which with its partners ran an incredible public education campaign to inform people about the potential impacts of the proposed project. Together, groups passed eleven Fiscal Court (county) resolutions opposing the pipeline, worked with lawmakers to introduce legislation that protected landowners, and won a court proceeding declaring that eminent domain could not be used to seize people's land for pipeline construction. As a result of all the public education efforts and grassroots community organizing, the Bluegrass Pipeline Company could not secure the land leases it needed to start construction. Similar exciting campaigns are taking place in states where pipelines are proposed. (See Chapter 16.)

In order to move its product abroad, the industry needs export facilities that will allow the export of natural gas in the form of LNG—projects that have engendered significant community opposition. The Port Ambrose project, off the coast of New York and New Jersey, has drawn national attention, with more than two hundred organizations and nearly thirty thousand people urging Governors Christie and Cuomo to veto the project.[70] In a tremendous victory for activists, Governor Cuomo vetoed it in November 2015, killing the project.

In the Finger Lakes region of New York, Crestwood Midstream is attempting to store millions of gallons of liquefied petroleum gas and compressed natural gas in depleted salt caverns near Seneca Lake. This irresponsible project would solve a storage problem for the company, allowing a repository en route to market—including possible export markets around the world.

The project has garnered massive resistance from local residents, more than two dozen municipalities in the area have passed resolutions against it, and the local business community—led by the Finger Lakes wineries—has emerged as a powerful voice against the storage plan. Over the course of more than a year, scores of activists have been arrested for civil disobedience, largely by blocking trucks from entering the construction area.[71] Sandra Steingraber and the grassroots group We Are Seneca Lake have led the direct actions that have resulted in numerous arrests. In a promising development, the local judge has been dismissing charges against the protesters.

Many other grassroots groups have been active in the campaign, including Gas Free Seneca, which has organized efforts to pressure Governor Cuomo to stop the project (a piece of the project requires state permits to move forward; the rest of it only needs federal approval from the Federal Energy Regulatory Commission). Gas Free Seneca, working with the winery owners, has also been instrumental in building out the business coalition against the project. At the same time, Gas Free Seneca has partnered with Earthjustice to pursue a legal strategy to stop the project.

Beyond Extreme Energy, a coalition effort by dozens of groups fighting projects that FERC will rubber-stamp, is holding direct actions at FERC headquarters in Washington, D.C., in an effort to raise awareness about the problems. Organizations that participate in Americans Against Fracking are talking to members of Congress about the need for legislation that will drastically reduce FERC's ability to make decisions without accountability.

This sampling of the grassroots mobilizations taking place around the country shows that people will organize to prevent their families, friends, and communities from being poisoned. They are willing to spend the time and resources needed to prevent harm and to work for the kind of future they want. The fight against fracking will only continue to escalate as communities experience the deadly impacts and as scientific evidence mounts showing that fracking is too inherently dangerous to pursue and that the only option, in light of climate disruption, is a sustainable energy future. As Beyond Extreme organizer Ted Glick says, "It's time to get serious about moving off of fossil fuels and onto a renewable energy path."[72]

21

A GLOBAL MOVEMENT TO BAN FRACKING

I am terrified for my children. I am fighting for their future.
—Willy Schuster, a farmer in Mosna, Romania [1]

Across the globe, wherever the Frackopoly's tentacles have reached, people are rising up to defend their communities and say no to fracking. In South Africa, Goldman Prize–winning activist Jonathan Deal, who has led a broad-based campaign to keep fracking out of the Karoo region, is emblematic of this opposition. He says, "The more I read and the more media reports there are and the more I see the growing backlash against fracking, the more convinced I am that there is no reason to go ahead [with fracking in the Karoo]." Deal has sacrificed just about everything—especially his economic well-being—to fight fracking, including devoting his prize money to the cause. [2]

A powerful anti-fracking movement has also emerged across Europe, in response to the Frackopoly's American-style lobbying and influence-peddling activities. In 2014 Friends of the Earth Europe's report, *Fracking Brussels,* exposed the tactics of the shale gas lobby in Europe, revealing a web of relationships between industry players on both sides of the Atlantic. Antoine Simon, shale gas campaigner for the organization, says that the industry has essentially launched an underground offensive to silence concerns about the dangers of fracking.

When Bulgarians heard in 2011 that Chevron had been given a five-year deal to frack millions of acres, grassroots activists such as Borislav Sandov were infuriated. Several massive demonstrations were organized in Sofia, leading to an overwhelming vote in the nation's legislature to ban fracking and withdraw Chevron's permits. [3] Meanwhile, in Romania, thousands of people were demonstrating to oppose a Chevron fracking project, prompting the parliament to consider a shale gas moratorium.[4]

Former U.S. secretary of state Hillary Clinton swooped into Sofia to defend fracking, promising that the United States would send its "best specialists . . . to present the benefits to the Bulgarian people." Clinton then deployed the special envoy for energy in Eurasia, Richard Morningstar, to read the riot act to wayward democratically elected officials in the region. Shortly after the arm-twisting, Romania's parliament voted down that country's fracking ban.[5] Bulgaria's legislature still defied the United States, but softened the ban legislation to clarify that fossil fuel companies could use conventional methods for natural gas production. Economy and energy minister Delyan Dobrev reiterated, "The change will by no way allow hydraulic fracturing for shale gas."[6]

In 2013 Chevron began its fracking adventures in eastern Romania, preparing to drill for shale gas near the town of Pungesti. Unlike in the United States, in Romania mineral rights are owned by the state rather than by individual property owners, meaning that support for fracking in the places where wells are drilled tends to be negligible. Local residents of Pungesti—many of them elderly farmers—blocked the roads to the drilling site and built a protest camp. Eventually hundreds of riot police were deployed to forcibly remove people, with local newspapers reporting that forty villagers had been beaten.[7]

Despite the persecution, activists bravely persisted, and by February 2015 Chevron announced that it was pulling out of Romania. Georgeta Ionescu, an environmental activist who has worked closely with the nation's foremost opponent of fracking, Orthodox priest Father Liau, commented: "In all those fights for life, communities must participate in political decision making, as they are the first ones to be affected." In defiance of the U.S. State Department's meddling, Ionescu said that "democracy is the best cure for our society" when communities are threatened.[8]

Farmers in Poland—the most pro-fracking nation in the European Union—have also organized to stop fracking. Barbara Siegieńczuk led a four-hundred-day blockade at a Chevron drilling site in 2013, getting help from nearby residents in setting up the protest camp. With natural gas prices low and resistance strong, Chevron announced in early 2015 that it would pull out of shale gas operations in Poland as well.[9]

Shale formations in southeastern Poland stretch across the border into western Ukraine, and Ukraine also has a long band of shale along its border with Russia in the east. In 2013 Ukraine signed two $10 billion fracking deals with Chevron and Shell.[10] And the drumbeat to frack has grown since Russia's annexation of the Crimea, as the eagerness to wean the country off Russian gas imports is used as a justification to exploit domestic shale resources. Yet despite the myriad challenges faced by Ukrainians, grassroots opponents have been working to ban fracking. In a victory for opponents, Chevron pulled out of its proposed project in 2014 because the country had failed to change its taxation law, as had been agreed during negotiations.[11]

As in other parts of Eastern Europe, the United States is strong-arming Ukraine on behalf of fossil fuel interests. Vice President Joe Biden visited the country in 2014, promoting an aid package that included help with developing both shale and conventional gas resources, saying, "We stand ready to assist you."[12] Biden's son Hunter, along with David Leiter, former Senate chief of staff to John Kerry, and Devon Archer, a former adviser to Kerry's presidential campaign, all have been hired to work in varying capacities for the Ukrainian energy company Burisma Holdings.[13]

Pavlo Khazan, with Friends of the Earth Ukraine, stated: "The Ukrainian people have never agreed to shale gas. . . . Now that [the former prime minister] has been ousted by the Ukrainian people, a new government must immediately end this contract with Shell." The group charges that the deal was based on corruption and that fracking operations are marked by "harmful techniques unacceptable in many European countries," with "open reservoirs for toxic fracking water."[14]

Friends of the Earth Europe and Food & Water Europe, an affiliate of Food & Water Watch, have been working together with many members of the European Parliament to stop these dangerous practices and to ban fracking in the EU. In 2012 more than a third of parliamentarians voted in support of a moratorium on fracking in the parliament's first vote on shale gas. Although the moratorium amendment fell short of a majority, the final version of the parliament's reports on shale gas identified the climate, environmental, and health risks associated with unconventional gas. Food & Water Europe policy officer Geert Decock commented that "extreme energy like shale gas will hinder, not facilitate, the transition to a much-needed low-carbon energy future."[15]

In late 2013, advocates for renewable energy in the European Parliament called for mandatory environmental impact assessments for both shale gas exploration and extraction, an effort defeated by "a strong blocking minority of Member States," said Andrea Zanoni, an Italian member of the European Parliament. She added that pro-fracking advocates' "determination to exclude citizens and local governments from decision-making will only increase . . . the justified . . . distrust in this form of energy."[16] In 2015, during the debate about energy security, parliamentarians in the pocket of the fossil fuel industry managed to insert pro-fracking code words into the draft policy platform.[17] This is part of a larger attack on renewables that activists are resisting in Germany, a country with a strong commitment to renewable energy. (See Chapter 18.)

Fortunately, several progressive members of the European Parliament submitted amendments that support a moratorium on shale gas, giving anti-fracking activists another chance to fight back. Members have organized numerous briefings and events on the problems with fracking and have brought grassroots activists from around the EU to meetings about the issues they face. This struggle over fracking at the EU level will continue into the future, as grassroots activists organize to prevent shale operations in their countries.

France became the first national government to ban fracking in 2011 when the French parliament passed a law that ultimately was upheld by France's highest court two years later. Maxime Combes, who is an economist and member of ATTAC France, explains that the mass movement, which included large demonstrations in Paris, began with community groups organizing in the region where fracking was slated to take place. Josh Fox's film *Gasland* was shown hundreds of times, helping to spur a movement that included local groups, national associations, and environmental, health, and social organizations. French environment minister Philippe Martin commented, "With this decision, the ban on hydraulic fracturing is absolute," and he added, "Beyond the question of fracking, shale gas is a carbon emitter. We must set our priorities on renewable energies."[18]

Several regions in Spain banned fracking, but the Spanish supreme court ultimately overruled the measures. So in northeastern Spain, in response to activist pressure, Catalonia's officials were creative in developing language that has resulted in a de facto ban. No fracking permits will be issued if the fracking could negatively affect the area's geology, environment, landscape, or socioeconomic status.[19] Activists are continuing to organize against fracking in light of the resurgence of the progressive political party Podemos, which offers new hopes for significant reform.

As the threat of fracking grew in the UK, the bold network Frack Off was formed to support the growing resistance. In 2011 the well-connected British company Cuadrilla began test drilling in northwest Britain, near Blackpool in Lancashire.[20] Local residents Tony Young, Doreen Stopforth, Eve McNamara, and others were outraged and began organizing to stop the project. Soon after the test drilling began, earthquakes hit the area, and a moratorium on drilling was declared. A report sponsored by the company found that drilling had been the cause, but it claimed that the unusual conditions leading to the tremors were "unlikely to occur again."[21] In the summer of 2015 Lancashire rejected Cuadrilla's drilling applications, but the company continued to push to frack the biggest shale play in the UK.[22] Many groups have emerged to fight fracking, including the Ribble Estuary Against Fracking, Residents Action on Fylde Fracking, and Frack Free Greater Manchester.

In 2013, after the moratorium was lifted, Cuadrilla began to test drilling in Balcombe, located thirty-four miles from London. Over the next year the village became the focal point of an extraordinary fight against fracking that featured mass protests. Hundreds of activists were cleared from the well-organized protest camp near the site, and many people were arrested.[23] Wife-and-husband team Kathryn McWhirter and Charles Metcalfe, widely known wine experts, never dreamed that they would become almost full-time activists. Living close to the drilling site, they were instrumental in organizing the Frack Free Balcombe Residents Association and in supplying the protest camp with food, materials, and moral support. McWhirter says that she and the other residents "have been politicized by this, people who would never have protested before."[24] The protests delayed drilling activities, and Cuadrilla's license expired.[25]

Prime minister David Cameron has continued to push fracking forward despite the fact that public support for it has dropped to below 50 percent. Fracking was a major issue in the country's May 2015 elections. Friends of the Earth and Greenpeace organized the "Frack Free Promise," in which more than a thousand candidates for office agreed to oppose fracking if elected.[26] Meanwhile, other countries in the United Kingdom are moving in a different direction, with Scotland and Wales moving to place moratoriums on fracking.[27]

Resistance to fracking is growing in the Republic of Ireland and in Northern Ireland (part of the UK) because, as journalist Greg Palast said on a recent visit, "fracking here would be insane, Ireland is like one big flood plain."[28] Maureen Seaberg, a writer who works with No Fracking

Ireland, has noted that despite the violent conflicts of the past, a great solidarity has emerged among community activists from the two countries.[29] Some of the strongest resistance has been in Leitrim, a county in the Irish Republic that adjoins Northern Ireland, where members of Love Leitrim have been organizing for several years. In a major victory in 2014, Leitrim's county councilors stood with the people, voting to ban fracking.[30] Meanwhile, Good Energies Alliance Ireland was organized in 2010 to educate the public and policy makers on the dangers of fracking and the need to replace dirty energy with energy-efficient technologies and renewables.

In Australia, concerns about fracking escalated in 2010 when farmers began speaking out about irresponsible water use and the impacts of fracking chemicals on livestock, crops, and water resources. People across the nation began organizing over the next several years to "lock the gate" on fracking and fossil fuel development. Indigenous people requested that the United Nation's Special Rapporteur on the Rights of Indigenous Peoples intervene on their behalf because of the industry's impact on their land, water, and sacred areas. In 2015, as part of the Global Frackdown to the climate talks in Paris, Dr. Mariann Lloyd-Smith, a senior advisor to the Australian public interest group National Toxics Network, embarked on an international speaking tour around their report, *Unconventional Gas Exploration and Production: Human Health Impacts and Environmental Legacy*. By 2016, the Lock the Gate Alliance has grown to 250 local groups from all across Australia and 40,000 supporters.

On the other side of the globe, several Latin American governments—Argentina, Brazil, Chile, and Colombia—are touting fracking as a way to build their economies.[31] Resistance has grown quickly in Argentina, where fossil fuel development began in Neuquén province in 2008. Since that time, the nation's largest energy firm, YPF, was partially renationalized ahead of signing a $1.2 billion deal with Chevron that would mean fifteen hundred wells by 2017. Drilling began in the Vaca Muerta, where indigenous residents briefly took over drilling rigs in protest. Lefxaru Hahuel, a representative of the Mapuche community, explained, "We wanted to send a message to the companies and the government to say we are against an initiative that will have a serious impact on our grounds."[32]

A broad-based coalition, the Multisectorial Against Hydro-fracturing of Neuquén, has led mass street demonstrations in Neuquén that have been met by tear gas and rubber bullets. The assault on fragile ecosystems across Argentina, like the nationally protected territory of Auca Mahuida in Patagonia, near where YPF announced another oil and gas discovery, is spurring momentum in a national movement against fracking, while activists across the country have passed more than thirty local bans.[33]

Shale gas development also has taken off in Mexico, just across the border from Texas. Until the Mexican Alliance Against Fracking launched in August 2013, the public knew little about fracking. This has changed, with some communities declaring "frack-free zones" and the introduction of national legislation to ban fracking in Mexico.[34] Although conditions in Mexico's congress are not yet favorable for passage of the bill, growing awareness of the risks of fracking is creating a national debate. Since tenders for extracting shale gas have been issued, outrage is growing in the areas to be fracked.

Similar to other parts of North America, almost every Canadian province is experiencing an expansion of drilling and fracking. This assault on people and the environment has been met by strong and unified opposition from First Nation communities. Since 2009 the Unist'ot'en Camp, established on ancestral land in northern British Columbia, has successfully prevented multiple pipelines from crossing its territory.[35] For several months, members of the Lax Kw'alaams Nation have been occupying their traditional territory on Lelu Island, located near Prince Rupert, British Columbia, preventing construction of a liquid natural gas terminal. Hereditary Chief Donald Wesley says, "Our rights and title have not been looked at, we've never been consulted on the activities that are taking place."[36]

The Council of Canadians has campaigned for many years to stop unconventional oil and gas extraction, including fracking, tar sands, LNG terminals, and pipelines. Working in many parts of Canada with local community groups, it has passed municipal resolutions against fracking in many communities across the nation. Such efforts have impacted public opinion, especially in Atlantic Canada, where most provinces are now under a fracking moratorium. In 2014 the council released the results of an EKOS Research poll finding that 70 percent of Canadians support "a national moratorium on fracking until it is scientifically proven to be safe." Maude Barlow, the national chairperson for the council, says, "Regardless of age, region or education, people from coast to coast are calling for an end to fracking." Emma Lui, water campaigner for the council, called on Prime Minister Justin Trudeau to support a moratorium on fracking. She said, "Based on these numbers, political parties may want to rethink their positions to put them in line with what the population wants."[37]

In 2012 Quebec implemented a moratorium on fracking that has since spurred Lone Pine Resources, a U.S. oil and gas firm, to file a lawsuit against the Canadian government. The American company is using the controversial Investor State Dispute Settlement process that is part of the North American Free Trade Agreement (NAFTA) to sue Canada. Lone Pine claims the fracking moratorium is prohibited under NAFTA because it "violated Lone Pine's legitimate expectation of a stable business and legal environment" and that the Quebec government in particular infringed on the firm's "valuable right to mine for oil and gas under the St. Lawrence River."[38] This case exemplifies how international trade and investment agreements can prioritize corporate interests over public health and environmental regulations established through local democratic processes.

Food & Water Watch, with staff in Europe and Latin America, was well positioned to help connect these different movements with those in the United States. In 2012 the Global Frackdown was launched to organize a day of action to ban fracking. The first Global Frackdown exceeded organizers' expectations, with upward of two hundred actions in more than twenty countries around the world. Thousands marched in France, hundreds rallied in South Africa, and actions were held across Argentina, Spain, and Australia. The day of action has continued to grow. In 2013 there were more than 250 actions, and in 2014 more than three hundred actions took place in more than thirty countries, representing every continent.

In 2015, rather than engaging in just one day of international action, hundreds of groups across the world made their voices heard throughout the month of November in the lead-up to the United Nations Conference on Climate Change in Paris. Activists told their elected leaders that all fossil fuels needed to stay in the ground if climate chaos is to be avoided. "Fracking amounts to inaction," they said, "and it is anathema to developing sustainable energy systems available to all and premised on the efficient use of safe, abundant, affordable and renewable energy resources. . . . At the Paris climate summit, it must be made clear that fracking for shale gas, tight gas, coalbed methane and tight oil, as well as other extreme fossil fuel extraction methods, are incompatible with climate stability."[39]

As this book goes to press in February 2016, it is important to note that the international movement to stop fracking and to keep fossil fuels in the ground is growing stronger. One hundred and fifty frontline and organizational leaders from around the world met at an activist anti-fracking summit, "Not Here Not Anywhere," held during the Paris climate talks. Convened by Stop the Frack Attack, Friends of the Earth Europe, Earthworks, Attac France, and Food & Water Watch, the meeting brought impacted people and activists from forty nations. People on the front lines of fracking testified to the growing resistance in Indonesia, Thailand, and Africa. The meeting also gave voice to many indigenous people on the terrible health, environmental, and social impacts on their communities in North America; South America; and Algeria, Nigeria, and other parts of Africa.

Robby Diesu, who helped coordinate the conference, said, "What happens when you get fracktivists from around the world together in one room? Magic."[40]

Jennifer Krill, executive director of Earthworks, summed it up: "The summit enabled front-line activists from far-flung corners of the world to build new relationships to support our shared struggle for clean water, breathable air, and healthy communities against big oil."[41]

Photo courtesy of Food & Water Watch

22

THE WAY FORWARD

Human progress is neither automatic nor inevitable. . . . Every step toward the goal of justice requires sacrifice, suffering, and struggle; the tireless exertions and passionate concern of dedicated individuals.
—Martin Luther King Jr.[1]

Humanity faces a bleak future if we do not act to reverse runaway global climate disruption. The cumulative effects of climate chaos are already visible—violent storms, drought, floods, and unpredictable and changing weather patterns. Scientists warn that if we do not act swiftly to keep fossil fuels in the ground, our children and grandchildren will experience disrupted food supplies and a significant loss of animal and plant species by 2050, with up to 70 percent gone by the end of the century.[2] William J. Snape III at the Center for Biological Diversity cautions, "Life on Earth as we know it is under siege. Significant and probably irreversible changes to the natural world are now occurring. . . . The rapid advent of global warming and associated climate change makes the job of saving native plants, animals, and habitats even more difficult. Human beings need biological diversity to survive and prosper, but our natural support system is fraying."[3]

In the United States, the nation's political leaders are failing to take the brave and farsighted actions necessary to prevent this human-induced tragedy. Republicans who shill for the fossil fuel industry deny that a problem exists, while the leadership of the Democratic Party promotes half measures and market-based schemes to address the crisis.

President Obama's two terms offered many opportunities to stand tall against the greedy energy interests and their Wall Street funders. But under his watch, he championed a lethal "all of the above" energy strategy and advanced the use of fracked natural gas and oil. Rather than fighting to quickly transition to the use of efficient technologies, wind energy, and solar power, the administration's Clean Power Plan rules favor gas-fired electricity plants and pollution trading schemes. If finalized, the draft methane standards proposed by the EPA will grandfather in the thousands of existing wells and the associated infrastructure, sending vast amounts of methane into the atmosphere. And even these insufficient measures could be turned back, depending on the elections over the next few years.

Fighting for the World We Want

The solution is not for well-meaning politicians to support weaker and weaker policies, bending over backward to negotiate and accommodate the fossil fuel industry. We need leaders who are willing to speak truth to power and to fight for turning back climate change and the other environmental and social problems that we face.

Clearly, developing our own leaders or giving liberal-minded politicians the backbone to address climate change and all of the other social, economic, and environmental problems we face must be part of a broad-based, long-term strategy for restoring our democracy and getting money out of politics. Building the political power necessary to dramatically change our political system requires organizing around bold solutions that inspire people to become involved and to demand action. When people win a victory that addresses a problem that seemed insurmountable, they are motivated to work harder to achieve even bigger goals. This is how long-term change takes place, not by cutting deals and compromising with polluters.

Tackling the climate emergency requires the same approach. We must move beyond hard-to-understand trading schemes that are ultimately for the benefit of Wall Street and on to a strategy that requires the climate polluters to stop profiting by using the atmosphere and air as a private waste dump. This must be a top priority in the short term, or all of these critical problems will become worse—or even become unsolvable. Working to ban fracking is an excellent step in the battle to protect public health and our precious water, air, and land resources—and to reverse the ravages of climate change. This important issue has already inspired tens of thousands of people to get involved. If the large green groups adopted this call to action and stopped engaging in the uninspiring politics of the possible, it could completely change the dynamics of the environmental movement.

It could make the movement a real partner in bringing about a new era of progressive change, addressing the many social, economic, and environmental inequities that mark our nation.

Mainstream green groups and their funders are so committed to fracked natural gas that they have inexplicably failed to oppose the use of the dangerous technology even for oil production, although 81 percent of fracking in recent times has been for oil.[4] More often than not, they have cheered half-measures and embraced a philosophy dependent on negotiation with polluters, rather than building the long-term political power to hold them accountable. This strategy has been promoted by funders such as the Energy Foundation that use their dollars to moderate grassroots environmental activism. There is no appetite for fundamentally changing the economic system and building a movement powerful enough to challenge the status quo. There is no appetite for confronting and changing a political system that favors the creation of larger and larger monopolies that have the economic and political power to pervert public policy. There is no appetite for calling out Wall Street's role as the most powerful of all political forces in pushing policies that wreck the environment, negatively impact public health, and create greater and greater inequities.

It seems that the very organizations that should be working to make politicians accountable to their base—the people who vote them into office—have no stomach for a real fight. Many feel that the current shape of the political system, with a batch of Republicans bent on destroying the planet, has left us with no choice but to support centrist and right-of-center Democrats. A defeatist groupthink has taken hold in the environmental community, sucking away the appetite for a unified campaign against fracking or efforts to tackle climate disfunction in a more meaningful way. Too often the leaders of the environmental community have capitulated, rationalizing, "Don't let the perfect be the enemy of the good." But we are a very, very long way from the perfect today, and the good is just slightly better than the bad.

Fortunately, there are many Democrats who are willing to stand up and say no to fracking and the abuses of the fossil fuel industry. On Earth Day, April 22, 2015, Wisconsin congressman Mark Pocan and Illinois congresswoman Jan Schakowsky introduced a bill to ban fracking on public lands. This legislation stands in bold opposition to the oil and gas industry and its supporters in Congress who are working to *increase* fracking and other fossil fuel extraction on our public lands. As this book goes to press, big green groups such as the Natural Resources Defense Council and the Environmental Defense Fund have not supported this commonsense legislation. But we are hopeful that as the evidence about fracking continues to mount, they will see the potential of fighting for this legislation.

Now, I am not implying that the decision makers at the big greens are not well intended or not interested in protecting the environment, or that they are not committed to forestalling the disaster of climate change. I also am not suggesting that their large environmental foundation funders who see fracked natural gas as a bridge fuel do not believe that this is the best we can hope for in light of the political challenges. We surely do live in a political climate where well-meaning advocates have been beaten down and where public opinion is shaped by a media and other institutions with direct ties to the vested interests.

But ought we not demand better? Shouldn't nonpartisan public interest and environmental groups insist on the accountability of Democrats as well as Republicans? Shouldn't we be working shoulder to shoulder with folks at the grassroots, whose lives are often on the line, to stop the abuses of the fracking industry?

If we don't have a vision of a much better future and begin a massive organizing effort to achieve it, who will? We will be left without a democracy and with a greatly diminished natural world racked with chaotic weather and marked by even more inequities. And without a major push for public policy changes, we will not move into a renewable energy future.

The stark fact remains that we are not anywhere near where we need to be on renewable energy. From 2010 to 2014 wind energy averaged 3.6 percent of U.S. electricity generation and solar only 0.2 percent.[5] While it appears that the growth of renewables has skyrocketed if we assess current numbers as a percentage of previous numbers, this is misleading. For instance, since 1995 solar power has grown almost 3,500 percent. But jumping from 0 percent to 0.2 percent of total power generation is hardly a figure to be proud of.

Any real progress in renewables is because of regulatory and legislative changes that advocates fought for, certainly not because of deregulation or wholesale markets or retail choice of suppliers. Energy expert Tyson Slocum, director of Public Citizen's energy program, explains, "Growth in the deployment of renewables is due to the technologies' continued falling costs, coupled with government incentives and mandates for their use.

Deregulated markets discourage wind and solar. Utility deregulation in the 1990s spurred the creation of Regional Transmission Organizations, privately run entities that write the rules for and operate wholesale power markets. These rules, particularly capacity auctions, present barriers to renewables' utilization, as the market structures are operated to maximize financial benefits for incumbent fossil fuel generators."[6]

An examination of the two states with the most solar and wind power bears this out. In California, which has embraced a strong renewable portfolio standard—a regulation that requires utilities to produce a specified percentage of electricity from renewable sources—solar and wind energy accounted for 12 percent of production in 2014. In Texas, another state with such a standard, wind and solar account for 9 percent of the energy produced. These percentages show that we should have an even more ambitious standard for the entire nation. And it should be based on alternative energy that is truly renewable and that does not encourage other environmentally damaging activities. Corn-based ethanol, manure-to-energy, waste-to-energy, and even nuclear power are often included in renewable portfolio standards even though these energy sources have too many damaging effects to be considered truly sustainable.[7]

Unfortunately, while renewable power is growing, natural gas generation is growing much faster, at the same time as coal-generated electricity is declining. We need to work to ensure that *all* fossil fuels stay in the ground. (See Introduction.) In 2014, natural gas generated more than 26 percent of U.S. electricity, a 118 percent increase since 1997.[8] The Clean Power Plan rules and the weak methane regulations that the Obama administration supports—and which some green groups are pushing for—will greatly increase the share of fracked gas generation, at the expense of renewable energy.

The evidence on fracking is clear. Impacts from drilling and fracking create significant health and environmental risks, and a wildly unstable climate endangers life on earth. Climate science supports the critical need for bringing an end to our dependence on fossil fuels. A brave and united environmental front that forcefully challenges the legitimacy of the oil and gas industry and the direct ways that fossil fuels are supplanting renewable energy could change the course of history.

We know that we can win amazing victories when the goal is far-reaching enough to inspire people to devote their time and energy to a cause bigger than themselves. Throughout the history of our nation, people have made progress by joining together to address major inequities and threats, from child labor and civil rights to passage of the nation's environmental laws and winning gay rights. Hundreds of communities across the United States and around the world are rising to the occasion with actions against fracking. In New York, our movement proved the naysayers wrong. Calling for a ban and fighting for it greatly widened the political space, and ultimately we built the political power to win a major round in the battle.

Ushering in this new era will mean moving away from touting ineffective carbon trading schemes, and instead putting all of our efforts into fast-forwarding the necessary shift away from fossil fuels. To ensure this shift, we must have a bold and visionary platform that includes policy changes that are hard to imagine today, but which can be achieved by working together. This platform should include policy changes at all levels of government, from the local to the federal and international. The necessary energy-related policy changes go way beyond the scope of this book, from adopting strict vehicle efficiency standards to eliminating nuclear power and investing in energy-efficient building retrofits. But a top goal must be leaving fossil fuels in the ground and reorienting the production and use of electricity.

To do this, we must mount a massive grassroots organizing effort to:

- Keep all fossil fuels in the ground.
- Ban fracking and all associated activities, including mining for sand and disposing of waste.
- Discontinue the building of fossil fuel infrastructure, including pipelines, processing facilities, and LNG plants.
- Reinstate the oil export ban.
- Require the federal government to develop a truly clean energy plan that can transition the nation to 100 percent renewable energy by 2035.
- Eliminate all policy mechanisms that favor natural gas and other dirty energy sources over renewable and energy-efficient technologies.
- Fully investigate claims of contamination from drilling and fracking, and require companies to remediate the damage and to fairly compensate affected residents.
- End all oil-and-gas-industry exemptions from environmental and public health laws.
- Terminate all public funding of the oil and gas industry and other dirty energy sources, including the billions of dollars in tax breaks.

- Stop fossil fuel exports and the construction of infrastructure to support these exports.
- Enact aggressive energy conservation mandates with major public investments in and widespread deployment of energy-saving solutions.
- Establish an ambitious mandate (a combination of federal and state requirements) for 100 percent clean energy that includes deploying and incentivizing renewable energy and energy efficiency technologies.
- Modernize the U.S. electricity grid and the policies that govern it so that renewable energy can be deployed and so that distributed renewable power can be fully utilized.
- Enact strong fuel-efficiency standards and mandates for using advanced-technology vehicles and make massive investments in public transportation and other transportation alternatives.
- Make sweeping investments in research and development for the next generation of clean energy and energy-efficient solutions.
- Restore strong protections in our commodities markets that prevent Wall Street speculators from profiteering and artificially driving fossil fuel production.
- Prevent energy and petroleum company mergers that accelerate environmental degradation, gouge consumers, and allow fossil fuel companies to become even more politically powerful.

We can make these changes if we are willing to unite and stand up together. The road to a sustainable future is clear, and the technologies are ready and cost-efficient. The only thing holding us back is the lack of political will. And with the crisis at hand, this is no excuse for failing to fight for the future we want for generations to come. We must move forward fearlessly to build a mass movement with the political power necessary to create a truly sustainable energy future. We must do this—it's a matter of life and death.

NOTES

The following abbreviations are used in the notes:

BLM U.S. Bureau of Land Management
DOE U.S. Department of Energy
DOJ U.S. Department of Justice
EDF   Environmental Defense Fund
EIA   U.S. Energy Information Administration
EPA   U.S. Environmental Protection Agency
SEC   U.S. Securities and Exchange Commission
USGS U.S. Geological Survey

Introduction

The introduction draws upon a letter that I wrote in the beginning of the Food & Water Watch report *The Urgent Case for a Ban on Fracking* (Washington, DC: 2015).

1. A.R. Brandt et al., "Methane Leaks from North American Natural Gas Systems," supplementary materials, *Science* 343, no. 733 (February 14, 2014): 29.

2. Gunnar Myhre et al., "Anthropogenic and Natural Radiative Forcing," in *Climate Change 2013: The Physical Science Basis. Contribution of Working Group I to the Fifth Assessment Report of the Intergovernmental Panel on Climate Change*, ed. T.F. Stocker et al. (Cambridge: Cambridge University Press), 714.

3. Robert W. Howarth, "A Bridge to Nowhere: Methane Emissions and the Greenhouse Gas Footprint of Natural Gas," *Energy Science and Engineering* 2, no. 2 (2014): 47, 56.

4. Calculation based on 2012 inventory of 2010 greenhouse gas emissions by EIA estimate of 2010 U.S. natural gas consumption and an assessment of EPA's underestimation of emissions from the life cycle of natural gas production to end use, factoring in natural gas as 90 percent methane. EPA, "Inventory of U.S. Greenhouse Gas Emissions and Sinks: 1990–2010," EPA 430-R-12-001, April 15, 2012, 2-5; EIA, "Monthly Energy Review," August 2015, 81; Scot M. Miller et al., "Anthropogenic Emissions of Methane in the United States," *Proceedings of the National Academy of Sciences* 110, no. 50 (December 10, 2013): 20022; Ramón A. Alvarez et al., "Greater Focus Needed on Methane Leakage from Natural Gas Infrastructure," supporting information, *Proceedings of the National Academy of Sciences* 109, no. 17 (April 24, 2012): 1.

5. Kate Konschnik and Mark Boling, "Shale Gas Development: A Smart Regulation Approach," *Environmental Science and Technology* 48, no. 15 (February 24, 2014): 8404.

6. EPA, "Assessment of the Potential Impacts of Hydraulic Fracturing for Oil and Gas on Drinking Water Resources," EPA/600/R-15/047a, June 2015, 4–7.

7. Konschnick and Boling, "Shale Gas Development," 8404; Jean-Phillippe Nicot et al., "Current and Projected Water Use in the Texas Mining and Oil and Gas Industry," University of Texas at Austin, Jackson School of Geosciences, prepared for Texas Water Development Board, June 2011, 54, 72.

8. Committee on Energy and Commerce, U.S. House of Representatives, "Chemicals Used in Hydraulic Fracturing," Minority Staff Report, April 2011, 2, 8; Christopher D. Kassotis et al., "Estrogen and Androgen Receptor Activities of Hydraulic Fracturing Chemicals and Surface and Ground Water in a Drilling-Dense Region," *Endocrinology* 155, no. 3 (March 2014): 899, 902, 904; Patrick Riley, "Bonita Springs City Council Votes to Pass Anti-fracking Ordinance," *Naples* (FL) *Daily News*, July 15, 2015; David R. Baker, "Acidizing Could Rival Fracking in Monterey Shale," *San Francisco Chronicle*, August 25, 2013.

9. EPA, "EPA's Full Draft Assessment of the Potential Impacts of Hydraulic Fracturing for Oil and Gas on Drinking Water Resources," June 4, 2015, 7-4.

10. Rivka Galchen, "Weather Underground," *New Yorker*, April 13, 2015.

11. Tom Randall, "This Animated Map Shows How Moving Oil by Rail Has Exploded in Just the Last 5 Years," Bloomberg, April 6, 2015.

12. Kim Mackrael and Justin Giovannetti, "Three People, Rail Company Face Charges in Lac-Mégantic Disaster," *Toronto Globe and Mail*, May 12, 2014.

13. Jad Mouwad, "New Oil Train Rules Are Hit from All Sides," *New York Times*, May 1, 2015.

14. Jake Hays and Seth B.C. Shonkoff, "Toward an Understanding of the Environmental and Public Health Impacts of Shale Gas Development: An Analysis of the Peer-Reviewed Scientific Literature, 2009–2015," PSE Healthy Energy, working paper 12-2014, June 2015, 2, 9.

15. Russell Gold and Tom McGinty, "Energy Boom Puts Wells in America's Backyards," *Wall Street Journal*, October 25, 2013.

16. Eric J. Esswein et al., "Occupational Exposures to Respirable Crystalline Silica During Hydraulic Fracturing," *Journal of Occupational and Environmental Hygiene* 10, no. 7 (July 2013): 347.

17. John L. Adgate, Bernard D. Goldstein, and Lisa M. McKenzie, "Potential Public Health Hazards, Exposures and Health Effects from Unconventional Natural Gas Development," *Environmental Science and Technology* 48, no. 15 (2014): 8310.

18. EPA 2015, ES-5.

19. Calculation based on Baker Hughes's U.S. rig counts for specific basins identified by EIA as tight oil and/or shale gas basins; oil rig share of all fracked rigs from January 2013 to June 2015. Baker Hughes, "North America Rotary Rig Count (January 2000–Current): U.S. Rig Count by Basin," September 11, 2015; EIA, "Technically Recoverable Shale Oil and Shale Gas Resources: An Assessment of 137 Shale Formations in 41 Countries Outside the United States," June 2013, 13, 14, 2–26.

20. EIA, "Annual Energy Outlook 2012: With Projections to 2035," DOE/EIA-0383, June 25, 2012, 59.

21. Asjylyn Loder, "Shakeout Threatens Shale Patch as Frackers Go for Broke," *Bloomberg*, May 27, 2014; Jeff Barron, "As Cash Flow Flattens, Major Energy Companies Increase Debt, Sell Assets," *Today in Energy*, July 29, 2014.

22. Ben German, "Energy Secretary: Natural Gas Helps Battle Climate Change—for Now," *The Hill*, August 1, 2013.

23. Sally Jewell, Secretary of the Interior, remarks at the National Press Club, October 31, 2013.

24. Amy Harder, "Colorado's Elections Were Fracked," *National Journal*, November 6, 2013.

25. Alan Neuhauser, "New York, Citing Health Risks, Moves to Ban Fracking," *U.S. News & World Report*, December 17, 2014.

26. Food & Water Watch analysis of EIA, "March 2015 Monthly Energy Review," DOE/EIA-0035(2015/03), Table 7.2a, "Electricity Net Generation: Total (All Sectors)," March 26, 2015, 105.

27. Lincoln F. Pratson, Drew Haerer, and Dalia Patiño-Echeverri, "Fuel Prices, Emission Standards, and Generation Costs for Coal vs. Natural Gas Power Plants," *Environmental Science and Technology* 47, no. 9 (2013): 4926.

28. EIA, *Monthly Energy Review*, March 2015, Table 7.2, and prior years.

29. EIA, "Annual Energy Outlook 2015 with Projections to 2040," April 2015, 24–25.

30. Ibid., A-18, A-31.

31. Linda Stamato, "Money and Muscle: The Koch Brothers and Their Billions of Dollars Are Making America More Dangerous," *Newark Star-Ledger*, April 6, 2014; Tom Hamburger, Kathleen Hennessey, and Neela Banerjee, "Koch Brothers Now at Heart of GOP Power," *Los Angeles Times*, February 6, 2011.

32. Matthew Continetti, "The Paranoid Style in Liberal Politics: The Left's Obsession with the Koch Brothers," *Weekly Standard*, April 4, 2011.

33. U.S. Commodities Future Trading Commission, personal communication with author, April 16, 2015; "News Summary," *Journal of Commerce*, April 4, 1990, 2A.

34. Pipeline and Hazardous Materials Safety Administration, "Data & Statistics: Pipeline Mileage and Facilities," U.S. Department of Transportation, accessed August 2015, phmsa.dot.gov/pipeline/library/data-stats.

35. Ambassador C. Boyden Gray, "Uncharted Territory: What Are the Consequences of President Obama's Unprecedented 'Recess Appointments,'" testimony before the Committee on Oversight and Government Reform, U.S. House of Representatives, February 1, 2012, 11; J. Owen Saunders, "North American Deregulation of Electricity: Sharing Regulatory Sovereignty," *Texas International Law Journal* 36, no. 167 (2001): 169.

36. Jeffrey H. Birnbaum, "Players: C. Boyden Gray. A Moving Force in Fight for Bush's Judicial Nominees," *Washington Post*, May 24, 2005; George W. Bush, "Personnel Announcement," press release, January 17, 2006; George W. Bush, "President Bush Selects C. Boyden Gray as Special Envoy for European Union Affairs," press release, January 11, 2008.

37. Ed Mendel, "Shake-up Could Be Coming in Electricity; PUC Considers Expanding 'Direct Access' to Buy Power," *San Diego Union-Tribune*, March 10, 2008; Dale Kasler, "State's Power-Plant Fight with JPMorgan Chase Is a Legacy of Deregulation Mess," *Sacramento Bee*, December 10, 2012; Lester Lave, Jay Apt, and Seth Blumsack, "Deregulation/Restructuring Part I: Reregulation Will Not Fix the Problems," *Electricity Journal* 20, no. 8 (October 2007): 10; Jay Hancock, "Md. Regulators Take Small Step Toward Electricity Reregulation," *Baltimore Sun*, October 4, 2011.

38. Center for Responsive Politics, "Electricity Deregulation," accessed August 2015, www.opensecrets.org/news/issues/electricity/index.php.

39. Jeffrey St. Clair and Alexander Cockburn, "Power Play: The Biggest Game in Town," *Minneapolis City Pages*, March 12, 1997.

40. Exelon Corporation, SEC Form 10-K, fiscal year ended December 31, 2014, 6–10; Excelon Corporation, "Excelon Recognized for Industry Leading Sustainability Performance for Tenth Year in a Row," press release, September 14, 2015.

41. Ivan Penn, "Duke Energy Mulls Fracking Charge," *Tampa Bay Times*, December 2, 2014; Duke Energy, SEC Form 10-K, fiscal year ended December 31, 2014, 9, 38; Duke Energy, "Duke Energy, U.S. Government Agree to End Clean Air Act Litigation," press release, September 10, 2015.

42. NextEra Energy Inc., SEC Form 10-K, fiscal year ended December 31, 2014, 6, 9, 14, 18.

43. Mary Ellen Klas, "Regulators Allow FPL to Invest in Natural Gas Fracking," *Miami Herald*, December 18, 2014.

1. In the Beginning

1. James Drape, "Petroleum—Something of Its History," *American Gas Light Journal*, August 5, 1901, 211.

2. G. Etiope et al., "The Geological Links of the Ancient Delphic Oracle (Greece): A Reappraisal of Natural Gas Occurrence and Origin," *Geology* 34, no. 10 (October 2006): 821–24.

3. Heather Brown, EC/R Inc., "Composition of Natural Gas for Use in the Oil and Natural Gas Sector Rulemaking," memorandum to Bruce Moore, U.S. EPA, June 29, 2011; Agency for Toxic Substances and Disease Registry, "Interaction Profile for: Benzene, Toluene, Ethylbenzene, and Xylenes (BTEX)," U.S. Department of Health and Human Services, May 2004, 1–2.

4. Robert G. Temple, "The Chinese Scientific Genius," *The Courier*, October 1988, 25.

5. M.S. Vassiliou, *The Historical Dictionary of the Petroleum Industry* (Plymouth, UK: Scarecrow Press, 2009), 168–69.

6. U.S. Census Bureau, "Special Report: Mines and Quarries 1902," 1905, 399.

7. Douglas Wayne Houck, *Energy and Light in Nineteenth-Century Western New York* (Charleston, SC: History Press, 2014), 12, 15, 44–45, 47; Ken Milam, "Fredonia,

N.Y.?," American Association of Petroleum Geologists, *AAPG Explorer*, September 2011, 24.

8. Houck, *Energy and Light*, 55–57; Milam, "Fredonia, N.Y.?," 22, 24.

9. Ibid.

10. Kendall Beaton, "Dr. Gesner's Kerosene: The Start of American Oil Refining," *Business History Review*, March 29, 1955, 28.

11. Parke Dickey, "The First Oil Well," *Journal of Petroleum Technology* 11, no. 1 (January 1959): 22–23; Judah Ginsberg, "The Development of the Pennsylvania Oil Industry," American Chemical Society, 2009, 2–3.

12. Charles Austin Whiteshot, *The Oil-Well Driller: A History of the World's Greatest Enterprise, the Oil Industry* (Morgantown, WV: Acme, 1905), 50; Dickey, "First Oil Well," 21–22.

13. Whiteshot, *Oil-Well Driller*, 48.

14. Dickey, "First Oil Well," 23.

15. Whiteshot, *Oil-Well Driller*, 49, 54; Ginsberg, "Development of the Pennsylvania Oil Industry," 3; George Elvin, *Post-Petroleum Design* (New York: Routledge, 2009), 3.

16. Tasneem Abbasi and S.A. Abbasi, *Renewable Energy Sources: Their Impact on Global Warming and Pollution* (Delhi: PHI Learning, 2010), 13.

17. National Fuel Gas Company, "Annual Report, 2002," 14.

18. National Fuel Gas Company, SEC Form 10-K, fiscal year ended September 30, 2014, 21–22, 110.

19. Ralph D. Gray, *Alloys and Automobiles: The Life of Elwood Haynes* (Indianapolis: Indiana Historical Society, 1979), 35–36, 42–51, 117.

20. Scott M. Harkins et al., "U.S. Production of Manufactured Gases: Assessment of Past Disposal Practices," Research Triangle Institute, commissioned for EPA, EPA/600/2-88/012, February 1988, i, ES-1, ES-3, 1, 72, 298.

21. DOE, "Secondary Energy Infobook," 2007, 28.

22. Sherie Mershon and Tim Palucka, "A Century of Innovation: From the U.S. Bureau of Mines to the National Energy Technology Laboratory," National Energy Technology Laboratory, DOE, 2010, 56–57.

23. U.S. Department of the Interior, Bureau of Mines, "Fifth Annual Report by the Director of the Bureau of Mines," 1915, 3, 77; Mershon and Palucka, "Century of Innovation," 25.

24. Mershon and Palucka, "Century of Innovation," 26–27, 35–37.

25. J.C. Speight, *Natural Gas: A Basic Handbook* (Houston: Gulf, 2007), 24; Richard E. Ricker, "Analysis of Pipeline Steel Corrosion Data from NBS (NIST) Studies Conducted Between 1922–1940 and Relevance to Pipeline Management," *Journal of Research of the National Institute of Standards and Technology* 115, no. 5 (September–October 2010): 376; Rexmond C. Cochrane, "Measures for Progress: A History of the National Bureau of Standards," National Bureau of Standards, U.S. Department of Commerce, 1974, 120–22.

26. John Hrastar, *Liquid Natural Gas in the United States: A History* (Jefferson, NC: McFarland, 2014), 71.

27. Ibid., 71; Peoples Gas Light and Coke Company, "100 Years of Gas Service in Chicago," 1950, 16–17.

28. Rodney P. Carisle and August W. Giebelhaus, C&W Associates, prepared for DOE, "Bartlesville Energy Research Center: The Federal Government in Petroleum Research 1918–1983," DOE/BC/10126-1, 1985, 2–4.

29. Mershon and Palucka, "Century of Innovation," 33.

30. Carisle and Giebelhaus, "Bartlesville Energy Research Center," 24.

31. Mershon and Palucka, "Century of Innovation," 56–59.

32. Ibid., 60; 49 CFR §192.625, Pipeline and Hazardous Materials Safety Administration—Odorization of Gas, originally published 35 FR 13257, August 19, 1970.

33. Mershon and Palucka, "Century of Innovation,"148–49.

34. David Miller, "The Historical Development of Oil and Gas Laws in the United States," *California Law Review* 51, no. 3 (August 1963): 524.

35. Mary C. Rabbitt, "The United States Geological Survey: 1879–1989," USGS Circular 1050, 1989, 1, 10, 34.

36. Texas Eastern Transmission Corporation, "The Big Inch and the Little Big Inch Pipelines," May 2000, 1, 19; Christopher J. Castaneda and Clarence M. Smith, *Gas Pipelines and the Emergence of America's Regulatory State* (Cambridge: Cambridge University Press, 2003), 128.

37. National Park Service, Historic American Engineering Record, "War Emergency Pipeline (Inch Lines): Inch Line Historic District," 1976, 22, 24.

38. "Texas Eastern Buyout Approved," *Los Angeles Times*, June 28, 1989; Bill Mintz and David Ivanovich, "Firm's Handle Now PanEnergy; Panhandle Eastern Seeks to Broaden Marketing Image," *Houston Chronicle*, January 3, 1996; Ted Reed, "How Deals Are Transforming Duke Energy," *Charlotte Observer*, March 29, 1999; Tom Fowler, "Spectra Ready to Trade; Duke Energy Spinoff Scheduled to Hit NYSE Today," *Houston Chronicle*, January 3, 2007.

39. A.C. Hartley, "Operation Pluto," *Proceedings of the Institution of Mechanical Engineers* 154 (June 1946): 433, 438.

40. Mershon and Palucka, "Century of Innovation," 259–60.

41. Edward Walsh, "Carter Is Staking 1st-Year Success on Energy Bill," *Washington Post*, October 16, 1977; Department of Energy Organization Act, P.L. 95-91, 91 Stat. 565 (1977).

42. Mershon and Palucka, "Century of Innovation," 262.

43. Zhongmin Wang and Alan Krupnick, Resources for the Future, "US Shale Gas Development: What Led to the Boom?," Issue Brief 13-04, May 2013, 4.

44. Albert B. Yost II, "Eastern Gas Shales Research," in *Proceedings of the Natural Gas R&D Contractors Review Meeting*, ed. C.A. Komar, R.D. Malone, and C.W. Byrer, U.S. Department of Commerce, National Technical Information Service, DOE/METC-89/6103, Morgantown, WV, April 18–19, 1989, 47.

45. Crude Oil Windfall Profit Tax Act of 1980, P.L. 96-23, §231, 94 Stat. 229 (1980); Staff of the Joint Committee on Taxation, U.S. Congress, "General Explanation of the Windfall Profit Tax of 1980" (JCS-1-81), January 31, 1981, 7; EIA, "The Majors' Shift to Natural Gas," September 2001, 4–5, 7; EIA, "Energy Policy Act Transportation Study: Interim Report on Natural Gas Flows and Rates," October 1995, 17.

46. Fred Sissine, "Renewable Energy R&D Funding History," Congressional Research Service, CRS 7-5700, October 10, 2014, 5.

2. Setting the Stage

1. Roger Lowenstein, "Before There Was Enron, There Was Insull," *New York Times*, March 19, 2006.

2. Robert L. Bradley Jr., *Edison to Enron: Energy Markets and Political Strategies* (Hoboken, NJ: Wiley-Scrivener, 2011), 187.

3. Ibid., 122, 124–25.

4. Cutler J. Cleveland, ed., *Concise Encyclopedia of the History of Energy* (San Diego: Elsevier, 2009), 168–69.

5. Arthur M. Schlesinger Jr., *The Age of Roosevelt: The Politics of Upheaval* (New York: Houghton Mifflin, 1960), 3:304.

6. Lowenstein, "Before There Was Enron."

7. M. Elizabeth Sanders, *The Regulation of Natural Gas: Policy and Politics, 1938–1978* (Philadelphia: Temple University Press, 1981), 26.

8. Ibid., 28.

9. U.S. Federal Trade Commission, "Annual Report for the Fiscal Year Ended June 30, 1935," 1935, 27.

10. Sanders, *Regulation of Natural Gas*, 28.

11. Schlesinger, *Age of Roosevelt*, 3:302, 315, 320, 324.

12. Ibid., 320.

13. Sanders, *Regulation of Natural Gas*, 38; Schlesinger, *Age of Roosevelt*, 3:324.

14. EIA, "Public Utility Holding Company Act of 1935: 1935–1992," January 1993, 11–12.

15. Mark Holt and Carol Glover, "Energy Policy Act of 2005: Summary and Analysis of Enacted Provision," U.S. Congressional Research Service, March 8, 2006, 82–84.

16. Sanders, *Regulation of Natural Gas*, 42–45.

17. Paul W. Parfomak, "Interstate Natural Gas Pipelines: Process and Timing of FERC Permit Application Review," U.S. Congressional Research Service, January 16, 2015, 1.

18. Cleveland, *Concise Encyclopedia*, 171.

19. Richard H.K. Vietor, *Energy Policy in America Since 1945: A Study of Business-Government Relations* (Cambridge: Cambridge University Press, 1984), 72–73.

20. "Robert S. Kerr," *Tulsa World*, February 2, 1963; John Shiffman et al., "The Lavish and Leveraged Life of Aubrey McClendon," Reuters, June 7, 2012.

21. Vietor, *Energy Policy*, 76–77.

22. Bradford Ross and Bernard A. Foster Jr., "Phillips and the Natural Gas Act," *Law and Contemporary Problems* 19 (1954): 396; Vietor, *Energy Policy*, 79.

23. Vietor, *Energy Policy*, 80–81.

24. Robert A. Caro, *Master of the Senate: The Years of Lyndon Johnson* (New York: Vintage, 2003), chap. 10–12.

25. Sanders, *Regulation of Natural Gas*, 86–87; Vietor, *Energy Policy*, 78–80.

26. Ibid.

27. U.S. Supreme Court, *Phillips Petroleum Co. v. Wisconsin* (1954).

28. Senator J. William Fulbright, *Congressional Record*, Senate 117, January 17, 1956, 668.

29. "Republicans: Take a Letter," *Time*, February 24, 1958.

30. James L. Merriner, "Illinois' Liberal Giant, Paul Douglas," *Chicago Tribune*, March 9, 2003; Institute of Government and Public Affairs, University of Illinois at Urbana-Champaign, "Biography of Paul H. Douglas," accessed August 2015, igpa .uillinois.edu/ethics/biography.

31. Senator Paul H. Douglas, "The Case for the Consumer of Natural Gas," *Georgetown Law Journal* 44 (1955–56): 577, 585.

32. Ibid., 590–92, 598.

33. Sanders, *Regulation of Natural Gas*, 105.

34. Vietor, *Energy Policy*, 84.

35. Sanders, *Regulation of Natural Gas*, 107.

36. Ibid., 107, 112–13.

3. The Natural Gas Heist

1. President Richard M. Nixon, "Remarks at the Seafarers International Union Biennial Convention," Public Papers of the Presidents no. 340, November 26, 1973.

2. Andy Kroll, "Follow the Dark Money," *Mother Jones*, July–August 2012.

3. Robert Sherrill, *The Oil Follies of 1970–1980* (New York: Anchor Press/ Doubleday, 1983), 44–47. I am indebted to this excellent book for much of the information in this chapter. This book is must-reading for anyone interested in oil and gas issues.

4. Ibid., 50.

5. Senator Frank Moss, *Congressional Record*, Senate, September 21, 1972, S15576.

6. Bryan Gruley and Rebecca Smith, "Anatomy of a Fall: Keys to Success Left Kenneth Lay Open to Disaster," *Wall Street Journal*, April 26, 2002; Vikas Bajaj and Kurt Eichenwald, "Kenneth L. Lay, 64, Enron Founder and Symbol of Corporate Excess, Dies," *New York Times*, July 6, 2006.

7. Robert L. Bradley Jr., *Edison to Enron: Energy Markets and Political Strategies* (Salem, MA: Scrivener, 2011), 293, 295.

8. U.S. Supreme Court, *Permian Basin Area Rate Cases* (1968).

9. *Federal Trade Commission v. Texaco Inc.*, 555 F2d 862 (1977).

10. William B. Picket, "Philip Hart: The Conscience of the Senate," *Indiana Magazine of History* 92, no. 4 (1996): 376–77.

11. Andrew T. Karron, "Hart and Minds," *Harvard Crimson*, January 11, 1977; Joseph Alsop, "School Busing: Noose for Liberals?," *Milwaukee Journal*, December 2, 1971.

12. William D. Smith, "Breakup of Oil Industry Stirs Dispute in Capital," *New York Times*, June 15, 1976.

13. Subcommittee on Antitrust and Monopoly, Committee on the Judiciary, U.S. Senate, Hearing on Competition and Concentration in the Natural Gas Industry, Part 1, June 26, 27, and 28, 1973, 1–8.

14. Jack Anderson, "Nassikas Ignored Economists' Warnings," *Lewiston* (ME) *Daily Sun*, June 15, 1971.

15. "The Gas Shortage Fuels a Fight," *Businessweek*, August 1, 1970; "Man-Made Fuel Crisis," *New York Times*, October 2, 1970.

16. Sherrill, *Oil Follies*, 51.

17. American Gas Association, "Our Country's Gas Supplies: What the Gas Industry Is Doing to Be Sure Your Home Has Enough Gas," advertisement, *Life*, October 22, 1971.

18. U.S. Department of Commerce, "Statistical Abstract of the United States 1973," July 1973, Table 1111, 660.

19. U.S. Comptroller General, "Need for Improving the Regulation of the Natural Gas Industry and Management of Internal Operations," GGD-74-106, September 13, 1974, 31–39, 49.

20. Shell Oil, "How in All Conscience Can Anyone Call These Excess Profits?," advertisement, *Milwaukee Journal*, January 18, 1974.

21. Subcommittee on Oversight and Investigations, Committee on Interstate and Foreign Commerce, U.S. House of Representatives, Hearings on Natural Gas Supply in the United States, June 9, 13, 26, and 27, 1975, part 1, 8, 17–25.

22. Subcommittee on Antitrust and Monopoly, Hearing on Competition and Concentration in the Natural Gas Industry, 482–84.

23. Michael R. Lemov, *People's Warrior: John Moss and the Fight for Freedom of Information and Consumer Rights* (Hackensack, NJ: Fairleigh Dickinson University Press, 2011), chap. 1.

24. Ibid., xviii.

25. Subcommittee on Oversight and Investigations, Committee on Interstate and Foreign Commerce, U.S. House of Representatives, Hearing on Allegations of Withholding of "Behind-the-Pipe" Natural Gas Reserves, February 22 and 23, 1977, 90.

26. Lemov, *People's Warrior*, ix.

27. Robert Sherrill, "The Natural Gas Swindle," *The Nation*, January 24, 1976, 70.

28. G. Kevin Jones, "Continental Shelf Oil and Gas Development During the Reagan Administration—Part I," *Western New England Law Review* 12, no. 1 (1990): 6–7.

29. Committee on Interior and Insular Affairs, U.S. Senate, "Report to the Federal Trade Commission on Federal Energy Land Policy: Efficiency, Revenue, and Competition," 1976, 455–65; Arthur Siddon, "Senate Reveals How Firms Hiked Oil Price for Tax Cuts," *Chicago Tribune*, January 31, 1974.

30. William E. Clayton, United Press International, "Oil Company Profits: Are They Gouging Us or Hurting for Money?," *Lexington* (NC) *Dispatch*, March 14, 1974.

31. Sherrill, "Natural Gas Swindle," 71.

32. "Probers Hint Firm Delayed Well Repairs," *Miami News*, July 24, 1975.

33. Sherrill, *Oil Follies*, 295.

34. Subcommittee on Oversight and Investigations, Hearings on Natural Gas Supply in the United States, 10.

35. Subcommittee on Energy and Power, Committee on Interstate and Foreign Commerce, U.S. House of Representatives, "Long-Term Natural Gas Legislation:

Compilation of Statements of Witnesses Before the Subcommittee on Energy and Power 1976," February 1976, 479, 484, 486.

36. Subcommittee on Oversight and Investigations, Hearings on Natural Gas Supply in the United States, 18.

37. Sherrill, "Natural Gas Swindle," 70.

38. Sherrill, *Oil Follies*, 328.

39. Ibid., 329.

40. Richard L. Lyons, "Mondale Helps Break Gas Pricing Filibuster," *Washington Post*, October 4, 1977.

41. Ibid.; Richard L. Lyons, "Senate Votes to Decontrol Natural Gas Prices," *Washington Post*, October 5, 1977; EIA, "Historical Natural Gas Annual 1930 Through 2000," DOE/EIA-E-0110(00), December 2001, 11.

42. Sherrill, *Oil Follies*, 385, 388, 394.

43. EIA, "Historical Natural Gas Annual," 11.

4. Seeking the Roots of the Frackopoly

1. Gaylord Nelson, *Beyond Earth Day: Fulfilling the Promise* (Madison: University of Wisconsin Press, 2002).

2. Robert Sherrill, "The Real McCloy: The Chairman: John J. McCloy, The Making of the American Establishment," *Los Angeles Times*, April 19, 1992.

3. Joseph Finder, "Ultimate Insider, Ultimate Outsider," *New York Times*, April 12, 1992.

4. Kai Bird, *The Chairman: John J. McCloy: The Making of the American Establishment* (New York: Simon & Schuster, 1992), 288, 462, 483, 549.

5. Bruce Raphael, *King Energy: The Rise and Fall of an Industrial Empire Gone Awry* (Lincoln, NE: Writers Club Press, 2000), 148–49.

6. Bird, *Chairman*, 517.

7. Daniel Yergin, *The Prize: The Epic Quest for Oil, Money and Power* (New York: Touchstone, 1992), 37, 45, 95.

8. Anthony Sampson, *The Seven Sisters: The Great Oil Companies and the World They Shaped* (New York: Viking Press, 1975), 24–26; Yergin, *Prize*, 37–38.

9. Yergin, *Prize*, 44–45.

10. See Glenn Porter, ed., "The Papers of John D. Rockefeller Sr.: Part 2: Business Investments Correspondence," Rockefeller University, 1992.

11. Yergin, *Prize*, 40–43.

12. Ida Tarbell, *The History of the Standard Oil Company*, 2 vols. (New York: McClure, Phillips, 1905).

13. Barry C. Lynn, *Cornered: The New Monopoly Capitalism and the Economics of Destruction* (Hoboken, NJ: John Wiley and Sons, 2010), 107.

14. President Theodore Roosevelt, "State of the Union Address," December 7, 1903.

15. Sampson, *Seven Sisters*, 27–28.

16. *Standard Oil Co. of New Jersey et al., v. United States*, transcript of stenographer's minutes of the oral argument of Frank B. Kellogg, on behalf of the

United States, Supreme Court of the United States, no. 398, October Term, 1910, 8, 60.

17. John T. Flynn, *God's Gold: The Story of Rockefeller and His Times* (New York: Harcourt, Brace, 1932), 447.

18. Yergin, *Prize*, 110–13.

19. Sampson, *Seven Sisters*, 32–34, 62; "Standard Oil Elects W.C. Teagle President," *New York Times*, November 16, 1917.

20. Sampson, *Seven Sisters*, 44–48.

21. Yergin, *Prize*, 148–49, 156–62.

22. Sampson, *Seven Sisters*, 59–60.

23. Patrick Bishop, "Britain's Legacy to the Tortured Ottoman Empire," *The Telegraph*, February 1, 2014.

24. Nicholas George Malavis, *Bless the Pure and Humble: Texas Lawyers and Oil Regulation, 1919–1936* (College Station: Texas A&M University Press, 1996), 25.

25. Colin Gordon, *New Deals: Business, Labor, and Politics in America, 1920–1935* (Cambridge: Cambridge University Press, 1994), 58.

26. John A. Morello, *Selling the President, 1920: Albert D. Lasker, Advertising, and the Election of Warren G. Harding* (Westport, CT: Praeger, 2001), 6–7.

27. Sampson, *Seven Sisters*, 78.

28. Robert Schlesinger, *White House Ghosts: Presidents and Their Speechwriters* (New York: Simon & Schuster, 2008), 3.

29. Rachel A. Schurman and Paul E. Sabin, "Public Policy, Oil Production, and Energy Consumption in Twentieth-Century California," Minerals Management Service, U.S. Department of the Interior, October 2003, 172–76.

30. Coolidge's letter of appointment to Secretaries of War, Navy, Interior, and Commerce, quoted in "Cut-Throat Oil Production Is Our National Disgrace," *San Francisco Examiner*, August 14, 1928, cited in Schurman and Sabin, "Public Policy," 172.

31. Sampson, *Seven Sisters*, 78.

32. Ibid., 65–69.

33. Ibid., 69–77.

34. Ibid., 78.

35. Ralph L. Nelson, *Merger Movements in American Industry, 1895–1956* (Princeton, NJ: Princeton University Press, 1959), Table C-7, 166–67.

36. Adolf A. Berle Jr. and Gardiner C. Means, *The Modern Corporation and Private Property* (New York: Macmillan, 1934), 32.

37. Richard J. Jenson, "The Causes and Cures of Unemployment in the Great Depression," *Journal of Interdisciplinary History* 19, no. 4 (Spring 1989): 557.

38. Linsey K. Hanson and Timothy J. Essenburg, eds., *The New Faces of American Poverty: A Reference Guide to the Great Recession* (Santa Barbara, CA: ABC-CLIO, 2014), 1:74.

39. Colin Gordon, *New Deals: Business, Labor, and Politics in America, 1920–1935* (Cambridge: Cambridge University Press, 1994), 155.

40. Sampson, *Seven Sisters*, 78.

41. Spencer Weber Waller, "The Antitrust Legacy of Thurman Arnold," *St. Johns Law Review* 78 (2004): 574–79.

42. Sampson, *Seven Sisters*, 78–80.

43. Ibid., 123–24.

44. Ibid.

45. Ibid., 124–25.

46. Bird, *Chairman*, 409, 429.

47. Sampson, *Seven Sisters*, 128–33.

48. Ibid., 52–59, 113–39.

49. Ibid., 124–30.

50. Antonia Juhasz, *The Tyranny of Oil: The World's Most Powerful Industry and What We Must Do to Stop It* (New York: William Morrow, 2009), 85–87.

51. Sampson, *Seven Sisters*, 156–63.

52. Bird, *Chairman*, 516–18.

53. Ibid., 517.

54. Sampson, *Seven Sisters*, 166.

55. Bird, *Chairman*, 518.

56. Sampson, *Seven Sisters*, 133–35.

57. Ibid., 203–4.

58. Bird, *Chairman*, 613–15.

59. Ibid., 625–26.

60. Ibid., 625–27.

61. Ibid., 626–27.

62. Bird, *Chairman*, 627; Sampson, *Seven Sisters*, 215.

63. Dean Walcutt, President of Certified Oil Company, testimony before the Subcommittee on Antitrust and Monopoly, U.S. Senate Committee on the Judiciary, May 3, 4, 5, 11, 12, 1977, 185; Alan Brinkley, *Liberalism and Its Discontents* (Cambridge, MA: Harvard University Press, 1998), 207.

64. Sanders, *Regulation of Natural Gas*, 216–17; Bird, *Chairman*, 628.

65. Bird, *Chairman*, 629–30.

66. Euclid A. Rose, "OPEC's Dominance of the Global Oil Market: The Rise of the World's Dependency on Oil," *Middle East Journal* 58, no. 3 (Summer 2004): 432–33.

67. Sampson, *Seven Sisters*, 177–81.

68. Bird, *Chairman*, 632.

69. Sampson, *Seven Sisters*, 186.

70. Rose, "OPEC's Dominance," 434.

71. Committee on Finance, U.S. Senate, "1974 Profitability of Selected Major Oil Company Operations," June 25, 1974, Table 1, Table 2.

72. Sampson, *Seven Sisters*, 277.

73. 663 F.2d 120. 213 U.S. App. D.C. 356, 1980–81 Trade Cases 63,577, *Exxon Corporation, Appellant v. Federal Trade Commission, et al.*, October 3, 1980.

74. Edward Cowan, "Attorneys Quit F.T.C. Oil Case," *New York Times*, June 26, 1978.

75. Attorneys General of California, Arizona, Connecticut, the District of Columbia, Illinois, Louisiana, Massachusetts, Mississippi, New Mexico, the Northern Mariana Islands, Ohio, Oregon, Rhode Island, Utah, Washington, West Virginia, Communication to European Commission, Directorate-General for Competition, Comments on the Review of Damages Actions for Breach of the EC Antitrust Rules, April 21, 2006, 5.

76. Juhasz, *Tyranny of Oil*, 99–100.

77. Bird, *Chairman*, 641, 644–52.

78. Bill Peterson, "PACs Gave $19.3 Million to '80 Favorites," *Washington Post*, March 29, 1981.

79. Dolly Langdon, "Demoted and Defanged, Consumer Watchdog Mike Pertschuk Keeps On Kicking About the Hard-Sell Sins of Big Business," *People*, May 2, 1983.

5. The Frackopoly Comes to Power

1. Steve Forbes, "Varney and Company," Fox Business Network, March 4, 2011.

2. President Richard Nixon, conversation with Lido Anthony Iacocca, Henry Ford II, and John S. Ehrlichman, April 27, 1971, transcript, Nixon Presidential Materials, National Archives.

3. U.S. Supreme Court, *First National Bank of Boston v. Bellotti* (1978).

4. Lewis F. Powell Jr., "Confidential Memorandum: Attack on American Free Enterprise System," memorandum to Eugene B. Sydnor Jr., U.S. Chamber of Commerce, August 23, 1971, 2–3, 6.

5. Henry A. Giroux, "The Powell Memo and the Teaching Machines of Right-Wing Extremists," Truthout, October 1, 2009.

6. Nicholas Wapshott, *Ronald Reagan and Margaret Thatcher: A Political Marriage* (New York: Sentinel, 2007), 55.

7. Mike Davis, "The New Right's Road to Power," *New Left Review*, July–August 1981, 8.

8. Bob Colacello, "Ronnie and Nancy: Part 1," *Vanity Fair*, July 1998.

9. Edward Boyer, "William French Smith, 73, Dies; Reagan Adviser and Atty. Gen," *Los Angeles Times*, October 30, 1990; Richard Lyons, "William French Smith Dies, 73; Reagan's First Attorney General," *New York Times*, October 30, 1990.

10. George L. Priest and William Ranney Levi, "Stevens and Antitrust," *National Law Journal*, May 24, 2010.

11. John McGee, "Predatory Price Cutting: The Standard Oil (N.J.) Case," *Journal of Law and Economics* 1 (October 1958).

12. Barry C. Lynn, *Cornered: The New Monopoly Capitalism and the Economics of Destruction* (Hoboken, NJ: John Wiley and Sons, 2010), 137.

13. Paul H. Brietzke, "Robert Bork, the Antitrust Paradox: A Policy at War with Itself," *Valparaiso Law Review* 13, no. 2 (Winter 1979): 403, 411–12.

14. See Barak Y. Orbach, "The Antitrust Consumer Welfare Paradox," *Journal of Competition Law and Economics* 7, no. 1 (December 2010).

15. Willard F. Mueller, "The New Attack on Antitrust," Conference on Management and Public Policy Toward Business, University of Florida, WP-90, April 4, 1986, 2–4.

16. Michael M. Weinstein, "W.F. Baxter, 69, Ex-antitrust Chief, Is Dead," *New York Times*, December 2, 1998.

17. William Kleinknecht, *The Man Who Sold the World: Ronald Reagan and the Betrayal of Main Street America* (New York: Nation Books, 2009), 140.

18. Lynn, *Cornered*, 137–38.

19. Michael A. Livermore and Richard L. Revesz, "Regulatory Review, Capture, and Agency Inaction," New York University School of Law, working paper no. 12-28, September 2012, 44; Robert D. Hersey, "Continuity Is Observed in U.S. Antitrust Policy," *New York Times*, January 9, 1982.

20. Subcommittee on Oversight and Investigations, Committee on Energy and Commerce, U.S. House of Representatives, "Report on the Performance of the Federal Trade Commission, 1977–1984," September 1984.

21. Irvin Molotsky, "At the F.T.C., the Trade in Mud Is Brisk," *New York Times*, August 29, 1984.

22. Michael Pertschuk, interview with author, 2012.

23. J. Fred Weston, Brian A. Johnson, and Juan A. Siu, "Mergers and Restructuring in the World Oil Industry," *Journal of Energy Finance and Development* 4 (1999): 154.

24. Patricia Sullivan, "Anne Gorsuch Burford, 62, Dies; Reagan EPA Director," *Washington Post*, July 22, 2004; Douglas Martin, "Anne Gorsuch Buford, 62, Reagan E.P.A. Chief, Dies," *New York Times*, July 22, 2004; David W. Barnes, "Back Door Cost-Benefit Analysis Under a Safety-First Clean Air Act," *National Resources Journal* 23 (October 1983): 829.

25. Jeff Welsch, "Thank You, James Watt, for All You Did for Greater Yellowstone," *High Country News*, August 1, 2013.

26. Ann Blackman, "Interior Secretary James Watt: You Either Like Him or You Hate Him," Associated Press, June 9, 1982; David Grimes, "Born-Again James Watt Wows Christian Retreat Crowd," *Sarasota* (FL) *Herald-Tribune*, August 31, 1984.

27. Lou Cannon, *President Reagan: The Role of a Lifetime* (New York: Public-Affairs, 1991), 469.

28. Welsch, "Thank You."

29. James E. Katz, "U.S. Energy Policy Impact of the Reagan Administration," *Energy Policy* 12, no. 2 (June 1984): 142.

30. David Biello, "Where Did Carter's White House Solar Panels Go?," *Scientific American*, August 6, 2010.

31. James B. Stewart, "When Media Mergers Limit More than Competition," *New York Times*, July 25, 2014.

32. Robert D. Hershey, "F.C.C. Votes Down Fairness Doctrine in a 4–0 Decision," *New York Times*, August 5, 1987.

33. Susan Whitehall, "Rather Offers No Apologies," *Detroit News*, May 1, 2012.

34. Ben H. Bagdikian, *The Media Monopoly*, 6th ed. (Boston: Beacon Press, 2000), 45.

6. The Road to Ruin

1. Paul Koberstein, "You Can Trust Enron," *Cascadia* (OR) *Times*, March 1997.

2. EIA, "Electric Power Annual 2013," March 2015, Table 3.1.A.

3. Paul M. Healy and Krishna G. Palepu, "The Fall of Enron," *Journal of Economic Perspectives* 17, no. 2 (Spring 2003): 4, 6; "Enron's Bankruptcy: Wasted Energy," *The Economist*, December 6, 2001.

4. Kenneth Lay, "Natural Gas: The Cost Effective Link Between Robust Economic Growth and Aggressive Environmental Protection," remarks at the Global Warming and the Earth Summit, Alliance to Save Energy Conference, June 23, 1992, 2.

5. Leslie Wayne, "Enron's Many Strands: The Politics; Enron, Preaching Deregulation, Worked the Statehouse Circuit," *New York Times*, February 9, 2002; Mark Dowie, *American Foundations: An Investigative History* (Cambridge, MA: MIT Press, 2001), 145, 148–54; EDF, "Environmental Defense Fund Urges Electricity Customers to 'Go Green,' " press release, March 31, 1998.

6. Sharon Beder, "How Environmentalists Sold Out to Help Enron," *PR Watch*, third quarter 2003, 5–6.

7. Dowie, *American Foundations*, 148–54.

8. Judy Keen, "Bush, Lay Kept Emotional Distance," *USA Today*, February 26, 2002; "Bush and Enron's Collapse," *The Economist*, January 11, 2002.

9. Bethany McClean and Peter Elkind, *The Smartest Guys in the Room: The Amazing Rise and Scandalous Fall of Enron* (New York: Penguin, 2004), 4–5.

10. Laura Goldberg and Mary Flood, "The Rise of Ken Lay as Dramatic as His Fall," *Houston Chronicle*, February 3, 2002.

11. McClean and Elkind, *Smartest Guys*, 5.

12. Robert L. Bradley, *Edison to Enron: Energy Markets and Political Strategies* (Salem, MA: Scrivener, 2011), 292

13. Ibid., 291.

14. Ibid., 291–92; McClean and Elkind, *Smartest Guys*, 5.

15. Robert Sherrill, "Energy 'Crisis' a Phony Emergency?," *Spokane Spokesman-Review*, October 21, 1979, H2; J.Y. Smith, "Rogers C.B. Morton Dies, Politician, Farmer, Outdoorsman," *Washington Post*, April 20, 1979.

16. "Oilmen Insist Offshore Fields Must Be Tapped," *Lakeland* (FL) *Ledger*, September 16, 1973.

17. "Jack Bowen, Once CEO of Florida Gas and Transco, Dies," *Pipeline & Gas Journal*, March 2011.

18. Bradley, *Edison to Enron*, 304; McClean and Elkind, *Smartest Guys*, 6–7.

19. Bradley, *Edison to Enron*, 303, 303n29.

20. Ibid., 206–308, 311.

21. McClean and Elkind, *Smartest Guys*, 7–8.

22. Bradley, *Edison to Enron*, 344; Paul Taylor, "Reagan Won't Ask Quick Natural Gas Decontrol," *Washington Post*, March 2, 1982.

23. Ward Morehouse III, "Natural Gas Decontrol Moves to Front Burner," *Christian Science Monitor*, March 1, 1982.

24. Michael McManus, "Public Must Protest Hikes in Natural Gas Cost," *Beaver County* (PA) *Times*, December 14, 1982.

25. See J. Michael Medina, "The Take-or-Pay Wars: A Further Status Report," *Oklahoma Law Review* 41, no. 381 (Fall 1988).

26. Bradley, *Edison to Enron*, 338–40.

27. Toni Mack, "The Other Enron Story," *Forbes*, October 14, 2002.

28. John Wyeth Griggs, "Restructuring the Natural Gas Industry: Order No. 436 and Other Regulatory Initiatives," *Energy Law Journal* 7, no. 71 (1986): 81–86.

29. Michael Arndt, "Natural Gas Rule Slows the Flow, Price Rise Tests Market Strategies," *Chicago Tribune*, January 10, 1988; President George H.W. Bush, "Statement on Signing the Natural Gas Wellhead Decontrol Act of 1989," P.L. 101-60, July 26, 1989.

30. "Nation's Natural Gas Industry Now Officially Deregulated," *Los Angeles Times*, July 31, 1992; Arthur Gottschalk, "Rules Approved to Restructure Natural Gas Pipeline Industry," *Journal of Commerce*, April 9, 1992.

31. Bradley, *Edison to Enron*, 477.

32. McClean and Elkind, *Smartest Guys*, 11–14.

33. Ibid., 11, 19–24, 36–38, 112–13.

34. Jonathan Weil and John Wilke, "Systemic Failure by SEC Is Seen in Enron Debacle," *Wall Street Journal*, October 7, 2002; "Bush and Enron's Collapse," *The Economist*, January 11, 2002.

35. Christopher Helman, "Here's What the Analyst Who Uncovered Enron Thinks About Chesapeake," *Forbes*, June 6, 2012.

36. Elizabeth Nichols, "U.S. Nuclear Power and the Success of the American Anti-nuclear Movement," *Berkeley Journal of Sociology* 32 (1987): 167, 180–81.

37. Gary McWilliams, "The Quiet Man Who's Jolting Utilities," *Businessweek*, June 8, 1997.

38. 61 Fed. Reg. 21540, May 10, 1996.

39. Allen R. Myerson, "Enron, Seeking to Be a Household Name, Plans to Start Its Campaign on Super Bowl Sunday," *New York Times*, January 14, 1997; "The Quiet Man Who's Jolting Utilities," *Businessweek*, June 8, 1997.

40. Linda Stamato, "Money and Muscle: The Koch Brothers and Their Billions of Dollars Are Making America More Dangerous," *Newark Star-Ledger*, April 6, 2014; Tom Hamburger, Kathleen Hennessey, and Neela Banerjee, "Koch Brothers Now at Heart of GOP Power," *Los Angeles Times*, February 6, 2011; Christian Bourge, "Enron Fall May Affect Think Tank Funding," United Press International, January 31, 2002.

41. Viskas Bajaj and Kurt Eichenwald, "Kenneth L. Lay, 64, Enron Founder and Symbol of Corporate Excess, Dies," *New York Times*, July 6, 2006; M. Asif Ismail, "A Most Favored Corporation: Enron Prevailed in Federal, State Lobbying Effort in 49 States," Center for Public Integrity, January 6, 2003.

42. John Hendry, *Ethics and Finance: An Introduction* (Cambridge: Cambridge University Press, 2013), 267

43. Tyson Slocum, "Blind Faith: How Deregulation and Enron's Influence over Government Looted Billions from Americans," Critical Mass Energy Project, Public Citizen, December 2001, 3.

44. Commodity Futures Modernization Act (S. 2697), 106th Congress, co-sponsored by Sen. Phil Gramm (R-Tex.); Center for Responsive Politics, "Senator Phil Gramm (R-Tex.), Career Profile (Since 1989)," accessed August 2015, www.open secrets.org.

45. Slocum, "Blind Faith," 22, 28.

46. Gramm-Leach-Bliley Act, P.L. 106-102, November 12, 1999.

47. UBS, "UBS Announces the Retirement of Senator Phil Gramm as Vice Chairman of the Investment Bank," press release, February 10, 2012.

48. "Who Deserves the Most Blame: 25 People to Blame for the Financial Crisis," *Time*, February 11, 2009.

49. Ismail, "Most Favored Corporation."

50. Robert L. Bradley, *Capitalism at Work: Business, Government and Energy* (Salem, MA: M&M Scrivener, 2009), 188.

51. Michael Weisskopf, "The White House: That Invisible Mack Sure Can Leave His Mark," *Time*, September 1, 1997.

52. James K. Glassman, "Turning Green," *Wall Street Journal*, February 14, 2002.

53. Larry Bell, "The U.N.'s Global Warming War on Capitalism: An Important History Lesson," *Forbes*, January 22, 2013.

54. Executive Office of the President, "President Nominates FERC Commissioners," press release, April 12, 1993; *Congressional Record* 143, no. 76 (June 5, 1997): S5384; DOE, Office of the Executive Secretariat, Correspondence Control Ticket, "Enron Corp. Requests a Meeting with Deputy Secretary to Discuss Some DOE Issues June 23, or 24th," control no. 97-009335, June 19, 1997; DOE, Office of the Executive Secretariat, Correspondence Control Ticket, "Letter to Secretary from Cynthia C. Sandherr," control no. 1998-001620.

55. Ismail, "Most Favored Corporation"; McClean and Elkind, *Smartest Guys*, 87; Jeanne Cummings, "Enron's Washington Clout Before Collapse Draws Scrutiny," *Wall Street Journal*, January 15, 2002; Kenneth Lay, Enron, letter to President George H.W. Bush, April 3, 1992.

56. John Nichols, "Enron: What Dick Cheney Knew," *The Nation*, April 15, 2002; Energy Policy Act of 2005, P.L. 109-58, August 8, 2005, §322, §368, §390, §1221; "The Halliburton Loophole," *New York Times*, November 3, 2009.

57. Ralph Cavanagh, "The Future of America's Electric Utilities: Reconciling Deregulation and Least-Cost Planning," *Electricity Journal* 4, no. 4 (May 1991): 27, 28.

58. Robert F. Worth, "Kerry's Attacks on Enron Draw Return Fire," *New York Times*, July 10, 2004; John H. Cushman Jr., "Environmental Study Center Created to Honor Late Senator," *New York Times*, December 15, 1995; Heinz Family Foundation, "The Heinz Awards—3rd: Ralph Cavanagh," 1995, www.heinzawards.net /recipients/ralph-cavanagh.

59. Dowie, *American Foundations*, 145, 148, 150–55; Jeffrey St. Clair and Alexander Cockburn, "Power Play: The Biggest Game in Town," *Minneapolis–St. Paul City Pages*, March 12, 1997; "California Backs Into the Future," *Wall Street Journal*, November 3, 1998.

60. Energy Commission, "Quarterly Fuel and Energy Report 2014."

61. California Renewables Portfolio Standard Program, Senate Bill no. 1078, Approved by Governor, September 12, 2002; California Renewable Energy Act, Senate Bill 108, Approved by Governor, September 26, 2006; California Energy Act 2011, Senate Bill 2, Approved by Governor, April 12, 2011.

62. Environmental Law & Policy Center, "Legislators Call for Stronger Environmental Provisions in Electricity Deregulation Bill," press release, October 10, 1999.

63. Julie Wernau, "Fracking Regulations Passed in Springfield," *Chicago Tribune*, May 31, 2013; Kari Lydersen, "In Illinois, Environmentalists and Industry Compromise on Fracking," *Midwest Energy News*, February 22, 2013.

64. Energy Foundation, "Annual Report, 2000," 10, 11.

65. Eric Heitz and Hal Harvey, "Utility Industry Restructuring: New Levers for Sustainable Energy in the Great Utility Debate: A Briefing for Foundations," Energy Foundation, October 2, 1995, 10–11; MB Financial Inc., SEC filing DEF-14A, April 10, 2015, 7; MD Financial Inc., "MB Financial, Inc. Approves Dividend on Its Series A Preferred Stock," press release, June 3, 2015.

66. For example: Energy Foundation, International Revenue Service I-990 form, Schedule I, Part II: 2012 Grant #295 ("To review experience of U.S. shale gas development and regulation for dialogue and exchange with key Chinese stakeholders on shale gas"); 2011 Grant #158 ("To support strong federal EPA standards for oil and gas drilling"); 2010 Grant #436 ("To develop a roadmap for increasing the use of responsibly-produced natural gas for power generation").

67. John Howat, senior policy analyst, National Consumer Law Center, personal communication with author, February 20, 2014.

68. Lynn Hargis, personal communication with author, February 26, 2014.

69. Evan Halper, "Koch Brothers, Big Utilities Attack Solar, Green Energy Policies," *Los Angeles Times*, April 19, 2014.

7. Mitchell Makes a Fortune

1. John Bartlett, *Familiar Quotations*, 16th ed. (New York: Little, Brown, 1992), 539.

2. Robin Sidel and Chip Cummins, "Devon Energy to Acquire Mitchell in $3.1 Billion Cash-and-Stock Deal," *Wall Street Journal*, August 14, 2001; Devon Energy Corp., "Devon Energy Completes Acquisition of Mitchell Energy," press release, January 24, 2000.

3. Texans for Public Justice, "Checks and Imbalances: How Texas Supreme Court Justices Raised $11 Million," April 11, 2000, sec. V, part F.

4. Molly Ivins, "There's Something About Carole Keeton Rylander," *Bryan* (OH) *Times*, August 13, 1998.

5. Russell Gold, *The Boom: How Fracking Ignited the American Energy Revolution and Changed the World* (New York: Simon & Schuster, 2014), 101–11; *Mitchell Energy Corp. v. Bartlett*, 958 SW 2d 430 (1997).

6. Gold, *Boom*, 107.

7. Joseph W. Kutchin, *How Mitchell Energy and Development Corp. Got Its Start and How It Grew: An Oral History and Narrative Overview—Updated* (Boca Raton, FL: Universal, 2001), 69; *Mitchell Energy Corp. v. Bartlett.*

8. Kutchin, *How Mitchell Energy*, 68.

9. Gold, *Boom*, 97–111, 325, 326.

10. Ibid., 100–101.

11. "Mitchell/Chesapeake's Louisiana Tow Line to Flow 250,000 Mcf/Day to Eunice," *Inside F.E.R.C.'s Gas Market Report*, September 20, 1996.

12. "Stadium Debates Are Nothing New in Houston," *Houston Business Journal*, September 1, 1996.

13. Center for American and International Law, Institute for Energy Law, John Rogers Award, accessed August 2015, www.cailaw.org/institute-for-energy-law /about-us/awards/rogers-award.html.

14. National Petroleum Council, "Natural Gas: Meeting the Challenges of the Nation's Growing Natural Gas Demand. Volume I: Summary Report," December 1999, A-4–A-10.

15. Ibid., 1.

16. Ibid., 18.

17. EIA, "U.S. Crude Oil, Natural Gas and Dry Developmental Wells Drilled," accessed July 6, 2015, www.eia.gov/dnav/ng/hist/e_ertw0_xwcd_nus_cA.htm; Matt Cook, "Douglas-Westwood Forecast: 35% Increase in Well Completion Count from 2013–2020 Drive Only 17% Rise in Oil, Gas Output," *Drilling Contractor*, April 22, 2014.

18. EPA, "EPA's Full Draft Assessment of the Potential Impacts of Hydraulic Fracturing for Oil and Gas on Drinking Water Resources," June 4, 2015, ES-5.

19. National Petroleum Council, "Natural Gas," Joe Foster letter, 10, 27.

20. Kutchin, *How Mitchell Energy*, 342.

21. Gold, *Boom*, 134; Kutchin, *How Mitchell Energy*, 374, 465.

22. Gregory Zuckerman, "Breakthrough: The Accidental Discovery That Revolutionized American Energy," *The Atlantic*, November 6, 2013.

23. Kutchin, *How Mitchell Energy*, 363–68.

24. Gregory Zuckerman, *The Frackers: The Outrageous Inside Story of the New Billionaire Wildcatters* (New York: Penguin, 2013), 22–26.

25. Elizabeth M. Sanders, *The Regulation of Natural Gas: Policy and Politics, 1938–1978* (Philadelphia: Temple University Press, 1981), 40; Kutchin, *How Mitchell Energy*, 21; Zuckerman, *Frackers*, 26.

26. Kutchin, *How Mitchell Energy*, 21, 58, 201–2.

27. "Mitchell on Gas Survey Committee," *Galveston Daily News*, June 15, 1971.

28. "Mitchell Predicts Natural Gas Deregulation in 1975," *Galveston Daily News*, January 9, 1975.

29. Associated Press, "Gas Companies Charged with Lying," *Florence* (AL) *Times*, June 14, 1975.

30. Jack Anderson, "Gas Firm Crackdown Sought," *Toledo Blade*, February 14, 1977.

31. Subcommittee on Oversight and Investigations, Committee on Interstate and Foreign Commerce, U.S. House of Representatives, "Questions and Answers About the Nature and Causes of the Natural Gas Shortage," February 1976, 4.

32. Jack Anderson and Les Whitten, "Congress Pushes for Crackdown on Gas Squeeze," *St. Petersburg Times*, February 14, 1977; "Natural-Gas Firm Exec Faces Perjury Charges," *Miami Times*, July 24, 1975.

33. Kutchin, *How Mitchell Energy*, 58.

34. "Mitchell Opined on Policies Tied to Economics and Energy," *Houston Chronicle*, August 3, 2013.

35. Kutchin, *How Mitchell Energy*, 65.

36. Ibid., 65–66.

37. James Conca, "The Fracking Solution Is a Good Cement Job," *Forbes*, September 10, 2012.

38. Kutchin, *How Mitchell Energy*, 66–68.

39. Gold, *Boom*, 133.

40. Alex Trembath et al., "Where the Shale Gas Revolution Came From," Breakthrough Institute, May 2012, 2.

41. John M. Golden and Hannah J. Wiseman, "The Fracking Revolution: Shale Gas as a Case Study in Innovation Policy," *Emory Law Journal* 64, no. 955 (2015): 1010–6. See also, for example, "Unique Method of Hydraulic Fracturing," patent no. US 540284; "Hydraulic Fracturing Method Using Sintered Bauxite Propping Agent," patent no. US 4068718; "Compositions and Methods for Hydraulic Fracturing," patent no. US 6169058 B1.

42. Zuckerman, "Breakthrough"; Gold, *Boom*, 117–24.

43. Christopher Helman, "Billionaire Father of Fracking Says Government Should Step Up Regulation," *Forbes*, July 19, 2012.

44. "An Interview with George Mitchell: The Industry Can No Longer Simply Focus on the Benefits of Shale Gas," *The Economist*, August 1, 2013.

45. Cynthia and George Mitchell Foundation, "Shale Sustainability," accessed July 2015, cgmf.org/p/shale-sustainability-program.html.

46. Cynthia and George Mitchell Foundation, "Foundation Creates $6 Million Texas Energy and Climate Change Program," press release, February 6, 2008.

47. "The Father of Fracking," *Economist*, August 3, 2013.

48. Cited in Loren Steffy, "The Energy Hunter," *Texas Monthly*, November 2013.

8. Devon: Big Fish Polluting a Small Pond

1. Eugene Robinson, "What the Planet Needed," *Washington Post*, November 14, 2014.

2. Adam Wilmoth, "Well Done; Bartlesville Boomed Thanks to Nellie's Crude Success," *Daily Oklahoman*, April 1, 2007; Richard Mize, "Before It Was Oklahoma . . . ," *Daily Oklahoman*, April 22, 2007.

3. Suzanne Goldenberg, "Terror Charges Faced by Oklahoma Fossil Fuel Protesters 'Outrageous,' " *The Guardian*, January 10, 2014.

4. Great Plains Tar Sands Resistance, "Statement from Moriah Stephenson, One of the Two Activists Facing Potential 'Terrorism Hoax' Charges," press release, January 7, 2014.

5. Kurt Hochenauer, University of Oklahoma, interview with author, March 19, 2014.

6. Scott Thompson, "Rogers County Woman Who Fought Black Fox Plant Left Lasting Legacy," KOTV Channel 6, Tulsa, April 28, 2011.

7. Myrna Oliver, "Firm to Settle Silkwood Case: Kerr-McGee Will Pay $1.38 Million to Estate," *Los Angeles Times*, August 23, 1986.

8. Earl Hatley, Grand Riverkeeper, interview with author, 2015.

9. Al Pickett, "New Technology Allows Mid-Continent's Operators to Capture New Reserves," *American Oil & Gas Reporter*, August 24, 2015; Jeff Mullen, "Mississippi Lime Is Still Producing for the Area," *Enid* (OK) *News & Eagle*, April 9, 2015.

10. "Mississippi Lime Moves into Mainstream Oil Production in Two Years," *Exploration & Production Magazine*, June 11, 2012; Ryan Dezember, "Sandridge Inks $1 Billion Drilling Pact with Respol," *Wall Street Journal*, December 22, 2011; Continental Resources Inc., SEC Form 10-K, fiscal year ended December 31, 2014, 14.

11. Scott Weeden, "Oklahoma Reverses 25-Year Decline in Oil Production," *Exploration & Production Magazine*, January 1, 2013.

12. Devon Energy, "Devon Energy Announces $2.2 Billion Transaction on Five New Venture Plays," press release, January 3, 2012.

13. Nicholas Rapp and Scott DeCarlo, "The Global 500: Growth Moves to the East," *Fortune*, August 1, 2015; Devon Energy Corporation, SEC Form 10-K, fiscal year ended December 31, 2014, 3, 6.

14. Joe Wertz, "Hazy Guidance over Fracking Water Lines Confounds Commissioners and Cowboys," StateImpact Oklahoma, NPR, December 19, 2013.

15. Adam Wilmoth, "Oklahoma's Oil Production Growing Fast," *Daily Oklahoman*, November 27, 2013.

16. Wertz, "Hazy Guidance."

17. See William L. Ellworth et al., "Increasing Seismicity in the U.S. Midcontinent: Implications for Earthquake Hazard," *Leading Edge*, June 2015; F. Rall Walsh III and Mark D. Zoback, "Oklahoma's Recent Earthquakes and Saltwater Disposal," *Science Advances* 1, no. 5 (June 18, 2015); K.M. Keranen et al., "Sharp Increase in Central Oklahoma Seismicity Since 2008 Induced by Massive Wastewater Injection," *Science* 345, no. 6195 (July 3, 2014); William L. Ellsworth, "Injection-Induced Earthquakes," *Science* 431, no. 6142 (July 12, 2013); USGS, "Earthquake Swarm Continues in Central Oklahoma," press release, October 22, 2013; Liam Herringshaw, Durham Energy Institute, "What Size of Earthquakes Can Be Caused by Fracking?," press release, April 2013.

18. USGS, "Record Number of Oklahoma Tremors Raise Possibility of Damaging Earthquakes," press release, May 5, 2014; Walsh and Zoback, "Oklahoma's Recent Earthquakes."

19. Mike Soraghan, "Drilling-Heavy Okla. Ranked 2nd Last Year for Quakes," *EnergyWire*, February 20, 2014; USGS, "Earthquake Swarm Continues in Central Oklahoma," press release, October 22, 2013.

20. Walsh and Zoback, "Oklahoma's Recent Earthquakes," 1.

21. Analysis of earthquake data from the Oklahoma Geological Survey, "Earthquake Catalogue, Years 2000–2014," accessed January 2015, www.okgeosurvey1 .gov/pages/earthquakes/catalogs.php.

22. Daniel Gilbert, "Energy Companies Can Be Sued over Earthquakes, Oklahoma Supreme Court Says," *Wall Street Journal*, June 30, 2015.

23. Peter Moskowitz, "Earthquake Spike Pushes Oklahoma to Consider Tighter Fracking Regulations," *The Guardian*, June 25, 2015.

24. USGS, "Induced Earthquakes," accessed November 5, 2014, earthquake .usgs.gov/research/induced.

25. Ellsworth et al., "Increasing Seismicity," 619, 624.

26. Joe Wertz, "In Rural Oklahoma, Drilling Hits Close to Home," StateImpact Oklahoma, NPR, December 21, 2012; Oklahoma state statute, 52 OK Stat. §52-320.1 (2014).

27. Oklahoma state statute, 52 OK Stat. §52-87.1(e) (2014).

28. Oklahoma Corporation Commission, "Frequently Asked Questions: Mineral Owners Escrow Account Unknown or Unlocatable Mineral Owners," accessed August 2015, www.occeweb.com/moeasearch/faq.aspx.

29. Tulsa Association of Petroleum Landmen, newsletter, September 2014, 17.

30. Oklahoma City Association of Professional Landmen, "President's Letter," *OCAPL Record*, December 2014.

31. Roger A. Soape, "Challenges for Professional Landmen," *Oil & Gas Financial Journal*, March 13, 2014.

32. Jay F. Marks, "Oil Industry Rallies at Oklahoma State Capitol," *Daily Oklahoman*, April 10, 2014.

33. Jeff McDougall, Wildcatters Club of Oklahoma, "OIPA: Your Industry, Your Voice," presentation at OIPA Fall 2009 Conference, October 6, 2009, 2, 21.

34. S. Res. 159, Senate Resolution recognizing the fiftieth anniversary of the Oklahoma Independent Petroleum Association, *Congressional Record*, May 26, 2005, S6064.

35. Committee on Environment and Public Works (hereafter EPW), U.S. Senate, "Inhofe Receives Unanimous Support to Be Chairman of EPW Committee," press release, January 9, 2015.

36. EPW, "The Chain of Environmental Command: How a Club of Billionaires and Their Foundations Control the Environmental Movement and Obama's EPA," Minority Staff Report, July 30, 2014, 248–50.

37. EPW, "Setting the Record Straight: Hydraulic Fracturing and America's Energy Revolution," Minority Staff Report, October 23, 2014, iv.

38. President Barack Obama, "State of the Union," January 28, 2014.

39. Center for Responsive Politics, "Sen. James M. Inhofe: Top 5 Industries 1986–2016," accessed August 2015, www.opensecrets.org.

40. Devon Energy Corp., SEC Form 10-K, fiscal year ended December 31, 2014, 12–13; Jay F. Marks, "Oklahoma Energy Company Marks 40th Anniversary," *Daily Oklahoman*, March 11, 2011.

41. Randy Krehbiel, "Sky Changer," *Oklahoma Today*, January–February 2013.

42. John A. Sullivan, "John W. Nichols, Co-founder of Devon Energy Dies, 93," *Oil and Gas Investor*, August 5, 2008; Stephen Miller, "Former Accountant Worked to Build Devon Energy into Industry Giant," *Wall Street Journal*, August 9, 2008.

43. Miller, "Former Accountant"; Krehbiel, "Sky Changer," 41–42.

44. "Most Admired CEOs Profile: J. Larry Nichols, Oklahoma City–Based Devon Energy," *Oklahoma City Journal Record*, February 18, 2010; Devon Energy, "Devon Energy Corporation Announces Formation of Devon Resource Investors," press release, May 30, 1985.

45. Devon Energy Corp., SEC Form 10-K, fiscal year ended December 31, 2014, 3; Marks, "Oklahoma Energy Company"; Devon Energy, "Devon Energy Completes Acquisition of Eagle Ford Assets from GeoSouthern Energy," press release, February 28, 2014; Devon Energy Corp., "Devon Energy and PennzEnergy Announce Completion of Merger," press release, August 17, 1999; Devon Energy Corp., "Devon Energy and Ocean Energy Complete Merger; Creating Largest U.S. Independent Oil and Gas Producer," press release, April 25, 2003.

46. Jeremy Pelofsky, "Insight: African Leader's Son Tests U.S. Anti-corruption Push," Reuters, December 2, 2011; Ken Silverstein, "U.S. Investigates Oil Firms' Deals in West Africa," *Los Angeles Times*, May 22, 2004.

47. Devon Energy Corporation, 2006 Annual Report, 82; Ben Casselman and Jason Womack, "Devon Energy to Sell International, Gulf of Mexico Assets," *Wall Street Journal*, November 17, 2009; Devon Energy, "Devon to Divest Assets and Terminate Operations in West Africa," press release, January 23, 2007.

48. Tess Stynes, "Devon Energy Swings to Profit on Increased Production, Prices," *Wall Street Journal*, February 19, 2014.

49. Enlink Midstream Partners, LP, SEC Form 10-K, fiscal year ended December 31, 2014, 56.

50. Sarah Terry-Cobo, "Reaction to Devon Earnings Rude, Analyst Says," *Oklahoma City Journal Record*, August 5, 2015; Stephanie Yang, "Canada Is on the Brink of a 'Very Unusual Recession,'" CNBC, August 6, 2015; Mark Hanson, "Devon's Focus Is Now on Its North American Onshore Assets, Supported by a Rock-Solid Balance Sheet," Morningstar, Inc. analyst report, August 5, 2015.

51. Center for Responsive Politics, Lobbying Spending Database, "Devon Energy, 2013 and 2014."

52. Center for Responsive Politics, "Rep. Mary Fallin: Summary Data 2005–2008"; American Legislative Exchange Council, press release, April 26, 2013.

53. Randy Ellis, "Gov. Mary Fallin, Oklahoma Lawmakers React to Tax Proposal from Devon, Chesapeake, Continental," *Daily Oklahoman*, May 4, 2014; Paul Monies, "Gov. Mary Fallin Signs Bill Preventing Oklahoma Cities from Enacting Drilling Bans," *Daily Oklahoman*, May 30, 2015.

54. Center for Responsive Politics, "Devon Energy: Summary 2000–2014"; Jackie Kucinich, "Cole Backed for Approps; Boehner to Uphold Pledge to Ousted NRCC Chairman," *Roll Call*, December 8, 2008.

55. Office of U.S. Congressman Tom Cole, "Energy," accessed August 2015, cole.house.gov/issue/energy.

56. Jacob McCleland, "Rep. Tom Cole on Fast Track Approval, Crude Oil Exports," KGOU 106.3 FM (Norman, OK), May 11, 2015.

57. Brandon Williamson and Kristin Van Veen-Hincke, "Congressional Spotlight—Tom Cole (R-OK)," *Well Servicing Magazine*, September–October 2010.

58. Oklahoma State Statute, Title 68, OK Stat. §68-2357.22; National Conference of State Legislatures, "State Incentives and Fees for Natural Gas Vehicles," November 2014, 10.

59. Benjamin Elgin, Benjamin Haas, and Phil Kuntz, "Fracking Secrets by Thousands Keep U.S. Clueless on Wells," Bloomberg, November 10, 2012.

60. On non-attainment issues, Devon lobbied the U.S. House of Representatives, the U.S. Senate, the DOE, the U.S. Department of the Interior, the EPA, the Office of Science and Technology Policy, and the Council on Environmental Quality. See Devon Energy Production Company, L.P., U.S. House of Representatives, U.S. Senate, LD-2 disclosure form filing, April 22, 2013; Devon Energy Production Company, L.P., LD-2 disclosure form filing, January 21, 2014.

61. Sidney Austin LLP, "Re: Request for Partial Reconsideration and Stay of EPA's Final Rule Titled 'Air Quality Designations for the 2008 Ozone National Ambient Air Quality Standards,' " letter to EPA administrator Lisa P. Jackson, July 20, 2012, 2.

62. Joe Leonard, Devon Energy Corporation, "America's Energy Future, Part I: A Review of Unnecessary and Burdensome Regulations," testimony before the Committee on Oversight and Government Reform, U.S. House of Representatives, July 13, 2012, 64.

63. Tom Schoenberg, "Devon Energy, Texas Sue EPA over Ozone Limits Set by Bush," Bloomberg News, July 23, 2012.

64. Alex Mills, "EPA's Tightened Oil-Gas Rules Political Payback," *Wichita Falls* (TX) *Times Record*, August 23, 2015.

65. Devon lobbied the House and Senate about "sue and settle" in 2013. See Devon Energy Production Company, LP, LD-2 disclosure form filing, January 21, 2014; Committee on the Judiciary, U.S. House of Representatives, Report to Accompany H.R. 1493, Sunshine for Regulatory Decrees and Settlement's Act of 2013, Report 113-230, September 26, 2013, "Dissenting Views."

66. Eric Lipton, "Energy and Regulators on One Team," *New York Times*, December 7, 2014.

67. Devon Energy Production Company, LD-2 disclosure form filing, April 22, 2013.

68. Matthew Tresaugue, "Energy Firms' Plan to Protect Chickens from Ruffling Feathers," *Houston Chronicle*, February 22, 2014.

69. Russell Gold, "Save a Chicken, Drill a Well," *Wall Street Journal*, July 19, 2013; David Festa, "Letter of the Day: Economic and Environmental Cooperation," *Lubbock* (TX) *Avalanche-Journal*, March 17, 2013.

70. Scott Streater, "FWS Finalizes 'Landmark' Lesser Prairie Chicken Protections from Drilling," *Greenwire*, March 3, 2014.

71. Earl Hatley, interview with author, 2015.

72. Barbara VanHanken, interview with author, 2015.

9. Chesapeake Energy: High-Rolling Fracking Drama

1. Warren Buffett, "Buy American. I Am," *New York Times*, October 16, 2008.

2. John Shiffman, Anna Driver, and Brian Grow, "Special Report: The Lavish and Leveraged Life of Aubrey McClendon," Reuters, June 7, 2012.

3. Jeff Goodell, "The Big Fracking Bubble: The Scam Behind Aubrey McClendon's Gas Boom," *Rolling Stone*, March 1, 2012.

4. Natural Gas Supply Association, "Top 40 Natural Gas Producers 2015—1st Quarter," July 2015.

5. Christopher Helman, "The Two Sides of Aubrey McClendon, America's Most Reckless Billionaire," *Forbes*, October 24, 2011.

6. Goodell, "Big Fracking Bubble."

7. Shiffman et al., "Special Report."

8. Zachary Midler et al., "Chesapeake's 1% Tax Rate Shows Cost of Drilling Subsidy," Bloomberg, July 2, 2012.

9. Center for Responsive Politics, "Chesapeake Energy, Summary and Total 1990–2014," accessed August 2015, available at www.opensecrets.org.

10. Russell Gold, *The Boom* (New York: Simon & Schuster, 2014), 166; Darren Samuelsohn, "Fred Upton Finds It's Good to Be the Chairman," *Politico*, March 15, 2012.

11. Representative Fred Upton, U.S. House of Representatives, "2013 Financial Disclosure Statement," May 22, 2014, 3.

12. Center for Responsive Politics, "Rep. Fred Upton, Top 100 Donors, Election Cycles 1999–2014," accessed August 2015, www.opensecrets.org.

13. David Whitford, "Meet Mr. Gas," *Fortune*, May 1, 2008.

14. National Institute on Money in State Politics, "Chesapeake Energy," accessed August 2015, www.followthemoney.org.

15. Will Bunch, "How a Natural-Gas Tycoon Tapped into Corbett," *Philadelphia Daily News*, June 29, 2011.

16. Goodell, "Big Fracking Bubble."

17. Edward McAllister, "Driller Halts Pennsylvania Fracking After Blowout," Reuters, April 21, 2011; Susan Phillips, "Bradford County Blow-Out Costs Chesapeake More Than $250K," StateImpact Pennsylvania, NPR, February 9, 2012.

18. Goodell, "Big Fracking Bubble."

19. Laura Olson, "Chesapeake Energy Hit with Big Fine over Gas Drilling Accidents," *Pittsburgh Post-Gazette*, May 18, 2011.

20. Chris Amico et al., "Shale Play: Natural Gas Drilling in Pennsylvania," StateImpact Pennsylvania, NPR, accessed August 2015, stateimpact.npr.org/pennsylvania/drilling.

21. "Chesapeake Delay Contributed to Wyoming Well Blowout," Reuters, May 10, 2012.

22. "Year after Wyoming Blowout, No Fines for Chesapeake," Associated Press, April 11, 2013.

23. Anna Driver, "SEC Steps Up Probe of Chesapeake, CEO McClendon," Reuters, March 1, 2013.

24. Daniel Gilbert, "SEC Ends Investigation of Chesapeake Ex-CEO Aubrey McClendon," *Wall Street Journal*, May 7, 2014.

25. Joshua Schneyer, Brian Grow, and Anna Driver, "Chesapeake, Encana Face Criminal Antitrust Charges in Michigan," Reuters, March 5, 2014.

26. Christopher Helman, "Aubrey McClendon: Fracking's Cowboy Rides Again," *Forbes*, June 15, 2015.

27. Abrahm Lustgarten, "Chesapeake Energy's $5 Billion Shuffle," *ProPublica*, March 13, 2014.

28. Ibid.

29. Christopher Helman, " 'Screwing Royalty Owners Means Chesapeake Is Stealing Cash,' " *Forbes*, March 17, 2014.

30. Ben Lefebvre, "Sinopec to Buy Stake in Chesapeake Energy Asset," *Wall Street Journal*, February 25, 2013.

31. Agustino Fontevecchia, "Ex-billionaire McClendon Out at Chesapeake over Differences with Board," *Forbes*, January 29, 2013.

32. Jack Anderson, "Oilmen to Drain Ocean?," *Tuscaloosa* (AL) *News*, November 2, 1975; "Robert S. Kerr," *Tulsa World*, February 2, 1963.

33. Juliet Eilperin, "A Frightening Map of Where Kerr-McGee Polluted," *Washington Post*, April 5, 2014.

34. Anadarko Petroleum Corporation, "Anadarko Completes Kerr-McGee Acquisition," press release, August 10, 2006; "Chesapeake Taps Anadarko Veteran to Succeed McClendon," *Natural Gas Intelligence*, May 21, 2013.

35. Steven Church, Tiffany Kary, and Bradley Olson, "Anadarko's Kerr-McGee Held Liable in Tronox Spinoff," Bloomberg, December 12, 2013; *Natural Gas Intelligence*, May 21, 2013; Clifford Krauss, "Anadarko Pays Billions in Settling Toxins Case," *New York Times*, April 3, 2014.

36. Grant Slater, "Chesapeake's Aubrey McClendon Aims to Cement Legacy with Sprawling Campus," *Oklahoma Gazette*, August 6, 2009.

37. Gregory Zuckerman, *The Frackers: The Outrageous Inside Story of the New Billionaire Wildcatters* (New York: Penguin, 2013), 124–26.

38. SEC, "Aubrey M. Kerr, Jr. and James W. McTiernan Enjoined," *SEC News Digest*, March 28, 1983; Zuckerman, *Frackers*, 126.

39. Zuckerman, *Frackers*, 126, 126–28.

40. Rick Robinson, "Oil Company Grows to Maturity," *Daily Oklahoman*, July 21, 2002.

41. Zuckerman, *Frackers*, 128–30.

42. Ibid., 130–35.

43. Railroad Commission of Texas, "Blowouts and Well Control Problems: All Blowouts 1990–1995," accessed March 28, 2014, www.rrc.state.tx.us/data/drilling /blowouts/allblowouts90-95.php.

44. Zuckerman, *Frackers*, 138; "Higher Crude Oil and Gas Prices Buoy Exxon and Shell Earnings," *New York Times*, January 22, 1997.

45. Gold, *Boom*, 176–77.

46. Zuckerman, *Frackers*, 140–42.

47. "Class Action Suit Against Chesapeake Dismissed," *Natural Gas Intelligence*, March 7, 2000.

48. Slater, "Chesapeake's Aubrey McClendon."

49. Whitford, "Meet Mr. Gas."

50. Gold, *Boom*, 178; James Peltz, "Stock Spotlight: Deregulation, Expansion Propel Calpine's Climb," *Los Angeles Times*, September 9, 1999.

51. Michael Hiltzik, "Calpine's Troubles Rooted in Power Crisis," *Los Angeles Times*, December 19, 2005.

52. Juliet Eilperin and Steven Mufson, "Alliance Between Natural Gas Industry, Environmental Groups Fractures," *Washington Post*, February 19, 2012.

53. Bryan Walsh, "Exclusive: How the Sierra Club Took Millions from the Natural Gas Industry—and Why They Stopped," *Time*, February 2, 2012.

54. Gold, *Boom*, 180–82, 331–32.

55. See Congressional Budget Office, "Causes and Lessons of the California Electricity Crisis," September 2001; Jason Leopold, "Enron Linked to California Blackouts," *CBS Marketwatch*, May 16, 2002.

56. "2 Power Companies to Settle Claims," *Los Angeles Times*, June 22, 2007.

57. Gold, *Boom*, 184, 195–97, 207.

58. Shiffman et al., "Special Report."

59. "Chesapeake Energy Will Pay $2.3 Billion to Acquire Gas Reserves in Appalachian Basin," *Oil & Gas Financial Journal*, November 1, 2005; Chesapeake Energy Corp., SEC Form 10-K, fiscal year ended December 31, 2005, 33.

60. Ray Tyson, "Chesapeake Buys Columbia Natural Resources," *Petroleum News*, October 9, 2005.

61. Governor Joe Manchin III, "Governor Welcomes Chesapeake Energy to State, as Energy Leader Acquires Columbia Natural Resources," press release, November 18, 2005.

62. Ken Ward Jr., "Roane County Gas Royalties Case Settled," *Charleston Gazette*, October 24, 2008.

63. Chris Dickerson, "Gas Companies Agree to Pay $380 Million to Settle Roane Royalty Case," *West Virginia Record*, October 24, 2008.

64. Center for Responsive Politics, "Senator Joe Manchin, Top 20 Contributors 2009–2014," accessed August 2015, www.opensecrets.org; Ward, "Roane County Gas Royalties Case Settled."

65. Chesapeake Energy, "Chesapeake Energy Corporation Announces Plan to Reorganize Its Eastern Division Operation in Charleston, West Virginia," press release, February 26, 2009.

66. U.S. Department of Justice, "Energy Company to Pay $3.2 Million Penalty to Resolve Clean Water Violations in West Virginia," press release, December 19, 2013.

67. "The Forbes 400 Richest People in America: #155 Tom Ward," *Forbes*, September 17, 2008; Christopher Helman, "The Sordid Deal That Created the Okla. City Thunder," *Forbes*, June 13, 2012; Zuckerman, *Frackers*, 222.

68. Zuckerman, *Frackers*, 218–20.

69. Ibid.

70. Joshua Schneyer, Jeanine Prezioso, and David Sheppard, "Special Report: Inside Chesapeake, CEO Ran $200 Million Hedge Fund," Reuters, May 2, 2012.

71. Ibid.

72. Ibid.

73. Ibid.

74. U.S. Bureau of Labor Statistics, Census of Fatal Occupational Injuries, "Fatal Occupational Injuries, Total Hours Worked and Fatal Occupational Injuries by Selected Worker Characteristics, Occupations, and Industries, Civilian Workers, 2012," 2014.

75. Lise Olsen, "Pain of Oil Boom: Top Texas Firms in Oilfield Accident Claims," Houston Chronicle, February 22, 2014.

76. Gayathri Vaidyanathan, "Death on the Gas Field Illustrates High Risks of the Rush to Drill," Energywire, February 21, 2013.

77. Lise Olsen, "Injured Oil Worker 'Lived in Hell for 2½ Years,'" Houston Chronicle, February 22, 2014.

78. James Loewenstein, "OSHA Investigation into Sullivan County Fatality Is Under Way; Nomac Drilling Fined 7K Following Separate Probe," Tonawanda (PA) Daily Review, February 9, 2011.

79. Occupational Safety and Health Administration, "US Department of Labor's OSHA Cites Nomac Drilling for Failing to Provide Fall Protection to Workers on Well Derricks in Trenton, ND," press release, April 25, 2013.

80. Jay F. Marks, "Seventy Seven Energy, Former Subsidiary of Oklahoma City–Based Chesapeake Energy, Begins Trading," Daily Oklahoman, July 1, 2014.

81. Christopher Helman, "The Dim Outlook for Chesapeake Energy," Forbes, August 10, 2015.

82. Erin Ailworth and Daniel Gilbert, "Chesapeake to Sell Gas Assets for $5.38 Billion," Wall Street Journal, October 16, 2014; Cadie Thompson, "Chesapeake Energy Cuts 800 Employees," CNBC, October 8, 2013; Joe Wertz, "Chesapeake Energy Lays Off 800 Employees," StateImpact Oklahoma, NPR, October 8, 2013.

83. Helman, "Aubrey McClendon."

84. Ibid.

85. Ibid.

10. When Will the Bakken Boom Go Bust for Good?

1. Ryan Holeywell, "North Dakota's Oil Boom Is a Blessing and a Curse," Governing, August 2011.

2. Janet K. Pitman, Leigh C. Price, and Julie A. LeFever, "Diagenesis and Fracture Development in the Bakken Formation, Williston Basin: Implications for Reservoir Quality in the Middle Member," USGS, November 2001, 2, 4, 6; James MacPherson, "N.D. Study Estimates 167 Billion Barrels of Oil in Bakken," Associated Press, April 28, 2008.

3. EPA, "EPA's Full Draft Assessment of the Potential Impacts of Hydraulic Fracturing for Oil and Gas on Drinking Water Resources," June 2015, 7-1, 7-16.

4. Curt Anderson, "Disasters Show Holes in 'Freedom to Farm' Law," Associated Press, August 1, 1998.

5. National Agricultural Statistical Service, "1997 Census of Agriculture—State Data: North Dakota," U.S. Department of Agriculture, March 1999, Table 42; National Agricultural Statistical Service, "2012 Census of Agriculture—State Data: North Dakota," U.S. Department of Agriculture, May 2014, Table 25.

6. National Agricultural Statistical Service, "2012 Census of Agriculture—State Data: North Dakota," Table 5, 14.

7. Western Organization of Resource Councils, "Gone for Good: Fracking and Water Loss in the West," 2013, 11, 16.

8. Lauren Donovan, "Radioactive Oil Patch Waste on the Loose in N.D.," *Bismarck Tribune*, January 19, 2013; Western Organization of Resource Councils, "Gone for Good," 17.

9. U.S. Census Bureau, "Annual Estimates of the Resident Population, April 1, 2000–July 1, 2014"; U.S. Census Bureau, "Table 2: Cumulative Estimates of Resident Population Change for the United States, Regions, States, and Puerto Rico and Region and State Rankings: April 1, 2010–July 1, 2014," December 2014.

10. Jude Sheerin and Anna Bressanin, "North Dakota Oil Boom: American Dream on Ice," BBC News, March 12, 2014.

11. Federal Bureau of Investigation, "Crime in the United States, 2013," U.S. Department of Justice, November 2014, Table 4, Table 8.

12. Kevin Begos, "Traffic Accidents Are a Deadly Side Effect to Fracking Boom," Associated Press, May 6, 2014.

13. Steven Mufson, "In North Dakota, the Gritty Side of an Oil Boom," *Washington Post*, July 18, 2012.

14. Audrey Putz, Alex Finken, and Gary A. Goreham, "Sustainability in Natural Resource–Dependent Regions That Experienced Boom-Bust-Recovery Cycles: Lessons Learned from a Review of the Literature," North Dakota State University, Fargo, July 2011, 19; Bartley Kives, "Welcome to Williston, North Dakota: America's New Gold Rush City," *The Guardian*, July 28, 2014.

15. Becky Kramer, "Oil Industry Man Camps Offer No-Stress Living," *Spokane* (WA) *Spokesman-Review*, April 29, 2012; Jessica Holdman, "Companies Make Temporary Housing a Permanent Business," *Bismark* (ND) *Tribune*, August 11, 2012.

16. A.G. Sulzberger, "Oil Rigs Bring Camps of Men to the Prairie," *New York Times*, November 25, 2011; amenities listed on Target Logistics website, accessed August 2015, www.targetlogistics.net/tioga.php.

17. Chris Reidy, "Boston's Target Logistics Management Agrees to Be Acquired in a Deal Worth Up to $625m," *Boston Globe*, February 14, 2013.

18. David Wethe and Kelly Gilblom, "The Oil Industry's 'Man-Camps' Are Dying," Bloomberg *Businessweek*, April 15, 2015.

19. Robert Johnson, "You've Never Seen Anything Like This North Dakota Oil Boomtown," *Business Insider*, March 7, 2012; Jacob Wascalus, "North Dakota Oil Boom Squeezes Seniors Who Rent," *CommunityDividend*, October 2012.

20. David Baily, "In North Dakota, Hard to Tell an Oil Millionaire from Regular Joe," Reuters, October 3, 2012; U.S. Census Bureau, "Per Capita Income in Past 12

Months, Table B19301," 2010 and 2013, adjusted for inflation with Consumer Price Index calculator at U.S. Bureau of Labor Statistics.

21. EIA, "North Dakota State Energy Profile," December 18, 2014.

22. E. Russell Lloyd, "Contributions to Economic Geology, 1912, Part II, Mineral Fuels—the Cannonball River Lignite Field, Morton, Adams, and Mettinger Counties, North Dakota," USGS, Bulletin 541-G, 1914, 243, 250, 262; Richard Rubin, "In North Dakota, Boom, Bust and Oil," *New York Times*, August 6, 2015; James MacPherson, "ND Oil Boom Started in a Wheat Field," Associated Press, August 30, 2008.

23. James MacPherson, "The Oil Millionaire Farmers of North Dakota," Associated Press, October 19, 2008.

24. Lloyd W. Sveen, "Oil Boom in Northwest," *Chicago Tribune*, May 24, 1953; Charles H. Waldren, Elmer G. Meldahl, and LaVern L. McGowan, "North Dakota—Oil State," *North Dakota Geological Survey Bulletin 28* (1955): 105–6.

25. "Son of Bakken Formation Namesake Remains Reserved," Associated Press, December 3, 2012.

26. "Court Rules Amerada's Holders Were Misled in Merger with Hess," *Wall Street Journal*, August 2, 1976.

27. Gerald Eskenaz, "Leon Hess, Who Built a Major Oil Company and Owned the Jets, Is Dead, 85," *New York Times*, May 8, 1999; Richard K. Vietor, *Energy Policy in America Since 1945* (Cambridge: Cambridge University Press, 1984), 135.

28. Joy Blackburn, "Hovensa Lays Off Final 101 Employees," *Virgin Islands Daily News*, March 22, 2015; Joy Blackburn, "V.I. Hires Legal Team to Take on HOVENSA," *Virgin Islands Daily News*, June 25, 2015.

29. Leslie Eaton, "Triton Energy Settles Indonesia Bribery Case for $300,000," *New York Times*, February 28, 1997.

30. Richard Helman, "How Hess Lost $800 Million in the Eagle Ford Shale—and Other Reasons Shareholders Should Vote for Change," *Forbes*, April 26, 2013.

31. Richard Behar, "Hess Oil's Russian Mob Problem," *Forbes*, June 5, 2012.

32. Helman, "How Hess Lost $800 Million."

33. Michael J. de la Merced, "How Elliott and Hess Settled a Bitter Proxy Battle," *New York Times*, May 16, 2013.

34. Hess Corporation, SEC Form 10-K, fiscal year ended December 31, 2013, 4; Hess Corporation, "2013 Annual Report," 2.

35. "Hess Starting Up North Dakota Natgas Plant, May Boost Bakken Output," Reuters, March 14, 2014.

36. Continental Resources, "2014 Annual Report," 9; Jessica Holdman, "Keeping Up with Technology in Oil Country," *Bismarck* (ND) *Tribune*, May 11, 2014.

37. Nathan Vardi, "The Last American Wildcatter," *Forbes*, January 15, 2009.

38. Gregory Zuckerman, *The Frackers: The Outrageous Inside Story of the New Billionaire Wildcatters* (New York: Penguin, 2014), 164–66.

39. Vardi, "Last American Wildcatter."

40. Ibid.

41. EIA, "Growing Global Liquids Inventories Reflect Lower Crude Oil Prices," Today in Energy release, August 24, 2015; Continental Resources, "2014 Annual Report," 9.

42. Gregory Zuckerman, "Romney Taps Harold Hamm for Advisory Role," *Wall Street Journal*, March 1, 2012; Senator James Inhofe, "The World's 100 Most Influential People 2012: Harold Hamm—Wildcatter," *Time*, April 18, 2012.

43. Harold Hamm, Continental Resources Inc., "American Energy Independence Within a Decade and the Policies Necessary to Achieve It," testimony before Energy and Power Subcommittee, Energy and Commerce Committee, U.S. House of Representatives, September 13, 2012, 2, 7.

44. Citizens for Tax Justice, "Despite Claim of High Tax Rate, Continental Resources Paid Just 2.2% of Its Profits in Federal Income Taxes over the Past 5 Years," press release, September 13, 2012.

45. Taxpayers for Common Sense, "Understanding Oil and Gas Tax Subsidies," April 2014, 5, 8.

46. Continental Resources, SEC Form 10-K, fiscal year ended December 31, 2014, 2.

47. Amy Harder, "Harold Hamm on Oil, Climate Change, and His Divorce," *National Journal*, August 19, 2013.

48. Elizabeth Dilts and Sabina Zawadzki, "Bakken Crude Breakeven Prices as Low as $58/Bbl in 2014—Report," Reuters, April 2, 2014.

49. "The *Journal Record* Innovator of the Year Profile: Continental Resources, Inc," *Oklahoma City Journal Record*, April 7, 2011; Jay F. Marks, " 'Walking' Rig Helping Continental Drill for Oil in North Dakota," *Daily Oklahoman*, November 5, 2010.

50. Continental Resources, "Q2 2011 Continental Resources Inc. Earnings Conference Call—Final," *Fair Disclosure Wire*, August 4, 2011; Marks, " 'Walking' Rig."

51. Mike Ellerd, "Pad Drilling Leads Way," *Petroleum News Bakken*, January 6, 2013.

52. EIA, "Drilling Productivity Report," July 2015.

53. Russell Gold, "No End in Sight for Oil Glut," *Wall Street Journal*, August 21, 2015.

54. Blake Ellis, "When a Boomtown Goes Bust: 'Sudden Desertion,' " CNN Money, December 6, 2010.

55. Ibid.

56. Asjylyn Loder, "U.S. Shale-Oil Boom May Not Last as Fracking Wells Lack Staying Power," Bloomberg *Businessweek*, October 10, 2013.

57. J. David Hughes, "Drill, Baby, Drill: Can Unconventional Fuels Usher In a New Era of Energy Abundance?," Post Carbon Institute, 2013, 81.

58. Loder, "U.S. Shale-Oil Boom."

59. Ibid.

60. Ibid.

61. Don Morrison, interview with author, May 26, 2014.

62. "Turtle Mountain Tribal Council Bans Fracking," Indian Country Today Media Network, November 27, 2011.

63. Dakota Resource Council, "Dakota Resource Council (This Is Who We Are)," video, June 19, 2013, www.youtube.com/watch?v=z6T3f8KzHPQ.

64. Ibid.

65. Dakota Resource Council, "This Is Our Country: Living with the Wild West Oil Boom," video, vimeo.com/82246373.

11. Poisonous Legacy in Wyoming

1. Senator James Inhofe's office, "Inhofe and Vitter: EPA Hydraulic Fracturing Investigations 0 for 3," press release, June 20, 2013, accessed January 26, 2016, http://www.inhofe.senate.gov/newsroom/press-releases/inhofe-and-vitter-epa-hydraulic-fracturing-investigations-0-for-3.

2. John Fenton, personal communication with author, June 10, 2014.

3. Pinedale Field Office, "Mineral Occurrence and Development Report: Pinedale Resource Management Plan Planning Area," U.S. Bureau of Land Management, January 2003, 3-17–3-19.

4. Adam Lederer, "Project Wagon Wheel: A Nuclear Plowshare for Wyoming," *Annals of Wyoming* 70, no. 3 (Summer 1998): 26–27.

5. "AEC Supports Nuclear Blast Near Pinedale," *Casper* (WY) *Star-Tribune*, February 1, 1972.

6. Lederer, "Project Wagon Wheel," 27.

7. Jake Booher Jr., "American Scientists Studying Effects of First Industrial Nuclear Explosion," *Nashua* (NH) *Telegraph*, December 11, 1967.

8. Sherie Mershon and Tim Palucka, "A Century of Innovation," National Energy Technology Laboratory, 2010, 225, 226.

9. Gordon Gauss, "N-blast Could Create New Natural Gas Industry," *Eugene* (OR) *Register-Guard*, August 27, 1969.

10. Scott C. Yates, "Boom Years," *Westword*, February 26, 1998.

11. Lederer, "Project Wagon Wheel," 26.

12. Mershon and Palucka, "Century of Innovation," 226.

13. Lederer, "Project Wagon Wheel," 32.

14. "Group Opposed Nuclear Test," *Sumter* (SC) *Daily Item*, February 8, 1973.

15. Lederer, "Project Wagon Wheel," 29–32.

16. "A-test in Wyoming Put Off for at Least a Year," *Milwaukee Journal*, February 6, 1973.

17. Neil A. "Mick" McMurray, interview with Ann Noble, in "Wyoming's Energy Booms and Busts: Sublette County," American Heritage Center's Alan K. Simpson Institute for Western Politics and Leadership, University of Wyoming, November 27, 2010.

18. "Kern River Pipeline to Start Shipping Fuel to California Within Few Weeks," *Salt Lake City Deseret News*, January 25, 1992; "Wyoming Gas May Be Headed to California," *Lodi* (CA) *News-Sentinel*, April 1, 1989; Susan Klann, "Markets Seeking Inspiration for Commodity-Price Support," *Denver Post*, April 14, 1997.

19. Leslie Haines and William Pike, eds., "Oil and Gas in the Rockies: Wildcatters and Legends," Independent Petroleum Association of Mountain States, 2004, 48; Robert M. Cluff and Suzanne G. Cluff, "The Origin of Jonah Field, Northern

Green River Basin, Wyoming," in *Jonah Field: Case Study of a Giant Tight-Gas Fluvial Reservoir*, ed. J.W. Robinson and K.W. Shanley (Tulsa, OK: American Association of Petroleum Geologists, 2004), 128, 129.

20. Albert Energy Company, "AEC's Acquisition of McMurry Oil Company and Other Private Interests Closes as Scheduled," press release, June 1, 2000; Encana Corporation, SEC Form 40-F, fiscal year ending December 31, 2002, 2, 4; "Canada's Encana Posts Quarterly Loss Due to $1.3 Bln Charge," Reuters, July 24, 2015.

21. U.S. Bureau of Land Management (hereafter BLM), "Final: Supplemental Environmental Impact Statement for Pinedale Anticline Oil and Gas Exploration and Development Project—Vol. I," June 2008, 3–91; BLM, "Record of Decision: Final Supplemental Environmental Impact Statement for the Pinedale Anticline Oil and Gas Exploration and Development Project," September 2008, 23.

22. Abrahm Lustgarten, "Buried Secrets: Is Natural Gas Drilling Endangering U.S. Water Supplies?," *ProPublica*, November 13, 2008.

23. BLM, "Final: Supplemental Environmental Impact Statement," 3-123–3-153; BLM, "Record of Decision," 4.

24. Hall Sawyer and Ryan Nielson, "Mule Deer Monitoring in the Pinedale Anticline Project Area: 2010 Annual Report," Western Ecosystems Technology, Inc., September 14, 2010, 14, 16–18.

25. Jamie Smith Hopkins, "As New Ozone Rules Loom, Smog in Rural West Rivals Los Angeles," *National Geographic*, March 12, 2015.

26. S. Oltmans et al., "Anatomy of Wintertime Ozone Associated with Oil and Natural Gas Extraction Activity in Wyoming and Utah," *Elementa: Science of the Anthropocene* 2 (March 4, 2014): 1, 13.

27. Jeff Gearino, "DEQ Issues Ozone Alert for Pinedale," *Casper Star-Tribune*, February 3, 2009.

28. Jeffrey Jacquet, "Energy Boomtowns and Natural Gas: Implications for Marcellus Shale Local Governments and Rural Communities," Northeast Regional Center for Rural Development, Pennsylvania State University, January 2009, 33, 34–44.

29. Leah Todd, "Gas Drilling Slowdown Means Quiet Bust for Pinedale," *Casper Star-Tribune*, April 1, 2013.

30. John and Catherine Fenton, interview with author, 2015.

31. The split estate (surface and mineral rights) bond requirement gives surface but not mineral rights owners compensation for drilling. Since 1995, surface rights owners received $2,000 per well, but the bond was raised to $10,000 per well in 2014. Laura Hancock, "Wyoming Committee Endorses Split-Estate Bonding Hike to $10,000," *Casper Star-Tribune*, February 17, 2014; Wyo. Stat. § 30-5-404(b).

32. Abrahm Lustgarten, "Hydrofracked: One Man's Quest for Answers About Natural Gas Drilling," *High Country News*, June 27, 2011.

33. Ibid.

34. Abrahm Lustgarten, "EPA's Abandoned Wyoming Fracking Study One Retreat of Many," *ProPublica*, July 3, 2013.

35. Abrahm Lustgarten and Sabrina Shankman, "Congress Tells EPA to Study Hydraulic Fracturing," *ProPublica*, November 10, 2009.

36. EPA, "EPA's Full Draft Assessment of the Potential Impacts of Hydraulic Fracturing for Oil and Gas on Drinking Water Resources," June 4, 2015, ES-6–ES-22; Weston W. Wilson, "Widespread and Systemic Contamination Found—at the EPA," *The Hill*, June 15, 2015; Neela Banerjee, "Can Fracking Pollute Drinking Water? Don't Ask the EPA," *InsideClimate News*, March 2, 2015.

37. Abrahm Lustgarten and Sabrina Shankman, "Congress Tells EPA to Study Hydraulic Fracturing," *ProPublica*, November 10, 2009.

38. Agency for Toxic Substances and Disease Registry, "Evaluation of Contaminants in Private Residential Well Water, Pavillion, Wyoming, Fremont County," Centers for Disease Control, August 31, 2010, 12, 15, 27.

39. EPA, "Draft: Investigation of Ground Water Contamination Near Pavillion, Wyoming," December 2001, xiii.

40. "Inhofe Asks EPA About Pavillion and Fracking," *Billings Gazette*, December 7, 2011.

41. David O. Williams, "Wyo. Fracking Contamination Case Eerily Similar to Colorado's Divide Creek Accident," *Colorado Independent*, September 18, 2009.

42. Ibid.

43. Kirk Johnson, "E.P.A. Links Tainted Water in Wyoming to Hydraulic Fracturing for Natural Gas," *New York Times*, December 8, 2011.

44. Mead Gruver, "Encana Mounts Response to EPA Fracking Report," Associated Press, December 21, 2011.

45. Johnson, "E.P.A. Links Tainted Water."

46. Senator James Inhofe, "Inhofe Statement on EPA Announcement on Hydraulic Fracturing," press release, December 8, 2011.

47. Johnson, "E.P.A. Links Tainted Water."

12. Politics, Betrayal, and Broken Communities

1. Wendell Berry, endorsement statement for Charles E. Little, in *The Dying of the Tree* (New York: Penguin, 1997).

2. Jack Z. Smith, "Couple Blame Range for Methane in Water," *Fort Worth Star-Telegram*, January 15, 2012; Jim Malewitz and Neena Satija, "A Push for New Look into Tainted Water's Source," *New York Times*, June 19, 2014; Brantley Hargrove, "How One Man's Flaming Water Fired Up a Battle Between Texas and the EPA," *Dallas Observer*, April 26, 2012.

3. Hargrove, "How One Man's Flaming Water."

4. Smith, "Couple Blame Range."

5. Hargrove, "How One Man's Flaming Water."

6. Ibid.

7. EPA, "In the Matter of Range Resources Corporation, Emergency Administrative Order," docket no. SDWA-06-2010-1208, December 7, 2010, 2, 4–6.

8. Range Resources Corp., SEC Form 10-K, fiscal year ended December 31, 2009, 19.

9. Range Resources Corp., "Range Achieves Record Production," press release, January 19, 2011.

10. Tom Fowler, "RRC Says EPA Acted Too Hastily in Water Case," *Midland* (TX) *Reporter-Telegram*, December 12, 2010.

11. Steven P. Lispsky, oral and videotaped deposition, Railroad Commission of Texas docket no. 78-028829, Merit Court Reporters, job no. 9625, January 14, 2011, 58.

12. EPA's Office of Inspector General, "Response to Congressional Inquiry Regarding the EPA's Emergency Order to the Range Resources Gas Drilling Company," December 20, 2013, 15.

13. Hargrove, "How One Man's Flaming Water."

14. Railroad Commission of Texas, Office of General Counsel, Oil and Gas docket no. 78-0268829: Commission Called Hearing to Consider Whether Operation of the Range Production Company Butler Unit Well N0.1H (RRC ID 263732) and Teal Unit Well N0.1H (RRC 10 253729) in the Newark, East (Barnett Shale) Field, Hood County, Texas, Are Causing or Contributing to Contamination of Certain Domestic Water Wells in Parker County, Texas, March 7, 2011, 11.

15. "Update 1—Range Resources to Sell Barnett Properties for $90 Mln," Reuters, February 28, 2011.

16. Mike Soraghan, "Sen. Inhofe Seeks Preservation of EPA Records in Agency's Natural Gas Dispute with Texas," *New York Times*, February 16, 2011.

17. Thomas H. Richter, amended affidavit of Thomas H. Richter, P.E., in support of plaintiff's original petition, *Lipsky v. Durant, Carter, Coleman LLC et al.*, cause no. CV-11-0798, District Court, Parker County, Texas, November 8, 2011, 2.

18. Mike Soraghan, "Enforcement: EPA Officials Ignored Engineer's Theory in Range Contamination Case," *Energywire*, February 20, 2013.

19. Abrahm Lustgarten, "Officials in Three States Pin Water Woes on Gas Drilling," *ProPublica*, April 26, 2009; Commonwealth of Pennsylvania, Department of Environmental Protection (hereafter PDEP), In the Matter of Cabot Oil & Gas, Consent Order and Settlement Agreement, December 15, 2010.

20. "Shale Play: Operators with Active Wells in Pennsylvania," StateImpact Pennsylvania, NPR, accessed August 2015, stateimpact.npr.org/pennsylvania/drilling/operators; Andrew Maykuth, "Long Fight over Fracking Still Divides Pa. Town," *Philadelphia Inquirer*, August 27, 2012.

21. PDEP, Notice of Violations: Re: Gas Migration Investigation, Dimock Township, Susquehanna County, February 27, 2009.

22. Abrahm Lustgarten, "Frack Fluid Spill in Dimock Contaminates Stream, Killing Fish," *ProPublica*, September 21, 2009; PDEP, "DEP Orders Cabot Oil and Gas to Cease All Gas Well Fracking in Susquehanna County," press release, September 25, 2009.

23. PDEP, Consent Order and Agreement, In the Matter of Cabot Oil and Gas Corporation, November 4, 2009, 4; Michael Rubinkam, "Pa. DEP Targets Texas Driller for Tainted Water," *Washington Post*, September 30, 2010.

24. Scott Detrow, "DEP's Dimock Decision Based on 2010 Agreement, Not Water Quality," StateImpact Pennsylvania, NPR, December 8, 2011; PDEP, Consent Order and Settlement Agreement, 8–9.

25. Laura Legere, "DEP: Cabot IK to Stop Dimock Water Deliveries," *Scranton Times-Tribune*, October 20, 2011.

26. Olivia Katrandjian, "Celebs and Officials Collect Emergency Water for Hydro-fracking Victims in Pennsylvania," ABC News, December 6, 2011.

27. Jon Hurdle, "Pennsylvania Report Left Out Data on Poisons in Water Near Gas Site," *New York Times*, November 2, 2012.

28. Abrahm Lustgarten, "Buried Secrets: Is Natural Gas Drilling Endangering U.S. Water Supplies?," *ProPublica*, November 13, 2008.

29. EPA, "EPA Initiates Hydraulic Fracturing Study: Agency Seeks Input from Science Advisory Board," press release, March 18, 2010.

30. Lustgarten, "Buried Secrets."

31. Weston Wilson, letter to Senators Wayne Allard and Ben Nighthorse Campbell and Representative Diana DeGette, October 8, 2004, 1.

32. Lustgarten, "Buried Secrets."

33. Mike Soraghan, "EPA Frack Study's Safety Findings Exaggerated, Bush EPA Official Says," *New York Times*, May 20, 2011.

34. EPA, "EPA Identifies Pennsylvania Sites for National Study on Hydraulic Fracturing," press release, June 23, 2011.

35. EPA, ATSDR, Record of Activity/Technical Assist, UID#1BD7, EPA Region 3 Water Protection Division, December 28, 2011, 1.

36. EPA, "EPA to Begin Sampling Water at Some Residences in Dimock, Pa," press release, January 19, 2012.

37. Scott Detrow, "Mike Krancer and the EPA: It's Complicated," StateImpact Pennsylvania, NPR, May 15, 2012.

38. "Republican Presidential Candidates Participate in Mike Huckabee Presidential Forum on Fox News, New York City," Political Transcript Wire, December 4, 2011.

39. President Barack Obama, "Remarks by the President in State of the Union Address," January 24, 2012.

40. Jeremy Fugleberg, "EPA Extends Public Comment Period on Pavillion Fracking Report," *Casper* (WY) *Star-Tribune*, January 20, 2012; 77 Fed. Reg. 3770 (January 25, 2012).

41. Susan Phillips, "EPA's Test Results Show Safe Drinking Water in Dimock," StateImpact Pennsylvania, NPR, March 15, 2012.

42. EPA, "EPA Completes Drinking Water Sampling in Dimock, Pa," press release, July 25, 2012.

43. Abrahm Lustgarten, "So, Is Dimock's Water Really Safe to Drink?," *ProPublica*, March 20, 2012.

44. Jack Z. Smith, "Owner of Contaminated Water Well in Parker County Loses in Court," *Fort Worth Star-Telegram*, February 18, 2012.

45. Christin Coyne, "Controversy Caused by Judge's Campaign Material," *Weatherford* (TX) *Democrat*, May 28, 2012; Randy Keck, "Towson Unseats Loftin in Judge's Race," *Aledo* (TX) *Community News*, May 29, 2012.

46. Ramit Plushnick-Masti, "EPA Changed Course After Oil Company Protested," Associated Press, January 16, 2013.

47. Mike Soraghan, "Enforcement: Former Pa. Gov. Rendell Pressed EPA in Range Pollution Case, Emails show," *Energywire*, February 5, 2013.

48. Ibid.

49. Barry Schlacter, "EPA Drops Action Against Range Resources over Parker County Wells," *Fort Worth Star-Telegram*, March 30, 2012.

50. 77 Fed. Reg. 19012 (March 29, 2012).

51. Rush Limbaugh, "Obama EPA Official Vows to 'Crucify' Oil and Gas Industry," *The Rush Limbaugh Show*, April 26, 2012.

52. Dina Cappiello, "EPA Official Armendariz Resigns over 'Crucify' Comment," Associated Press, April 30, 2012.

53. Lesa Jansen and Todd Sperry, "EPA Official Resigns over 'Crucify' Remark," CNN, April 30, 2012.

54. Cappiello, "EPA Official Armendariz Resigns."

55. Abrahm Lustgarten, "EPA's Abandoned Wyoming Fracking Study One Retreat of Many," *ProPublica*, July 8, 2013.

56. Cheniere Energy Inc., "Notice of Annual Meeting of Shareholders and Proxy Statement," April 24, 2015, 7–8.

57. Heather Zichal, "Facilitating Safe and Responsible Expansion of Natural Gas Production," White House blog, April 13, 2012.

58. President Barack Obama, Executive Order 13605, Supporting Safe and Responsible Development of Unconventional Domestic Natural Gas Resources, April 13, 2012.

59. Mike Soraghan, "White House: Top Obama Aide Worked the Pavillion Fracking Investigation," *Energywire*, September 11, 2013.

60. Mike Soraghan, "Hydraulic Fracturing: White House Huddled with Industry Before Changes to BLM Fracking Rule," *Energywire*, April 12, 2013.

61. Mike Soraghan, "Hydraulic Fracturing: White House Delaying BLM Rule at Industry's Request," *Energywire*, June 22, 2012.

62. Dave Share, "Dave McCurdy Brings Strong Credentials to AGA," *Pipeline & Gas Journal* 238, no. 12 (December 2011); Jim Snyder, "Obama's Aide on Climate Changes Seeking Oil, Gas Allies," Bloomberg, May 30, 2012.

63. Josh Hicks, "White House Names New Climate and Energy Chief to Replace Heather Zichal," *Washington Post*, November 8, 2013; Cheniere Energy Inc., "Notice of Annual Meeting," 5, 17.

64. EPA, "EPA Completes Drinking Water Sampling in Dimock, Pa," press release, July 25, 2012.

65. Susan Phillips, "LA Times: EPA Not in Agreement over Dimock," StateImpact Pennsylvania, NPR, July 28, 2013.

66. Neela Banerjee, "Message Is Mixed on Fracking," *Los Angeles Times*, July 28, 2013.

67. Ibid.

68. "Cabot Gets OK to Resume Fracking Operation in Dimock," *Pittsburgh Tribune-Review*, August 21, 2012.

69. Laura Legere, "Cabot, Dimock Families Near Settlement on Gas Drilling Contamination," *Scranton* (PA) *Times-Tribune*, August 15, 2012.

70. Andrew Maykuth, "Long Fight over Fracking Still Divides Pa. Town," *Philadelphia Inquirer*, August 27, 2012.

71. Ray Kemble, interview with author, 2015.

72. Tom Wilber, "Cabot Settles Water Law Suit with Residents of Dimock, Pa.: Agreement Marks an Ending for Most While Some Fight On," *Shale Gas Review*, August 16, 2012.

73. USGS, "USGS Releases Reports on Groundwater-Quality Sampling Near Pavillion, Wyo," press release, September 26, 2012; Jeff Tollefson, "Is Fracking Behind Contamination in Wyoming Groundwater?," *Nature*, October 4, 2012.

74. 77 Fed. Reg. 62234, October 12, 2012.

75. Committee on Environment and Public Works, U.S. Senate, "New Senate Report Reveals Economic Pain of Obama—EPA Regulations Put on Hold Until After the Election," press release, October 18, 2012.

76. EPA, "Statement by EPA Administrator Lisa P. Jackson Announcing Her Leaving Cabinet After State of Union," press release, December 27, 2012.

77. Kevin Freking, "Lisa Jackson Resigns: EPA Administrator Stepping Down," Associated Press, December 27, 2012.

78. President Barack Obama, "Remarks by the President in State of the Union Address," February 12, 2013.

79. Juliet Eilpern, "Senate Confirms Gina McCarthy as EPA Administrator," *Washington Post*, July 18, 2013; Robert Nelson, "Ernest Moniz and Fracking Drive Environmentalists Off of the Rails," *Forbes*, March 26, 2013.

80. Zack Colman, "GOP Boycott Thwarts EPA Vote," *The Hill*, May 9, 2013; Senator James M. Inhofe, "Inhofe: McCarthy Vote Contingent Upon Response to Concerns with War on Fossil Fuels," press release, April 19, 2013.

81. Political Party Time, "Lunch for Jim Inhofe," National Republican Senatorial Committee, invitation to Senator Inhofe fund-raising lunch, Sunlight Foundation, May 9, 2013, accessed August 2015, politicalpartytime.org/party/34519; Fierce, Isakowitz, & Blalock, 2013 Lobbying Disclosure Act filings for BP America, Edison International, and Noble Energy.

82. EPA, "Wyoming to Lead Further Investigation of Water Quality Concerns Outside of Pavillion with Support of EPA," press release, June 20, 2013.

83. John Fenton, chair, Pavillion Area Concerned Citizens, letter to Wyoming governor Matt Mead, June 24, 2013.

84. Benjamin Storrow, "Wyoming Report: Pavillion Gas Wells Properly Drilled; More Study Needed," *Casper Star-Tribune*, August 6, 2014.

85. Lustgarten, "EPA's Abandoned Wyoming Fracking Study."

86. Juliet Eilpern, "Senate Confirms Gina McCarthy as EPA Administrator," *Washington Post*, July 18, 2013.

87. Earthworks et al., "Fracking-Harmed Residents from Across the U.S. Confront President Obama and EPA, Demand Reopening of Investigations of Poisoned Drinking Water in Pennsylvania, Texas and Wyoming," press release, September 25, 2013.

13. Sacrifice Zones in the Keystone State

1. George Orwell, *In Front of Your Nose*, vol. 4, *Essays, Journalism and Letters* (Jaffrey, NH: Nonpareil, 2000), 40.

2. Craig Stevens, interview with author, 2015.

3. Rachel Morgan, "Post-production Costs Hitting Leaseholders Hard," *Uniontown* (PA) *Herald-Standard*, July 9, 2013; Tom Wilbur, "Firm Pays $283M for Local Gas Rights," *Binghamton* (NY) *Press & Sun-Bulletin*, January 1, 2009.

4. Laura Legere, "Conservation Group Signs Lease Deal Next to Salt Springs State Park," *Scranton* (PA) *Times-Tribune*, August 10, 2010.

5. Natural Resources Defense Council, "Fracking's Most Wanted: Lifting the Veil on Oil and Gas Company Spills and Violations," April 2015, 7.

6. Susan Phillips, "EPA Fines Talisman Energy for Fracking Violations," StateImpact Pennsylvania, NPR, July 25, 2012.

7. Erich Schwartzel, "Fouled Waters: Woodlands Residents Search for Ways to Survive Without Clean Water," *Pittsburgh Post-Gazette*, August 18, 2012; Erich Schwartzel, "Woodlands Trying to Solve Its Own Problems," *Pittsburgh Post-Gazette*, December 20, 2012.

8. Rosanne Skirble, "Black, Foamy Water Worries Fracking Neighbors," Voice of America, December 11, 2011.

9. Kevin Begos, "Janet McIntyre, Pennsylvania Woman, Voices Contaminated Water Concerns," Associated Press, February 24, 2012.

10. Ibid.

11. Kimberlie McEvoy, letter to Pennsylvania governor Tom Corbett, September 1, 2011.

12. Sarah Hoyle, " 'Fracking' Protesters Say Drilling Jobs Not Worth the Environmental Risks," CNN, Septermber 20, 2011.

13. "Families Without Water Question if Rex Energy Is to Blame," KDKA Channel 2 CBS, Pittsburgh, March 1, 2012.

14. Iris Marie Bloom, " 'I Just Want Water': Demonstrators Confront Rex Energy in Butler County," Protecting Our Waters, March 2, 2012.

15. Anya Litvak, "Water Problems Lead to Lawsuit in Small Community of Woodlands," *Pittsburgh Post-Gazette*, September 26, 2013.

16. Bill O'Driscoll, "John Stolz Warns of Danger When Past, Present Drilling Practices Collide," *Pittsburgh City Paper*, May 21, 2014.

17. Jerry Zremski, "As Environmental Debate Rages over Fracking, People in Western Pennsylvania Express Dread," *Buffalo News*, May 17, 2014; Timothy Puko, "Fouled Water Strains Butler County Residents," *Pittsburgh Tribune-Review*, December 5, 2012.

18. Don Hopey, "Drillers Go Deep for Natural Gas," *Pittsburgh Post-Gazette*, July 20, 2008.

19. Food & Water Watch, "The Social Costs of Fracking: A Pennsylvania Case Study," September 2013, 3.

20. Dan Stets, "Troubled Times in Pa.'s Oil Patch," *Philadelphia Inquirer*, December 11, 1988.

21. Anna M. Clovis and Ross H. Pifer, "The Pennsylvania Oil and Gas Act: A Summary of the Statutory Provisions," Agricultural Law Resource and Reference Center, Penn State Dickenson School of Law, March 2009.

22. Shale Gas Roundtable, "Deliberations, Findings and Recommendations," August 2013, 65–66; Zoë Schlanger, "Gas Industry's Solutions to Toxic Wastewater: Spray It on Roads," *Newsweek*, March 2, 2015.

23. Dormant Oil and Gas Act, Pennsylvania, act no. 115, P.L. 1134, §2, July 11, 2006.

24. Oil and Gas Act of 2012, act no. 13, P.L. 87, §3304(b), February 14, 2012; Tom Yerace and Brian Bowling, "Localities Can Decide Where It Is OK to Drill Wells," *Pittsburgh Tribune Review*, February 27, 2009.

25. American Legislative Exchange Council, Model Policies, "An Act Granting the Authority of Rural Counties to Transition to Decentralized Land Use Regulation," approved by ALEC Board of Directors, September 19, 2010; Steve Horn, "Exposed: Pennsylvania Act 13 Overturned by Commonwealth Court, Originally an ALEC Model Bill," *DeSmogBlog*, July 27, 2012; Stacey Singer, "Altruist's Other Role: Antagonist," *Palm Beach Post*, February 19, 2012.

26. *Robinson Township et al. v. Commonwealth of Pennsylvania*, Supreme Court of Pennsylvania, Middle District, 52A.3d463 (Pa. Cmwlth 2012), decided December 19, 2013.

27. Susan Philips, "Public Utility Commission Appeals Commonwealth Court Decision on Act 13," StateImpact Pennsylvania, NPR, August 16, 2014.

28. Act [No. 13] of February 14, 2012, P.L. 87, §2302(b).

29. Pennsylvania Public Utility Commission, "Disbursements and Impact Fees," Act 13 Public Reporting, accessed August 2015, www.act13-reporting.puc.pa.gov.

30. Act [No. 13] of February 14, 2012, P.L. 87, §2314, §2505.

31. Act [No. 13] of February 14, 2012, P.L. 87, §2315(a).

32. Pennsylvania Public Utility Commission, "Disbursements and Impact Fees."

33. Sam Bernhardt, interview with author, 2015; Jennifer Reeger, "Funding Plan Puzzles Conservation Districts," *Pittsburgh Tribune Review*, March 10, 2013.

34. Act [No. 13] of February 14, 2012, P.L. 87, §3222.1(b)(10); Sandy Bauers, "Doctors Object to Secrecy in PA's New Natural Gas Law," *Philadelphia Enquirer*, April 13, 2012.

35. Kevin Begos, "Docs Say Drilling Law Hurts Health," Associated Press, April 11, 2012.

36. Kate Sheppard, "For Pennsylvania's Doctors, a Gag Order on Fracking Chemicals," *Mother Jones*, March 23, 2012.

37. Susan Phillips, "Pennsylvania Doctors Worry over Fracking 'Gag Rule,'" WHYY-Philadelphia, NPR, May 17, 2012.

38. Katie Colaneri, "Former State Health Employees Say They Were Silenced on Drilling," StateImpact Pennsylvania, NPR, June 19, 2014.

39. Ibid.

40. Iris Marie Bloom, "Doug Shields Decries PA Department of Health 'Gas Is Good' Policy," *Protecting Our Waters*, July 6, 2014.

41. Ellen Cantarow, "Fracking Ourselves to Death in Pennsylvania," *The Nation*, May 2, 2013.

42. Southwestern Pennsylvania Environmental Health Project, "Health Issues and Concerns Related to Unconventional Gas Development," June 2013.

43. Begos, "Docs Say Drilling Law."

44. Nadia Steinzor, Wilma Subra, and Lisa Sumi, "Gas Patch Roulette: How Shale Gas Development Risks Public Health in Pennsylvania," Earthworks' Oil & Gas Accountability Project, October 2012, 21, 25–26.

45. Ibid., 15.

46. Laurel Peltier, "Fracking's List of the Harmed: 1,208 and Counting," *The Examiner*, April 17, 2013.

47. Department of the Auditor General, "DEP's Performance in Monitoring Potential Impacts to Water Quality from Shale Gas Development, 2009–2012," Commonwealth of Pennsylvania, July 2014, iii, 6.

48. Laura Legere, "DEP: Oil and Gas Operations Damaged Water Supplies 209 Times Since End of '07," *Pittsburgh Post-Gazette*, July 22, 2014.

49. Susan Phillips and Reid Frazier, "DEP's New Oil and Gas Rules Irk Both Environmentalists and Industry," StateImpact Pennsylvania, NPR, August 12, 2015.

50. Lou D'Amico, Pennsylvania Independent Oil and Gas Association, "Comments on Draft Final Rules—Proposed Amendment to 25 Pa. Code Chapter 78, Subchapter C (Relating to Oil and Gas Wells), and Addition of New Chapter 78a," Pennsylvania Department of Environmental Protection, May 19, 2015, 19.

51. Marc Levy, "Fracking Towns See Crime, Carousing Surge Amid Gas Boom," Associated Press, October 27, 2011.

52. Marc Levy, "Towns See Crime, Carousing Surge Amid Gas Boom," Associated Press, October 26, 2011; Multi-state Shale Research Collaborative, "The Shale Tipping Point: The Relationship of Drilling to Crime, Traffic Fatalities, STDs, and Rents in Pennsylvania, West Virginia, and Ohio," December 2014, 25–34.

53. Kacey Deamer, "Fracking Leads to More Pa. Crime," *The Ithacan* (NY), November 11, 2011.

54. Food & Water Watch, "The Social Costs of Fracking," September 2013, 2, 8.

55. Ibid., 9.

56. National Highway Traffic Safety Administration, "National Statistics," accessed July 22, 2013, www-fars.nhtsa.dot.gov/Main/index; PennDOT, "Crashes in Pennsylvania by County and Year 2000–2011," Bureau of Highway Safety and Traffic Engineering; PennDOT, Bureau of Highway Safety and Traffic Engineering, "Heavy Truck Related Crashes (GVWR > 26,000 Lbs) in Pennsylvania by County and Year 2000–2011."

57. Food & Water Watch, "Social Costs of Fracking," 9.

58. Shmuel Abramzon et al., "Estimating the Consumptive Use Costs of Shale Natural Gas Extraction on Pennsylvania Roadways," *Journal of Infrastructure Systems*, February 18, 2014.

59. Ibid.

60. Karen Feridun, interview with author, 2015; Robert J. Vickers, "Democrats Square Off over Call for Fracking Moratorium in Pennsylvania," *Harrisburg Patriot-News*, August 17, 2013.

61. Karen Langley, "Anti-frackers Ask Wolf to Forget Shale Tax," *Pittsburgh Post-Gazette*, November 18, 2014.

14. Not a Drop Left to Drink

1. Rachel Carson, *Silent Spring* (1962; New York: Mariner Books, 1990), 39.

2. CWC Group, "CWC Group to Hold Global Water: Oil and Gas Summit in Dubai, May 22 and 23," press release, May 20, 2012.

3. Anthony DiPaola, "Dubai to Stick with Natural Gas as Main Source for Power," Bloomberg, April 18, 2011.

4. Food & Water Europe, "Veolia Environment: A Profile of the World's Largest Water Service Corporation," April 2011.

5. EPA, "EPA's Full Draft Assessment of the Potential Impacts of Hydraulic Fracturing for Oil and Gas on Drinking Water Resources," June 4, 2015, 7-4, 7-5.

6. Ibid., ES-19; Fakhru'l-Razi Ahmadun et al., "Review of Technologies for Oil and Gas Produced Water Treatment," *Journal of Hazardous Materials* 170, nos. 2–3 (2009): 532.

7. Ahmadun et al., "Review of Technologies," 535–46.

8. CWC Group, "CWC Group to Hold"; National Academy of Sciences, *Desalination: A National Perspective* (Washington, DC: National Academies Press, 2008), 34; Claudia H. Deutsch, "There's Money in Thirst," *New York Times*, August 10, 2006.

9. United Nations–Water, "Coping with Water Scarcity: Challenge of the Twenty-First Century," March 2007, 10.

10. "Maude Barlow Named 1st UN Water Adviser," CBC News, October 21, 2008; United Nations Deputy Secretary-General, "Hailing Election of 63rd General Assembly President, Deputy Secretary-General Calls for Joint Action by Upcoming Session in Forging Effective Responses to Problems," press release, June 4, 2008.

11. United Nations General Assembly, "64/292: The Human Right to Water and Sanitation: Resolution Adopted by the General Assembly on 29 July 2010," August 3, 2010, 1–3; Maude Barlow, "Our Right to Water: A People's Guide to Implementing the United Nations' Recognition of the Right to Water and Sanitation," n.d., 10–11.

12. Maude Barlow, interview with author, 2015.

13. Kate Konschnik and Mark Boling, "Shale Gas Development: A Smart Regulation Approach," *Environmental Science & Technology* 48, no. 15 (February 24, 2014): 8404.

14. Monika Freyman, "Hydraulic Fracturing and Water Stress: Water Demand by the Numbers," Ceres, February 2014, 4–5.

15. Laurent Esnault et al., "Linking Groundwater Use and Stress to Specific Crops Using the Groundwater Footprint in the Central Valley and High Plains Aquifer Systems, U.S.," *Water Resources Research* 50 (June 18, 2014).

16. Colorado Division of Water Resources, Colorado Water Conservation Board, and Colorado Oil and Gas Conservation Commission, "Water Sources and Demand for the Hydraulic Fracturing of Oil and Gas Wells in Colorado from 2010 Through 2015," n.d.

17. Bruce Finley, "Water Used for Oil and Gas Drilling in Colorado Increasing," *Denver Post*, June 21, 2012.

18. Colo. Rev. Stat. §37-45-102(2) (2015); Colo. Rev. Stat. §37-42-137 (2015).

19. Bruce Finley, "Fracking Bidders Top Farmers at Water Auction," *Denver Post*, April 2, 2012.

20. David Owen, "Where the River Runs Dry," *New Yorker*, May 25, 2015; Henry Brean, "Colorado River Could Reach the Sea for the First Time in Decades," *Las Vegas Review-Journal*, May 14, 2014.

21. Zack Ponce, "Hurt by Drought, NM Farmers Are Selling Off Water Intended for Irrigation to Oil and Gas Companies—for Fracking," *Carlsbad* (NM) *Current-Argus*, January 29, 2014.

22. Stella Davis, "NM Farmers Selling Water to Oil and Gas Developers," *Carlsbad Current-Argus*, July 1, 2013.

23. Freyman, "Hydraulic Fracturing and Water Stress," 5–6, 30–31.

24. Manjula V. Guru and James E. Horne, "The Ogallala Aquifer," Kerr Center for Sustainable Agriculture, 2000, 1, 4, 6–7, 21; Rex C. Buchanan et al., "The High Plains Aquifer," Kansas Geological Survey, December 2009, 4.

25. Nicole C. Brambila, "Drying Times: Could the Rapidly Depleting Ogallala Aquifer Run Dry?," *Lubbock* (TX) *Avalanche-Journal*, August 9, 2014.

26. Taelor A. Allen, "The South Texas Drought and the Future of Groundwater Use for Hydraulic Fracturing in the Eagle Ford Shale," *St. Mary's Law Journal* 44, no. 487 (January 2013): 496–502.

27. Kevin Welch, "Authority Seals Water Deal with Pickens," *Amarillo* (TX) *Globe-News*, December 30, 2011; Joe Nick Patoski, "Boone Pickens Wants to Sell You His Water," *Texas Monthly*, August 2001.

28. Staff person from a conservation district in the Texas Panhandle, personal communication with author, August 12, 2014.

29. Jean-Philippe Nicot, "Assessment of Industry Water-Use in the Barnett Shale Gas Play (Fort Worth Basin)," *Gulf Coast Association of Geologic Societies* 59 (2009): 549.

30. Ibid. See also Texas Water Development Board, "2011 Texas Water Use Survey Summary Estimates by County," accessed August 2015, www.twdb.state.tx.us /waterplanning/waterusesurvey/estimates.

31. Kate Galbraith, "In Texas, Water Use for Fracking Stirs Concerns," *Texas Tribune*, March 8, 2013.

32. Sally Entrekin et al., "Rapid Expansion of Natural Gas Development Poses a Threat to Surface Waters," *Frontiers in Ecology and the Environment* 9, no. 9 (November 2011): 506–9.

33. Evan Hansen, Dustin Mulvaney, and Meghan Betcher, "Water Resource Reporting and Water Footprint from Marcellus Shale Development in West Virginia and Pennsylvania," Downstream Strategies, prepared for Earthworks Gas & Oil Accountability Project, October 30, 2013, 17, 20.

34. U.S. Army Corps of Engineers, "Monongahela River Watershed Initial Watershed Assessment," September 2011, 46.

35. Jim Harger, "Group Says 'Fracking' Operation in Kalkaska County Is Forced to Buy Municipal Water," *Ann Arbor* (MI) *News*, June 5, 2013; Matt Troutman, "Fracking Water Falls Short," *Traverse City* (MI) *Record-Eagle*, June 13, 2013.

36. Marc Lifsher and Patrick McGreevy, "Brown Signs Bill on Fracking, Upsetting Both Sides of Oil Issue," *Los Angeles Times*, September 20, 2013.

37. Veronica Rocha, "Water-Use Restrictions Take Effect in California; Daily Fines Possible," *Los Angeles Times*, July 30, 2014.

38. Chris Megerian, Matt Stevens, and Bettina Boxall, "Brown Orders California's First Mandatory Water Restrictions: 'It's a Different World,' " *Los Angeles Times*, April 1, 2015; Evan Simon, "California's Drought Plan Mostly Lays Off Agriculture, Oil Industries," ABC News, April 6, 2015.

39. Julie Cart, "State Lawmakers Slam Oil Regulators After Embarrassing Lapses," *Los Angeles Times*, March 26, 2015.

40. Julie Cart, "Central Valley's Growing Concern: Crops Raised with Oil Field Water," *Los Angeles Times*, May 2, 2015.

41. Emily Pickrell, "Water Follows the Shale Trail," *Global Water Intelligence*, January 2010, 25.

42. Marcellus Shale Coalition, "Marcellus Shale Coalition Members," March 2012.

43. Jeff Sterba, "Q2 2011 American Water Works Co. Inc. Earnings Conference Call—Final," *Fair Disclosure Wire*, August 4, 2011.

44. Anna Prior, "CEO Interview: Aqua America," *MarketWatch*, July 12, 2011; Aqua America, "Aqua America Board Appoints Christopher H. Franklin CEO Effective July 1," press release, June 3, 2015.

45. Nicholas DeBenedictis, Aqua America Inc., letter to shareholders, September 2011, 1.

46. Pickrell, "Water Follows the Shale Trail."

47. "Produced Water Market: Opportunities in the Oil, Shale and Gas Sectors in North America," *Global Water Intelligence*, March 17, 2011, 100.

48. Yuliya Chernova, "In Fracking's Wake," *Wall Street Journal*, September 12, 2011.

49. Ibid.

50. Roger Real Drouin, "As Fracking Booms, Growing Concerns About Wastewater," *Yale Environment 360*, February 18, 2014.

51. Ian Urbina, "Regulation Lax as Gas Wells' Tainted Water Hits Rivers," *New York Times*, February 26, 2011.

52. Ibid.

53. EPA, "Effluent Limitations Guidelines and Standards for the Oil and Gas Extraction Point Source Category," proposed rule, 40 CFR 435, 80 Fed. Reg. 18557–80 (April 7, 2015).

54. 80 Fed. Reg. 18561 (April 7, 2015).

55. Lux Research Inc., "Frac Water Treatment Market Still Worth $1.9 Billion," press release, August 12, 2015.

56. Barbara Warner and Jennifer Shapiro, "Fractured, Fragmented Federalism: A Study in Fracking Regulatory Policy," *Journal of Federalism* 43, no. 3 (April 18, 2013): 474.

15. The Real Cost of Fracking Infrastructure

1. Amy Harder, "Approval of Natural-Gas Export Projects Gets Mixed Reaction from Lawmakers," *Wall Street Journal*, March 24, 2014.

2. Paul Parformak, "Interstate Natural Gas Pipelines: Process and Timing of FERC Permit Application Review," Congressional Research Service, January 15, 2015, 1; U.S. Government Accountability Office, "Federal Approval Process for Liquefied Natural Gas Exports," GAO-14-762, September 2014, 1–2.

3. Office of Fossil Energy (hereafter OFE), "Long Term Applications Received by DOE/FE to Export Domestically Produced LNG from the Lower-48 States," DOE, December 2, 2015; EIA, Natural Gas Summary: Total Consumption, accessed August 2015, www.eia.gov/naturalgas/data.cfm.

4. OFE, "Long Term Applications"; EIA, "Natural Gas Annual Supply and Disposition by State: Dry Production," accessed August 2015, www.eia.gov/dnav/ng/ng_sum_snd_a_EPG0_FPD_Mmcf_a.htm.

5. U.S. Government Accountability Office, "Federal Approval Process for Liquefied Natural Gas Exports," GAO-14-762, September 26, 2014, publicly released October 1, 2014, 2.

6. Timothy B. Wheeler, "Natural Gas Export Eyed for Bay Site," *Baltimore Sun*, February 11, 2012; Clifford Kraus, "A Bet on Natural Gas," *New York Times*, January 28, 2011.

7. National Energy Technology Laboratory, "Liquefied Natural Gas: Understanding the Basic Facts," DOE, August 2005, 3.

8. Dominion Resources, "Dominion Begins Construction Activities for Cove Point LNG Export Project," press release, October 30, 2014.

9. Richard Bass and Gordon Pickering, "The U.S. Has a Natural Gas Glut; Why Exporting It as LNG Is a Good Idea," *Forbes*, June 13, 2012.

10. Bill Cooper, Center for Liquefied Natural Gas, letter to the U.S. Congress, "Re. Managers Amendment to H.R. 6, the Domestic Prosperity and Global Freedom Act," June 24, 2014.

11. W. David Montgomery et al., "Macroeconomic Impacts of LNG Exports from the United States," NERA Economic Consulting, December 3, 2012, 2.

12. Joanne Omang, "Cove Point LNG Facility: An Industry Being Born; LNG Facility Near Completion," *Washington Post*, November 14, 1977; David Burnham, "G.A.O. Report Charging Lack of Federal Protection Is Basis of Hearings This Week," *New York Times*, February 20, 1978.

13. "Company News: Dominion to Cut 700 Jobs in Connection with Merger," *New York Times*, April 21, 2000; Phil Porter, "Utilities Reach Agreement, Nisource Wraps Deal for Columbia," *Columbus Dispatch*, February 29, 2000; Dan Gearino, "Industry News: Columbia Gas of Ohio Parent Company Splits," *Columbus Dispatch*,

July 3, 2015; Daniel Southerland, "Columbia Gas System Emerges from Chap. 11; Utility Plans to Expand, Form Alliances," *Washington Post*, November 29, 1995.

14. Raymond McCaffrey, "Plant Fully Operational Again; Cove Point Facility Starts Sending Gas Through Pipelines," *Washington Post*, August 28, 2003; Tom Pelton, "An Energy Boom in Calvert," *Baltimore Sun*, August 21, 2005.

15. Timothy B. Wheeler, "Court Refuses to Stop LNG Plant Construction," *Baltimore Sun*, June 18, 2015; Max Ehrenfreund, "The Stakes of Cove Point," *Washington Post*, December 7, 2014; Jennifer A. Dlouhy, "In Line to Export," *Houston Chronicle*, April 27, 2014.

16. Dominion Resources Inc., SEC Form 10-K, fiscal year ended December 31, 2014, 8.

17. Political Economy Research Institute at University of Massachusetts, Amherst, and Food & Water Watch, "A Toxic Flood," May 2013, Table 1, 10.

18. FERC, "Environmental Assessment for the Cove Point Liquefaction Project," May 2014, 3, 125–26, 184; Alan Suderman, "Dominion's Donations Partially Subsidized by Its Customers," Associated Press, August 22, 2015; Max Ehrenfreund, "Community Divided over Cove Point Natural Gas Terminal," *Washington Post*, December 6, 2014.

19. Paul W. Parfomak and Adam Vann, "Liquefied Natural Gas (LNG) Import Terminals: Siting, Safety, and Regulation," Congressional Research Service, CRS no. RL32205, December 14, 2009, 4–5.

20. Lyle Kendrick, "Some Calvert County Residents Question Cove Point LNG Tanks," Capital News Service (MD), January 31, 2014.

21. Chesapeake Climate Action Network, "Groups Slam Deferral Regulators over Flawed Environmental Review of Cove Point LNG Export Facility," press release, May 15, 2014.

22. Kristi Pihl, "Update: Evacuation Radius Near Plymouth Plant to Be Reduced," *Tri-City* (WA) *Herald*, March 31, 2014.

23. Earthjustice, "Hundreds Intervene in Proceedings over Federal Review of Constitution Pipeline Project," press release, July 17, 2013.

24. Ike Wilson, "Natural Gas Compressor Station Makes Progress," *Frederick News-Post*, April 5, 2014; EPA's Office of Inspector General, "EPA Needs to Improve Air Emissions Data for Oil and Natural Gas Production Sector," February 20, 2013, 2; R. Subramanian et al., "Methane Emissions from Natural Gas Compression Stations in the Transmission and Storage Sector: Measurements and Comparisons with the EPA Greenhouse Gas Reporting Program Protocol," *Environmental Science & Technology* 49, no. 5 (March 3, 2015).

25. Don Hopey, "Marcellus Gas Facilities, Near to One Another or Even Linked, Are Evaluated Individually for Pollution," *Pittsburgh Post-Gazette*, October 6, 2013.

26. Lou Kilzer, "Feds OK Export of Natural Gas," *Pittsburgh Post-Gazette*, May 21, 2011; FERC, "FERC Approves LNG Export Project," press release, April 16, 2012.

27. Zain Shauk, Caleb Melby, and Laura Marcinek, "Cheniere CEO's $142 Million Pay Delays Annual Meeting," Bloomberg, June 3, 2014; Gregory Zuckerman, "Export King," *Foreign Affairs*, November 8, 2013.

28. Gregory Zuckerman, *The Frackers: The Outrageous Inside Story of the New Billionaire Wildcatters* (New York: Penguin, 2013), 173, 175–77.

29. Ibid., 178–79.

30. John M. Glionna and Carla Hall, "Brentwood Sheds Another Trial Reminder," *Los Angeles Times*, July 2, 1997.

31. Zuckerman, "Export King."

32. Simon Romero, "Demand for Natural Gas Brings Big Import Plans, and Objections," *New York Times*, June 15, 2005; Zuckerman, *Frackers*, 185–86.

33. Walter F. Roche Jr., "Doors Opened for Gas Firm Tied to Neil Bush," *Los Angeles Times*, October 29, 2004; Abraham Group, "Cheniere Energy Engages the Abraham Group," press release, October 21, 2005.

34. Cheniere Energy Inc., SEC Form 10-K, fiscal year ended December 31, 2014, 124; John Deutch, "Obama's Second-Term Energy Policy Is Working," *Wall Street Journal*, August 18, 2014; Massachusetts Institute of Technology, "The Future of Natural Gas," June 6, 2011, v.

35. Cheniere Energy Inc., "Notice of Annual Meeting of Shareholders," April 24, 2015, 6–9; Cleco Corporation, "Cleco Adds Vicky A. Baily to Its Board of Directors," press release, June 13, 2013.

36. Zuckerman, *Frackers*, 258–60, 278–82.

37. Ibid., 361–63.

38. Ibid.

39. Charles Ebinger, Kevin Massy, and Govinda Avasarala, "Evaluating the Prospects for Increased Exports of Liquefied Natural Gas from the United States," Brookings Institution, January 2012, 23–24.

40. DOE, "Energy Department Conditionally Authorizes Oregon LNG to Export Liquefied Natural Gas," press release, July 31, 2014; DOE, "Energy Department Authorizes Jordan Cove to Export Liquefied Natural Gas," press release, March 24, 2014.

41. Pipeline and Hazardous Materials Safety Administration, "All PHSMA Pipeline Incidents (1995–2014)," U.S. Department of Transportation, data as of September 4, 2015.

42. Elana Schor and Andrew Rustuccia, " 'Pipelines Blow Up and People Die,' " *Politico*, April 21, 2015.

43. Christian Von Hirschhausen, "Infrastructure, Regulation, Investment and Security of Supply: A Case Study of the Restructured US Natural Gas Market," *Journal of Utilities Policy* 16 (2008): 4, 7.

44. Pipeline and Hazardous Materials Safety Administration, "Data and Statistics: Pipeline Mileage and Facilities," U.S. Department of Transportation, accessed August 2015, phmsa.dot.gov/pipeline/library/data-stats.

45. Pipeline and Hazardous Materials Safety Administration, "Onshore Gas Gathering," U.S. Department of Transportation, briefing paper, March 24, 2011, 2.

46. Center for Biological Diversity, "Lawsuit Filed to Stop 677-Mile Ruby Pipeline and Protect Endangered Fish," press release, July 30, 2010.

47. Paul Henson, Oregon State Supervisor, U.S. Department of the Interior, Fish and Wildlife Service (FWS), letter to Federal Energy Regulatory Commission, December 22, 2008.

48. FWS, Mountain-Prairie Region, transmittal of biological opinion for the Ruby Pipeline Project (docket no. CP09-54-000), June 8, 2010, 94.

49. Scott Sonner, "Conservationists Win Ruby Pipeline Appeal," Associated Press, October 22, 2014.

50. Ibid.

51. Scott Streater, "Natural Gas: BLM Reauthorizes Completed Wyo.-to-Ore. Pipeline Without New Mitigation," *Greenwire*, November 20, 2013.

52. James Tobin, "Natural Gas Market Centers and Hubs: A 2003 Update," EIA, October 2003, 1.

53. James Tobin, "Natural Gas Market Centers: A 2008 Update," EIA, April 2009, 8.

54. Oregon Department of Environmental Quality, "Jordan Cove Energy Project," fact sheet, April 2014; Tobin, "Natural Gas Market Centers: A 2008 Update," 3 (Figure 1), 11 (Figure 5).

55. Veresen, "Veresen Reaches Major Milestone on Jordan Cove Energy Project with Filing of Formal FERC Application," press release, May 22, 2013; Jonathan Thompson, "A Pipeline Built Years Ago May Start to Export Rocky Mountain Gas to Asia," *High Country News*, April 14, 2014.

56. Carisa Cegavske, "FERC Gets Earful from Pacific Connector Pipeline Foes, Fans at Roseburg Hearing on Draft Environmental Impact Statement," *Roseburg* (OR) *News-Review*, December 10, 2014.

57. Rogue Riverkeeper, "Liquefied Natural Gas Threatens Rogue River Basin," fact sheet.

58. Ibid.

59. Ted Sickinger, "Landowners Tell Proposed LNG Export Terminal in Coos Bay: 'Keep Your Pipeline Off My Property,' " *The Oregonian*, August 28, 2014.

60. Oregon International Port of Coos Bay, Special Commission Meeting, transcript, March 26, 2012, 22.

61. Ted Sickinger, "Jordan Cove LNG Terminal at Coos Bay Designed for Cascadia Quake, Tsunami Though Hazards Remain," *The Oregonian*, June 26, 2014.

62. Leucadia National Corporation, SEC Form 10-K, fiscal year ended December 31, 2014, 27; Leucadia National Corporation, Annual Report 2014, 14.

63. CH2Mhill, LNG Development Company, LLC and Oregon Pipeline Company, LLC, "Applicant-Prepared Draft Biological Assessment and Essential Fish Habitat Assessment for the Oregon LNG Terminal and Oregon Pipeline Project," docket nos. C09-6-001, CO09-7-001, December 2013, Appendix 15.

64. Oregon LNG, "Oregon LNG Bidirectional Project Resource Report 1—General Project Description," June 2013, 1–26.

65. ExxonMobil Corp, "ExxonMobil Technology Yields World's Largest LNG Carrier," press release, December 17, 2008.

66. Ted Sickinger, "LNG Developer Pulls the Plug on Bradwood Landing Project," *The Oregonian*, May 4, 2010.

67. Columbia Riverkeeper, "Bradwood Suspends LNG Project: LNG Opponents Declare Victory," press release, May 4, 2014.

68. FERC, "Oregon LNG and Washington Expansion Projects: Draft Environmental Impact Statement," vol. 1, DOE docket no. FE 1-48-LNG, August 2015, ES-2, 3–5.

69. "Gas Pipeline Exploded East of Auburn; Evacuation Ordered," *Seattle Times*, May 1, 2003; Pihl, "Update."

70. Pihl, "Update."

71. Greg Kocher, "Companies Halt Bluegrass Pipeline but Say Project Could Be Revived if Demand Increases," *Lexington* (KY) *Herald-Leader*, April 28, 2014.

72. Williams Companies, Inc., SEC Form 10-K filing, February 27, 2013, 10.

73. Parformak, "Interstate Natural Gas Pipelines," 3.

74. James Bruggers and Mike Wynn, "Bluegrass Pipeline Opposition Increases in Kentucky," *Louisville* (KY) *Courier-Journal*, August 8, 2013.

75. John MacCormack, "Pipeline Plan Raises Hackles in Land-Loving Big Bend," *San Antonio Express-News*, April 11, 2015; John Malewitz, "In Pristine Big Bend, a Pipeline Could Run Through It," *Texas Tribune*, July 14, 2015.

76. Spectra Energy, "Spectra Energy Places New Jersey–New York Natural Gas Pipeline into Service," press release, November 1, 2013; Eileen Stukane, "Gas Pipeline Protests No Longer Burn, but Could Problems Flare in Future?," *The Villager* (NY), March 12, 2015.

77. Peter Rugh, " 'We Have to Be the Carbon Tax'—an Interview with Tim De-Christopher," *Waging Nonviolence*, November 6, 2013.

16. Exxon: More Powerful Than Ever

1. Rex W. Tillerson, Council on Foreign Relations, transcript, June 27, 2012.

2. ExxonMobil, "ExxonMobil Earns $32.5 Billion in 2014; $6.6 Billion During Fourth Quarter," press release, February 2, 2015.

3. ExxonMobil Corporation, "Locations," accessed August 2015, corporate
.exxonmobil.com/en/company/worldwide-operations/locations; James Osborne, "Exxon Calm in the Storm," *Dallas Morning News*, August 6, 2015.

4. Raymond J. Learsy, *Over a Barrel: Breaking Oil's Grip on Our Future* (New York: Encounter Books, 2007), 112–13; Kristine Henry, " 'Evil Empire' Members to Share History Again Exxon's, Mobil's Origins Precede Breakup of Standard Oil Trust," *Baltimore Sun*, December 2, 1998; "Jersey Standard Lists Dip in Profits," *New York Times*, January 27, 1959; "Jersey Standard Lifts Its Profit," *New York Times*, January 28, 1965.

5. William D. Smith, "Spotlight: A Man of Oil—and Its Politics," *New York Times*, March 4, 1975; "Jersey Standard's Profits Pass $1 Billion Mark for First Time," *New York Times*, January 30, 1964.

6. Smith, "Spotlight"; Learsy, *Over a Barrel*, 112.

7. Learsy, *Over a Barrel*, 112–13.

8. Henry, " 'Evil Empire' Members to Share History."

9. Jad Mouawad, "Exxon Chairman Got Retirement Package Worth at Least $398 Million," *New York Times*, April 13, 2006; Jad Mouawad, "Lee Raymond, Exxon Mobil's Chief Since 1999 Merger, to Step Down at Year's End," *New York Times*, August 5, 2005.

10. "Lawrence Rawl, 76; Exxon Chief at Time of Alaskan Oil Spill Disaster," *Los Angeles Times*, February 15, 2005.

11. Allan Turner, "Tanker's Double Hull Prevented Disaster, Coast Guard Credits Sturdiness for Averting Spill Tanker: Single-Hulled Tankers Replaced After Exxon Valdez," *Houston Chronicle*, March 12, 2009.

12. Jennifer Latson, "America's Second-Worst Oil Spill Is Still Scarring the Shores of Alaska," *Time*, March 24, 2015.

13. Steve Coll, *Private Empire: ExxonMobil and American Power* (New York: Penguin, 2012), 12–13.

14. James Osborne, "Oil Spill Lawsuits Tarring Exxon," *Dallas Morning News*, September 15, 2013; Adam Liptak, "Damages Cut Against Exxon in Valdez Case," *New York Times*, June 26, 2008.

15. Coll, *Private Empire*, 34–35, 69–71.

16. Jonathan Owen and Paul Bignell, "Think-Tanks Take Oil Money and Use It to Fund Climate Deniers," *The Independent*, February 7, 2010.

17. Thaddeus Herrick, "Exxon CEO Lee Raymond's Stance on Global Warming Causes a Stir," *Wall Street Journal*, August 29, 2001.

18. John H. Cushman, "Industrial Group Plans to Battle Climate Reality," *New York Times*, April 26, 1998.

19. Greenpeace USA, "ExxonMobil's Continued Funding of Global Warming Denial Industry," May 2007, 6.

20. Suzanne Goldenburg, "Work of Prominent Climate Change Denier Was Funded by Energy Industry," *The Guardian*, February 21, 2015; ExxonMobil, "2007 Corporate Citizenship Report," 2007, 39.

21. Center for Responsive Politics, "Top Lobbying Spenders, All Years 1998–2015," accessed August 2015, www.opensecrets.org.

22. Alastair MacDonald, "U.S. Firms Lead EU Lobbying League," Reuters, April 30, 2015; EU Transparency Register, ExxonMobil Petroleum and Chemical, identification no. 0745650927-75, registry updated March 26, 2015, accessed August 2015, ec.europa.eu/transparencyregister.

23. Friends of the Earth Europe, "Fracking Brussels: A Who's Who of the EU Shale Gas Lobby," July 24, 2014, 7, 8.

24. Coll, *Private Empire*, 66–71.

25. Ibid., 68, 77.

26. Wenonah Hauter and Charlie Higley, " 'Black Gold' Merger Mania: How the Exxon/Mobil and BP Amoco/ARCO Mergers Threaten Consumers," Public Citizen, October 1999, 2.

27. Christopher Helman, "The World's Biggest Oil and Gas Companies—2015," *Forbes*, March 19, 2015; Nicholas Rapp and Scott DeCarlo, "The Global 500: Growth Moves to the East," *Fortune*, August 1, 2015.

28. "Iran Not Likely to Get High-Tech Oil Help," CNN, December 5, 2011; Andrew E. Kramer, "Memo to Exxon: Business with Russia Might Involve Guns and Balaclavas," *New York Times*, September 1, 2011.

29. Mark Drajem, "Boeing, Exxon Say New Iran Sanctions Would Hurt Global Sales," Bloomberg, May 13, 2010.

30. Alex Lawler and Peg Mackey, "Update 2: Iran Names 7 Western Oil Companies It Wants to Return," *Reuters*, December 4, 2013.

31. EIA, "Iran: International Energy Data and Analysis," June 19, 2015.

32. Indira Lakshmanan and Anthony DiPaola, "Growing Iran Oil Exports Challenge U.S. Nuclear Sanctions," *Bloomberg*, June 12, 2014.

33. Center for Responsive Politics, "Lobbying Spending Database—Exxon Mobil 2014, Summary and Bills," accessed August 2015, www.opensecrets.org.

34. Matthew Philips, "Post Crimea, Exxon's Partnership with Rosneft Feels Weird," *Bloomberg*, March 20, 2014.

35. Thomas Nilsen, "Discovers Kara Sea Oil a Week Before Sanctions," *Barents Observer*, September 29, 2014.

36. Capitol Legistics, ExxonMobil Corporation client, Clerk of the U.S. House of Representatives, Secretary of the U.S. Senate, Lobby Disclosure Act of 1995 Form LD-2, October 20, 2014.

37. Timothy Gardner, "Exxon Winds Down Drilling as U.S. Sanctions Hit Russia," *Reuters*, September 19, 2014.

38. Jake Rudnitsky and Stephen Bierman, "Exxon Fracking Siberia to Help Putin Maintain Oil Clout," *Bloomberg*, June 14, 2012.

39. Coll, *Private Empire*, 191.

40. Christopher Helman, "A Bird's Eye View of Exxon's Giant New Houston Complex," *Forbes*, December 4, 2012; Emily Wilkinson, "High-Profile Projects Deliver, Others Underway," *Houston Business Journal*, September 4, 2015; Rapp and DeCarlo, "Global 500."

41. Coll, *Private Empire*, 580.

42. Brian O'Keefe, "Exxon's Big Bet on Shale Gas," *Fortune*, April 16, 2012.

43. Coll, *Private Empire*, 580–82.

44. Ibid., 576–82.

45. Russell Gold, "Exxon Bets Big on Gas with Deal for XTO," *Wall Street Journal*, December 15, 2009.

46. ExxonMobil Corporation, SEC Form 10-Q, quarterly period ended June 30, 2010, 6.

47. SEC, Modernization of Oil and Gas Reporting, 74 Fed. Reg. 2158–9, 2163, January 14, 2009.

48. Katie Howell, "House Panel Looks into Effects of Exxon-XTO Merger," *New York Times*, January 19, 2010; Gold, "Exxon Bets Big."

49. Orhan Coskin, "Update 1—ExxonMobil in Talks with Turkey over Shale Gas Exploration," *Reuters*, June 23, 2014; Justin Scheck and Selina Williams, "Non-U.S. shales prove difficult to crack," *Wall Street Journal*, March 18, 2015; "Ukraine Signs Shale Gas Deal with ExxonMobil," *Reuters*, September 30, 2011.

50. Marc Naumann and Anne Philippi, "ExxonMobil in Europe's Shale Gas Fields: Quitting Early or Fighting It Out?," *Journal of European Management and Public Affairs Studies* 1, no. 2 (2014): 32–33.

51. Ibid.

52. Karolin Schaps and Vera Eckert, "Germany Overtakes Britain as Europe's Biggest Gas User," *Reuters*, October 2, 2013; Coll, *Private Empire*, 587.

53. Naumann and Philippi, "ExxonMobil in Europe's Shale Gas Fields," 34.

54. Daniel Kummetz, "Neun Lecks-Null Information," *Die Tageszeitung*, January 10, 2011; European Parliament, Directorate General for Internal Policies, Policy Department A: Economic and Scientific Policy, "Impacts of Shale Gas and Shale Oil Extraction on the Environment and Human Health," June 2011, 30; Julio Godoy, "Can Europe Derail the Shale Gas Express?," InterPress Service, February 13, 2012.

55. Andy Gheorghiu, personal communication with author, September 8, 2013.

56. Elizabeth Douglass, "U.S. Ranks Near Bottom on Energy Efficiency; Germany Tops List," *InsideClimate News*, July 18, 2014.

57. Catherine Stupp, "Germans Line Up Against Fracking, Spurred by Fears of a U.S.-Style Boom," *InsideClimate News*, October 14, 2014.

58. Matthew Karnitschnig, "Germany's Expensive Gamble on Renewable Energy," *Wall Street Journal*, August 26, 2014; Philip Oltermann, "German Beermakers Look Like Winning Their Battle to Stop Fracking," *The Guardian*, June 17, 2014.

59. Naumann and Philippi, "ExxonMobil in Europe's Shale Gas Fields," 35.

60. Ibid., 36.

61. Melissa Eddy and Stanley Reed, "Germany Takes Step Toward Permitting Fracking," *New York Times*, June 6, 2014.

62. Stupp, "Germans Line Up."

63. Arthur Neslen, "Germany Moves to Legalise Fracking," *The Guardian*, February 14, 2015.

64. Deutsche Umwelthilfe, "Fracking in Germany: Federal Legislative Proposal Does Not Manage the Risks Involved (in Fracking)," press release, February 12, 2015.

65. Stefan Nicola, "German Beer Brewers Win Fracking Protection for Spring," Bloomberg, February 26, 2015.

66. Oltermann, "German Beermakers."

67. Nicola, "German Beer Brewers."

68. Stupp, "Germans Line Up."

69. J.S. Simon, ExxonMobil Corporation, testimony before the Select Committee on Energy Independence and Global Warming, U.S. House of Representatives, April 1, 2008, 2.

17. The Climate Change Heist

1. Robert Christy, *Proverbs, Maxims and Phrases of All Ages* (New York: Knickerbocker Press, 1907), 345.

2. Joby Warrik, "New Rule Targets Pollution from Coal," *Washington Post*, August 2, 2015; Chris Mooney, "The Facts of the Clean Power Plan," *Washington Post*, August 2, 2015.

3. Katie Fehrenbacher, "These Are the Winners and Losers in Obama's Plan to Slash Carbon from Power Plants," *Fortune*, August 3, 2015.

4. EPA, "Carbon Pollution Emission Guidelines for Existing Stationary Sources: Electric Utility Generating Units," proposed rule, proposed August 3, 2015, 33, 1033, 1043, 1071; Coral Davenport, "For States That Don't File Carbon-Cutting Plans,

E.P.A. Will Impose 'Model Rule,' " January 7, 2015; P. Friedlingstein et al., "Persistent Growth of CO_2 Emissions and Implications for Reaching Climate Targets," *Nature Geoscience Review* 7 (2014): 710–13.

5. Gina McCarthy, "Administrator Gina McCarthy, Remarks Announcing Clean Power Plan, as Prepared," EPA, June 2, 2014.

6. Jenny Heeter and Lori Bird, "Including Alternative Resources in State Renewable Portfolio Standards: Current Design and Implementation Experience," National Renewable Energy Laboratory, DOE, November 2012, 6–7.

7. EPA, "Carbon Pollution Emission Guidelines."

8. EPA, "Regulatory Impact Analysis for the Clean Power Plan Final Rule," August 2015, 3–28.

9. Gunnar Myhre et al., "Anthropogenic and Natural Radiative Forcing," in T.F. Stocker et al., *Climate Change 2013: The Physical Science Basis: Contribution of Working Group I to the Fifth Assessment Report of the Intergovernmental Panel on Climate Change* (Cambridge: Cambridge University Press, 2013), 714.

10. Robert W. Howarth, Renee Santoro, and Anthony Ingraffea, "Methane and the Greenhouse-Gas Footprint of Natural Gas from Shale Formations: A Letter," *Climatic Change* 106 (2011): 679–80, 686.

11. Ibid., 679, 687.

12. Robert W. Howarth, personal communication with author, 2015.

13. EPA, "BP Exploration [Alaska] Pleads Guilty to Hazardous Substance Crime, Will Pay $22 Million, Establish Nationwide Environmental Management System," press release, September 23, 1999.

14. Robert W. Howarth, personal communication with author, 2015.

15. Anthony Ingraffea, personal communication with author, 2015.

16. Howarth et al., "Methane," 683.

17. Ibid., 680–81.

18. Tom Zeller, "Studies Say Natural Gas Has Its Own Environmental Problems," *New York Times*, April 11, 2011; Howarth et al., "Methane," 679.

19. Bryan Walsh, "People Who Mattered: Mark Ruffalo, Anthony Ingraffea, Robert Howarth," *Time*, December 14, 2011.

20. Zeller, "Studies Say Natural Gas ."

21. Tom Zeller, "Cornell Gas Study Stirs Heated Debate," *New York Times*, April 18, 2011.

22. MIT Energy Initiative, "MIT's Ernest J. Moniz Becomes Secretary of Energy," *Energy Futures*, Spring 2013, 2; MIT Energy Initiative, "MITEI Members," *Energy Futures*, Spring 2015, 44.

23. Lawrence M. Cathles III et al., "A Commentary on 'The Greenhouse-Gas Footprint of Natural Gas in Shale Formations' by Robert W. Howarth, Renee Santoro, and Anthony Ingraffea," *Climatic Change* 113 (2012).

24. Global Warming Petition Project, accessed August 2015, www.petition project.org/signers_by_last_name.php?run=C.

25. Robert W. Howarth, Renee Santoro, and Anthony Ingraffea, "Venting and Leaking of Methane from Shale Gas Development: Response to Cathles et al.," *Climatic Change* 113 (2012): 537.

26. A.R. Brandt et al., "Methane Leaks from North American Natural Gas Systems," *Science* 343 (February 14, 2014): 733.

27. Ibid., supplementary materials, 41–42.

28. Gabrielle Pétron et al., "Estimations of Emissions from Oil and Natural Gas Operations in Northeastern Colorado," presented at the 2012 International Emission Inventory Conference, Tampa, FL, August 13–16, 2012; Gabrielle Pétron, "Estimation of Emissions from Oil and Natural Gas Operations in Northeastern Colorado," n.d., www.epa.gov/ttnchie1/conference/ei20/session6/gpetron.pdf.

29. Cooperative Institute for Research in Environmental Sciences, "CIRES, NOAA observe significant methane leaks in a Utah natural gas field," press release, August 5, 2013.

30. Dana R. Caulton et al., "Toward a Better Understanding and Quantification of Methane Emissions from Shale Gas Development," *Proceedings of the National Academy of Sciences* 111, no. 17 (April 29, 2014): 6240.

31. Anthony R. Ingraffea et al., "Assessment and Risk Analysis of Casing and Cement Impairment in Oil and Gas Wells in Pennsylvania, 2000–2012," *Proceedings of the National Academy of Sciences* 111, no. 30 (July 29, 2014): 10958.

32. Bobby Magill, "Huge Methane Leaks Add Doubt on Gas as 'Bridge' Fuel," *Climate Central*, April 15, 2014.

33. Robert W. Howarth, "A Bridge to Nowhere: Methane Emissions and the Greenhouse Gas Footprint of Natural Gas," *Energy Science & Engineering* 2, no. 2 (2014): 47, 56.

34. Zain Shauk, "Prominent Producers Join Methane Leak Study," *Houston Chronicle*, October 11, 2012; EDF, "Methane Research: The 16 Study Series," fact sheet, 2015.

35. Renee Schoof, "As Natural Gas Production Grows, Questions Arise About Methane Leaks," *Bozeman* (MT) *Daily Chronicle*, March 25, 2012.

36. These companies include Statoil, Anadarko, Apache Corporation, BG Group, Chevron, Encana Oil & Gas, ExxonMobil's XTO, Hess Corporation, Noble Energy, Pioneer Natural Resources, Shell Oil Co., Southwestern Energy, and Talisman Energy. EDF, "Statoil Joins Methane Detectors Challenge with Technology Pilots on Horizon," press release, July 30, 2015; Shauk, "Prominent Producers."

37. David T. Allen et al., "Measurements of Methane Emissions at Natural Gas Production Sites in the United States," *Proceedings of the National Academy of Sciences* 110, no. 44 (October 29, 2013): 17773.

38. EPA, "Oil and Natural Gas Sector: New Source Performance Standards and National Emissions Standards for Hazardous Air Pollutants Reviews," final rule, 77 Fed. Reg. 49492, August 16, 2012; Allen et al., "Measurements of Methane Emissions," 17770.

39. Russell Gold, "U.S. Overstates Leaks by Gas-Drillers, Says Study," *Wall Street Journal*, September 16, 2013.

40. Anthony J. Marchese, "Methane Emissions from United States Natural Gas Gathering and Processing," *Environmental Science & Technology* 49 (August 18, 2015): 10723.

41. John Schwartz, "Methane Leaks in Natural-Gas Supply Chain Far Exceed Estimates, Study Says," *New York Times*, August 18, 2015.

42. White House, "Fact Sheet: Administration Takes Steps Forward on Climate Action Plan by Announcing Actions to Cut Methane Emissions," press release, January 14, 2015.

43. John Podesta, "New Actions to Reduce Methane Emissions Will Curb Climate Change, Cut Down on Wasted Energy," *Counsel to the President* (blog), January 14, 2015.

44. EPA, "Oil and Natural Gas Sector," 17.

45. Robert W. Howarth, "Perspectives on Air Emissions of Methane and Climatic Warming Risk from Hydraulic Fracturing and Shale Gas Development: Implications for Policy," *Energy and Emission Control Technologies*, October 2015, abstract.

18. Pollution Trading: A Shell Game

1. Brent Fewell, "An Interview with EDF's Fred Krupp—A Leading Voice in Today's Environmental Wilderness," Conserve Fewell, May 6, 2015, conservefewell .org/an-interview-with-edfs-fred-krupp-a-leading-voice-in-todays-environmental -wilderness.

2. Fred Krupp and Miriam Horn, *Earth: The Sequel* (New York: W.W. Norton, 2008), 179.

3. EDF, "How Cap and Trade Works," accessed August 2015, www.edf.org /climate/how-cap-and-trade-works.

4. Krupp and Horn, *Earth*, 178.

5. California Code of Regulations, Title 10, §95810.

6. California Air Resources Board, "California's Cap-and-Trade Program: Fuel Facts," December 2014.

7. Susan Phillips, "Maryland Governor Proposes Stringent Fracking Regulations," StateImpact Pennsylvania, NPR, November 25, 2014.

8. Coral Davenport, "Championing Environment, Francis Takes Aim at Global Capitalism," *New York Times*, June 18, 2015.

9. Coral Davenport, "President Said to Be Planning to Use Executive Authority on Carbon Rule," *New York Times*, May 28, 2014.

10. Eduard Gismatullin, "Shell Call for Global Expansion of Cap-and-Trade CO_2 Programs," Bloomberg, November 13, 2009.

11. Matt Taibbi, "The Great American Bubble Machine," *Rolling Stone*, July 9–23, 2009, 100.

12. Justin Gillis, "A Price Tag on Carbon as a Climate Rescue Plan," *New York Times*, May 30, 2014.

13. Taibbi, "Great American Bubble Machine," 100.

14. Steve Horn, personal communication with author, March 9, 2015.

15. Jean-Philippe Brisson, Latham & Watkins, LLP, "Outstanding Design Flaws in California's Cap-and-Trade Program," white paper, October 16, 2014, 1.

16. Danny Cullenward and David Weiskopf, "Resource Shuffling and the California Carbon Market," working paper, Stanford Law School, Environmental and Natural Resources Law and Policy Program, July 18, 2013, 2.

17. Ibid., 1, 12–16.

18. European Commission (EC), "EU Emissions Trading System (EU ETS)," October 2013, 1; "The EU Emissions Trading System (EU ETS)," European Parliament, Committee on the Environment, Public Health and Food Safety, draft report on amending Directive 2003/87/EC. no. 2012/0202(COD), November 23, 2012, 6–8.

19. Martin Walter, "The Impact of Corruption on Climate Change: Threatening Emissions Trading Mechanisms?," United Nations Global Environmental Alert Service, March 2013, 2–5.

20. Ben Schiller, "Is It Time to Overhaul Europe's Carbon Trading Scheme?," *The Guardian*, April 28, 2011.

21. "Green Fleeces, Red Faces: A Theft of Carbon Credits Embarrasses an Entire Market," *The Economist*, February 3, 2011.

22. Gillis, "Price Tag on Carbon."

23. Jonathan L. Ramseur, "The Role of Offsets in a Greenhouse Gas Emissions Cap-and-Trade Program: Potential Benefits and Concerns," Congressional Research Service, no. RL34436, April 4, 2008, 1–3; Environmental Crime Programme, "Guide to Carbon Trading Crime," INTERPOL, June 2013, 2, 11; U.S. Government Accountability Office (hereafter GAO), "Climate Change Issues: Options for Addressing Challenges to Carbon Offset Quality," GAO-11-345, February 2011, 7–17.

24. GAO, "Carbon Offsets: The U.S. Voluntary Market Is Growing, But Quality Assurance Poses Challenges for Market Participants," GAO-08-1048, August 2008, 7.

25. EPA, "EPA Settlement Protects Arkansas Community, Company Will Invest $750,000 for Environmental Project," press release, May 13, 2014; Rory Carroll, "California Investigating Validity of 4.3 Mln Carbon Credits," Reuters, June 5, 2014.

26. Phillips, "Maryland Governor Proposes."

27. 42 USC § 7651(a) to §7651(o); Zachary Colie, " 'Cap-and-Trade' Model Eyed for Greenhouse Gases," *San Francisco Chronicle*, December 3, 2007.

28. EPA, "Clearing the Air: The Facts About Capping and Trading Emissions," May 2002, 5.

29. Brian Tokar, "The Myths of 'Green Capitalism,' " *New Politics* 14, no. 4 (Winter 2014).

30. Lauraine G. Chestnut and David M. Mills, "A Fresh Look at the Benefits and Costs of the U.S. Acid Rain Program," *Journal of Environmental Management* 77 (2005): 253–54.

31. European Union, "Assessment of the Effectiveness of European Air Quality Policies and Measures: Case Study 1," project for Directorate-General Environment, conducted by Milieu Ltd, the Danish National Environmental Research Institute, and the Center for Clean Air Policy, October 4, 2004, 7, 20.

32. Chestnut and Mills, "Fresh Look," 255.

33. Richard Conniff, "The Political History of Cap and Trade," *Smithsonian*, August 2009.

34. Tokar, "Myths of 'Green Capitalism.'"

35. See Michael A. Livermore and Richard L. Revesz, "Interest Groups and Environmental Policy: Inconsistent Positions and Missed Opportunities," *Environmental Law Review* 45 (2015): 6n16. Among the early economists promoting the idea were John H. Dales, who is usually credited with the idea in his *Pollution, Property and Prices* (Toronto: University of Toronto Press, 1968), and Thomas D. Crocker, "The Structuring of Atmospheric Pollution Control Systems," in Harold Wolozin, ed., *The Economics of Air Pollution* (New York: W.W. Norton, 1968). See also John H. Dales, "Land, Water, and Ownership," *Canadian Journal of Economics* 1, no. 4 (1968), on advocating transferable permits as a market-based solution to depletion and pollution problems; and W. David Montgomery, "Markets in Licenses and Efficient Pollution Control Programs," *Journal of Economic Theory* 5, no. 395 (1972), on providing a theoretical framework for the use of allowance markets to address pollution.

36. Tokar, "Myths of 'Green Capitalism.'"

37. Ibid.

38. EPA, "Selected Management Articles: Public Policy Mechanisms: Non-regulatory Options for Environmental Protection," EPA/IMSD/91-006, June 1991, 29–30.

39. Tokar, "Myths of 'Green Capitalism.'"

40. Philip Shabecoff, "An Emergence of Political Will on Acid Rain," *New York Times*, February 19, 1989.

41. Jeffrey H. Birnbaum, "Players: C. Boyden Gray: A Moving Force in Fight for Bush's Judicial Nominees," *Washington Post*, May 24, 2005.

42. Sara Fritz, "*Los Angeles Times* Interview: C. Boyden Gray—on Clinton's Conduct as President and Starr's as Independent Counsel," *Los Angeles Times*, August 2, 1998.

43. Eric Pianin, "Suits Against Power Firms Justified, Justice Dept. Says," *Washington Post*, January 16, 2002; Neela Banerjee, "Energy Giants Push to Weaken Pollution Rule," *New York Times*, April 13, 2002; Gary Polakovic and Elizabeth Shogren, "Smog Rules May Be Eased," *Los Angeles Times*, July 27, 2001.

44. Elizabeth Becker, "White House Undermined Chemical Tests, Report Says," *New York Times*, April 2, 2004; "U.S., Other Nations Concerned by European Chemical Rules," States News Service, August 1, 2006.

45. Joe Davis, "Debates Polluted by Ambiguities, but Dukakis Comes Out Cleaner," *Deseret News* (UT), November 4, 1988.

46. President Ronald Reagan, "Message to the Congress on 'a Quest for Excellence,'" January 27, 1987.

47. James Verini, "The Devil's Advocate," *New Republic*, September 24, 2007.

48. Conniff, "Political History of Cap and Trade."

49. Brian Tokar, "Trading Away the Earth: Pollution Credits and the Perils of 'Free Market Environmentalism,'" *Dollars and Sense*, March–April 1996; Al From, "Recruiting Bill Clinton," *The Atlantic*, December 3, 2013.

50. Tokar, "Myths of 'Green Capitalism.'"

51. Robert N. Stavins, curriculum vitae, accessed March 2015, scholar.harvard.edu/stavins/biocv.

52. Richard Schmalensee and Robert N. Stavins, "The SO$_2$ Allowance Trading System: The Ironic History of a Grand Policy Experiment," *Journal of Economic Perspectives* 27, no. 1 (Winter 2013): 103.

53. Sharon Begley, "Adam Smith Turns Green," *Newsweek*, June 9, 1991; EDF, "30th Anniversary Report," 1997, 16.

54. Fred Krupp, "The Making of a Market-Minded Environmentalist," *Strategy + Business*, no. 51 (Summer 2008): 3.

55. Conniff, "Political History of Cap and Trade."

56. Ambassador C. Boyden Gray, "Uncharted Territory: What Are the Consequences of President Obama's Unprecedented 'Recess Appointments,'" testimony before the Committee on Oversight and Government Reform, U.S. House of Representatives, February 1, 2012, 11; J. Owen Saunders, "North American Deregulation of Electricity: Sharing Regulatory Sovereignty," *Texas International Law Journal* 36, no. 167 (2001): 169.

57. Kenneth Lay, Enron, letter to President George W. Bush, April 3, 1992, 1.

58. Al Gore, *Earth in the Balance: Ecology and the Human Spirit* (Boston: Houghton Mifflin, 1992), 347.

59. John J. Fialka, "How a Republican Anti-pollution Measure, Expanded by Democrats, Got Rooted in Europe and China," *ClimateWire*, November 17, 2011.

60. Timothy E. Wirth, C. Boyden Gray, and John D. Podesta, "The Future of Energy Policy," *Foreign Affairs* 82, no. 4 (July–August 2003): 142.

61. President George W. Bush, "Personnel Announcement," press release, January 17, 2006; President George W. Bush, "President Bush Selects C. Boyden Gray as Special Envoy for European Union Affairs," press release, January 11, 2008.

62. Ambassador C. Boyden Gray, "Trust America on Climate Change," *Financial Times*, September 26, 2007.

63. Thomas Dunlap, *DDT: Scientists, Citizens, and Public Policy* (Princeton, NJ: Princeton University Press, 1981), 143–44; Gilbert Rogin, "All He Wants to Save Is the World," *Sports Illustrated*, February 3, 1969; Stony Brook University, "Environmental Defense Fund Archive, Collection 232, Historical Note," Special Collections and University Archives.

64. Richard Gottlieb, *Forcing the Spring: The Transformation of the American Environmental Movement* (Washington, DC: Island Press, 2005), 190–91.

65. Ibid., 192.

66. Ibid., 192–93.

67. Ibid., 192–96.

68. Krupp, "Making of a Market-Minded Environmentalist," 2; Bill Slocum, "Unlikely Allies," *Greenwich Magazine*, May 2007.

69. Slocum, "Unlikely Allies."

70. Priscilla Roberts, "John J. McCloy—Architect of the American Century," in *The Human Tradition in America Since 1945*, ed. David L. Anderson (Wilmington, DE: Scholarly Resources, 2003), 17.

71. Susan Welsh, "The German Marshall Fund: Reviving the Morgenthau Plan," *Executive Intelligence Review* 8, no. 10 (March 10, 1981): 40–42.

72. Nicholas Siegel, "The German Marshall Fund of the United States: A Brief History," May 2012, 11–12.

73. Ibid., 12, 18–20; Peterson Institute for International Economics, brochure, February 2012.

74. National Governors Association, resolution, August 2001, cited in White House, "Executive Summary—Clear Skies Initiative," February 14, 2002.

75. Frank E. Loy, "Statement for the Record by Frank E. Loy, Under Secretary of State–Designate for Global Affairs," testimony before Committee on Foreign Relations, U.S. Senate, October 2, 1998.

76. Emma Ross, "Global Warming Negotiations Fail to Reach Agreement," Associated Press, November 25, 2000.

77. James A. Barnes, "Obama's Inner Circle," *National Journal*, March 29, 2008; "Sweet: Obama, at Sun-Times Request, Releases Names of Finance Committee Members, Senate Interns," *Chicago Sun-Times*, March 24, 2008; President Barack Obama, "President Obama Announces More Key Administration Posts," press release, July 11, 2011.

78. "The Directors," *Fortune*, April 23, 2009; EDF, "The Way Forward: 2014 Annual Report," 2014, 50.

79. Resources for the Future (hereafter RFF), "2014 Annual Report," 2015, 21; Columbia Energy Group, "Columbia Names Philip Sharp, Former Congressman, as Advisor on Consumer Choice, Energy Deregulation," press release, October 12, 1999.

80. FoundationSearch, "Grant Visualizer," accessed September 2014, www .foundationsearch.com; Energy Foundation, Internal Revenue Service Form 990, November 7, 2014, Schedule I, Part II, 28, 29; RFF, "Center for Energy and Climate Economics," accessed August 2015, www.rff.org/about/rffs-center-energy-and -climate-economics; Clayton Munnings et al., "Assessing the Design of Three Pilot Programs for Carbon Trading in China," RFF, discussion paper no. RFF DP 14-36, October 2014, 1.

81. RFF, "The Risks of Shale Gas Development: How RFF Is Identifying a Pathway Toward Responsible Development," *Resources* 179 (February 16, 2012).

19. Hard-Fought Victory in New York

1. Thomas Kaplan, "Citing Health Risks, Cuomo Bans Fracking in New York State," *New York Times*, December 17, 2014

2. Ibid.

3. Fred von Wiegen, "Poll Shows New York Voters Favor Fracking Ban," *Finger Lakes Daily News*, December 23, 2014.

4. Quinnipiac University Polling Institute, "New York Voters Back Fracking, Despite Concerns, Quinnipiac Poll Finds; More Women in Government Means Fewer Sex Scandals," press release, August 11, 2011.

5. New York Department of Environmental Conservation (hereafter NY DEC), "Final Supplemental Generic Environmental Impact Statement on the Oil, Gas and Solution Mining Regulatory Program," finding statement, June 2015, 5.

6. Ibid., 6.

7. Sarah Hoye, "New York Governor Pauses 'Fracking,'" CNN, December 13, 2010.

8. Suzanne Goldenberg, "Josh Fox's Gasland II to Expose Power Politics of Fracking," *The Guardian*, July 3, 2013.

9. Mark Ruffalo, "Lessons from Dimock, PA: Calling for a Moratorium on Natural Gas Drilling in New York," *Huffington Post*, August 3, 2010.

10. Brian Nearing, "Lawyer Lauded over Fracking Battle," *Albany Times-Union*, April 29, 2014.

11. Lindsay Abrams, "The Real Secret to Beating the Koch Brothers: How Our Broken Political System Can Still Be Won," *Salon*, April 29, 2014.

12. Casey Seiler, "Sing, Baby, Sing for Drill Delay," *Albany Times-Union*, July 21, 2010; Karen DeWitt, "Pete Seeger, Mark Ruffalo, Among Advocates for Hydro Fracking Moratorium," WXXI News 1370 AM, NPR, n.d.

13. Abrahm Lustgarten, "New York Senate Passes Temporary Ban on Hydraulic Fracturing," *ProPublica*, August 4, 2010; Hoye, "New York Governor Pauses."

14. Hoye, "New York Governor Pauses."

15. David Braun, personal communication with author, 2015.

16. Eric Weltman, "How New York Activists Banned Fracking," *In These Times*, February 27, 2015.

17. Danny Hakim and Nicholas Confessore, "Cuomo Will Seek to Lift Ban on Hydraulic Fracturing," *New York Times*, June 30, 2011.

18. Jon Campbell, "Cuomo's Office Expands Fracking Review, Sets July 1 End Date," *Ithaca* (NY) *Journal*, May 29, 2011.

19. Jon Campbell, "DEC Alters Fracking Proposals," *Rochester* (NY) *Democrat and Chronicle*, July 1, 2011; NY DEC, "Revised Draft Supplemental Generic Environmental Impact Statement on the Oil, Gas and Solution Mining Regulatory Program," September 7, 2011, Executive Summary, 20.

20. Food & Water Watch, "49 Groups Call on Cuomo for Statewide Fracking Ban," press release, July 7, 2011.

21. "NY DEC to Hold Hearings on Proposed Rules for Gas Drillers," WCBS-TV Channel 2, New York, September 28, 2011.

22. NY DEC, "Final Supplemental Generic Environmental Impact Statement," 6.

23. Ithaca College, "Ithaca College Distinguished Scholar Sandra Steingraber Receives National Award," press release, September 14, 2011; New Yorkers Against Fracking (hereafter NYAF), "National, State, and Local Groups Launch Statewide Coalition 'New Yorkers Against Fracking,'" press release, March 14, 2012.

24. Weltman, "How New York Activists Banned Fracking."

25. Ibid.

26. Danny Hakim, "Cuomo Proposal Would Restrict Gas Drilling to a Struggling Area," *New York Times*, June 13, 2012.

27. NYAF, "Proposal to Allow 'Limited' Fracking Draws Opposition from Around the State," press release, June 20, 2012.

28. NYAF, "New Yorkers Against Fracking Condemns Cuomo Administration Plan to Allow 'Limited' Drilling," press release, June 13, 2012.

29. NYAF, "Over a Thousand Businesses Across the State Call on Governor Cuomo to Reject Fracking," August 23, 2012.

30. Rick Karlin, "Hundreds March in Opposition to Fracking," *Albany Times-Union*, August 28, 2012.

31. Jacob Gershman, "Pressure Rises for Decision on Drilling," *Wall Street Journal*, September 28, 2012.

32. "Revised Hydrofracking Regulations Are Released in New York State," Associated Press, November 29, 2012; Lara O. Haluszczak, Arthur W. Rose, and Lee R. Kump, "Geochemical Evaluation of Flowback Brine from Marcellus Gas Wells in Pennsylvania, USA," *Applied Geochemistry*, October 2012.

33. NY DEC, "Final Supplemental Generic Environmental Impact Statement," 42; Brian Nearing, "Cuomo Aims, 2014 Decision on Gas Fracking," *Albany Times-Union*, January 5, 2014; NYAF, "Over 1,500 New Yorkers Descend on Albany for Governor Cuomo's State of the State Address to Rally Against Fracking," press release, January 9, 2013.

34. Mary Esch, "DEC Chief: No Timetable Set on Fracking Decision," Associated Press, February 4, 2013; Siena College, "Siena College Poll: NY and Southern Tier Voters Nearly Evenly Divided on Fracking; Opponents More Passionate Than Supporters," February 4, 2013.

35. NYAF, "Dozens of NYC Faith Leaders Call on Gov. Cuomo to Protect State from Fracking at Office Pray-In," press release, February 6, 2013.

36. Kenneth Lovett, "Anti-fracking Campaign Ads Drill Governor Cuomo," *New York Daily News*, February 11, 2013.

37. NYAF, "Health Professionals, National and Statewide Leaders to Affirm Gov. Cuomo's Decision to Call Fracking Time Out, Urge Him to Let Public Health Studies of Fracking Finish Before Making Decision," press release, February 26, 2013.

38. NYAF, "ExxonMobil Tries to Buy Way into New York Global Oil and Gas Company Dropped $2 Million on Fracking Ads; New Yorkers Not Buying It; Polls Show New Yorkers Still Don't Want Fracking," press release, March 28, 2013.

39. NYAF, "Re: Conflict of Interest Raised by Ecology and Environment, Inc.'s Role as Signatory on IOGA of NY Letter to Governor Cuomo," April 22, 2013.

40. Casey Seiler, "Anti-fracking Groups Rally," *Albany Times-Union*, June 18, 2013.

41. NYAF, "Yoko Ono and Sean Lennon Launch 'Artists Against Fracking' on *The Late Night with Jimmy Fallon Show*," press release, June, 2013.

42. NYAF, "Syracuse City Councilor, PA Elected Official and Fracking-Harmed PA Residents to Ask President Obama to Reopen EPA Investigation of Fracking-Related Contaminated Drinking Water in Pennsylvania," press release, August 21, 2013.

43. Concerned Health Professionals of New York, "Compendium of Scientific, Medical, and Media Findings Demonstrating Risks and Harms of Fracking (Unconventional Gas and Oil Extraction)," December 11, 2014; PSE Healthy Energy, "Toward an Understanding of the Environmental and Public Health Impacts of

Shale Gas Development: An Analysis of the Peer-Reviewed Scientific Literature, 2009–2014," December 2014, 7.

44. Paul Grondahl, "Cuomo Speech Draws Anti-frackers, Political Hangers-On," *Albany Times-Union*, January 8, 2014.

45. NYAF, "Statement Re: Oil and Gas Industry Ad Campaign Focused on New York," press release, April 17, 2014.

46. Beth Young, "Challenging Cuomo, Zephyr Teachout Comes to Sag Harbor," *East End Beacon* (NY), August 23, 2014.

47. Jon Campbell, "Cuomo: Fracking Protesters Are 'Everywhere,' " *Binghamton* (NY) *Press & Sun-Bulletin*, September 10, 2014.

48. Thomas Kaplan, "Cuomo Defeats Teachout, Liberal Rival, in the Democratic Primary," *New York Times*, September 9, 2014.

49. Tom Precious, "Cuomo Wins with Fewest Votes Since FDR," *Buffalo News*, November 5, 2014.

50. Kaplan, "Citing Health Risks."

51. New York Department of Health, "A Public Health Review of High Volume Hydraulic Fracturing," December 2014.

52. Alan Neuhauser, "New York, Citing Health Risks, Moves to Ban Fracking," *U.S. News & World Report*, December 17, 2014.

20. The Ban Movement Grows, Stretching Coast to Coast

1. Amalgamated Clothing Workers of America, Proceedings of the Third Biennial Convention of the Amalgamated Clothing Workers of America, Baltimore, Maryland, May 13–18, 1919, 53.

2. Susan Phillips, "What New York's Fracking Ban Means for Drilling Along the Delaware River," StateImpact Pennsylvania, NPR, December 18, 2014; Steve McConnell, "Governor Rips DBRC over Gas Drilling Ban," *Scranton* (PA) *Times-Tribune*, June 29, 2013; Joshua Roseneau, "Ahead of Vote in Trenton, Activists Weigh In Against Fracking," *Trenton* (NJ) *Times*, November 15, 2011.

3. Ilya Marritz, "Christie Vetoes NJ Fracking Ban, but Orders Moratorium," WNYC 93.9 FM, August 25, 2011.

4. *State of New York v. United States Army Corps of Engineers et al.*, Complaint, U.S. District Court, Eastern District of New York, May 30, 2011; John Campbell, "Schneiderman's Delaware River Basin Fracking Lawsuit Tossed," Bloomberg, September 25, 2012.

5. Mike Davis, "Activists Want Delaware River Basin Commission's Temporary Fracking Ban Made Permanent," *Trenton Times*, September 13, 2012; Delaware River Basin Commission, "DBRC Will Not Act on Draft Natural Gas Regulations at September 21 Meeting," press release, September 6, 2011.

6. Mike Davis, "River Activists: Ban Fracking for Good," *Trenton Times*, September 13, 2012.

7. Ibid.

8. Tom Avril, "DRBC Delays Controversial Vote on Fracking Rules," *Philadelphia Inquirer*, November 19, 2011; Governor Jack A. Markell, letter to Delaware River

Basin commissioners re: Delaware River Basin Commission's natural gas development regulations, November 17, 2011.

9. Susan Phillips, "What Wolf's Win Means for Energy and the Environment," StateImpact Pennsylvania, NPR, November 4, 2014.

10. "Vermont Fracking Ban: Green Mountain State Is First in U.S. to Restrict Gas Drilling Technique," Associated Press, May 16, 2012.

11. Emma Hinchliffe, "Hillsdale Bans Fracking, Mainly to Send a Message," *Bergen County* (NJ) *Record*, June 15, 2014; Brent Johnson, "Following Two Vetoes, Bill to Ban Fracking Waste Heads Back to Christie," *Newark Star-Ledger*, June 29, 2014.

12. Bruce Finley, "Colorado Oil Drilling Boom Intensifies as Voter Initiatives Multiply," *Denver Post*, April 15, 2014.

13. Bruce Finley, "Oil and Gas Spills Surge, Two a Day, Residents Often Not Notified," *Denver Post*, July 29, 2014.

14. Bruce Finley, "Drilling Spills Reaching Colorado Groundwater; State Mulls Test Rules," *Denver Post*, December 9, 2012.

15. Christopher D. Kassotis et al., "Estrogen and Androgen Receptor Activities of Hydraulic Fracturing Chemicals and Surface and Ground Water in a Drilling-Dense Region," *Endocrinology* 155, no. 3 (March 2014): 899, 902, 904.

16. Lisa M. McKenzie et al., "Birth Outcomes and Maternal Residential Proximity to Natural Gas Development in Rural Colorado," *Environmental Health Perspectives* 122, no. 4 (April 2014).

17. *Board of County Commissioners, La Plata County v. Bowen/Edwards Associates, Inc.*, Supreme Court of Colorado, 830 P.2d 1045 (1992); *Voss v. Lundvall Bros., Inc.* Supreme Court of Colorado, 830 P.2d 1061 (1991).

18. Zahra Hirji, "Small Colorado Town Picks Big-Time Fight over Fracking," *InsideClimate News*, July 22, 2014.

19. Jefferson Dodge, "People of the Year: Longmont Anti-fracking Citizens' Group Our Longmont," *Boulder Weekly*, December 27, 2012.

20. Joel Rosenblatt and Jennifer Oldham, "Longmont's Fracking Ban Tossed as Colorado Vote Looms," Bloomberg, July 25, 2014.

21. *Colorado Oil and Gas Association et al. v. City of Longmont, Colorado et al.*, District Court, Boulder County, Order Granting Motions for Summary Judgment, 2013CV63, July 24, 2014, 13.

22. Alison Noon, "Sides Square Off over $900,000 Spent on Colorado Anti-fracking Measures," *Denver Post*, November 5, 2013: Megan Quinn, "Broomfield Fracking: Recount Finds 5-Year Ban Wins by 20 Votes," *Boulder Daily Camera*, December 3, 2013.

23. Noon, "Sides Square Off."

24. Amy Harder, "House Passes Bill Speeding Up Liquefied Natural-Gas Exports," *Wall Street Journal*, June 25, 2014.

25. Julie Cart, "Central Valley's Growing Concern: Crops Raised with Oil Field Water," *Los Angeles Times*, May 2, 2015.

26. California State Water Resources Control Board Workshop, transcript, April 8, 2015.

27. Josh Harkinson, "These Popular Fruit and Veggie Brands May Be Grown with Oil Wastewater," *Mother Jones*, July 24, 2015.

28. EIA, "Petroleum and Other Liquids: Crude Oil Production," accessed September 2, 2015, www.eia.gov/dnav/pet/pet_crd_crpdn_adc_mbblpd_a.htm; EIA, "Top 100 U.S. Oil and Gas Fields," March 2015; John Kemp, "California's New Oil Rush," Reuters, January 2, 2013; Peter Fimrite and Evan Sernoffsky, "Spill Reopens Old Wounds," *San Francisco Chronicle*, May 22, 2015.

29. Los Angeles Times Editorial Board, "Editorial: Does Fracking Cause Quakes? California Needs to Know," *Los Angeles Times*, April 20, 2014.

30. Emily Alpert Reyes, "L.A. City Council Takes Step Toward Fracking Ban," *Los Angeles Times*, February 28, 2014; Emily Alpert Reyes, "L.A. Lawmakers Press for Action on Fracking Ban Despite New Report," *Los Angeles Times*, November 13, 2014.

31. Matt Bigler, "Santa Cruz First County in State to Ban Fracking," KCBS 740 AM/106.9 FM, May 21, 2014; Dana Feldman, "Beverly Hills Becomes First in California to Ban Fracking," May 7, 2014.

32. Christine Mai-Duc, "Carson Imposes Moratorium on Oil Drilling over Fear of Fracking," *Los Angeles Times*, March 19, 2014; Christine Mai-Duc, "City of Carson Changes Mind on New Oil Drilling Ban," *Los Angeles Times*, May 1, 2014; Christine Mai-Duc, "Massive Oil Drilling Project in Carson Is Dropped," *Los Angeles Times*, January 26, 2015.

33. Howard Mintz, "San Benito County's Measure J: Voters Back Anti-fracking Ban," *San Jose Mercury News*, November 4, 2014; "San Benito County Voters Pass Fracking Ban with Measure J," KSBW-TV Channel 8, November 5, 2014.

34. Glenda Anderson, "Mendocino County Voters Ban Fracking," *Santa Clara Press-Democrat*, November 5, 2014; Michael Larkin, "Hermosa Beach Residents Reject Oil Drilling Proposal," KNBC-TV Channel 4, March 4, 2015.

35. Anderson, "Mendocino County Voters Ban Fracking"; Mike Sprague, "Election 2015: La Habra Heights Anti-oil Initiative Loses," *Whittier* (CA) *Daily News*, March 3, 2015.

36. California Department of Oil, Gas and Geothermal Resources, "SB 4 Well Stimulation Treatment Regulations: Final Text of Regulations," July 1, 2015.

37. Erin Cox and Michael Dresser, "Hogan, Brown Clash on Education, Economy, Environment," *Baltimore Sun*, October 18, 2014.

38. John Wagner, "O'Malley Says He Is Ready to Allow 'Fracking' in Western Maryland, with Strict Safeguards," *Washington Post*, November 25, 2014.

39. Erin Cox, "Assembly Votes to Ban Fracking for Two Years," *Baltimore Sun*, April 10, 2015; Sarah Fleischman, "Fracking Moratorium Passes House," *Montgomery* (MD) *Gazette*, April 1, 2015; Baltimore Sun Editorial Board, "Fracking Deserves a Pause," *Baltimore Sun*, March 24, 2015.

40. Josh Hicks, "Md. Fracking Moratorium to Become Law Without Hogan's Signature," *Washington Post*, May 29, 2015; Food & Water Watch, "Edward Norton Lends Support to Maryland Fracking Moratorium in New Advocacy Radio Ad," press release, April 7, 2015.

41. Florida Department of Environmental Protection, "DEP to File Suit Against Dan A. Hughes Company to Shut Down Operations at Collier-Hogan," press release,

July 15, 2014; Dave Paresh, "Oil Drilling Near Everglades Prompts Worries About Fracking, Water," *Los Angeles Times*, May 2, 2014; June Fletcher, "Dan A. Hughes Defends Environmental Record; Vows to Exit South Florida," *Naples* (FL) *Daily News*, September 23, 2014.

42. Thomas St. Myer, "BOCC Sides with Anti-fracking Crowd," *Pensacola* (FL) *News-Journal*, August 20, 2015; Brian Lee, "Ban Fracking in Florida," *Tallahassee* (FL) *Democrat*, April 1, 2015: Jeff Burlew, "Senate Panel OKs Fracking Bills Despite Vocal Opposition," *Tallahassee Democrat*, April 1, 2015.

43. Randy Lee Loftis, "Dallas OKs Gas Drilling Rules That Are Among Nation's Tightest," *Dallas Morning News*, December 11, 2013.

44. Peggy Heinkel-Wolfe, "Denton Fracking Ban Passed in a Landslide," *Dallas Morning News*, November 5, 2014; Max B. Baker, "Denton City Council Repeals Fracking Ban," *Fort Worth Star-Telegram*, June 16, 2015; Marc W. McCord, "The Most Blatant Assault on Home Rule Authority in Texas' History," *Dallas Morning News*, May 22, 2015.

45. Wayne County Commission, resolution no. 2011-432, September 22, 2011; Detroit City Council, resolution to oppose hydraulic fracturing, July 22, 2011; "Cannon Township Enacts Ordinances to Regulate Ancillary Oil and Gas Activities as Part of FLOW's Model Local Ordinance Program," *Rockford* (MI) *Squire*, January 23, 2015.

46. Jim Harger, "Attorney General Bill Schuette Accuses Big Oil Companies of Collusion on Oil and Gas Leases," *Grand Rapids Press*, March 4, 2014; Brian Grow and Joshua Schneyer, "Chesapeake Reaches $25 Million Michigan Settlement over Leasing Charges," Reuters, April 24, 2015.

47. Garret Ellison, "Why Michigan Won't Shut Down the Mackinac Straits Oil Pipeline," *Grand Rapids Press*, August 6, 2015.

48. Julie Wernau, "Environmentalists Feel Betrayed by Proposed Fracking Rules," *Chicago Tribune*, November 17, 2013; Katherine Bagley, "Fracking Bill Triggers Rift Among Illinois Green Groups," *InsideClimate News*, June 17, 2013.

49. Tim Landis, "Regulators Weigh 35,000 Comments on Fracking Rules," *Springfield* (IL) *State Journal-Register*, May 1, 2014; Julie Wernau, *Chicago Tribune*, "Fracking Rules for Illinois Published After Long Battle," November 14, 2014.

50. Daniel Gilbert and Alison Sider, "Ohio Geologists Link Fracking with Earthquakes," *Wall Street Journal*, April 11, 2014; Laura Arenschield, "Fracking Waste Stirs Controversy in Athens," *Columbus Dispatch*, April 5, 2015.

51. Athens City Council, ordinance no. 0-52-12, May 7, 2012; Broadview Heights City Council, ordinance no. 115-12, September 4, 2012; Cincinnati City Council, Res. 56-2012, December 5, 2012; Mansfield City Council, Ord. 12-178, October 23, 2012; Oberlin City Council, res. no. R12-09 CMS, June 4, 2012.

52. *State ex rel. Morrison v. Beck Energy Corp.*, Slip Opinion no. 2015-Ohio-485, para. 75.

53. Jeffery C. Reid and Robert C. Milici, "Hydrocarbon Source Rocks in the Deep River and Dan River Triassic Basins, North Carolina," USGS, Open-File Rpt. 2008-1108, 2008, 1–2; N.C. Gen. Stat §27-113-387–§27-113-388 (Repealed); "Fracking Might Impair Water Quality," *Chapel Hill* (NC) *Herald*, July 22, 2011.

54. "N.C. General Assembly Retains Fracking Moratorium," *Anson* (NC) *Record*, July 31, 2013; General Assembly of North Carolina, Session 2011, Session Law 2012-143 §143B-293.1, §130A-29.

55. John Murawski, "N.C. Senate Approves Fracking Bill," *Raleigh* (NC) *News & Observer*, June 21, 2012.

56. John Murawski, "Fracking Bill Becomes Law Amid Errant Vote," *Raleigh News & Observer*, July 3, 2012.

57. Zach Potter, "With Delay Over, Lee Could See Drilling by Fall," *Sanford* (NC) *Herald*, March 18, 2015; Environment North Carolina, "More Than 50,000 North Carolinians Tell Governor McCrory: Ban Fracking," press release, October 15, 2014; Mark Barrett, "Environmentalists Target 3 State Officials," *Ashville* (NC) *Citizen-Times*, October 1, 2014; Craig Jarvis, "Environmentalists' TV Campaign Expands Targets," *Raleigh News & Observer*, June 30, 2014; "4 GOP Incumbent Losses Among NC House Races," Associated Press, November 5, 2014.

58. Billy Ball, "Chatham County Approves Two-Year Moratorium on Fracking," *Durham–Chapel Hill* (NC) *Indy Week*, August 18, 2015.

59. Brian Voerding, "Fracking Sand Faces Stiff Opposition in Midwest," *Winona* (MN) *Daily News*, April 1, 2013.

60. Matt McKinney, "Mining Tension Tears Up County," *Minneapolis Star-Tribune*, March 30, 2015; "Goodhue County Extends Sand Mining Moratorium," *Winona Daily News*, August 8, 2013; Steve Karnowski, "Natural Gas, Oil Boom Spurs Sand Mining in Midwest," Associated Press, January 6, 2012; Chris Rogers, "Sand Mining Revival in Winona County?," *Winona Post*, May 28, 2014.

61. Chris Rogers, "Petition for Township Ban on Frac Sand," *Winona Post*, June 15, 2015; Tony Kennedy, "Lake Pepin Towns Seek to Ban Sand Mining," *Minneapolis Star-Tribune*, May 23, 3013; "Red Wing Mayor Hired by Frac Sand Lobbying Group," Associated Press, February 6, 2013.

62. Tony Kennedy, "Dayton Says He Can't Enact Frac Sand Ban," *Minneapolis Star-Tribune*, April 23, 2014; Minnesota Department of Natural Resources, "Trout Stream Setback Permit and Silica Sand Reclamation Rulemaking Projects Move Forward," press release, August 8, 2013.

63. Johanna Rupprecht, personal communication with author, April 30, 2015.

64. *Zwiefelhofer et al. v. Town of Cooks Valley, Wisconsin*, Supreme Court of Wisconsin. no. 2010AP2398, decided February 8, 2012.

65. Michael Phillis, "Frac Sand Mining Splits Wisconsin Communities," *Milwaukee Journal-Sentinel*, July 28, 2013; Karen Rivedal, "Transparency, Good Regulation Needed as Wisconsin Sand Mines Multiply, Expert Says," *Wisconsin State Journal*, April 20, 2014.

66. Tony Kennedy, "June 19: Pepin County Board Adopts Frac-Free Zone Along Lake Pepin," *Minneapolis Star Tribune*, July 12, 2013.

67. Wisconsin Network for Peace and Justice, "Citizens Groups to Lawmakers: Stop Frac Sand Mining and SB 349," press release, January 20, 2014.

68. Amber Rouse, "Sand Mining Fractures Opinion in Northeast Iowa," *Dubuque* (IA) *Telegraph-Herald*, September 2, 2014; "Planning and Zoning Sets Public Hearing on Frac Sand," *Decorah* (IA) *Journal*, April 11, 2013.

69. Iowa Citizens for Community Improvement Action Fund, "Iowa Policy Project's Frac Sand Mine Report Uses CAFO Case-Studies as Warning, Call for Local Control," press release, January 30, 2014, cciaction.org/in-the-news/farming-environment/iowa-policy-projects-frac-sand-mine-report-uses-cafo-case-studies-as-warning-call-for-local-control.

70. Jonathan Lemire, "Officials, Activists Oppose Ocean Gas Terminal," Associated Press, March 16, 2015; Adam Uzialko, "Clock Stops on Port Ambrose Application," *Long Branch* (NJ) *Atlanticville*, April 2, 2015; Joan Gralla, "Rally Opposes Gas Port Plan Off Long Beach," *Newsday*, May 17, 2015; Food & Water Watch, "Hundreds of National, State and Local Groups Urge Christie and Cuomo to Veto Port Ambrose LNG Plan," press release, March 16, 2015.

71. Jesse McKinley, "What Pairs Well with a Finger Lakes White? Not Propane, Vintners Say," *New York Times*, December 26, 2014; Tom Wilber, "Clash at Meeting over Gas Storage," *Binghamton* (NY) *Press & Sun-Bulletin*, July 9, 2015; Bob Jamieson, "10 Charged in Crestwood Gate Blockade," *Ithaca* (NY) *Journal*, July 30, 2015.

72. Ted Glick, "Stop Fracked Gas Exports Now!," *Grist*, May 18, 2014.

21. A Global Movement to Ban Fracking

1. Jim Wickins, "Romanian Rendezvous," *The Indypendent*, April 4, 2014.

2. John Yeld, "Karoo Man Fracks the Nod at Awards," *Cape Argus*, April 16, 2013; Ufrieda Ho, "Ex-Joburger Takes on Fight for Karoo," *The Star* (Johannesburg), September 14, 2011.

3. Eric Watkins, "Bulgaria Grants Chevron Shale Gas Exploration Permit," *Oil & Gas Journal*, June 16, 2011; "Bulgaria's Rulers Promise Shale Gas Ban, Protesters Claim," Sofia News Agency, January 14, 2012; "Bulgarian Environmentalists Seek Statutory Ban on Shale Gas Development," Sofia News Agency, February 23, 2012; "Update 1—Bulgaria Bans Shale Oil and Gas Drilling," Reuters, January 18, 2012.

4. "Romania Promises Shale Gas, Gold Mine Rethinks," Reuters, May 4, 2012.

5. Mariah Blake, "How Hillary Clinton's State Department Sold Fracking to the World," *Mother Jones*, September–October 2014.

6. Ibid.; "Bulgaria Eases Oil and Gas Fracking Ban," Reuters, June 14, 2012.

7. Luke Dale-Harris and Vlad Ursulean, "Police Remove Protesters from Chevron's Fracking Site in Romania," *The Guardian*, December 5, 2013.

8. Selina Williams, "Chevron to Give Up Romanian Shale-Gas Interests," *Wall Street Journal*, February 20, 2015; Democracy International, "Direct Democracy Is the Best Cure for Our Society: Interview with Georgeta Ionescu," September 26, 2013.

9. Arthur Nelson, "Poland's Shale Gas Revolution Evaporates in Face of Environmental Protests," *The Guardian*, January 12, 2015; Stanley Reed, "Chevron to Abandon Shale Natural Gas Adventure in Poland," *New York Times*, January 30, 2015.

10. Pavel Polityuk and Richard Balmforth, "Ukraine Signs $10 Billion Shale Gas Deal with Chevron," Reuters, November 5, 2013; Ladka Mortkowitz Bauerova and

Kateryna Choursina, "Shell to Drill First Wells in $10 Billion Ukrainian Project," Bloomberg, November 8, 2013.

11. Katya Gorchinskaya, "Chevron Pulls Out of Gas Extraction in Western Ukraine," *Kyiv Post*, December 15, 2014.

12. Laura Barron-Lopez, "US Sends Experts to Tackle Ukraine's Energy Needs," *The Hill*, April 22, 2014; White House, "Fact Sheet: U.S. Crisis Support Package for Ukraine," press release, April 21, 2014.

13. Michael Scherer, "Ukrainian Employer of Joe Biden's Son Hires a D.C. Lobbyist," *Time*, July 7, 2014.

14. Friends of the Earth Europe, "Ukraine: Shell, Shale Gas and Corruption," February 26, 2014.

15. Food & Water Europe, "MEPs Call for Stricter Environmental Standards for Fracking in Europe but Fall Short of Endorsing a Moratorium," press release, November 21, 2012.

16. Committee on the Environment, Public Health and Food Safety, European Parliament, "Environmental Impact Assessment Directive: Agreement Reached with EU Ministers," press release, December 20, 2013.

17. European Parliament, "Report on Energy Security Strategy: Committee on Industry, Research and Industry," plenary sitting: A8-0164, May 18, 2015, 11, 27, 40, 49.

18. "France Cements Fracking Ban," *The Guardian*, October 11, 2013.

19. Inés Benitez, "Growing Mobilization Against the Introduction of Fracking in Spain," Inter Press Service, June 2, 2015; Dani Cordero, "Catalonia Changes the Law to Ban Fracking," *El País*, February 1, 2014.

20. Terry Macalister, "Vast Reserves of Shale Gas Revealed in UK," *The Guardian*, September 21, 2011.

21. "Fracking Tests Near Blackpool 'Likely Cause' of Tremors," BBC News, November 2, 2011; "Moratorium on Fracking a 'No Brainer,' " *Blackpool Gazette*, July 23, 2014.

22. Adam Vaughan, "Cuadrilla to Appeal Against Fracking Refusal by Lancashire County Council," *The Guardian*, July 23, 2015.

23. Paula Dittrick, "The UK Government Lifted a Temporary Moratorium on Hydraulic Fracturing," *Oil & Gas Journal*, December 13, 2012; "Balcombe Oil Drilling Starts After Fracking Protests," BBC, August 2, 2013; Sarah Young, "Police Detain Protesters at Anti-fracking Demo," Reuters, August 19, 2013; "Anti-fracking Protesters Pull Out of Balcombe Camp," Press Association (UK), September 30, 2013.

24. Frack Free Surrey, "Fracking: Facts, Figures and Falsehoods," press release, November 25, 2014.

25. Fiona Harvey, "Company at Heart of Fracking Protests Applies for New Drilling Licenses," *The Guardian*, September 3, 2013.

26. Karolin Schaps, "Heat Rises on Britain to Change Shale Gas Laws After Projects Blocked," Reuters, July 15, 2015; University of Nottingham, "Support for Fracking Drops for Third Time in a Row with Conservatives Most in Favour," press release, May 20, 2014; Will McCallum, "Under the Radar, the Party Grassroots Aren't as Pro-fracking as Their Leaders Would Like," *New Statesman*, April 2015.

27. Libby Brooks, "Scotland Announces Moratorium on Fracking for Shale Gas," *The Guardian*, January 28, 2015; "Wales Votes Against Shale Gas Fracking," Reuters, February 4, 2015.

28. Maureen Seaberg, "Why Fracking Ireland Is Different," *Huffington Post*, September 26, 2014; Aodhan Fagan, "Fracking: Drilling Will Not Be Allowed in Northern Ireland Unless It's Proven Safe," *Belfast Telegraph*, July 30, 2014; Roanan McGreevy, "Majority of Submissions to EPA Oppose Fracking," *Irish Times*, November 28, 2013.

29. Seaberg, "Why Fracking Ireland Is Different."

30. "Leitrim County Councillors Vote to Ban Fracking," *Leitram Journal* (Ireland), January 14, 2014.

31. David R. Mares, "Shale Gas in Latin America: Opportunities and Challenges," Inter-American Dialogue, working paper, July 2013.

32. "Fracking Controversy Arrives in Argentina," *Buenos Aires Herald*, July 21, 2013; Vladimir Hernandez, "YPF Nationalization: Is Argentina Playing with Fire?," BBC, April 17, 2012.

33. "YPF Makes Oil and Gas Discovery in Patagonia," Reuters, August 24, 2014.

34. Claire Ribando Seelke et al., "Mexico's Oil and Gas Sector: Background, Reform Efforts, and Implications for the United States," Congressional Research Service, July 30, 2015, 12, 17; Emilio Godoy, "Opponents of Fracking Seek to Thwart Shale Gas Finance," Inter Press Service, August 18, 2013.

35. Tony Manno, "Special Report: Unsurrendered, Part One: The Stronghold," *Yes Magazine*, November 2014.

36. "Lelu Island LNG Project Divides First Nations as Protest Continues," *Daybreak North*, CBC News, November 12, 2015.

37. Council of Canadians, "Global Frackdown Starts: Majority of Canadians Want Fracking Moratorium, Says EKOS Poll," press release, October 8, 2014.

38. *Lone Pine Resources Inc. v. The Government of Canada*, ICSID Case No. UNCT/15/2, Notice of Arbitration, September 6, 2013, para. 55.

39. Global Frackdown letter to elected officials, December 2015.

40. Robby Diesu, e-mail correspondence, December 13, 2015.

41. Jennifer Krill, e-mail correspondence, December 13, 2015.

22. The Way Forward

1. Martin Luther King Jr., *Stride Toward Freedom: The Montgomery Story* (Boston: Beacon Press, 2010), 190.

2. Rajendra K. Pachauri et al., Intergovernmental Panel on Climate Change, "Climate Change 2014: Synthesis Report," 2015.

3. William J. Snape III, "Joining the Convention on Biological Diversity," *Sustainable Development Law & Policy*, Spring 2010, 6.

4. Calculation based on Baker Hughes's U.S. rig counts for specific basins identified by EIA as tight oil and/or shale gas basins; oil rig share of all fracked rigs from January 2013 to June 2015. Baker Hughes, "North America Rotary Rig Count (January 2000–Current): U.S. Rig Count by Basin," September 11, 2015; EIA,

"Technically Recoverable Shale Oil and Shale Gas Resources: An Assessment of 137 Shale Formations in 41 Countries Outside the United States," June 2013, 13, 14, 2–26.

5. EIA, *Monthly Energy Review*, March 2015, Table 7.2, and prior years.

6. Tyson Slocum, director of Public Citizen's Energy Program, personal communication with author, April 17, 2015.

7. EIA, "Most States Have Renewable Portfolio Standards," *Today in Energy*, February 3, 2011; Jenny Heeter and Lori Bird, "Including Alternative Resources in State Renewable Portfolio Standards: Current Design and Implementation Experience," National Renewable Energy Laboratory, November 2012, 6–7.

8. EIA, *Monthly Energy Review*, March 2015.

INDEX

About the Author

Wenonah Hauter is the executive director of Food & Water Watch, a D.C.-based watchdog organization focused on corporate and government accountability relating to food, water, and the environment. She has worked and written extensively on food, water, energy, and environmental issues at the national, state, and local levels. She owns a working farm in The Plains, Virginia.

Publishing in the Public Interest

Thank you for reading this book published by The New Press. The New Press is a nonprofit, public interest publisher. New Press books and authors play a crucial role in sparking conversations about the key political and social issues of our day.

We hope you enjoyed this book and that you will stay in touch with The New Press. Here are a few ways to stay up to date with our books, events, and the issues we cover:

- Sign up at www.thenewpress.com/subscribe to receive updates on New Press authors and issues and to be notified about local events
- Like us on Facebook: www.facebook.com/newpressbooks
- Follow us on Twitter: www.twitter.com/thenewpress
- Please consider buying New Press books for yourself; for friends and family; or to donate to schools, libraries, community centers, prison libraries, and other organizations involved with the issues our authors write about.

The New Press is a 501(c)(3) nonprofit organization. You can also support our work with a tax-deductible gift by visiting www.thenewpress.com/donate.